Gender in Chinese Music

Eastman/Rochester Studies in Ethnomusicology

Ellen Koskoff, Series Editor
Eastman School of Music

(ISSN: 2161-0290)

Burma's Pop Music Industry:
Creators, Distributors, Censors
Heather MacLachlan

Yorùbá Music in the Twentieth Century:
Identity, Agency and Performance Practice
Bode Omojola

Javanese Gamelan and the West
Sumarsam

Gender in Chinese Music
Edited by Rachel Harris, Rowan Pease, and Shzr Ee Tan

Gender in Chinese Music

Edited by Rachel Harris,
Rowan Pease, and Shzr Ee Tan

UNIVERSITY OF ROCHESTER PRESS

Copyright © 2013 by the Editors and Contributors

All Rights Reserved. Except as permitted under current legislation, no part of this work may be photocopied, stored in a retrieval system, published, performed in public, adapted, broadcast, transmitted, recorded, or reproduced in any form or by any means, without the prior permission of the copyright owner.

First published 2013
Transferred to digital printing and reprinted in paperback 2015

University of Rochester Press
668 Mt. Hope Avenue, Rochester, NY 14620, USA
www.urpress.com
and Boydell & Brewer Limited
PO Box 9, Woodbridge, Suffolk IP12 3DF, UK
www.boydellandbrewer.com

hardcover ISBN-13: 978-1-58046-443-7
paperback ISBN-13: 978-1-58046-544-1
ISSN: 2161-0290

Library of Congress Cataloging-in-Publication Data
Gender in Chinese music / edited by Rachel Harris, Rowan Pease, and Shzr Ee Tan.
    pages cm — (Eastman/Rochester studies in ethnomusicology, ISSN 2161-0290 ; v. 4)
    Includes bibliographical references and index.
    ISBN 978-1-58046-443-7 (hardcover : alk. paper) 1. Gender identity in music. 2. Music—China—History and criticism. 3. Music—Social aspects—China. I. Harris, Rachel (Rachel A.), author, editor of compilation. II. Pease, Rowan, author, editor of compilation. III. Tan, Shzr Ee, author, editor of compilation. IV. Series: Eastman/Rochester studies in ethnomusicology ; v. 4.
    ML3917.C6G46 2013
    780.81'0951—dc23

2013021896

A catalogue record for this title is available from the British Library.

This publication is printed on acid-free paper.
Printed in the United States of America

To Antoinet Schimmelpenninck
Sinologist and Musicologist
(1962–2012)

Contents

	Introduction *Rachel Harris and Rowan Pease*	1
1	Gender and Music in Local Communities *Stephen Jones*	26
2	The Pleasures of Print: Illustrated Songbooks from the Late Ming Courtesan World *Judith T. Zeitlin*	41
3	From Courtesans to Modern Hostesses: Music and Construction of Gender in the Entertainment Industry in China *Tiantian Zheng*	66
4	An Interview with Zhang Han, Karaoke Bar Host *Shzr Ee Tan*	82
5	Impulsive Scholars and Sentimental Heroes: Contemporary *Kunqu* Discourses of Traditional Chinese Masculinities *Joseph Lam*	87
6	An Interview with Madame Zinnia Kwok, Amateur Opera Singer *Shzr Ee Tan*	107
7	Men Behaving Badly? Shawm Bands of North China *Stephen Jones*	112
8	An Interview with Coco Zhao, Shanghai Jazz Singer *Ruard Absaroka*	127
9	New Chinese Masculinities on the Piano: Lang Lang and Li Yundi *Shzr Ee Tan*	132
10	An Interview with Aloysius Lee, Fan of Singer Faye Wong *Shzr Ee Tan*	152
11	"I Prefer a Man Who Is Fresh like a Jumping Fish": Gender Issues in *Shan'ge*, Chinese Popular Rural Song *Frank Kouwenhoven and Antoinet Schimmelpenninck*	156

12 An Interview with Liu Sola, Composer, Singer, Visual Artist, and Novelist 177
    Shzr Ee Tan

13 Broken Voices: Ethnic Singing and Gender 181
    Rowan Pease

14 An Interview with Li Sisong, Producer and Songwriter 201
    Shzr Ee Tan

15 "Mother's Daughter": Gender Narratives in Nuosu-Yi Women's Musical Expressive Forms 205
    Olivia Kraef

16 An Interview with Xiao Mei, Ethnomusicologist 224
    Shzr Ee Tan

17 "Doing Satan's Business": Negotiating Gendered Concepts of Music and Ritual in Rural Xinjiang 229
    Rachel Harris

18 Bodies, Gender, and Worldviews: *Me-mot* Spirit Mediums in the Jingxi Region of Guangxi 247
    Xiao Mei

19 Vegetarian Sisters: New Configurations of Gender in Buddhism in Southern Fujian 265
    Hwee-San Tan

Selected Bibliography 287

List of Contributors 297

Index 301

Introduction

Rachel Harris and Rowan Pease

Between 2004 and 2006, a TV pop idol show produced by a daring provincial satellite station, Hunan Satellite TV, sponsored by the Mengniu Dairy Company, took China by storm. The delightfully named Mengniu (Mongolian cow) Yoghurt "Super Girl" (*Chaoji Nüsheng*) contests featured young women from the provinces, many of them without formal musical training. For many fans, it was the lack of polish of the performers, and the lack of predictability of the voting results, that made the program addictive: the show had more than four hundred million viewers. Unlike China's leader Hu Jintao—as Western media commentators were quick to point out—the winners were popularly elected, via text message, and the final contest of 2006 drew more than ten million votes nationwide. In 2005, the competition was won by twenty-one-year-old Li Yuchun, who went on to become China's first homegrown superstar of the twenty-first century. Li was very different from the conventional image of a mainstream Chinese pop diva: lanky, always in trousers and loose shirts, no makeup, and spiky hair. It was widely believed that Li won on personality and image, rather than vocal talent. Like reality-show stars elsewhere, Li Yuchun was most admired for being individual and authentic—and for crying. Her fan base was young girls who described themselves as her "girlfriends," and fantasy fiction posted on fan websites depicted her in lesbian relationships. Li Yuchun was not the only contestant on this show challenging ideas of female public behavior. Second-placed "Bibi" Zhou Bichang, like Li, also sang mainly male songs during the competition. She wore baggy hip-hop clothing, with cropped hair and spectacles, and like Li had a fan base of "girlfriends." Like Li, her albums eschewed traditional romantic ballads, with assertively titled tracks such as "Wow" and "*Han*" (Sweat), the latter about global warming.

These androgynous superstars sparked national debates about talent, beauty, sexuality, femininity, and democracy. They and their fans provide a springboard from which to outline some of this volume's themes. If nothing else, they reveal that gender roles are continually being negotiated and renegotiated in China and that musical performance is a significant medium where these negotiations are played out. Within the space of half a century, women have been idealized as "iron girls" (represented by the immortal Tie Mei of the revolutionary opera *Red Lantern*), reclaimed their femininity in the reform era (notably in the glorious frills and trills of the Taiwanese pop star Deng Lijun), and now welcome a contravention of social norms in the tomboy look of Li and Zhou. It would be unwise to assume that such swift and radical changes are only a recent phenomenon, as though gender were a static concept in premodern China. As Tani Barlow argues, one cannot appeal to "Chinese women" as a transhistorical presence: femininity has been constructed differently throughout Chinese history.[1]

This book is not just about women, though. For its 2007 season, Hunan TV set up a Super Boy contest, but the government imposed restrictions on the show: text voting was tolerated but not the drama and the tears, which are as much a part of Chinese idol competitions as they are in US equivalents. In April 2007 the state broadcasting administration issued a set of rules, first banning the use of the word *super*, so that the competition was to be known as the "Happy Boys Voices" (*Kuaile Nansheng*) competition. Besides limiting its size and attempting to eliminate corruption, the rules "prohibit manners, language, hairstyles, accessories, and costumes that do not conform to the values held by the masses" and ban the "pursuit of weirdness." Also prohibited were screaming fans, crying losers, and "cruel or arrogant judges." The show's producers eliminated so-called girly boys, who predominated at the audition stage, in favor of so-called tuff boys, saying that they were more in keeping with the program's stipulated "Chinese values" and "happy image."[2] Here is an example of how the state also intervenes in questions of gender and music, especially where they relate to sexuality; again, this is true not only of the modern era but also throughout imperial history, from the famous Confucian prescriptions against the "licentious music" performed by women,[3] to the Emperor Qianlong's 1722 ban on female public performance.

Geographical Scope of This Volume

Li Yuchun looks like a rocker, but musically she covers a variety of styles, from rap to ballads, reggae, and tango. Is this Chinese music? The conception of "Chinese music" in this volume is wide-ranging and inclusive. It is no longer possible, if it ever was, to take the nation-state as a privileged and self-evident site of investigation. Li Yuchun drew support in Hong Kong and Taiwan, as well as from the global Chinese diaspora, who were able to share each stage of the competition on Internet sites such as YouTube and its Chinese equivalent Tudou. As its popularity grew, the Super Girls contest drew the attention of Western newspapers: reporters eagerly sought signs of subversion in the public's taste and hope for democracy in the enthusiastic adoption of text message voting. Li Yuchun became known abroad as Chris Lee; she launched the 2006 London Chinatown celebrations. Her 2008 album, the assertively titled *Mine* (*Wo de*), was recorded in New York studios using internationally renowned production and song-writing teams, and it was released on the label Taihe Rye, which was co-owned by a South Korean telecom company. Yet, despite Li being immersed in the global music industry, as British listeners, we feel there is an incongruity between Li's image and her (to Western ears) conservative lyrics; the album's mixture of musical styles is also unusual. In its aim for a mass domestic audience, *Mine* remains distinctively Chinese. Li's album shows that we must think transnationally and consider alternative forms of modernity in the non-West. The links between "local" formations and the West are fundamental to our study.

Previous Approaches to Gender in Chinese Music

Like musicology in general, English-language ethnomusicological studies of Chinese musical traditions have largely taken male music as their subject, whether court and ritual genres, instrumental music, twentieth-century composition, or minority musics. As Gail Hershatter argues, the study of gender is not so much an end in itself but a valuable tool for reassessing, enriching, and "making trouble for" all kinds of disciplines within Chinese and of course other studies.[4] In recent years a few studies on gender in Chinese music have attempted to redress this imbalance. Most notably, in a Garland encyclopedia entry, Su Zheng writes that the extraordinary achievements of Chinese women musicians are widely ignored, dismissed, minimized, and misinterpreted in Chinese and Western scholarship, despite an abundance of historical materials that document their musical contributions.[5] She highlights the discovery of twenty bodies of young women performers unearthed in the Marquis Yi of Zeng tomb, noting that though much has been made of a sixty-four-piece bell-chime set also in this tomb, there has been little interest in the lives of these women. Su Zheng's laudable feminist project to write "forgotten" women back into history, redressing marginalization, offers the possibility of a more complete documentation of female participation in and contribution to music in China. Since the publication of her article in 2001, efforts in this direction are beginning to grow in numbers and influence.

As the leading Chinese musicologist Xiao Mei notes, speaking to Shzr Ee Tan for this volume in 2008, the field of Chinese musicology is still "a man's world." The four-volume collection of modern musicians' biographies[6] has only forty-seven women out of 314 entries, and thirty of those are singers. Very few women are listed in the folk-song volumes of the *Anthology of Folk Music of the Chinese Peoples*.[7] This reflects their lesser public role but also prevailing scholarly understandings of what constitutes music and music making. Writing in 2001, Su Zheng mentions two historical studies with a focus on female music making as pioneering attempts to rewrite the historical record.[8] Since then, gender studies have begun to take root in China: a 2009 international conference on gender studies in Shanghai's Fudan University included a range of approaches to gender from literary analysis to fieldwork-based studies. Notable is a new focus on masculinities and a few papers drawing on queer theory. In the field of musicology, young women are now joining the discipline in greater numbers; with an increasing awareness of international trends in ethnomusicology, gender is becoming an issue. China's leading musicology journals have published articles introducing the state of gender theory in Western ethnomusicology.[9] Xiao Mei's own recent work, featured in this volume, focuses on rural female spirit mediums among ethnic minority groups. These female musicians are doubly marginalized in scholarship and political power structures but hold important social roles in rural life across Han and minority cultures. Xiao leads a distinct trend for younger scholars to engage in field-based work with ethnic minority women's traditions.[10] In the field of Han Chinese traditions, Wu Fan's work on temple fairs in north Shanxi includes perceptive comments on gender, addressing not only the male world of local temple committees, Daoists, and shawm bands but also the female family members and female mediums, worshippers, and deities.[11] Chinese scholars, both male and female, are also increasingly publishing on gender issues in contemporary and pop music.[12]

Of the few English language studies of Chinese musical traditions to focus on gender, Joseph Lam's work on historical texts of the early Han and late Ming periods does the most to address the questions raised by Zheng. Lam explores the apparent contradiction between the fierce denigration of "women's music" in the classics and its popularity as evidenced by numerous references in the textual record.[13] Yang Mu's groundbreaking work on sexuality and folk song, especially his work on the *hua'er* festivals of Gansu, provides a welcome antidote to the tendency in Chinese musicology to sanitize ethnographic accounts,[14] though Frank Kouwenhoven and Antoinet Schimmelpenninck in this volume go much further. Jonathan Stock contributes an admirable attempt to relate questions of gender to vocal style in Shanghai opera.[15] However, in contrast to the burgeoning interest within ethnomusicology over the last twenty years, the work on gender in Chinese music is still strikingly sparse.[16] We are cautious of an overly positivist view of Chinese women's music making. Stephen Jones in this volume warns against overstating women's agency in Chinese music and ignoring the harsh realities of inequality and oppression experienced by these silenced voices. Little surprise, then, that it is marriage laments that have so far offered the most fertile ground for the study of gender and expressive culture in rural society,[17] although these contributions come from anthropologists and folklorists who provide little discussion of music; Anne McLaren, for example, characterizes the laments not so much as songs as "stylized sobbing."[18] Discussion of gender is more central in several studies of popular

Chinese music, most prominently in the work of Nimrod Baranovitch,[19] who reveals, for instance, that, despite the apparent liberation of women's voices in the 1980s, the music industry was as masculinized in the reform era as it was in Maoist China. Jeroen de Kloet's 2010 book offers further insights into gender in Beijing's macho rock scene and the ways in which female rockers negotiate gender stereotypes.[20] Marc Moskowitz focuses primarily on Taiwanese Mandopop songs, arguing that these songs, with their themes of loneliness and sorrow, provide vocabularies for the articulation of alternative versions of masculinity, expressing more female or androgynous sensibilities.[21] Some recent articles have used queer theory as a lens to examine Taiwanese popular culture.[22] Other groundbreaking studies come not from musicologists but from historians examining homosexuality and transgender identities in Chinese opera.[23] A theme running through all of these studies, as our vignette of Li suggests, is of transformations of self and of social constructions of gender.

Approaches to Gender in Ethnomusicology

The discipline of ethnomusicology is perhaps uniquely able to examine music and gender not only through analysis of music as text but through study of lived experience, agency, and practice.[24] Music serves as a particularly rich field for the analysis of gender because of its important role in the construction and articulation of identities. As popular music scholar Simon Frith argues, identity is not a thing but a process, an experiential process that is most vividly grasped *as music*. In his investigations into how and why music articulates identity, Frith interconnects music's experiential and referential powers with its inherent ability to express the individual in the social and the social in the individual.[25] He notes that music can be both fantastic (an idealization of self and society) and real (in the process of actual bodily music making). These twin poles of gender identities—representations and lived experience—are likewise frequently referred to in the literature on gender in China.[26]

The field of gender studies in ethnomusicology has advanced swiftly in the last few decades. Earlier volumes focused on the hitherto neglected areas of female expressivity. Koskoff's influential edited volume *Women and Music in Cross-Cultural Perspective* examines how music both reflects and constructs gender, how women are present or absent in music, and how the public and private domains of music are gendered. The many case studies in Koskoff's volume explore the related spheres of the exclusion of women from musical activity and the social value placed on types of performance gendered male or female. Koskoff argues that across cultures "music is devalued by association with sexually active women" while female sexuality itself may be devalued by association with music.[27] Such themes are certainly apparent in China, where rural women may be excluded from rituals (the primary site of musical performance in rural China) because of pollution taboos associated with menstrual blood, while the fleeting high status enjoyed by high-class *yueji*, female musicians and courtesans, was of course highly contingent on their relationships to male power holders (for an elegant deconstruction of these relations, see Judith Zeitlin in this volume). Koskoff suggests four categories of performance of intergender relations: confirmation, apparent confirmation, protests that maintain the order, and challenges to the order.[28] These categories are still interesting to ponder, although expressive culture rarely fits neatly into such schema. Should the Super Girls contest be seen as a ritual reversal that reinforces rules by symbolic subversion where women preside over the dangerous sphere of the dance?[29] Or is the presence of not one but two contrasting lesbian performers a confirmation of women's new social role as a rapidly segmenting, ego-driven consumer group within market-driven China, as outlined by Jing Wang?[30] Symbolic and real change cannot be separated, neither can construction and reflection.

More recent approaches have recognized the role of musical performance in constructing and maintaining a whole range of gendered identities. Judith Butler's work on gender and performativity has been influential in developing these approaches. Butler argues that gender does not exist as an "ideal" or an "essence" but instead is constituted from a series of performed acts that actually create the notion of gender: "gender is, thus, a construction that regularly conceals its genesis; the tacit collective agreement to perform, produce, and sustain discrete and polar genders as cultural fictions is obscured by the credibility of those productions—and the punishments that attend not agreeing or believing in them; the construction 'compels' our belief in its necessity and naturalness."[31] The duality of lived experience versus representations of gender is collapsed in Butler's approach to gender theory. For her, "performativity is not a singular act, but a repetition and a ritual, which achieves its effects through its naturalization in the context of a body."[32] This emphasis on gender performativity is strongly realized in Jane Sugarman's ethnographic study of Prespa wedding songs in Bulgaria. Sugarman reminds us that we need to focus on the capacity of musical traditions not merely to reinforce gender relations within other domains but to actively engender those individuals who participate in them. Gender is intrinsic to our musical performances, and any musical performance is thus also a performance of gender. Sugarman analyzes texts, vocal style, and ornamentation and their communication of attributes signified as male or female. She discusses gendered emotional qualities and the division of performance space, arguing for an understanding of singing as the practice of patriarchy.[33]

Although the understanding of multiple and shifting constructs of gender is well established within the discipline, masculinities are still less discussed, notwithstanding the work of Louise Meintjes in Zulu song and dance,[34] Viet Erlmann on *isicathamiya*,[35] and Pacini Hernandez on Dominican *Bachata*.[36]

There is a longer tradition within popular music studies addressing different forms of masculinity, and we have found many of these studies useful for our approach to this volume. One significant recent contribution in this field is Freya Jarman-Ivens's edited volume *Oh Boy*, which takes the male as its object of scrutiny and thereby illuminates the multiple and malleable variations on this supposedly normative gender. Jarman-Ivens considers all gender formations the "results of careful and sustained practice . . . not simply formations, but "*per*-form-ations,"[37] despite a tendency to define masculinity as "nonperformative." Our understanding of masculinity is broad: China's Super Girls remind us that "masculinity does not belong to men [and] has not been produced only by men."[38]

The literature on rock and masculinity is also useful for its interest in the gendering of musical sound. Simon Frith and Angela McRobbie's article "Rock and Sexuality" discusses the overtly masculine performance conventions of "cock rock": loud, rhythmically insistent, and built around techniques of arousal and climax.[39] Similarly Robert Walser in his writing on heavy metal describes "impressive feats on the electric guitar, counterposed with the experience of power and control that is built up through vocal extremes, guitar power chords, distortion, and sheer volume of bass and drums." Such sounds, he argues, are produced out of "fantasies of masculine virtuosity and control."[40] Several articles in this volume emphasize the importance of listening to gender, placing musical sound at the heart of our analysis, rather than discussing only the visual aspects of musical performance conventions and the surrounding social structures. Susan McClary's pioneering work in the field of Western art music first drew attention to the notion of gendered musical structures,[41] but as the literature on rock and masculinity suggests, other aspects of musical sound are perhaps more significant in their ability to carry, and be decoded as, gendered messages. The discourse surrounding music links detail of musical style—for example, the use of melisma as opposed to playing it "straight"—directly to moral judgments and notions of authenticity and value. In this volume, Stephen Jones considers how the musical structure of the Shanxi shawm band suites might reveal underlying gendered ideologies, but a shift in focus, to a consideration of style and especially timbre, proves perhaps more fruitful. As Walser argues, harsh, abrasive timbres contribute to the Western cultural association between rock and masculinity: "timbre instantly signals genre and affect."[42] In this volume, Rowan Pease also draws attention to timbre, especially to vocal quality. As she argues, it is the way of singing that attracts audiences much more than what they sing, and timbre is the most recognizable aspect of song, instantly linked by listeners to categories of class, race, and gender.

Baranovitch traces the changing vocal style of Chinese female singers from the forceful, high-pitched production of the Cultural Revolution–era model operas to the breathy pop style of 1980s Canto-Mandopop singers like Deng Lijun, arguing that her huge popularity was based on her ability to supply the much-needed sounds of a softer, romantic femininity to Chinese listeners in the aftermath of that period of political extremism and violence.[43] Yet soft and breathy vocal styles can equally purvey hard-line political messages. Mu Rongxuan, with her song "Don't Be Too CNN," became the voice of popular Chinese outrage against the Western media in May 2008. With her soft singing style and acoustic guitar accompaniment, she vocalized a wave of Chinese nationalist anger as she railed against the "lies" of the Western media concerning the Tibet protests surrounding the Olympic torch relay.

But clearly caution must be exercised here; while the Shanxi shawm bands sound extremely macho to our ears, we cannot assume that their Shanxi audiences make the same associations. Even where discussing Chinese rock, we cannot necessarily assume that similar sounds of rock and heavy metal signify the same for Chinese audiences as they do for Western audiences.

Theorizing Gender and Music in China

Tullia Magrini's edited volume on gender and music in the Mediterranean[44] offers a rich array of ethnographic studies from across the region, identifying as its dominant and unifying theme the twin concepts of shame and honor, classic tropes of Mediterranean anthropology. What themes might we identify in the field of gender and music in China? One theme running through much research is the well-worn trope whereby tradition is gendered as feminine and modernity as masculine. The twin concepts of tradition and modernity are, of course, twentieth-century constructions, and it is interesting to trace the twentieth-century development of professional Chinese traditional music (*minyue*) performance, and its shifting gender profile, in the light of this perception. When the "masters" of various instrumental traditions were invited into the newly built conservatories in the 1950s, they were almost exclusively male, but the gender balance quickly began to shift. In the contemporary conservatories it is striking that the prominent performers of Western classical music, the more highly valued tradition, regarded as international and progressive, are most commonly male (see Tan's discussion of the pianists Lang Lang and Li Yundi in this volume), while *minyue* departments, regarded within the conservatories as less prestigious and less dynamic, have become strongly feminized. Stringed instruments in particular, such as the *pipa* and *zheng*, are now almost the exclusive domain of women, with a parade of glamorous virtuoso star performers and thousands of students from better-off families, much in the way that the piano served as an ideal feminine accomplishment in Victorian England. Even the classically male world of the seven-string zither *qin* has been penetrated by female performers within the conservatories. The most striking example of this feminization of *minyue* is the glamorous, highly packaged Twelve Girls Band, which achieved widespread popularity with its shifting profile of unnamed and interchangeable nubile young performers of traditional instruments and their contemporary fusion renditions of *minyue*. Less glitzy than the Twelve Girls, but a more widespread phenomenon, are the many older Chinese women, organizers of amateur groups, who act as preservers of traditional genres.[45] This has been best documented in the Chinese diaspora; for example, in articles about Grace Liu, who promotes and preserves Cantonese opera in England,[46] and Tsar Teh-yun, who maintains the *qin* tradition in Hong Kong.[47]

Related to this phenomenon is the gendered alterity of (male) self versus (female) other, a feature frequently noted in studies of the feminized and exoticized minority nationality song-and-dance troupe performances. Dru Gladney discusses representations of ethnic minority women in the spheres of Chinese art, film, music, and dance and argues that they are titillating in ways not permitted for representations of Han women.[48] Louisa Schein writes with insight of the position of the "divas" of professional ethnic minority performance, who proudly relate how they sang for Chairman Mao in the Great Hall of the People. She presents these encounters and others in which Miao peasant hotel maids in Guizhou put on ethnic costumes, perform songs, and pop food into the mouths of urban male tourists, as rituals of internal orientalism.[49] Rowan Pease and Olivia Kraef in this volume make original contributions to this debate. Yet it is not only feminine minority representations that are packaged and sold in contemporary China; minority masculinities are also alluring to Han consumers, as Baranovitch argues in his study of Teng Ge'er the Mongolian rocker.[50] The contemporary Beijing rock scene is rich in examples of minority rockers who draw on the links in the popular Chinese imagination between ethnic minorities, nature, and authenticity, from the extreme sounds of the Inner Mongolian heavy metal group Voodoo Kungfu, with their references to shamanism and use of the Mongolian horse-head fiddle,[51] to the more playful northwestern Uyghur group Jam, with their rock interpretations of the Uyghur Muqam.

These studies of the relationships among performance, ethnicity, and gender remind us that gendered sounds are also underpinned by politics. As we saw in our opening vignettes describing the Mengniu Yoghurt Super Girls and the spin-off Happy Boy Voices, the Chinese state still seeks to direct and control representations of gender in popular music performance, as in many other spheres. The government's anxieties over the representation of masculinity within the Happy Boy Voices competition reveal that the emasculated "sick man of East Asia" status imposed by colonial modernity still casts its shadow over China. In the existing literature, Baranovitch has been most alert to the relationship among politics, gender, and musical sound, arguing that the macho sounds (and the frequent misogyny) of Beijing's 1990s rock scene may be read as a direct reaction to the sense of emasculation experienced by the male musicians on this scene in the face of a controlling state and their nationalist sense of China's "backwardness."[52] Zheng Tiantian's chapter on karaoke bars in this volume also picks up this theme, arguing that the male entrepreneurs who patronize karaoke bars consume musical performances of extreme gendered subjugation by prostitutes in order to counter this sense of emasculation produced by the political system.[53] De Kloet's discussion of the Beijing rock scene also emphasizes the postcolonial and gendered sensibility of male rockers, who appropriate and localize the "hard" sounds of rock and authenticate themselves in opposition to "soft," feminized pop.[54]

The more recent generation of bands, however, shows signs of breaking away from this dualizing tendency. The highly cosmopolitan bands of the early twenty-first-century "new movement," such as Sober and the new punk group New Pants (Xin kuzi), mix Chinese and English lyrics and deploy parody and irony in a deliberate negation of rock ideology.[55] The first decade of the twenty-first century has also provided more space for assertive female musicians in the Beijing scene, with singers like Luo Qi, with her well-publicized "bad girl" lifestyle providing, as de Kloet argues, a dramatization of gender, or the female punk band Hang on the Box who sing (in English) "Asshole I'm Not Your Baby."[56]

Gender Dualisms and Their Problems

Just as contemporary approaches to gender in Western contexts argue against the tendency to reduce the complexities of gender relations to dualisms, likewise it is necessary to guard against this tendency in Chinese contexts, particularly since traditional beliefs tend toward a seductive series of oppositions. The shade-light yin-yang dichotomy of Chinese cosmology is sometimes simplistically conflated with female-male genders, although their meanings were far more fluid. Susan Brownell and Jeffrey Wasserstrom explain that, within Confucian orthodoxy, yin and yang referred to complementary hierarchical human relationships, including those between two males, such as between a minister and his ruler. In Tani Barlow's theorization of Chinese gender,[57] it becomes apparent that the man-woman (*nanxing-nüxing*) binary "scientific" categorization was a mid-nineteenth-century introduction to colonial modern China and that in imperial China male-female were understood within kinship (*jia*) relations, thus mother-father, brother-sister, rather than man-woman. Indeed, the importance of social gender over anatomical sex is a recurrent theme in Chinese gender studies, for instance: "The possession of a penis was *primarily* important not because of male sexual pleasure, but because of what it represented . . . the patriarchal power that had been passed down the patriline from father to son according to the rules of Confucian filial piety."[58] Confucian hierarchies provide much of the drama of Chinese music theatre, opera, and narrative song forms. Dynastic politics, historical intrigues, and battles provide much thematic material, as do more romantic representations of upright scholars, tragic lovers (such as the famous *kunqu* opera *Peony Pavilion* [*Mudanting*]), loyal wives and concubines (for example, the Beijing opera *Farewell my Concubine* [*Bawang bieji*]). These operas carry dominant messages but also subvert them where romantic love triumphs over filial piety, where cross-dressing women warriors or scholars take to the stage, or where rulers are shown to be corrupt.

Another enduring dyad in Chinese thought is that of "civil" (*wen*) and "martial" (*wu*), a classification that is applied to many forms of Chinese instrumental music (e.g., the opposition between *sizhu* "silk-and-bamboo" and *guchui* "drumming and blowing") as well as to designate individual pieces within many opera and instrumental repertoires. Kam Louie in his theorization of Chinese masculinity uses the *wen-wu* dyad to argue that, contrary to the modern nationalist fear of male "weakness," the "soft" scholarly male represented power in imperial China. Within the temples of China, *wen* is seen in the cult of worship of Confucius (Kongzi); *wen* is also represented by the figure of the young Confucian scholar (*caizi*), reproduced in so many literary, operatic, and narrative forms, who can achieve success in the imperial exams system and get the girl. *Wu* is seen in the cult of the god Guan Gong and in the *haohan* (good fellow) bandit heroes of Yuan dynasty novels: nonelite, loyal followers whose emotional ties are to their brothers, not to women or family, whose sexuality is subsumed to the cause and frequently expressed in violence.[59] There is a risk of oversimplification in transferring these elegant, but possibly essentialist, dualities onto lived experience. Yet they offer alternative non-Western discourses of gender to contemporary urban Chinese audiences. Lam in this volume argues for a more nuanced view of *wen* and *wu* in the context of *kunqu* opera, while Tan maps its modern popular culture manifestations onto the constructed images of contemporary piano idols.

In instrumental music, the *qin* inscribes in sound, and serves as an icon of, *wen* masculinity. For *qin* players (who in imperial times belonged mostly to the male elite class of literati), musical performance was a practice of self-cultivation, to be undertaken in solitude or among small select gatherings. The *qin* is closely associated with Confucius, and its sounds, when played by a virtuous man, conveyed the ideals of harmony and good governance.[60] Scores are interpreted and performed (*dapu*) in the tradition of Chinese scholarship,[61] and the instruments themselves, valuable works of art, carry with them their own genealogies. Even the instrument's construction reflects gender ideologies; we find *yin-yang* cosmology symbolically represented in the dragon pool and phoenix pond carved into its underside. In the Confucian literature, we also find the *qin* as a symbol of idealized friendship between elite men. The term *zhiyin* (friendship, lit. knowing the sound) refers to the third-century story of the great *qin* player, Bo Ya. He smashed his instrument after the death of his friend, Zhong Ziqi, who perfectly understood the moods he evoked with his playing. Bo Ya had perfected his art in solitude, marooned on an island where he learned from sounds of nature, and in this we see that the *qin* is also emblematic of Daoist ideals: the interaction of man and nature. The popular *qin* piece *Fisherman and Woodcutter Talk* (*yuqiao wenda*) evokes these figures as exemplars of the same ideals: the woodcarver slices along the grain of the wood, "in tune" with its inner nature, while the fisherman sits calm and still amidst nature, awaiting the bite of the fish. The sounds of the *qin*, intimate and delicate, slow and contemplative, with their many subtle variations of timbre, are inseparable from this richly layered ideological discourse.

Yet no genre can be described as pure *wen*. The *qin* repertoire includes pieces that reference tales of bloody filial revenge, notably the still popular *Guanglingsan* attributed to the third-century scholar Ji Kang, which conveys the assassination of the king of Han by Nie Zhen. Likewise, Bell Yung's biographies of the revered female *qin* player Tsar Teh-yun ("the last of China's literati") illustrate that men did not have the monopoly over *wen*. As a young woman, Tsar was marginalized in elegant *yaji* gatherings,[62] yet she remained strict in her adherence to the tradition of the *qin* and its associated accomplishments and values, which she passed on to disciples of all ages, genders, and nationalities from her home in Hong Kong.

If the *qin* so neatly gives voice to idealized *wen* masculinity, there is no such overt musical ascription for *wu* masculinity. Might we seek the values of loyalty, brotherhood, and physical strength in the shawm bands widespread across rural China? While the amateur *qin* player disdains money, the shawm bands are professionals: the pursuit of money is one of the attributes negatively ascribed to *wu* masculinity.[63] With their extremely loud volume and showy displays of virtuosity, the extrovert, macho sounds seem the opposite of the intimate *qin*. The players belong to a low-class hereditary group. At life-cycle rituals they play at the doorstep, unlike the more elite Daoist *shengguan* groups. Their low status is affirmed in a list of the most despised: "bastards, opera actors, and blowers-and-drummers."[64] Like the bandit heroes, exemplars of *wu*, they are outcasts, and their lifestyles are prone to violence.[65]

Sex and Transformations

Music in China, as everywhere else, is strongly related to sex, in terms of performance contexts, associations, and meanings and, especially for women musicians, as a dual profession. Musical erotica appears frequently in the historical literature. Take, for example, the seventeenth-century miscellany *Yugu Diaohuang* and its depiction of a man and woman seated together "blowing the *xiao* and plucking the strings": both popular metaphors for oral sex. In her study of seventeeth-century courtesans (*ji*) Zeitlin argues that *ji*, at the lower as well as the higher end of the social scale, were performing artists, primarily singers, as well as sex workers. Zeitlin regards the higher-status *ji* as literate and skilled musicians, able to set the poetry composed by male patrons to music. For her, these encounters are "collaborative and improvisational music-making," which she theorizes as an example of a gift economy involving financial, sexual, and artistic exchanges. The strength of the association between song and prostitution in this period is such that a talent for singing implies a lack of virtue.[66] There are interesting parallels between Zeitlin's work and the ethnographic research done by Yang Mu in the very different context of the *hua'er* folk song festivals in rural Gansu.[67] Singing at these festivals, he argues, is an opportunity to communicate sexual feelings, to pursue desires, and perhaps engage in sexual affairs. He observes that *hua'er* makes the awkwardness and difficulty of approaching the opposite sex feel "natural and appropriate."[68] Yang also notes the taboo on singing inside the home: "because of the sensual nature of *hua'er* singing it is traditionally restricted to the fields outside of villages. Singing at home or inside the village is regarded as lecherous and immoral because it might imply asking for sex."[69] Despite such taboos, sexuality and religion are not mutually exclusive. In this volume, Kouwenhoven and Schimmelpenninck describe the way *hua'er* are used to facilitate sexual contact and even pregnancy at temple fairs, under the protection of the gods, as the elders inside pray for fertility.

What is perhaps most striking in the field of gender in Chinese music is the fluidity, adaptability, and ceaseless transformations in the performance of gender across so many musical genres, periods, and social contexts. It is here that Butler's notion of performativity is most apt. Studies of marriage laments—sung performances that mark the rupture of women's transfer from their maternal home to their new family—highlight women's lived experience of liminality inherent in the social system of female exogamy:

> As my dress is soiled,
> There is no place to wash.
> When I ask the bitch where to wash,
> The bitch bids me to wash in the fields;
> When the wash water is finished,
> I must walk through the pig's piss.
> When I ask the bitch where to dry it,
> The bitch summons me to where three roads part;
> As I dry it up high,
> The bitch calls out not so high;
> But as I dry it down low,
> I fear the little rascal's dirty affections.[70]

As Rubie Watson argues, marriage for men means harmony and hierarchy; for women it means alienation and possibly death (in childbirth or potentially through maltreatment by the new family is severe). Laments express the tensions and contradictions (fears, longing, and anger) of those who must live of the periphery of two worlds but belong fully to neither. Watson argues that "laments give expression to an individual experience that is momentarily externalised through public performance, they do not resolve contradictions but celebrate them . . . the power of laments lies in their conflation of cultural form and personal style."[71]

Moving from personal to historical transformations, clearly Chinese opera, in its myriad regional variations, is the most obvious place to look for representations of gender. Opera is fertile ground for analysis, both in its delineation of gendered role types and in the aberrations, the areas of unease that are most revealing about norms and boundaries of gender categories, sex, and sexuality. Again we must avoid an assumption of historical stasis: across different dynasties we find fluctuating attitudes to both female and male performers, different representations of masculinity and femininity, and changing roles for the performers. The Qing period brought restrictions on public performance for women and hence the rise of male performers of female roles (*dan*), who were also deeply involved in male prostitution.[72] As the theatre scholar Min Tian argues, female impersonation was considered less dangerous and subversive than performances by real women, because Confucian doctrine emphasized the segregation of women from men to preserve the patriarchal social hierarchy.[73] Likewise, male prostitution was not considered subversive since, in the context of Qing China, sexual "morality" was a matter of male-female relations and the regulation of sexuality was really about regulating women's sexual behavior (in particular, preserving or disposing of their chastity); consequently, what men did with other men meant little in terms of the social morality of the time.[74]

In her groundbreaking study of homosexuality in late Qing China, Cuncun Wu finds that late Qing actors belonged to the lowest class of *jianmin* (mean people or outcasts) along with slaves, prostitutes, and yamen runners. Boys sold into the profession usually belonged to destitute or disaster-ridden families. "When a family sold a boy into the acting profession, the weight of the decision was enormous, as the child's legal status, and the status of his descendants, would suffer a humiliating decline from which it was difficult to recover."[75] The *dan* were the primary attraction for operagoers. Rich and powerful men were seated at the front of the theatre, and they invited *dan* to their table after the performance before publically taking them on to private entertainments.[76] Wu describes the production of *dan* as the feminization of subaltern males. Effeminate, pale, and delicate-looking boys were selected for *dan* training. They cultivated a pale complexion and an elegant and seductive gait, and they were admired in countless poems for their slender necks and bashful, gentle, girlish manner. They wore women's hair styles and sometimes performed on small stilts to imitate bound feet.[77]

The gender transformations of the *dan* between the late nineteenth and early twentieth centuries make a fascinating case study in the ideological changes sweeping across China during this period. Wu and Mark Stevenson write of the low-class, effeminate, rigorously cultivated catamite body of the *dan* actors who performed bawdy feminine stereotypes and displayed their naked white flesh for the entertainment of the crowd.[78] Mei Lanfang's grandfather, Mei Qiaoling, was one of the most celebrated *dan* of the 1870s, a favorite of Emperor Guangxu. He famously displayed his ample fair flesh in roles including a bathing scene where he played imperial consort Yang Yuhuan. He also ran Jinghe house, a renowned entertainment establishment that was situated at the center of the sex trade in Beijing.[79] The nineteenth-century *dan* were erased from history under the pressures of modernization in the early twentieth century, and they were replaced by the towering figure of Mei Lanfang. Mei distanced his sexuality, covered himself in elaborate costumes, and promoted virtuous female roles, transforming the performance of female roles into art and himself into a national icon.

The mid-twentieth century saw another momentous shift in gendered public performance with the rise of the all-female Yue opera in 1930s Shanghai. Their audiences represented a large segment of the female population of this rising cosmopolitan city. In her study of the genre, historian Jin Jiang argues that Yue opera represented an effort to explore dramatic changes in sex, gender, and family relationships in a rapidly modernizing city, and it helped the new urban dweller connect with these changes.[80] Yue opera fans were notorious for their unrestrained public displays of passion for their favorite female performers of male roles. By this time, public morality had shifted, and an all-female troupe could act "more naturally and passionately without restraint, while it was awkward to do so with male actors."[81] Mme Zinnia Kwok corroborates this point in her account of playing male roles in amateur Cantonese opera (chapter 6 of this volume).

These are intriguing tales of transformations, but in the accounts of these scholars the music of these operas and the sounds produced by these performers, which surely must be relevant to their communication of gender to their audiences, are barely in evidence. Wu goes so far as to claim that audiences were far more attentive to the effeminate appearance of *dan* than they were to their operatic skills, citing a nineteenth-century diarist who complains, "The melodies for *sheng* and *dan* are best sung in deep tones. However, the voices of the boy-actors are not mature enough and they only approximate the melody by following the tune of the *xiao* (vertical bamboo flute). Of course everyone in the audience is attracted to the theatre more for their beauty than their singing."[82] Yet the diarist's complaint surely reveals a connoisseurship at play, an appreciation of how the melodies of Beijing opera should sound, even if this ideal was not realized by the young *dan* performers. Stock goes some way to rescue us from our musicological frustration by discussing the rise of female performers in the less well-known genre of *huju* opera in mid-twentieth-century Shanghai. He argues that the operas as performed by female impersonators were constructions of difference, signifying femininity and full of stereotypes and bawdy innuendo. When real women took to the public stage, they sought instead to communicate authentic emotion. Stock analyzes this transformation in affect through a comparison of the vocal style of a female and a male performer, focusing on ornamentation, pitch range, and tone quality.[83]

Marjorie Garber argues that transvestites have a "male subjectivity in drag, a man-made femininity";[84] they either parody or celebrate femininity to make their bodies a site for male desire. Stock's analysis shares this perception, and in the popular opera form *huju* it is reasonable to believe that female impersonators were primarily parodying their subjects. But as we have seen above, in elite Chinese opera, ways of performing femininity go well beyond parody: male actors perform ideal representations of femininity and even become nationalist symbols. As Min argues, the inherited, male-defined language of Beijing opera performance has been prescribed not only for generations of male *dan* actors but also for the relative newcomers: female performers of female roles.[85] In this volume, Lam's study of a female performer of male roles in twentieth-century *kunqu* opera suggests that audiences may give greater weight to schools of performance and the inherited style of renowned teachers than to the biological sex of the performer.

In recent years, cross-dressing in Chinese opera has undergone something of a renaissance, as revealed in Lam's discussion, and male performers of female roles have become prominent celebrities in Chinese popular culture at the beginning of the twenty-first century. It remains the work of future studies to probe how contemporary listeners hear the emotions expressed by these actors. For example, Li Yugang's popularity seems to owe less to bawdy representations of womanhood than to the effeminate pop idols beloved by teenage fans and opposed by the state. Li won the 2006 reality talent show *Xingguang dadao* (Star Boulevard), which was national state broadcaster China Central Television's (CCTV) "healthy" rival to the Super Girl contest. A beautiful boy with a suitably moving backstory to satisfy the fans, he is nevertheless a state-sanctioned upholder of tradition. Appeasing all tastes, his operatic singing comes either straight or packaged in rhythm and blues, as he transforms fluidly between virtuous maiden and modern youth.

Chapters in This Volume

Stephen Jones's broad consideration of gender and music in local communities serves as a subintroduction to this volume. This trenchantly argued piece draws our attention to local traditions, gender, and power in the countryside, noting women's exclusion from the majority of traditional genres, just as they are still excluded from most public, power-holding roles in village society. Drawing on Susan McClary's work, Jones searches through Chinese traditions for examples of gendered musical features. He dismisses the statements on music and social order found in the Confucian classics, arguing that they bear little or no relation to the specifics of musical organization or style. It is perhaps in accordance with established gender stereotypes that our most contentious chapter is penned by a man, but Jones' contribution may also be read as an example of first-wave feminism, an interrogation and critique of the repression of women under patriarchy. Either way, this angry voice is an essential counterpoint to the more measured tones and more strategic readings of gender by the female contributors to this volume.

Judith Zeitlin's chapter provides another essential counterpoint in the form of a literary-historical approach to Ming musical, literary, and visual culture in the context of exchanges between courtesans and their clients and between male editors (habitual visitors to the pleasure quarter) and their readers. Treating the pleasure quarter as a site of cultural production, Zeitlin shows how "culture," "music," and "sex" were closely intertwined in anthologies of illustrated verse (*sanqu*) from this period. *Sanqu*, typically written by men to be performed by courtesans, offered a privileged site where men could write desire straightforwardly in a male voice. Citing Richard Middleton's writing on the pleasures of repetition in pop music, Zeitlin asks how the formulaic nature of these lyrics and their constant replay of conventionalized situations and emotions contribute to the image of the courtesan world they evoke.

Zheng Tiantian's chapter brings this scene up to date in a much rawer way with a view of contemporary "courtesan musical culture" in the karaoke bars of postsocialist China. She provides devastating insights into the use of musical performance in the production of the new entrepreneurial masculinity with memorable images of hostesses massaging the egos (figuratively) and the penises (literally) of their clients, singing with fake tears of their undying loyalty toward a philandering lover. Zheng juxtaposes her fieldwork insights with a survey of historical literature relating to courtesan culture to argue that courtesans in the premodern era enjoyed relatively higher status through their reputation as skilled artists and arbiters of their clients' social status. Arguing that revolutionary-era iconography of women produced a crisis of masculinity in China, Zheng's portrayal leaves us in no doubt that karaoke bar culture is tipping back the balance. Zheng finds so many continuities in the functions of affirming male social status served by the courtesan houses of imperial times and contemporary karaoke bars that one is compelled to wonder to what extent gendered power relations really differ across these different periods.

Joseph Lam draws on Louie's model of *wen* and *wu* masculinities in his discussion of contemporary *kunqu* performers. By analyzing specific scenes acted by two prominent performers, Lam draws attention to the subtleties of *kunqu*'s communication of gender through text, melody, and physical gesture. For Lam, the most successful characters portrayed in *kunqu* display aspects of both *wen* and *wu*: martial heroes may display emotion under duress; young scholars may allow lust to temporarily overcome their good manners. Such contradictions provide dramatic interest and connect directly with the audience. Lam argues for the relevance of these performances in contemporary negotiations of Chinese masculinity.

Stephen Jones's second contribution to the volume focuses on the shawm bands (*guchui*) that are widespread across rural China, hereditary male groups who historically performed ritual music for the Confucian elite. Jones draws our attention to the ways in which class and gender intersect. Again, drawing on Louie's model of *wen* and *wu* masculinities, Jones describes the social status of the shawm players, social outcasts whose lives are marked by poverty and violence, and contrasts this with the ritual role of their music under imperial China, a role that served to uphold the Confucian hierarchy. Jones examines the repertoire, searching for aspects of musical structure and style that might relate to aspects of the masculinity he describes, noting how, for instance, the extraordinary volume and the bravado and use of dramatic devices, surprise, and tricks relates to the competitive nature of the bands, their readiness to fight their rivals both musically and physically.

As they achieve greater international cachet, China's pianists find themselves negotiating ethnicized concepts of masculinity, combating Western stereotypes of emotionless technical brilliance to become icons of China's cultural diplomacy. In her chapter, Shzr Ee Tan describes how two contemporary stars, Lang Lang and Li Yundi, combine traditional Chinese ideas of masculinity with a highly cosmopolitan blend of popular culture models to craft their two distinct public personas. Addressing different audiences abroad and within China, Lang adopts elements of *wu* and *chou* (clowning) to aggressively dazzle audiences, while becoming a leader of new Chinese pianism. Li, in his more restrained pianism and quieter career, impresses Western critics as a serious, *wen* musician, while entrancing female audiences with his blend of Byronic romance and the soft masculinity of East Asian pop idols. The female singers of *hua'er* and *shan'ge* described in Frank Kouwenhoven and Antoinet Schimmelpenninck's chapter seem little concerned with soft romance or literary concepts of masculinity. These rural women want a man "as fresh as a jumping fish," for pleasure and to create children. The authors argue that, unlike other female-associated genres, such as laments and wailing, *shan'ge* provide not only an outlet for sorrows and anger but a space to deal with intersex relations, to achieve fame, and also to actively, even humorously, plead for more balanced views on the position and concerns of women. This theoretical positioning contrasts with Jones's approach, representing "second wave" feminism with its strategic reading of the fissure and disjuncture in patriarchy-dominated texts, practices, and institutions in a way that is empowering to the subaltern.

It is, then, Rowan Pease's chapter on the changing vocal style of professional Korean singers in China that may serve as the best representative of third-wave feminist thought, in its interrogation of the ways in which musical style—especially vocal quality—serves as a marker of gendered identities that may shift over time, thus highlighting their performative and constructed nature. Originally performed by men, the *p'ansori* genre began to admit women performers during the early twentieth century. Women singers who underwent the rigors of training in *p'ansori* to develop the desired timbral qualities of huskiness and rasp found themselves sidelined in the professional troupe network set up in the 1950s, when a higher, brighter tone became the preferred marker of ethnic femininity. Through the new enthusiasm for "authentic" (*yuanshengtai*) performance, the more traditional vocal style has made a limited comeback, although, as Pease points out, successful singers are still careful to soften the more unfamiliar aspects of their performance.

It is striking that four of the chapters in this volume address non-Han music but perhaps not surprising, given the emphasis on minority music within China, from performance on national stage to new composition and scholarship. The themes and approaches of these four chapters are highly diverse, but they make similar observations. Olivia Kraef discusses the promotion of Nuosu-Yi music and culture (a subgroup of the Yi living in southwest Sichuan) through national media and for the tourist industry. As with Pease's discussion of Korean *p'ansori* singers, here again we find the feminization of a minority tradition in twentieth-century China, or more specifically an instrument: the Jew's harp *hxohxo*. As Pease notes, men dominate the creative and modern domains of music, and women dominate the traditional and interpretive domains; a phenomenon of course not limited to China. Kraef is relatively upbeat on the movement of Nuosu women into professional performance as singers in state troupes, or more recently into successful careers in pop. Unlike Gladney's and Schein's critiques of "internal orientalism" and the exoticization and eroticization of minority women, Kraef points to the great popularity of these singers within the Nuosu community and sees this as part of a wider liberating trend for Nuosu women that includes greater opportunities for education and employment.

In the Zhuang minority area of Guangxi in southwest China, Xiao Mei explores the gendered and ethnicized nature of ritual performance, focusing on *me-mot* female ritualists and male Daoist priests. The Daoists practice a religion that is external to Zhuang culture: it is text based, in the standard Chinese dialect of the wider region, while the *me-mot*'s performance is oral, based on the local Zhuang dialect, and shamanic in style, her efficacy located in her trance-based journeys to the other world. In terms of musical performance, likewise, the Daoist recitation is learned from an external source, fixed, and incomprehensible to local audiences. The *me-mot* draws on local folk-song style, which she adapts into the ritual structure, improvising verses in the local dialect, surrounded by an eager audience that follows her spiritual journey. Xiao Mei emphasizes that these two types of ritualists are complementary, even to the extent of collaborating in one ritual, and the illiterate *me-mot* needs the acknowledgment and support of the Daoist priest (the spiritual representative of imperial power in this region of China), in the form of his written talismans, to ensure her efficacy. It is fascinating that the familiar gender division of male representative of central power and disempowered minority female, so familiar in the realm of national culture (e.g., in images of Chairman Mao applauding minority female performers) is also reproduced in the local ritual practices of this distant corner of Guangxi province.

In contrast with Xiao Mei's view of Zhuang culture in which Chinese and minority elements coexist, Rachel Harris's depiction of Uyghur women's ritual in Xinjiang is almost entirely focused on the ways these practices relate outward to the wider Islamic world. This is a useful reminder that China's minority peoples face outward as much as they face inward, but in fact Harris's delineation of Uyghur women's weeping as culturally codified musical performance resonates with the many references throughout this volume to women's use of weeping in musical performance, from marriage laments to pop idol Li Yuchun to the prostitutes of Dalian. Harris's description of a demonstration of weeping Uyghur women in the aftermath of the 2009 Ürümchi riots shows how women can achieve agency in the national and international political arena through the performance of emotion. Her reflexive approach in this chapter provides a counterpoint to the interview with Xiao Mei in this volume, who also reflects on the gendered experience of doing fieldwork in China.

Hwee-San Tan's chapter on "vegetarian sisters," Buddhist lay women ritualists in southern Fujian, brings us back to the Han majority. Tan carefully describes the position of the vegetarian sisters within the complex picture of Buddhist practice in this region, tracing their development through twentieth-century history. Impelled by religious and social changes such as the single-child policy and greater orthodoxy in monastic practice, the vegetarian sisters have found an important niche in local ritual practice. Like Xiao, Tan perceives a gendered division of national and local practice: the women maintain the local style of hymn singing, which has been supplanted by the national style in male monastic practice. Also like Xiao, Tan considers the interdependency of male and female ritualists, but here transformative power is a male preserve: only a man can embody the King of Hell and open the throats of the hungry ghosts.

Interviews

Interspersed among the chapters are interviews with musicians, musicologists, enthusiasts, and listeners who provide first-person perspectives complementing the main articles, either in elaboration of similar subject matter or in coverage of themes not addressed elsewhere in the volume. Ranging from just over one page to several thousand words, the style of these edited interviews is inspired by Sang Ye's valuable collection of self-representations by Chinese citizens in

China Candid.[86] The aim is to provide a sense of immediacy for readers, as if they are in direct conversation with the speakers, but this is an editorial device. Some of these interviews have been revisited over the course of time, developing deeper and wider conversational threads that are collapsed into a seamless whole in the interviews.

Conducted by Shzr Ee Tan, who takes editorial responsibility for this part of the book, and by Ruard Absaroka, largely through face-to-face meetings but also via new media technologies now widespread in China, they are deeply personal and often unsettling accounts. Most of the interviews were conducted in Mandarin or Cantonese, although a few interviewees felt comfortable enough with their cosmopolitan personas to resist linguistic stereotype and conduct conversations in a mix of languages, including English. Several of the interviewees are based in the Chinese diaspora, providing a crucial perspective on Chinese music that is less directly addressed by the chapters.

A Skype conversation across three time zones with amateur Chinese opera singer Zinnia Kwok, facilitated by her daughter Joanna Lee, sees the older woman pondering the gender dynamics of singing male roles opposite Hong Kong's lady amateur singers (*taitai*), whose husbands might frown upon their wives flirting on stage with real men. In Singapore, pop producer Li Sisong discusses the gendered styling of pop idols, each tailor-made for a different record-buying demographic. A chat with jazz singer and cross-dresser Coco Zhao, held in a foot massage parlor, yields insights into the stigma as well as the emancipatory possibilities of being openly gay in Shanghai's contemporary music scene. Zhao is a sophisticated cosmopolitan, both in his musical performance and in his discussion of self and gender, playing on the elite Chinese tradition of homosexuality, in his reference to the "passions of the cut sleeve," and on Western-orientalist gendered assumptions, in his delighted account of the disappointment of a drag club audience until they realized that he was "actually" a man.

Collectively, these interviews form a striking mosaic of views on music and gender in contemporary China and its diaspora. Offering rich life stories, disquieting anecdotes, (occasionally) hard-swearing voices, and insightful reflections on practice and the industry, these narratives position individuals within as well as beyond boundaries of social class and political background. Together, they show that the traditional boundaries between "insider" and "outsider" knowledge in musical practice and appreciation are never watertight, and they shed new light on the constantly evolving constructions of gender in the world of Chinese music.

Notes

1. Tani E. Barlow, "Theorizing Woman: *Funü, Guojia, Jiating* (Chinese Woman, Chinese State, Chinese Family)," in *Body, Subject, and Power in China*, ed. Tani E. Barlow and Angela Zito (Chicago: University of Chicago Press, 1994), 253–90.

2. State broadcasting administration statement approving Hunan TV mounting of the 2007 Happy Boy event [Guangdian zongju tongyi Hunan dianshitai juban "Kuaile nansheng" pifu], April 6, 2007, http://www.gov.cn/gzdt/2007-04/06/content_573621.htm. In 2010, one contestant who cross-dressed and sang like a woman, Liu Zhu, performed in several rounds before being eliminated. In the ensuing media stir, it was not clear whether his elimination was due to his singing or transgression of gender norms.

3. Compare Joseph S. C. Lam, "The Presence and Absence of Female Musicians and Music in China," in *Women and Confucian Cultures in Premodern China, Korea, and Japan*, ed. Dorothy Ko, JaHyun Kim Haboush, and Joan R. Piggott (Berkeley: University of California Press, 2003), 27–52.

4. Gail Hershatter, *Women in China's Long Twentieth Century* (Berkeley: University of California Press, 2007), 107–18.

5. Su Zheng, "Women and Music II," in *Garland Encyclopedia of World Music*, vol. 7, *East Asia: China, Japan, and Korea*, ed. Robert C. Provine (London: Routledge, 2001), 405–10.

6. Zhongguo yishu yanjiuyuan yinyue yanjiusuo, ed., *Zhongguo jinxiandai yinyuejia zhuan* (Shenyang: Chunfeng wenyi chubanshe, 1994).

7. Stephen Jones, "Reading between the Lines: Reflections on the Massive *Anthology of Folk Music of the Chinese Peoples*," *Ethnomusicology* 47, no. 3 (2003).

8. Su Zheng, "Chinese Scholarship and Historical Source Materials: Twentieth Century." In *Garland Encyclopedia of World Music*, vol. 7, *East Asia: China, Japan, and Korea*, ed. Robert C. Provine (London: Routledge 2001), 135–46; Xiu Jun and Jian Jin, *Zhongguo yueji shi* (Beijing: Zhongguo wenlian chuban gongsi, 1993); Dai Ning, "Ming Qing shiqi Qinhuai qinglou yinyue wenhua chutan," *Zhongguo Yinyuexue* 3 (1997): 40–54.

9. Li Juan, "Minzu yinyuexue zhong de shehui xingbie yanjiu: Yige xinke dute que yijiu bianyuan de yanjiu shijiao," *Zhongguo Yinyuexue* 1 (2006): 134–37.

10. See, for example, Yu Xia, "Yuexi tujiazu kujia ge de zhuti xinli fenxi," *Zhongnan Minzu Daxue Xuebao* 1 (2004): 152–55; Zhou Kaimo. "Minjian yishi zhong de nüxing juese: Yinyue xingwei jiqi xiangzheng yiyi," *Yinyue Yishu* 1 (2005): 64–72.

11. Wu Fan, *Yinyang yu gujiang: zai tiexu kongjian zhong* (Beijing: Wenhua yishu chubanshe, 2007), 235–76.

12. See, e.g., the analysis of female roles in China's revolutionary opera in Wang Baohua, "Shiqi nian zhong hongse geju nuxing xingxiang suzao de tezheng fenxi," *Zhongguo Yinyuexue* 4 (2006): 96–100.

13. Lam, "Presence and Absence."

14. Yang Mu, "On the *Hua'er* Songs of North-Western China," *Yearbook for Traditional Music* 26 (1994): 100–116; Yang Mu, "Erotic Musical Activity in Multiethnic China," *Ethnomusicology* 42, no. 2 (1998): 199–264.

15. Jonathan Stock, *Huju: Traditional Opera in Modern Shanghai* (Oxford: Oxford University Press, 2003), 86–96.

16. Other articles with references to gender issues in Chinese music include Cynthia P. Wong, "Women and Music I," in *Garland Encyclopedia of World Music*, vol. 7, *East Asia: China, Japan, and Korea*, ed. Robert C. Provine (London: Routledge, 2001), 401–4; Nora Yeh, "Wisdom of Ignorance: Women Performers in the Classical Chinese Music Traditions," in *Women, Gender, and Culture*, ed. Marcia Herndon and Susanne Ziegler (Wilhelmshaven: Florian Noetzel, 1990), 157–72; and Su Zheng, "Redefining Yin and Yang: Transformation of Gender/Sexual politics in Chinese Music," in *Audible Traces: Gender, Identity and Music*, ed. Elaine Barkin and Lydia Hamessley (Zurich: Carciofoli Verlagshaus, 1999), 153–76.

17. Fred C. Blake, "Death and Abuse in Chinese Marriage Laments: The Curse of Chinese Brides," *Asian Folklore Studies* 37 (1978): 13–33; Elizabeth L. Johnson, "Singing of Separation, Lamenting Loss: Hakka Women's Expressions of Separation and Reunion," in *Living with Separation in China: Anthropological Accounts*, ed. Charles Stafford (London: Routledge Curzon, 2003), 27–52; Anne E. McLaren, "Competing for Women: The Marriage Market as Reflected in Folk Performance in the Lower Yangzi Delta," *Intersections: Gender and Sexuality in Asia and the Pacific* 16 (2008), http://intersections. anu.edu.au/issue16/mclaren.htm; Anne E. McLaren, *Performing Grief: Bridal Laments in Rural China* (Honolulu, University of Hawaii Press, 2008); Rubie S. Watson, "Chinese Bridal Laments: The Claims of a Dutiful Daughter," in *Harmony and Counterpoint: Ritual Music in the Chinese Context*, ed. Bell Yung, Evelyn S. Rawski and Rubie S. Watson (Palo Alto, CA: Stanford University Press, 1996), 107–29.

18. Susan Auerbach suggests that the classification of women's laments in Greece as "nonmusic" is in itself emblematic of the devaluation of women's music. "From Singing to Lamenting: Women's Music Role in a Greek Village," in *Women and Music in Cross-Cultural Perspective*, ed. Ellen Koskoff (Champaign: University of Illinois Press, 1989), 27.

19. Nimrod Baranovitch, *China's New Voices: Popular Music, Ethnicity, Gender, and Politics, 1978–1997* (Berkeley: University of California Press, 2003).

20. Jeroen de Kloet, *China with a Cut: Globalisation, Urban Youth and Popular Culture* (Amsterdam: Amsterdam University Press, 2010).

21. Marc L. Moskowitz, *Cries of Joy, Songs of Sorrow: Chinese Pop Music and Its Cultural Connotations* (Honolulu: University of Hawaii Press, 2010).

22. Fran Martin, "The Perfect Lie: Sandee Chan and Lesbian Representability in Mandarin Pop Music," *Inter-Asia Cultural Studies* 4, no. 2 (2003): 264–79.

23. Cuncun Wu, "Beautiful Boys Made Up as Beautiful Girls: Anti-masculine Taste in Qing China," in *Asian Masculinities: The Meaning and Practice of Manhood in China and Japan*, ed. Kam Louie and Morris Low (London: Routledge Curzon, 2003), 19–40; Wu Cuncun, *Homoerotic Sensibilities in Late Imperial China* (London: Routledge Curzon, 2004); John Zou, "Cross-dressed Nation: Mei Lanfang and the Clothing of Modern Chinese Men," in *Embodied Modernities: Corporeality, Representation, and Chinese Cultures*, ed. Fran Martin and Larissa Meinrich (Honolulu: University of Hawaii Press, 2006), 79–97.

24. Jane Sugarman, *Engendering Song: Singing and Subjectivity at Prespa Albanian Weddings* (Chicago: University of Chicago Press, 1997), 32.

25. Simon Frith, "Music and Identity," in *Questions of Cultural Identity*, ed. Stuart Hall and Paul du Gay (London: Sage, 1996), 109–10.

26. Compare Susan Brownell and Jeffrey N. Wasserstrom, introduction to *Chinese Femininities/Chinese Masculinities: A Reader* (Berkeley: University of California Press, 2002), 1–41.

27. Ellen Koskoff, introduction to *Women and Music in Cross-Cultural Perspective* (Urbana: University of Illinois Press, 1989), 15.

28. Ibid., 10.

29. Compare Martin Stokes, introduction to *Ethnicity, Identity and Music: The Musical Construction of Place* (Oxford: Berg, 1994), 23.

30. Jing Wang, *Brand New China: Advertising, Media, and Commercial Culture* (Cambridge, MA: Harvard University Press, 2008), 77–79.

31. Judith Butler, *Gender Trouble: Feminism and the Subversion of Identity* (London: Routledge, 1990), 140.

32. Ibid., xv.

33. Sugarman, *Engendering Song*, 280.

34. Louise Meintjes, "Shoot the Sergeant, Shatter the Mountain: The Production of Masculinity in Zulu *Ngoma* Song and Dance in Post Apartheid South Africa," *Ethnomusicology Forum* 13, no. 2 (2004): 173–201.

35. Veit Erlmann, *Music, Modernity, and the Global Imagination: South Africa and the West* (London: Oxford University Press, 1999).

36. Deborah Pacini Hernandez, "'Cantando la Cama Vacia': Love, Sexuality and Gender Relationships in Dominican Bachata," *Popular Music* 9, no. 3 (1990): 351–67.

37. Freya Jarman-Ivens, introduction to *Oh Boy! Masculinities and Popular Music* (London: Routledge, 2007), 5.

38. Judith Halberstam, *Female Masculinity* (Durham, NC: Duke University Press, 1998), 241.

39. Simon Frith and Angela McRobbie, "Rock and Sexuality," *Screen Education* 29 (1978): 5–9, 12–15.

40. Robert Walser, *Running with the Devil: Power, Gender, and Madness in Heavy Metal Music* (Middletown, CT: Wesleyan University Press, 1993), 108–9.

41. Susan McClary, *Feminine Endings: Music, Gender and Sexuality* (Minnesota: University of Minnesota Press, 2002).

42. Walser, *Running with the Devil*, 41.

43. Baranovitch, *China's New Voices*, 10–11.

44. Tullia Magrini, ed. *Music and Gender: Perspectives from the Mediterranean* (Chicago: University of Chicago Press, 2003).

45. Compare chapters by Auerbach and others in Koskoff, *Women and Music*.

46. Tong Soon Lee, "Grace Liu and Cantonese Opera in England: Becoming Chinese Overseas," in *Lives in Chinese Music*, ed. Helen Rees (Urbana: University of Illinois Press, 2009), 119–44.

47. Bell Yung, "Tsar Teh-yun at Age 100: A Life of Qin Music, Poetry and Calligraphy," in *Lives in Chinese Music*, ed. Helen Rees (Urbana: University of Illinois Press, 2009), 69–90.

48. Dru Gladney, "Representing Nationality in China: Refiguring Majority/Minority Identities," *Journal of Asian Studies* 53, no. 1 (1994): 92–123.

49. Louisa Schein, *Minority Rules: The Miao and the Feminine in China's Cultural Politics* (Durham, NC: Duke University Press, 2000), 101.

50. Baranovitch, *China's New Voices*, 72–80.

51. de Kloet, *China with a Cut*, 59.

52. Baranovitch, *China's New Voices*, 128–31.

53. These musical responses to perceived social emasculation show interesting parallels to those described by Meintjes ("Shoot the Sergeant") and Hernandez ("Cantando la Cama"), albeit in very different political and economic situations.

54. de Kloet, *China with a Cut*, 193.

55. Ibid., 88.

56. Ibid., 110–15.

57. Barlow, "Theorizing Woman."

58. Brownell and Wasserstrom, *Chinese Femininities*, xx.

59. Kam Louie, *Theorising Chinese Masculinity: Society and Gender in China* (Cambridge: Cambridge University Press, 2002).

60. Compare Lam, "Presence and Absence."

61. Compare Bell Yung, "Da Pu: The Recreative Process for the Music of the Seven-string Zither." In *Music and Context: Essays in Honor of John Ward*, ed. Anne Shapiro (Cambridge, MA: Harvard University Press, 1985).

62. Bell Yung, *The Last of China's Literati: The Music, Poetry and Life of Tsar Teh-yun* (Hong Kong: Hong Kong University Press, 2008), 66; "Tsar Teh-yun at Age 100," 67.

63. Wu, "Beautiful Boys Made Up as Beautiful Girls," 93.

64. Stephen Jones, *Folk Music of China: Living Instrumental Traditions* (Oxford: Oxford University Press, 1995), 82.

65. Stephen Jones, *Ritual and Music of North China*, Vol. 2, *Shaanbei* (Aldershot: Ashgate, 2009), 165–66.

66. Judith Zeitlin, "Notes of the Flesh and the Courtesans' Song in 17th Century China," in *The Courtesans' Arts: Cross-Cultural Perspectives*, ed. Martha Feldman and Bonnie Gordon (Oxford: Oxford University Press, 2006).

67. Yang, "On the *Hua'er* Songs"; Yang, "Erotic Musical Activity."

68. Yang, "Erotic Musical Activity," 214.

69. Yang "On the *Hua'er* Songs," 108.

70. Marriage lament, cited in *Blake*, "Death and Abuse," 21–22.

71. Watson, "Chinese Bridal Laments," 129.

72. Wu, *Homoerotic Sensibilities*.

73. Min Tian, "Male *Dan*: The Paradox of Sex, Acting, and Perception of Female Impersonation in Traditional Chinese Theatre," *Asian Theatre Journal* 17, no. 1 (2000): 78.

74. Wu, *Homoerotic Sensibilities*, 74.

75. Ibid., 123.

76. Ibid., 134–39.

77. Ibid., 127–39.

78. Cuncun Wu and Mark Stevenson, "Male Love Lost: The Fate of Male Same-Sex Prostitution in Beijing in the Late Nineteenth and Early Twentieth Centuries," in *Embodied Modernities: Corporeality, Representation, and Chinese Cultures*, ed. Fran Martin and Larissa Heinrich (Honolulu: University of Hawaii Press), 2006.

79. Zou, *Cross Dressed Nation*.

80. Jin Jiang, *Women Playing Men: Yue Opera and Social Change in Twentieth-Century Shanghai* (Seattle: University of Washington Press, 2009), xiii.

81. Ibid., 83.

82. Wu, *Homoerotic Sensibilities*, 12.

83. Stock, *Huju*, 59–96.

84. Marjorie Garber, *Vested Interests: Cross-Dressing and Cultural Anxiety* (New York: Routledge, 1992), 96–97.

85. Min, "Male *Dan*."

86. Sang Ye, *China Candid: The People on the People's Republic*, edited by Geremie R. Barmé with Miriam Lang (Berkeley: University of California Press, 2006).

Chapter One

Gender and Music in Local Communities

Stephen Jones

Despite our groundbreaking access to China since the 1980s, including the vast countryside, one is still easily beguiled by the glossy images of modern metropolitan culture displayed in the media. So a reminder of the enduring values of local communities is apposite. In this chapter I discuss the Han majority of the population.

In their worthy goal of reinstating women into the story of Chinese music, the two articles by Cynthia P. Wong and Su Zheng on women and music in the *Garland Encyclopaedia of Music* (*East Asia volume*)[1] leave no space to spell out women's historical and ongoing submission in society. Though I am happy to accept Zheng's portrayal of Confucian culture as misogynistic, her "radical view" shouldn't mean airbrushing the evidence of the submission of women. This is as serious as (and not unrelated to) ignoring the ever-backward supply of water, healthcare, electricity, literacy, and transport available to much of the population. Along with celebrating women's musical contributions, and for all the complexities of women's ongoing struggle, it is worth stressing their ongoing exclusion from power and choice in public society, underlining the persistence of patriarchal tradition and the limited scope of modern progress.

Both Wong and Zheng illustrate women's contributions to early Chinese music history by referring to archeological excavations that show that female musicians were buried alive along with their dead master.[2] When women were allowed to survive their masters, they often worked as prostitutes. Zheng goes on to observe that, in ancient China, women could also be bestowed as a gift, and bought and sold—another enduring tradition today. What a lot of categories of prostitute upright Confucian men had to choose from[3]—and some were even chosen to be concubines! We should indeed incorporate all this into our account of Chinese music history, but I find little to celebrate here.

Wong and Zheng briefly point out women's progress in the twentieth century. To be sure, foot-binding was successfully stamped out, and arranged marriages became exceptional; female education was no longer limited to a tiny elite. Yet, despite government campaigns, female babies are still routinely murdered or abandoned. Under siege from the draconian birth-control policy, women and men alike attend rituals to pray to the gods to be granted a healthy son. Girls are a burden: since upon marriage they will be lost to another family, rural parents invest mainly in the welfare and education of sons. Economic progress has been uneven since the reform period. Scholars note many instances of regression in women's status: decollectivization and urban migration have been a mixed blessing. Women are still abducted and sold to poor older disabled men in less impoverished provinces; they continue to be subject to domestic abuse and are largely barred from public roles. Female leaders remain rare—at village, township, county, provincial, and national levels. Prostitution is rampant, though some women now rise to the artistic heights of working as karaoke hostesses (see Zheng Tiantian's chapter in this volume). Our accounts of women's roles in Chinese music cannot assume that readers know all this.[4] Any study of gender and music in China must include a broad assessment of women's progress, or regression, and this must be based on detailed local ethnography (both for expressive culture and the society that nourishes it), rather than plucking out instances of female stars.

Gender and Class

In China, as in most societies, gender images are dominated by men: even "femininity" in music has largely been dictated by men.[5] Men dominate women, but some classes of men dominate some other classes of men and women. Gender is hard to disentangle from class, and the ethos of any genre will further combine regional and historical factors.

Within China, gender values may be quite diverse. Looking at masculinity, concepts like *wen* and *wu* (civil and martial)[6] have been dominated by urban male literate images. The *wen-wu* construct involves women only marginally, with *wen* represented by the scholar and *wu* by the soldier or the righteous *haohan* 好汉 outlaw[7]—but we have scant data based on ethnography. The elite ideal may comprise a balance of *wu* at the service of *wen*, but if we are seeking widely practiced norms, such clearly delineated concepts may be hard to elicit among a semiliterate population. *Wen* men may often seem effeminate or emasculated,[8] but the vast majority of the population had little concern for such literate *wen* virtues. If those virtues were powerful, it was only a device to keep the lower classes in their place.

One might seek to identify the masculinities of the lower classes, including not just factory workers, peddlers, and soldiers but rural classes like artisans, hired and migrant laborers, and vagrants. We might read the production of masculinities into habits such as measuring prowess in terms of number of *mantou* rolls or bowls of noodles a man can eat or the amount of *baijiu* liquor he can drink. Male peasants are open about their bodies; physical strength, equipping men for labor, is admired.

In north China, whence much of my material derives, the *wen* pole is not much in evidence. Despite Confucian and Communist rhetoric, peasants are considered "backward." Their own protestations that they "have no culture" (*meiyou wenhua*) may mean merely that they have no formal education, but theirs is indeed largely a non-*wen* culture, even if they are exposed to "culture" like opera, Daoist liturgy, or local myth.

Of all people, peasants are aware of their poverty and lack of power, even aside from disparagement from the urban elite. Still, among them there are figures with relative prestige: selfless leaders like the (male) village party secretary in the 1950s or the (male) head of the temple committee—or in expressive culture, amateur leaders of ritual dance and singing, like the (male) "umbrella heads" of *yangge* groups. Since the 1990s, brave people determined to expose injustice and official corruption are respected, and in addition to the former categories involving public service, successful village entrepreneurs may be admired.[9] None of these quite possesses *wen*.

Local opera (performed mainly for temple fairs) is not only a *wen* force inculcating cultured values but is also a site for contesting such values: historically officials were constantly anxious at its portrayals of unethical behavior, and many of the most popular operas are martial (*wu*). The term *xiansheng* (master) is used for literate men, including bards in an oral tradition,[10] household Daoists, even *yinyang* 阴阳 geomancers. Whereas Daoist and Buddhist clerics were among the *xiajiuliu* lower classes 下九流 and priests resident in small local temples were often notorious opium addicts, hereditary households of Daoists tend to be more locally prestigious; though occupational, their work entails communicating with the gods and is literate (*wen*) to a considerable degree, even if their literacy is entirely based on learning the texts required for performing rituals efficaciously. At the bottom of the pile, virtual outcasts, are opera performers (*xizi*) and shawm bands (*chuishou* 吹手; see chapter 7 in this volume), along with other low-status men like coffin-bearers and cooks, all playing essential roles at life-cycle and calendric events.

Violence and Power

For all the civilized veneer, most of the "great events" (a masculine concept?) in imperial and modern history were driven by violence—all dynasties (including the Communist regime) were established through violence deriving from the countryside. But, aside from great events, both state and domestic violence have been endemic in imperial and modern eras.[11] Evident throughout William Hinton's work on a Shanxi village, the theme is pursued by Edward Friedman, Paul Pickowicz, and Mark Selden in their studies of a Hebei village;[12] they show how new forms of state violence post-1949 built on violent tendencies in Chinese society.

Violence is associated with many musical traditions in the world,[13] partly when they spring from a violent underworld, like jazz, tango, rebetika, gangsta rap, and so on. Violence may be peripheral to the music itself, as when performers and patrons are incidentally involved in violence and use music as an outlet. The jazz world was violent, but "cutting" contests were usually gentlemanly. Another situation is where the music encourages violence—either through the lyrics or ethos or through rivalry (see chapter 7 in this volume).

Violence is latent and often becomes overt in the raucous drinking and "guessing fists" games that so dominate rural restaurants—not least their soundscape. The popularity of shouting (often the local term for singing) connects with the loudness of much rural music (shawms, opera, not to mention firecrackers), contrasting with the sotto voce *wen* ideal of *qin* music. Some scholars[14] imply that the anti-*wen* Communist Party glorified *wu* through the peasantry; certainly, like imperial regimes, they encouraged the bullying and violence already endemic in peasant society even while purveying an image of the simple honest peasant.

One might also distinguish the violence of everyday life from implied legitimate power; the modeling of folk ritual on that of the elite has been called the "imperial metaphor."[15] Rural life (and indeed urban life until the 1950s) is structured and enlivened by the ritual of life-cycle and calendric events. Beyond the basic value of "excitement" (*re'nao* 热闹 lit. heat and noise) or *honghuo* 红火, the "red-hot sociality" of public ritual events,[16] such events celebrate conformity to a social hierarchy. Not merely a chaotic outpouring of folk exuberance, rituals are structured by the "orderliness" (*guiju* 规矩) of performance, including opera, ritual specialists, and shawm bands.[17] Ordinary peasants contributed to maintaining the rules of a hierarchical society that kept them in poverty, and they still obey ancient rules through displaying the five grades of mourning in their funeral attire, kowtowing, offering food, and so on. One may see all this as inculcating either social harmony or oppression.

Broadening Our Picture

If men are more visible as organizers of such rituals, women's roles are often significant. Before considering this, we need to see the broader picture at the grass roots. Only since the 1980s has urban migration significantly depleted the rural population—more than 80 percent of Chinese people were rural until then. For all the recent growth of cities and suburbs, in most counties in most provinces, at least 90 percent of the population is rural-based, with huge areas inland remaining very poor. Though today rural China tends to maintain traditional genres more, they were common to town and country until the 1950s. And while in general there are rather slim pickings for traditional musical activity in the major metropolitan centers, there are exceptions, such as Shanghai.[18] Ritual life continues to be vibrant in some highly industrializing areas, like the Putian plain on the southeast coast,[19] negotiating all the forces of modernity.

Beyond urban state institutions and media, local groups—whether communal or household based—represent the vast majority of cultural forms and music making.[20] Even the county opera troupes (whose state funding has dwindled since the 1980s) are in a small minority in any county compared to privately run groups, and they all depend for their living mostly on the rounds of local temple fairs.

Performance Genres

Thus if pop music and staged concert repertoires now dominate the media, they are only the tip of the iceberg. Traditional genres ubiquitous throughout local communities are documented in the several hundred thousand pages of the *Zhongguo minzu minjian yinyue jicheng* (Anthology of folk music of the Chinese peoples), our most basic source, however flawed.[21] In the West, our picture of local traditional music making remains incomplete. Rural societies encompass all kinds of performers—solo, household-based, and communal groups, both amateur and occupational. Amateurs include folk singers, percussion groups, and religious sects; occupational performers include narrative singers, opera troupes, shawm bands, household Daoists, and beggars. Amateur percussion ensembles are often related to martial arts and serve ritual purposes—heavenly generals mobilizing their troops.[22] Ceremonial music making looks to be far more common than entertainment in the life of local communities.

The male domination of such genres appears stark. In our discussions of instrumental music in China, the recent showcasing of women in conservatoire solo genres (*erhu, pipa, zheng*) may give a misleading impression of female dominance. Arguably, Western studies have tended to perpetuate the *wen* bias of Confucianism: apart from the *qin* zither (only ever played by a tiny minority compared to its vast exposure), other "refined" elite genres like *kunqu* opera and *sizhu* instrumental ensembles are favored over more "coarse" local operas, shawms, percussion, and so on, whose literate background is less apparent. *Sizhu* traditions may idealize *wen* characteristics in performing style. But again our genre sampling has been scant. One thinks of southeast China, for whose vibrant local ritual cultures we have an outstanding literature (Lagerwey, Dean, etc.), suggesting that the *sizhu* groups studied by Western scholars there are a minor part of the soundscape, compared to the diverse ritual and processional groups—not to mention the ubiquitous deafening firecrackers. The huge "gong-and-drum" groups around Chaozhou dominate the local soundscape, being closely involved in the major feuds and sometimes violent battles between communities, along with the closely related martial-arts groups. And for south Fujian, while Western music scholars have focused on the "refined" *nanyin* chamber genre, they have not addressed the shawm bands and percussion ensembles that accompany vast ritual parades while male spirit mediums skewer their cheeks in trance.[23]

In twenty years of documenting ritual groups, it has been distressingly possible for me not to meet any women at all; from rural cadres to temple committees, from shawm bands to ritual specialists, public roles are monopolized by men. Shawm bands, by far the most common genre in rural China, are male (see my chapter below). So—or so it may at first seem—are ritual specialists, such as household Daoists or ritual associations, performing vocal liturgy, ritual percussion, and sometimes melodic instrumental music.[24] The few exceptions to the male monopoly—nuns performing public liturgy, unmarried daughters taking part in their father's shawm band—only prove the rule.[25] Below, however, I note a substantial force of female ritual groups. Even for amateur urban entertainment genres like *Jiangnan sizhu* "silk-and-bamboo" ensembles in modern cosmopolitan Shanghai, women rarely participate.[26]

Vocal Music

At most points along the continuum from folk song through narrative singing to opera, again most Han Chinese vocal music in public contexts is likely to be male. Biographies in Chinese sources are an imperfect source, even apart from their superficiality. National dictionaries are less useful than the provincial volumes of the *Anthology*,[27] but here too we should beware selectivity. Very few women feature in the many biographies there; men are listed through their dominant role in local public contexts, whereas most of the women included may belong to state troupes. But this hardly reflects the realities of local communities.

As to opera, performers were traditionally an outcast group, like shawm bands, and in most places all male until the 1930s. Since then, women have been admitted to rural opera, even if they are rarely considered famous enough for a biography (the Shanxi volume of the *Zhongguo xiqu zhi* [Chinese opera monographs] gives 13 out of 188 biographies for women, all but one from the twentieth century), but, as I have argued, we should be interested in normative description, not just stars. Women have little power within the troupe; the troupe bosses are male, making the arrangements with the male temple committee and controlling the fees. Women are not listed for the responsible roles of composers, arrangers, and so on.

For narrative singing, I cannot agree that "*quyi*, regional music narratives traditionally dominated by men, are now predominantly performed by women."[28] Women are more visible in modern urban genres largely represented by state troupes. They did indeed constitute a substantial proportion of singers at amateur clubs I attended in Beijing in the 1990s; they have a more substantial role in narrative singing in the Shanghai region and seem to be increasingly dominating *nanyin* in Fujian. However, the vast majority of narrative-singing genres in the countryside, given their public nature (not to mention their primary ritual function of invoking blessings from the gods), are still performed by men.[29] Bards in Shaanbei, for example, are traditionally blind and male.[30] For Shanxi, Liu Hongqing's harrowing tale of the dysfunctional families of these performers in Zuoquan county[31] is revealing of the wretched fate of poor people generally and the burden of care on women.[32]

The umbrella category of folk song covers a wide range of contexts.[33] Men and women tend to sing different songs (such as men singing outdoor *shan'ge* 山歌, women singing *xiaodiao* 小调), with most public singing performed by men—for house building, drinking parties, work in the fields, and so on. So again, women's nugatory presence in the folk-song volumes of the *Anthology* may merely reflect their lesser public role in local societies. At weddings and funerals, though laments sung by the female kin (once a means of venting frustration against the Confucian system, however impotently) have become rarer, women may be found among groups of beggars performing songs.[34]

We need more material on the many occasional amateur festive percussion and dance groups in the "parish bands" (*shehuo* 社火) and "little opera" (*xiaoxi* 小戏) categories. Women have become more prevalent in urban *yangge*, but even in rural society they may now take part in genres like "boat on dry land" (*hanchuan* 旱船), and even if some of this is due to work-unit recruitment, it may constitute a substantial force. Women of all ages seem common in processional groups (even percussion ensembles) for ritual occasions in the southeast.

Ritual and Religion

Ritual, much of it religious, remains the main cultural engine of folk communities; most of the genres above are represented in ritual. Again, male domination is apparent—temple committees, household Daoists, funerary officiants, *yinyang* and *fengshui* masters. Women are often said to be unable to represent the community in communicating with the gods—their exclusion is starkly revealed in rain ceremonies, where, considered polluted and inauspicious, they are strictly forbidden even to witness the rituals.[35]

Yet ironically, it may transpire to be through religious behavior—seemingly a bastion of male hegemony—that women's power is most efficacious.[36] Some major female deities are worshipped—notably the Bodhisattva Guanyin and a host of local "Our Lady" (*niangniang*), "Granny" (*nainai*), and "old mother" (*laomu*) or "holy mother" (*shengmu*) deities—often promising fertility (healthy male births!). Given that ritual is the main engine for musical activity in the countryside, though women are never part of temple committees and not

Figure 1.1. Mediums and their disciples pray before they burn a boat, accompanied (*on left*) by members of ritual association. Houshan temple fair, Yixian, Hebei, 7th moon, 1993. Photograph by author.

heads of household for life-cycle rituals, they may comprise a majority of worshippers and patrons. It is perhaps at temple fairs that their role can be discerned most strongly. Apart from singing opera and wailing before the coffin and their roles as Buddhist and Daoist nuns, women are major supporters of temple life.[37] Women may further be strongly represented in local cults, and there may be more female groups of ritual specialists than we have noticed.[38] Sectarian and Christian groups may have a mixed membership, including performers of vocal liturgy.[39]

But it is as spirit mediums that I suspect women most commonly subvert male power. Amazingly widespread, both among the minorities and the Han Chinese, they have begun to attract scholarly attention as a major element of folk religion;[40] and they invariably sing. Though there are male mediums, such as the self-mortifying mediums who skewer their cheeks and flagellate themselves in trance under the direction of Daoists at the temple fairs of south Fujian[41] (*wu* at the service of *wen*?), in most areas female mediums seem to be in a considerable majority and may indeed possess local prestige. They often practice initially as healers for individuals, but this tends to overlap with public representation, as they instruct their clients (or their clients' offspring) to donate to the temple of the god possessing them and organize group attendance at temple fairs, often involving ritual singing. This may be a significant area where women forge a public role for themselves, even taking a leading role.[42]

The Sound of Music

The mechanics of music may be difficult to relate to society, but since Alan Lomax's cantometrics project it has been a beguiling mantra. Instrumental music may seem "abstract," offering few clues to discursive verbal "meaning," but Susan McClary, partly inspired by ethnomusicology,[43] shows how in the Western art music tradition it is neither abstract nor absolute, and it reflects social values, including gender roles. Penetratingly, she goes on to expose the dominant male agenda in Western art music since the baroque period.

Yet, in other patriarchal societies such as India, China, or the Islamic world, little seems to have been done to show how musical detail may reflect gender roles. Some societies might theorize gender less explicitly than in Western art music, but Confucian theorists insisted on linking music to meaning, both social and emotional; as the cornerstone of ritual (spreading from imperial court ritual throughout society), music should confirm the "proper" social hierarchy. Since McClary's work, one might expect to find "audible traces" of misogyny in Chinese music.[44] Ancient texts seem to promise more than they deliver: "When musical pitches are appropriately presented as high and low tones, and when musical phrases are arranged as beginnings and endings, music can be used to represent human affairs and activities, revealing principles behind intimate and remote relationships, high and low status, old and young ages, and males and females. Thus, there is a saying that music shows what is deep inside societies."[45] Unfortunately the sources are silent on *how* music might reveal such principles: whatever are these comments supposed to mean? If we are to cite them, surely we have to point out that their meaning is not semantic, discursive, or rational, hardly allowing meaningful musicological interpretation. Confucian texts themselves function as a kind of ritual of conformity; their mantric repetition inculcates unthinking obedience, but a musician can only dismiss them as empty mystification. If peasant musicians were to make such statements (they don't), at least one can politely request further explanation, specific examples of *how* "musical pitches are appropriately presented as high and low tones," and so on. The authors of ancient texts (incidentally, rarely musicians) cannot be so interrogated.[46]

Apart from the diverse entertainment genres of vocal and instrumental music favored by the Confucian elite, most of which were quite at odds with their austere theory, even the music used for their rituals is hard to relate to the theory—the core repertoire of the shawm bands may not be "popular," but it too seems far from Confucian ritual prescriptions. In my analysis of the repertoire of one shawm band,[47] I find scant clues to gender ideology, only magnificent creativity—a preserve of male outcasts working at the service of the Confucian elite.

Zheng aptly warns against imposing our Western concepts of gender onto traditional Chinese ones.[48] She describes *kunqu* opera melodies as androgynous, suggesting that, in drama and its music, women were far more equal than in the wider society; that melodies are more differentiated by age, and perhaps by intragender roles, than by gender; and that Chinese music was not gender specific until modern Western urban influences. But there is room for more detailed analysis of all kinds of vocal music, encompassing style, like that of Jonathan Stock on *Huju* opera.[49]

For instrumental music, are there any general qualities that reflect gender or social roles? Whereas modern conservatoire music mainly highlights solo virtuosity and emoting—derived from a view of the modern romanticism of Western art music—the more communal ethos of local music making is largely ensemble based. Might this tell us anything about changing patterns of gender? Can we argue, after Lomax, that heterophony (far from unique to China, of course) is more (or less) hierarchical than functional harmony?

Dyads such as *yin-yang*, *wen-wu*, and *cu-xi* (coarse-fine) do not seem to be helpful.[50] The *yin-yang* dyad is an operational category for rituals for the dead and the living and is crucial to geomancy, but it is hardly discussed in music. If correlations have been made in Confucian theory between *yin-yang* and pitches, no one seems to have noticed, nor is it discussed in the practice of living traditions. The *wen-wu* dichotomy is used more but still for general rather than specific musical features. *Wen* and *wu* operas are distinguished; *wuchang* may refer to the percussion as opposed to *wenchang* instrumental melody, although for the latter there is a further distinction between *sizhu* melodies and the *chuida* shawm pieces used for the entries of emperors and generals or for ceremonial occasions. In ritual ensembles, *wentan* 文坛 are ritual specialists performing vocal liturgy; *wutan* 武坛, the instrumental section, both percussion and melodic. "Martial" operas seem most popular. Style may be all-important, but I find no analysis of how martial and civil melodies may differ structurally in the logic of their melodic movement.

Though some regional differences may be identified in the use of scales, such as the northwestern preference for the *so* scale, they don't seem to relate to gender or class. In most traditional Han Chinese genres, we find a pentatonic basic set, with skillful use of metabole whereby the two further degrees of the heptatonic scale are used occasionally as passing notes or to create a feeling of temporary modulation. The preference for pentatonic scales is also a historical issue, with scales as shown in early notations appearing more heptatonic. Despite all the complexities of scale and mode in early elite vocal genres like *kunqu*, I find no historical evidence that certain scales were associated with gender. Even in living traditions, promising modal affects like the *kuyin* 哭音 weeping scale or *ruandiao* 软调 "soft mode" cannot necessarily be considered yin or feminine. Soft dynamic, slow tempo, or modern descriptions like lyrical or mellifluous, cannot be equated simply with femininity. It is hard to find meaning in the irregularity of phrasing[51] that is common to many genres. Nor are features such as conjunct or disjunct (smooth or angular) melodic contours or weak-beat or strong-beat cadences likely to map easily onto gender. One might base analysis on note weighting, discovering hierarchies of pitches, but this may not reveal social hierarchies.

So both social and musical study are needed, but with a far broader range of data than has hitherto been imagined. As long as we remain mesmerized by urban stage performances and by Confucian and Communist propaganda, we will never comprehend gender roles in the expressive cultures of the myriad local communities. But one point is clear: however much we unearth women's roles in local cultures and for all their "subversive strategies," as long as girl babies are murdered or abandoned, as long as women are kidnapped from poorer provinces and sold to older, sometimes disabled, men unable to afford a local bride, as long as women remain excluded from public power, women's ability to contribute to music making is likely to remain limited.

Notes

1. Cynthia P. Wong, "Women and Music I," and Su Zheng, "Women and Music II," in *Garland Encyclopedia of World Music*, vol. 7, *East Asia: China, Japan, and Korea*, ed. Robert C. Provine, Yosihiko Tokumaru, and J. Lawrence Witzleben (London: Routledge, 2002), 405–6.

2. Wong, "Women and Music I," 402; Zheng, "Women and Music II," 406. A disturbing (if remote) echo of this is in posthumous marriage (*minghun*), which has been reviving in northwest China since the 1980s; Stephen Jones, *Ritual and Music of North China*, vol. 2, *Shaanbei* (Aldershot, UK: Ashgate, 2009), 86. For unmarried men who die early (such as in the appallingly common mining accidents), a suitable unmarried dead female is found, and a wedding ceremony performed—accompanied by male shawm bands. Women (often disabled or from yet poorer provinces) may even be murdered to cater to this market.

3. Zheng, "Women and Music II," 405–6.

4. In an extensive literature, for a balanced survey, see Gail Hershatter, *Women in China's Long Twentieth Century* (Berkeley: University of California Press, 2007); for rural women since the reforms, including their urban migration, see Tamara Jacka, *Women's Work in Rural China: Change and Continuity in an Era of Reform* (Cambridge: Cambridge University Press, 1997). For a radical summary of women's regression under the reforms, see William Hinton, *Through a Glass Darkly: U.S. Views of the Chinese Revolution* (New York: Monthly Review Press, 2006), 195–97.

5. Susan McClary, *Feminine Endings: Music, Gender, and Sexuality* (Minneapolis: University of Minnesota Press, 1991).

6. Kam Louie, *Theorising Chinese Masculinity: Society and Gender in China* (Cambridge: Cambridge University Press, 2002).

7. David Ownby, "Approximations of Chinese Bandits: Perverse Rebels, Romantic Heroes, or Frustrated Bachelors?" in *Chinese Femininities, Chinese Masculinities: A Reader*, ed. Susan Brownell and Jeffrey N. Wasserstrom (Berkeley: University of California Press, 2002).

8. Louie, *Theorising Chinese Masculinity*.

9. For an intriguing mixture, see Adam Yuet Chau, *Miraculous Response: Doing Popular Religion in Contemporary China* (Palo Alto, CA: Stanford University Press, 2006), chap. 9; for charisma among local ritual leaders, note also Stephan Feuchtwang and Mingming Wang, *Grassroots Charisma: Four Local Leaders in China* (London: Routledge, 2001).

10. Jones, *Ritual and Music*, vol. 2.

11. One might reference imperial and modern government punishment systems, the birth-control policy, domestic violence, and the common practice of beating apprentices in opera troupes and temples. See, e.g., William Hinton, *Fanshen: A Documentary of Revolution in a Chinese Village*, New York: Vintage, 1966), 46–57 and throughout; Jonathan M. Lipman and Stevan Harrell, eds. *Violence in China: Essays in Culture and Counterculture* (Albany: State University of New York Press, 1990); many reports from Amnesty International; Jun Jing, *The Temple of Memories: History, Power, and Morality in a Chinese Village* (Palo Alto, CA: Stanford University Press, 1996); Xin Liu, *In One's Own Shadow: An Ethnographic Account of the Condition of Post-Reform Rural China* (Berkeley: University of California Press, 2000), 122–25, 143–50; Paul Pickowicz and Liping Wang, "Village Voices, Urban Activists: Women, Violence, and Gender Inequality in Rural China," in *Popular China: Unofficial Culture in a Globalizing Society*, ed. Perry Link, Richard Madsen, and Paul G. Pickowicz (New York: Rowman and Littlefield, 2002), 57–87. For state violence, note also, e.g., Jing, *Temple of Memories*, and Ralph Thaxton, *Catastrophe and Contention in Rural China: Mao's Great Leap Forward Famine and the Origins of Righteous Resistance in Da Fo Village* (Cambridge: Cambridge University Press). Elizabeth Perry, in her "Rural Violence in Socialist China," *China Quarterly* 103 (1985): 414–40, distinguishes reactive violence in the 1950s and competitive violence since the 1980s.

12. Edward Friedman, Paul Pickowicz, and Mark Selden, *Chinese Village, Socialist State* (New Haven, CT: Yale University Press, 1991), and *Revolution, Resistance, and Reform in Village China* (New Haven, CT: Yale University Press, 2005).

13. Bruce Johnson and Martin Cloonan, *The Dark Side of the Tune: Popular Music and Violence* (Aldershot, UK: Ashgate, 2009).

14. For example, Louie, *Theorising Chinese Masculinity*, 19–20.

15. For example, Stephan Feuchtwang, *The Imperial Metaphor: Popular Religion in China* (London: Routledge, 1992).

16. Chau, *Miraculous Response*, chap. 8.

17. In his ethnography of a Shaanxi village, Liu, *In One's Own Shadow*, distinguishes routine violence and violence in ritual contexts (122–25, 143–50); violence as a performative aspect of celebration, not conceived negatively (122), and "not confined to a particular social group defined by generation, age, or sex" (124), though he also suggests changing patterns (149–50). He gives the example of the blocking of the bride from entering the marital chamber (144, 147–48).

18. For example, Qi Kun, *Lishide shanshi: Shanghai Nanhui sizhuyue qingyinde chuancheng yu bianqian yanjiu* (Shanghai: Shanghai yinyuexueyuan chubanshe, 2007).

19. Kenneth Dean, *Ritual Alliances of the Putian Plain* (Leiden: Brill, 2009).

20. Kenneth Dean, in "China's Second Government: Regional Ritual Systems in Southeast China," in *Shehui, minzu yu wenhua zhanyan guoji yantaohui lunwenji* (Taipei: Hanxue yanjiu zhongxin, 2001) describes the communal ritual organizations

as "China's second government." Adam Yuet Chau, in "'Superstition Specialist Households'? The Household Idiom in Chinese Religious Practices," *Minsu Quyi* 153 (2006), also draws attention to the "household idiom" in religious practices—though still referring to male roles.

21. Stephen Jones, "Reading between the Lines: Reflections on the Massive *Anthology of Folk Music of the Chinese Peoples*," *Ethnomusicology* 47, no. 3 (2003): 287–337.

22. For Taiwan, cf. Donald S. Sutton, *Steps of Perfection: Exorcistic Performers and Chinese Religion in Twentieth-Century Taiwan* (Cambridge, MA: Harvard University Press, 2003).

23. Dean, *Ritual Alliances*.

24. Stephen Jones, *Folk Music of China: Living Instrumental Traditions* (Oxford: Oxford University Press, 1998); Stephen Jones, *Plucking the Winds: Lives of Village Musicians in Old and New China* (Leiden: CHIME Foundation, 2004); Stephen Jones, *Ritual and Music of North China, Shawm Bands in Shanxi* (Aldershot: Ashgate, 2007); Stephen Jones, *In Search of the Folk Daoists of North China* (Aldershot, UK: Ashgate, 2010); Helen Rees, *Echoes of History: Naxi Music in Modern China* (New York: Oxford University Press, 2000).

25. See, however, the stimulating Zhang Zhentao, "Nü yueshou yu nü changjia," *Xinghai yinyuexueyuan xuebao*, no. 3 (2009): 43–49.

26. Wong ("Women and Music I," 404) cites Witzleben to claim increasing female participation, but the latter passage actually shows that women were still very rare in the 1980s, and they remain so now. J. Lawrence Witzleben, *"Silk-and-Bamboo" Music in Shanghai: The Jiangnan Sizhu Instrumental Ensemble Tradition* (Kent, OH: Kent State University Press, 1995), 31.

27. For comments on the *Anthology* biographies, see Jones, "Reading between the Lines," 296–97.

28. Wong, "Women and Music I," 404; cf. Zheng, "Women and Music II," 408.

29. The 78 biographies of the Beijing volume of the *Zhongguo quyi zhi* include only three women. There are a mere seven women in the 230 biographies in the Jiangsu volume and six women out of 118 biographies for the Henan volume.

30. Jones, *Ritual and Music*, vol. 2.

31. Liu Hongqing, *Xiang tian er ge: Taihang mangyiren de gushi* (Beijing: Beijing chubanshe, 2004).

32. Zhang Yanqin, "Zhangzi shuoshu jiqi xijuhua qingxiang," *Minsu Quyi* 151 (2006), on narrative singers in a county in southeast Shanxi, shows a greater recent role for women.

33. Antoinet Schimmelpenninck, *Chinese Folk Songs and Folk Singers: Shan'ge Traditions in Southern Jiangsu* (Leiden: CHIME foundation, 1997), 89–95.

34. Jones, *Ritual and Music*, DVD §A1; Li Mei, "Jiang-Huai diqu qigai yinyue de chubu yanjiu," *Yinyue wenhua* 2001 (Beijing: Wenhua yishu chubanshe).

35. Xiao Mei, "Huwu hujie qi ganlin: Xibei (Shaanbei) diqu qiyu yishi yu yinyue diaocha zongshu," in *Zhongguo minjian yishi yinyue yanjiu, Xibei juan*, ed. Tsao Pen-yeh [Cao Benye] (Kunming: Yunnan renmin chubanshe, 2003), with DVD.

36. See Anne McLaren, "Women's Work and Ritual Space in China," in *Chinese Women, Living and Working*, ed. Anne McLaren (London: Routledge Curzon, 2004), 169–87, which is now being augmented by local case studies; see, e.g., issue 168 of *Minsu Quyi*, June 2010.

37. See, e.g., Adeline Herrou, *La vie entre soi: Les moines Taoïstes aujourd'hui en Chine* (Nanterre, France: Société d'ethnologie, 2005).

38. See, for example, Hwee-San Tan's chapter in this volume, and note the "scroll-reciting" *xuanjuan* groups in south Jiangsu; Qian Tiemin, "Jiangsu Wuxi xuanjuan yishi

yinyue yanjiu," in *Zhongguo minjian yishi yinyue yanjiu*, ed. Tsao Pen-yeh, vol. 1 and DVD; cf. Mark Bender, "A Description of *Jiangjing* (Telling Scriptures) Services in Jingjiang, China," *Asian Folklore Studies* 60, no. 1 (2001): 101–33. See also Erik Mueggler, *The Age of Wild Ghosts: Memory, Violence, and Place in Southwest China* (Berkeley: University of California Press, 2001), for his account of the ritual responses of a Yunnan minority people to state violence, famine, and the birth-control policy.

39. For the female takeover of a Protestant community and reflections on the gendered fieldworker, see Andrew Kipnis "Zouping Christianity as Gendered Critique? The Place of the Political in Ethnography," *Anthropology and Humanism* 27, no. 1 (2002): 80–96.

40. See, e.g., Ann S. Anagnost, "Politics and Magic in Contemporary China," *Modern China* 13, no. 1 (1987): 40–61.; Kang Xiaofei, "In the Name of Buddha: The Cult of the Fox in Contemporary Northern Shaanxi," *Minsu Quyi* 138 (2002): 67–109; Chau, *Miraculous Response*, 54–57; Yang Der-Ruey, "The Education of Taoist Priests in Contemporary Shanghai" (PhD diss., London School of Economics, 2003), 187–212; Fan Lizhu, "The Cult of the Silkworm Mother as a Core of Local Community Religion in a North China Village: Field Study in Zhiwuying, Baoding, Hebei," in *Religion in China Today*, ed. Daniel Overmyer (Cambridge University Press, 2003), 63–66; Jones, *Plucking the Winds*, 284–85; Thomas D. Dubois, *The Sacred Village: Social Change and Religious Life in Rural North China* (Honolulu: University of Hawaii Press, 2005), 65–85; Daniel Overmyer, *Local Religion in North China in the Twentieth Century: The Structure and Organization of Community Rituals and Beliefs* (Leiden: Brill, 2009), 83–92; Brigitte Baptandier, *The Lady of Linshui: A Chinese Female Cult* (Palo Alto, CA: Stanford University Press, 2008). These are just some references for the Han Chinese, with many more for the ethnic minorities, such as Xiao Mei's chapter 18 in this volume. Note also Barend ter Haar's bibliography http://website.leidenuniv.nl/~haarbjter/shamanism.htm; and the section on shamanism in Philip Clart's bibliography on religion http://www.uni-leipzig.de/~clartp/bibliography_CPR.html, both accessed February 7, 2013.

41. Dean, *Ritual Alliances*.

42. For the adaptation of male Daoist priests to female mediums in the ritual economy of Shanghai, see Yang, "Education of Taoist Priests," chap. 4.

43. McClary, *Feminine Endings*, 26.

44. Su Zheng, "Redefining Yin and Yang: Transformation of Gender/Sexual Politics in Chinese Music," in *Audible Traces: Gender, Identity, and Music*, ed. Elaine Barkin and Lydia Hamessley (Zurich: Carciofoli, 1999), 153–76; despite Lam's defense, Joseph S. C. Lam, "The Presence and Absence of Female Musicians and Music in China," in *Women and Confucian Cultures in Premodern China, Korea, and Japan*, ed. Dorothy Ko, JaHyun Kim Haboush, and Joan R. Piggott (Berkeley: University of California Press, 2003), 102.

45. Lam, "Presence and Absence," 99, citing the ancient *Record of Music*.

46. Alan Thrasher, *Sizhu Instrumental Music of South China: Ethos, Theory and Practice* (Leiden: Brill, 2009), seeks to relate Confucian ideology to living traditions of *sizhu* music, but his analysis discusses rather general ambient features rather than musical detail and refrains from problematizing the role of music in social and gender oppression.

47. Stephen Jones, "Living Early Composition: An Appreciation of Chinese Shawm Melody," in *Analysing East Asian Music: Patterns of Rhythm and Melody*, ed. Simon Mills, Musiké 4 (The Hague: Semar, 2010), 25–112.

48. Zheng, "Redefining Yin and Yang."

49. Jonathan Stock, *Huju: Traditional Opera in Modern Shanghai* (Oxford: Oxford University Press, 2003).

50. For general gender contrasts, Jacka, *Women's Work*, 15–20, refines the public-private debate by adopting the more emic "inner-outer" (*nei-wai*) distinction.

51. Compare Thrasher, *Sizhu*, 78–80; Jones, "Living Early Composition."

Chapter Two

The Pleasures of Print

Illustrated Songbooks from the Late Ming Courtesan World

Judith T. Zeitlin

> What lacks wings but can fly? Song. What is rootless but holds fast? Love. Song emerges from emptiness and so spreads everywhere. Love grows out of something concrete and always follows the bestowal of favors.
>
> —Liang Chenyu, "'Xiangbianman: Ji Wang Guifu' xu"

It is well established that the late Ming (roughly 1572–1644) was a high point of courtesan culture in China, that this culture was most dynamic in the southeastern cities of the lower Yangtze River delta region, and that musical performance, especially song, was a basic staple of the interaction between courtesans and their clients.[1] Until recently, studies of the late Ming courtesan world have been based mainly on representations of the pleasure quarter in fiction and drama; on poems to, by, or about a few celebrity courtesans; and especially on memoir literature composed in the early Qing after the fall of the Ming dynasty in 1644, such as Yu Huai's account of the Nanjing pleasure district, *Miscellaneous Records of the Plank Bridge* (*Banqiao zaji*). These memoirs come from a long line of nostalgic reminiscences of urban entertainment districts and entertainers. They are invariably written in hindsight, most often after the destruction of the quarter, from the twelfth-century *Dreams of Splendor in the Eastern Capital* (*Dongjing menghua lu*) after the fall of the northern Song capital Kaifeng to Stanley Kwan's 1987 ghost film *Rouge* (*Yanzhi kou*) on 1930s Hong Kong.

While this memoir literature provides useful materials for continuously thinking about issues such as memory, trauma, and nostalgia, a new type of scholarship has emerged in the past decade that explores direct links between the late Ming entertainment world and the trove of contemporaneous publications stemming from the courtesan world.² It is important to use these sources and not just rely on literature composed retrospectively during the early Qing, precisely because contemporaneity—being up-to-date—was such a crucial component of cultural life in the pleasure quarter, particularly when it came to song. Moreover, one reason for the spread of southeastern forms of courtesan culture across the empire during the late Ming was precisely that the cities of Nanjing, Hangzhou, and Suzhou, the locales of the most famous pleasure districts, were also centers of booming publishing industries. Books about the courtesan world geared to a contemporary market were produced in rapid succession during the first decades of the seventeenth century by editors capitalizing on their insider status and expertise within the demimonde for a public with a seemingly insatiable interest in anything related to *qing* (love, passion, desire, sentiment).

This essay is partly inspired by this new scholarly trend. But my focus is a specific historical problem concerning verbal and pictorial representations of songs and singing within late Ming courtesan culture and the conception of erotic love and music that such representations project. My evidence mainly comes from a particular type of late Ming printed source: anthologies of illustrated verse that presented themselves as high-end products of the social, sexual, and artistic interaction between bon vivant literati and top courtesans. Such books do not all adopt the same organization, format, or style of illustration, but they all include at least some examples of *sanqu* 散曲 (lyrics to freestanding arias composed as independent song rather than as part of an opera).

A short explanation of *sanqu* is necessary before I proceed to specific examples. Generally speaking, *sanqu* constitutes both a literary genre and a performance genre. As a literary genre, the songs identified as *sanqu* are printed in anthologies and can be treated as reading material or as manuals for writers in need of models to emulate. But, as a fashionable genre of late Ming sentimental verse, these songs were also closely associated with new composition and performance in the pleasure quarter; indeed "fashionable" or "contemporary" song (*shiqu* 时曲) was another possible term for them.³ "It's easy to tire of song-suites we're too familiar with hearing," as Feng Menglong 冯梦龙 explained to promote his anthology *The Celestial Air Played Anew* (*Taixia xinzou* 太霞新奏).⁴ The vogue for *sanqu* in this period was above all a by-product of the literati passion for *kunqu*, a musical system of tunes, instrumentation, and vocal styles associated with the Kunshan district outside Suzhou. *Sanqu* were one of the cornerstones of the courtesan's singing repertory at this time, the other two being arias excerpted from "operas" (*xiqu*) and "popular song" (*suqu* 俗曲). All of these are subsumed under the collective umbrella of sung verse known as *qu* or "aria." As with the earlier genre of *ci* (song lyric), the salient compositional feature of *qu* is writing new words to a preexisting melody, which is identified by a labeled tune title. For *sanqu* and *xiqu*, which were much stricter than popular song, this mode of versification required the lyricist to observe the individual rules governing rhyme, meter, and word tone prescribed for each tune pattern and to have some training in music (or at least to work with someone trained in music); conversely, to be capable of performing newly composed lyrics, a singer had to have some musical training in adjusting the words to the tune (or to work with someone trained in this art), something especially important and difficult in singing *kunqu*.

The most common paradigm in courtesan literature throughout the ages is that of literary men composing verses for these women to sing. During the late Ming, such verse took the form of *sanqu*, which explains in part why contemporaneous publications that billed themselves as products of the pleasure quarter consist so much of *sanqu* "presented as gifts" (*zeng*) to named courtesans. This dominant paradigm of a male lyricist and a female singer, however, tends to occlude the fact that many literary men were also avid singers and that courtesans particularly skilled in music and versification sometimes crafted their own lyrics to the arias they sang.[5]

I have discussed the learning, composition, and performance of songs by courtesans in earlier papers.[6] This essay tackles a related but different issue, namely, how songs and singing are represented in the *sanqu* anthologies—both in the texts and in pictures. Because these verses and images were created or commissioned by literati who were courtesan circle insiders and because the anthologies were compiled by the same group of men, we may consider such representations as the "self-fashioning" of the writers and audience for courtesans' songs.[7] This body of materials thus provides a unique opportunity to look into these men's own understanding of the artistic conventions and social implications of songs and singing in late Ming courtesan circles.

The biggest challenge facing any scholar who tackles these *sanqu* anthologies is the sheer repetitiveness and formulaic nature of the verse. I have previously argued that this formulaic quality may have facilitated impromptu composition and improvisational musical performance at gatherings in the pleasure quarter.[8] Such repetitiveness may also have had a certain pedagogical utility for novices learning to write or sing such verse or how to conduct themselves in the courtesan world. But since, as the illustrations and other factors attest, these anthologies were aimed at readers as well as singers and writers, here I also ask, How might repetitiveness have also contributed to the *reading* experience of sentimental songs and to the image of the courtesan world they create? What sort of master narratives about affairs in the pleasure quarter might be built up from this constant replay of the same situations and emotions? And what role might illustrations, themselves highly conventionalized, have played in reinforcing or undermining the repetitiveness of these songs?

The three sections of this essay that follow focus on three types of evidence in an attempt to answer these and other questions. The first section analyzes a little-known *sanqu* entitled "Ode on Singing" (Yongge 咏歌), published in the 1590s. The second section turns to the woodblock illustration that accompanies "Ode on Singing," as one of the few images in courtesan culture publications that portray the act of singing. The last section considers a specific late Ming *sanqu* collection as a whole. The example I have chosen is *Lyrics of Stylistic Brilliance* (*Caibi qingci* 彩笔情辞), published circa 1624, one of the more musically oriented, beautifully illustrated, and overtly commercial of the anthologies.

An Ode on Singing

How was the performance of *sanqu* conceptualized in printed verse during the late Ming? What qualities of the female singing voice were most prized and how was the male listener supposed to respond? "Ode on Singing," which was printed in elegant calligraphy with a matching woodblock illustration, helps provide some initial basic answers (fig. 2.1; for a complete translation of the suite, see app. 2.1). This *sanqu* was composed by the scholar-official Gu Zhengyi 顾正谊 (fl. 1575–1600 CE),[9] who was also a landscape painter and calligrapher of note; it is probable that the calligraphy and illustration were his design as well.[10] "Ode on Singing" was published in both his *Pictorial Catalogue of New Song-Lyrics* (*Yongwu xinci tupu* 咏物新词图谱) and his *New Songs from the House of a Flowering Brush* (*Bihualou xinsheng* 笔花楼新声). The contents of these two publications are nearly identical and consist entirely of Gu Zhengyi's own *sanqu*, each paired with an illustration. Although these books make no reference to technical musical considerations, the conceit is nonetheless that, as a contemporary performance genre, *sanqu* lyrics are not only for reading but for singing. As Yang Jili 杨继礼 gushes in one of the book's late Ming prefaces, "With the publication of these verses, [the demand will ensure that] merchants see the cost of paper rise and singers [complain] of chapped tongues."[11]

The "ode on things" (*yongwu*) was a venerable subgenre in Chinese poetry that could be treated in a variety of verse forms. Gu Zhengyi's "Ode on Singing" is noteworthy because singing was not a common topic for an ode on things, and because the act of singing is rarely depicted in printed illustrations. Moreover, because the point of an ode on things is to capture in words some distinct object or phenomenon and because the point of an illustration in a "pictorial catalogue" (*tupu*) is to visualize this phenomenon in an immediately recognizable form, "Ode on Singing" is valuable as a kind of primer, as a conglomerate of stock formulas and commonplace assumptions about the affect and purpose of a courtesan's song. The wit is that as an ode on singing cast in the form of a song, the ode itself performs what it purports to define.

"Ode on Singing" is an example of the "song-suite" (*taoshu*) type of *sanqu*, whose linked verses set to different tunes permit the creation of a loose temporal sequence punctuated by a series of refrains. Gu Zhengyi avails himself

Figure 2.1. "Ode on Singing." Gu Zhengyi, *Gu Zhongfang xinci tupu.* Courtesy of Peking University Library.

of this possibility to set out the most basic narrative of female singer and male listener, of courtesan and her would-be client, in which her performance of a song is the medium through which desire is expressed and seduction is transacted. But whose desire and where does it come from?

> *To the tune "Erlang shen" (The god Erlang)*
> Is she grieving for the passing of spring?
> I marvel whence comes the oriole's warble into this ornate chamber.
> Her soul about to melt, the lady by the lattice window already grown thin and wan.
> The twists and turns of these limpid tones divulged at once her springtime feelings.
> Each note full of longing, each line full of sadness.
> Where the gentle sound wafts, a sweet smell rises from her mouth.
> *Chorus*: How hard this is to bear.
>   Yes indeed, spring triggers millions of romantic feelings
>   in the human world. (v. 1a)

As in the epigraph to this essay, the "song emerges out of emptiness," seemingly out of nowhere, and by "lacking wings," "flies" like a bird into the lady's boudoir. The oriole's warble is a synecdoche for spring, itself a synonym for the free-floating lovesickness that is the theme of this verse, but the oriole's warble is also a metaphor describing the singer's pure and lovely voice, the "turns and twists" and "trills" so admired in vocal performance. The message of longing and sadness that the listener decodes in the song is typical of Chinese writing on music in which "the emotive quality of the music produced" is equated with the "emotional state of the musician."[12] The listener's response here is also typical of much Chinese writing about love, in which the man's own desire is projected backward as originating from his object of desire; it is also typical of the illusion a top courtesan's art is meant to foster, namely that it is she who voluntarily chooses her lover.

If the first stanza imagines the free-floating desire set into motion by "the oriole's warble," conveyed not only through sound but also through the "sweetness" of the singer's breath, the second stanza moves into the visual realm of physical performance. As the pleasure of looking is now conjoined with the pleasure of listening, the metaphorical song of the solitary oriole morphs into that of two lovebirds calling to one another: "I watch the play of her slim ivory fingers on the sandalwood clapper / I hear the mating calls of paired birds chirping outside the grove" (verse 1b).

Throughout the song suite, the most frequent attribute applied to the singing is "sorrow" (*chou*) not only because it fits the rhyme scheme but also because in the Chinese aesthetic code beautiful music was *supposed* to sound sad;[13] exclaiming over the "senseless feelings of sorrow" the singer "calls forth" (v. 2b) is thus to praise her artistry. But the constant litany of sadness and regret is also a function of singing in the pleasure quarter, where every new song plays back memories of old loves and is in part predicated on these memories. As Gu Zhengyi nicely phrases it: "New tunes keep on setting old griefs to music" (v. 2a). Song, love, and nostalgia are thus inextricably linked in a constant cycle of repetition.

Gu Zhengyi draws upon the well-developed poetic tradition of describing music by painting word pictures, mostly drawn from the natural world. Sometimes sound is specifically referenced, but sometimes the qualities of the singing are brought out through a purely visual conceit. For example, "new tunes" and "spring regrets" are likened to the image of "gossamer threads floating in the breeze entangled with tender willows / breaking off but still joined together; trying to halt yet still drifting on" (v. 2a). "Gossamer threads" (*qing si* 晴絲) is a set pun for "love-longing" (*qingsi* 情思); willows are a conventional symbol for courtesans; trees release their floss in the spring, and "breeze" connotes romance. Thus a paraphrase of the lines would be, aroused by amorous thoughts, I keep getting involved with courtesans; I try to stop but I keep on with my wastrel ways. More ingeniously, these lines also depict the pianissimo of spun-out notes, so attenuated that the voice seems to have ceased yet is still faintly audible. This sought-after vocal effect and the desire it arouses is mentioned again directly in the next stanza: "The sound suddenly stops, yet still lingers on" (v. 2b).

The eroticism deepens as the song-suite progresses. It is above all the choruses, however, that most clearly advance the amorous narrative. Once the opening chorus has established that the singing has succeeded in stirring up "spring" desires, the second chorus announces the listener's intention to continue the party all night long with the singer:

> Let's call for another round of wine
> And keep company
> Till the water clock drips out in the Han palace.

By the third chorus, the flirtation between singer and listener (referred to as Zhou Yu 周瑜, the proverbial connoisseur of music) has become an overt part of the performance, and the outcome of the evening, never really in doubt, is now inevitable.

> Her delicate voice trills.
> When Maestro Zhou throws her a glance
> She turns her head, suppressing a smile.

In the last tune, the concert reaches its end; the listener intends to pay the singer handsomely for her dazzling vocal performance, but not just yet, since he has more urgent things to attend to. As the final chorus explains:

> Being so besotted,
> We must repair to the bed curtains embroidered with mandarin ducks
> Inside the lady's bower of green and crimson.

Although the singing is long over, as the night wanes and dawn approaches, memories of the ethereal music still linger, and he is already imagining a repeat performance.

> Her song still echoes softly.
> At the horizon, the night's clouds are receding.
> The moon is setting over the bare rafters but is not yet gone.
> When will she sing "A Song of Yizhou" again?

The final coda proposes a duet between the two lovers with the listener now "matching" the courtesan's songs (here associated with the medieval songstress "Midnight" [Ziye]), but the real point of the coda is the message in the last line: "Just don't sing 'The Black Colt' and inflict the pain of parting." "The Black Colt" (Liju 丽驹) is an ancient song of farewell. By exhorting her *not* to sing this kind of song, he is in fact asserting the exact opposite, namely that "the pain of parting" is imminent and they will have to say goodbye. Such are the norms of love in the pleasure quarter.

Thus the "Ode on Singing" captures a truth about performance. The essence of singing is that although a song eventually comes to an end, it can begin again; it can be reprised by the same performer or sung by another. As an ode on things striving to capture the essence of singing, the song suite evokes the cyclical nature of song and desire as beginning anew each time, pointing to the shared repeatability of performance and falling in love in the pleasure quarter. The formulaic quality of the lyrics and the tunes simply reinforces this quality of repeatability. It is possible that this listener may come back and hear this singer again; but then again, he may choose to hear another—after all, as a line in the second stanza of the second tune observes, "Impossible to count all the flowers and willows in a single spring" (v. 2b).[14] This point becomes all the more piquant when we realize that song suites such as these were precisely the kind that a courtesan would have also repeatedly sung for different partners.

Picturing Song

Since antiquity, it had been understood that in musical performances designed for pleasure, the visual allure of the performer was as important as the sound produced.[15] The production of such music, most of all vocal music, put the body of the musician in the spotlight, and looking was considered an integral part of the listening experience, especially when the performer was a beautiful woman. The illustration accompanying "Ode on Singing" helps conjure up the visual scene of performance inevitably missing from the published song text. Conversely, the printed words of the song help fill in the sound inevitably missing from the pictorial rendition. Paired in this way, the illustration and the lyrics are mutually reinforcing, helping to recreate on the page an approximation of the multisensory presence of a singer's performance. It may not be too far-fetched to imagine that the courtesan in the illustration could even be understood as singing the very words to the song printed in the accompanying text.

The finely crafted illustration portrays a classic garden setting dominated by a large perforated Taihu rock upon which two gentlemen, clearly literati, are seated. To the right of the older, bearded man is a table upon which are arranged a book in a rectangular case, a jar full of writing brushes, and some ceramic crackleware—all markers of class and refinement to reinforce the elegance of the occasion. The attention of both men is fixed on the singer, a beautiful lady depicted in profile, who is seated on a small Taihu rock across from them, holding a round fan. Behind her on a chair sits her accompanist, another beautiful lady, who is playing a *xiao* (vertical flute), her slim fingers prominently displayed. The two musicians are clearly courtesans because no woman from good family would exhibit herself to the gaze of men in this fashion. The young man sits raptly, with his sleeves twisted bashfully in his lap, but the older man is more animated and confident, his raised hand gesturing to the singer as though to suggest he knows a thing or two about music. Behind the two men, peeping through a perforation in the rock, is a servant boy surreptitiously enjoying the performance.

The illustration is clearly not intended as a faithful rendition of the matching song suite's precise lines, although the fan the singer holds recalls "the peach blossom fan" mentioned in the second verse, behind which "her face is soft and warm" (v. 2b). The pictorial composition mainly follows its own visual logic, most prominently by adding a second male listener to balance the female flute player, and the garden setting itself. During the late Ming, the garden was a highly prized luxury, a symbol of cultivated elegance and sociality, and one possible site for playing and singing music, whether in a courtesan establishment or in a private wealthy home. As represented in fiction and drama at least, the garden was also a primary place for amorous assignations. Garden settings for figures are ubiquitous in printed illustrations from this period. It was a common trope in ribald illustrations to feature a peeper, and the perforations in garden rocks were often profitably put to this use.[16] The peeping servant boy planted in the composition here not only adds visual wit but suggests the erotic subtext of the musical performance as well.

The serious concert in the garden was a stock visual composition that Gu Zhengyi had at his disposal to depict a courtesan singer; another surviving example of this type, but of a rehearsal without an audience, is the portrait of a courtesan composing an aria in *Seductive Courtesans of Suzhou* (*Wuji baimei* 吴姬百媚, 1617 preface).[17] The other visual composition used to illustrate singing in the pleasure quarter is the drinking party. Gu Zhengyi utilizes this formula in his *Pictorial Catalogue of a Hundred Odes on Things* (*Baiyong tupu* 百咏图谱), a book that features poems rather than songs, in which he includes a poem entitled simply "Singing" (Ge 歌).

> Midnight begins a new song.
> Her delicate voice twists like an oriole at dawn.
> The notes follow like snowflakes slowly flying,
> Gently wafting like petals lightly falling.
> Softly they wind 'round the rafters, a boundless stream from behind her fan.
> Maestro Zhou's judgment is never wrong.
> With one glance he knows she harbors feelings for him.[18]

Virtually every element of this poem is recycled in Gu Zhengyi's *sanqu* on the same topic, which indicates how formulaic his diction in each one was meant to be, despite the difference in genre. The contrast between the two lies mainly in the matching illustrations. Although the accompanying picture to "Singing" also features a courtesan singer with male literati as listeners, they are shown engaged in a drinking party (see fig. 2.2). This was a stock situation for depicting musical merry making in the pleasure quarter, as found also in *A Ranked Compilation of Flowers* (*Pinhua jian* 品花笺), an early seventeenth-century compendium of the connoisseurship literature on pleasure, and in another compendium on courtesans, *The Debonair Reader* (*Sasa bian* 洒洒编).[19] In Gu Zhengyi's illustration, the party, which is taking place at night, is clearly already quite advanced. Seated across the table from the singer are two courtesan accompanists, one playing the vertical flute, the other beating out the rhythm on clappers. To balance the number of female musicians again, this time three male clients are depicted. One of them leans on his elbow, his arm around the singer as he gazes raptly at her; he is either completely captivated or else just drunk.

The pictorial catalogue with its one-to-one correspondence between "picture" (*tu*) and text that Gu Zhengyi favored was not adopted by the early seventeenth-century illustrated *sanqu* anthologies. Instead, these subsequent editors chose the format of having fewer but more complex illustrations, which freely elaborated on a line or two drawn from the songs in the more impressionistic manner of a "painting" (*hua*).[20] In these anthologies, even though many of the *sanqu* describe the circumstances of their composition and performance or praise the singing ability of an individual courtesan or describe the celestial

Figure 2.2. "Singing." Gu Zhengyi, *Gu Zhongfang baiyong tupu*. Courtesy of Peking University Library.

sound of her voice, illustrations depicting the songs being sung are conspicuously absent. What then is the relationship, if any, of these illustrations to the realm of song and emotion represented in these books?

The Realm of Song and Emotion

The remainder of this essay examines how the complex interaction among illustration, text, and format depicts the relationship between song and love in Zhang Xu's 张栩 edited volume *Love Lyrics of Stylistic Brilliance*. This book consists solely of *sanqu* written for courtesans, including examples that Zhang Xu wrote in the context of his own liaisons, though virtually nothing is known about him other than what can be gleaned from the pages of this anthology.[21] He was a native of Hangzhou, where the book was produced and printed around 1624, and the fancy diction he used for his prefaces and blurbs shows that he was well educated and eager to show it. He was also clearly interested in music, since *Love Lyrics* includes *dianban* 点板 metrical notation, the only form of musical notation used in Ming imprints of *qu*. This form of metrical punctuation, which marked the strong and soft beats, was always optional. It was meant to help people figure out how to match the words with the tune pattern, something especially tricky with *kunqu*; how effective such notation actually was as an aid, however, was a matter of debate even in its own time.[22]

What is clear is that the inclusion of *dianban* notation was important as an upward strategy of self-differentiation. Like Zhou Zhibiao's 周之标 *A Medley of Southeastern Airs* (*Wuyu cuiya* 吴歈萃雅) and Feng Menglong's *A Celestial Air Played Anew*, *Love Lyrics* presents itself as a novel endeavor to apply the rigorous editorial and literary standards demanded of prestigious collections of mainstream verse to the compilation of risqué *sanqu* composed and performed in a courtesan milieu. At the same time, Zhang Xu overtly directed his anthology to an audience of "singer-readers" (*gelanzhe* 歌览者) and adopted various organizational and typographical formats to facilitate singing in order to enhance its perceived value to consumers as a performance aid.

For late Ming printed collections of *sanqu*, the addition of *dianban* notation was, along with illustrations, a major selling point.[23] The exceptionally beautiful illustrations in *Love Lyrics* were produced by the famed Huang family of Hui carvers, who also did the pictures for the first two *Songs of the Southeast* anthologies (*Wusao ji* 吴骚集, edited by Wang Zhideng 王穉登, and *Wusao erji* 吴骚二集, edited by Zhang Qi 張琦 and Wang Huixuan 王煇選), both earlier *sanqu* collections published in Hangzhou. The first *Songs of the Southeast* is even credited with having initiated the late Ming vogue for illustrated *sanqu* collections.[24]

Zhang Xu must have been familiar with these predecessors, but he does not acknowledge them or their influence. Instead his *Love Lyrics of Stylistic Brilliance* was frank in attempting to capitalize on the success of another illustrated anthology printed in Hangzhou, *Stylish Verse from the Green Bower* (*Qinglou yunyu* 青楼韵语), compiled by Zhang Mengzheng 张梦征, a Hangzhou editor, publisher, and painter, who also designed the very fine illustrations carved by the Huang family.[25] The association between the two books evidently stuck, since *Love Lyrics* was reprinted several years later (without crediting Zhang Xu) under the title *Expanded Edition of Stylish Verse from the Green Bower* (*Qinglou yunyu guangji* 青楼韵语广记).[26]

    Stylish Verse from the Green Bower is not principally a *sanqu* collection, although it does include a goodly number of them. The book's claim to fame was that it was one of very few publications exclusively to showcase the literary output of courtesans themselves. (*Green bower* is a poetic term for a brothel.) This anthology's popularity was no doubt abetted by the editor's decision to cannibalize a well-known anonymous work entitled *The Classic of Whoring* (*Piaojing* 嫖经) to provide the rubrics under which he grouped the courtesan's verse.[27] The result is a cacophonous but playful mixture of different registers and tones: *The Classic of Whoring*, the courtesan's verses, the exquisite illustrations, and running commentaries that alternate between idealization and contempt and between extremes of sentimentality and cynicism.

    In contrast to *Stylish Verse*, Zhang Xu is absolutely committed to idealism and sentimentality in his romantic portrayal of courtesans (a section on "teasing and satire" is the one exception) because his focus is not on the courtesans themselves but on literary men of sensibility and talent like himself who find inspiration in them and express their emotions in song. As the bookseller's blurb on the cover proclaims: "This collection consists entirely of works by literary men from two dynasties: hence, *Stylistic Brilliance*. All the works are arias composed for courtesans in the 'green bower': hence, *Love Lyrics*. Brought together here are northern- and southern-style song-suites and single-stanza songs. Based on extensive and rigorous search and classified by category."[28] As advertised, this compendium differs from *Stylish Verse* on two major grounds: it includes works not written *by* courtesans but written *to* them, and it consists entirely of *sanqu* rather than verse with a smattering of arias. What Zhang Xu specifically borrowed from *Stylish Verse* was the idea of organizing the songs under thematic rubrics describing the course of a love affair, although his headings are more clearly organized and his introductory blurbs are naturally much more elevated in tone and style than those from *The Classic of Whoring*. To these thematic headings, he added musical guidelines, organizing the *sanqu* within each rubric by labeled tune title as well as providing *dianban* notation for each aria. Compared to the confusing layout of *Stylish Verse*, *Love Lyrics* offers neat and harmonious divisions that reinforce the uniform tone of elegance and authority for both its targeted audiences, singers and readers.

    Likewise, the beautiful illustrations interspersed in *Love Lyrics*, though similar in style, quality, and format to those in *Stylish Verse*, enhance *Love Lyrics*' intended effect of harmony and refinement, rather than interjecting another clashing stratum as in *Stylish Verse*.²⁹ In this respect the pictures in *Love Lyrics* live up to the lofty (though stereotyped) claims that Zhang Xu makes for them: "The illustrations are all from the hands of famous painters, who have modeled them after ancient styles and carefully imitated the *yi* 意 (meaning, intent, idea) of the lyrics. It took several days to complete each picture. Thereafter I sought fine craftsmen to carve each one in exquisite detail. The spirit of these pictures is profound, the figures and scenery dazzling. They're completely different from those careless rush jobs nowadays."³⁰ As is typical of the seventeenth-century illustrated *sanqu* collections from Hangzhou, the pictures, as Zhang Xu states, are meant to depict the idea of the lyrics, that is, to depict the situation and mood of the lyrics for a given category. The illustrations in *Love Lyrics* are particularly interesting in the way they visualize the male experience of love and desire fueling the songs. By far the most common way to depict desire in the Chinese poetic and pictorial tradition is in the person of a solitary woman in her empty boudoir longing for an absent lover. *Sanqu* were privileged places (though not the only ones, to be sure) where men had the option of writing desire straightforwardly in a male voice,³¹ even if—or because—the lyrics were expected (or at least imagined) to be sung by women. Zhang Xu's preface makes something like this argument in his attempt to one-up *Stylish Verse* and champion the transcendent value of "love" (*qing*) in his book's title.³² The reason for the popularity of *Stylish Verses*, he says, is not that the collection is about courtesans per se but that it consists of verse and songs composed by courtesans that express their feelings of love. By this measure his new compendium of songs by literary men must surely be superior because "past and present, it has always been that literary men have the biggest hearts of all, and that when it comes to writing about love, they invariably entrust it to song."³³

The illustrations in *Love Lyrics* substantiate Zhang Xu's ambition to showcase love-struck literati with "big hearts." The compendium not only includes the usual scenes of a courtesan waiting with just a maid for company or two lovers cuddling together (fig. 2.3) but also, more unusually, several that show a gentleman sitting by himself in a state of palpable desire and longing. One such picture (fig. 2.4), for the first of two sections on "Recalling with Emotion" (*juan* [chap.] 8), shows a small male figure sitting alone inside a little room nestled amid a towering stand of pines. He is poignantly gazing out across a vast expanse of river at the foamy waves furiously rolling up. Far away, another small gentleman figure, accompanied only by a servant boy, stands on a small overlook staring out at the same scene.³⁴ The caption reads: "At sunset misty waves on the river are swift and strong, / But how can they withstand the force of the west wind?"³⁵ Even more than the caption, Zhang Xu's introductory blurb to "Recollecting with Emotion" provides the textual "meaning" for the illustrator to "imitate" in his pictorial rendition:

Figure 2.3. "Modulation and Harmony." Zhang Xu, *Caibi qingci, juan* 4. Reproduced with permission from the National Palace Museum, Taiwan.

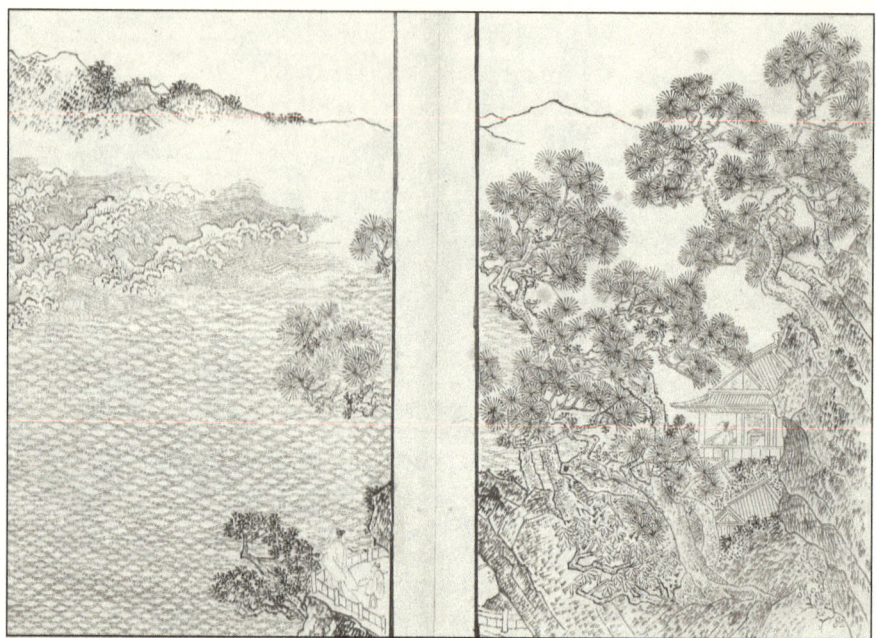

Figure 2.4. "Recalling with Emotion, Part 1." Zhang Xu, *Caibi qingci, juan* 8. Reproduced with permission from the National Palace Museum, Taiwan.

> There are a hundred different reasons why we feel things. If you are smitten by some external force, then everything will turn to melancholy and you will be unable to fix your heart or mind on anything else. Upon assessing this sort of emotional state, it generally turns out to be of the [romantic] entanglement sort. But now, where has that intimate relationship gone? All you can do is pace back and forth—who is there to talk to? And so you give voice to your prolonged depression and modulate the tune with the notes of the scale; you describe your innermost torment and harmonize the song with strings and winds.[36]

In this formulation, music is valued not only as a way to express genuine feelings but also as a means of regulating the emotions. Such classic Confucian ideas about music often went hand in glove with maintaining the division between "proper" and "licentious" music. The ideology of *qing* (love) championed throughout *Love Lyrics* and other like-minded late Ming publications was intended precisely to demonstrate the propriety of what was usually dismissed as licentiousness. The simultaneous venting and modulation of passion through music is a favorite theme of Zhang Xu's not only in the blurbs that precede each section[37] but also in the autobiographical prefaces attached to some of his own song suites in the collection.[38] It was only natural for him

Figure 2.5. "Writing a Letter." Zhang Xu, *Caibi qingci*, *juan* 12. Reproduced with permission from the National Palace Museum, Taiwan.

Figure 2.6. "Recalling with Emotion, Part 2." Zhang Xu, *Caibi qingci*, juan 9. Reproduced with permission from the National Palace Museum, Taiwan.

to take advantage of the many set convergences between terms for love and music, in which "harmonizing" was the goal of both pursuits.[39]

In the sequence of headings in *Love Lyrics*, "Recalling with Emotion" follows the stages of "Being in Love" (*juan* 5), "Obstacles" (*juan* 6) and "Parting" (*juan* 7). As such, the context for the emotional travail the poet is suffering from and that he must "give voice to" in the ensuing songs in this section is clear. The illustrator visualizes this torment of desire as violent frothing waves, which acquire an unmistakable sexual force as the metaphorical projection of the male figure's inner feelings and the release for which he yearns. A similar image of churning waves to represent the male figure's internal desires is utilized in the illustration for the section "Sending Letters" (*juan* 12), which depicts a young scholar at a writing desk set with a blank piece of paper before him (fig. 2.5), but here the visual metaphor is deflected onto the screen behind him.[40] Reinforcing the image on the screen are a towering willow intertwined with a blossoming tree and flower-spangled bed curtains draped in the back room, which further help clarify the message of the song to be inscribed in the letter as well as its destined recipient. Conversely, the illustration for the "Recalling with Emotion," part 2 (*juan* 9) abandons the visual metaphor of frothing waves but retains the compositional logic of the illustration for part 1 (*juan* 8). In this milder formulation of desire, the forlorn scholar is staring after a pair of love birds winging through the sky to externalize what is in his heart (fig. 2.6). Once again, as in the opening epigraph, song is imagined as freely taking flight while love holds the sufferer rooted to the spot.

Sanqu, Repetition, and Pleasure

As in other illustrated anthologies of *sanqu* from the late Ming, what we find are disparate renderings over and over again of stock situations and feelings. It is possible that this narrow variation on a circumscribed set of themes was itself important in creating an emotional effect in the listener or reader because it is known that familiarity, especially with regard to music and poetry, will often produce a strong sensation of pleasure, especially when spiked with a little novelty.[41] This again may partly explain why nostalgia—a yearning for the familiar reimagined—is so ubiquitous in these *sanqu*.

The repetitiveness of the lyrics also reinforces the sense that a love affair with a courtesan follows a natural course and therefore a predictable trajectory. Relations in the pleasure quarters are by definition understood as impermanent (the word often used is *biantai* 变态), and therefore have a beginning, middle, and an end. The set stages marked through the topical headings in *Love Lyrics* sketch the basic contours of a literary man's affair with a courtesan: courtship (through presenting gifts of song texts), rendezvous, being in love, obstacles, parting, remembering, meeting again, longing again, mourning the death of the beloved.[42] See appendix 2.2 for the full list of headings.

The rubrics are not all the same in all the *sanqu* anthologies, nor are all the anthologies organized according to such a clear sequence, but still always discernible are the phases of courtship, being together, parting, and remembrance. (In keeping with sentimental pop songs everywhere, as well as the expectation of nostalgia and sadness in late Ming *sanqu*, there is a lot of emphasis on the regrets and longings after the breakup of an affair). The illustrations in a book like *Love Lyrics* are quite infrequent, especially compared to the number of *sanqu*. They may therefore reinforce the headings to help mark out the path of an affair, which is sometimes in danger of being overwhelmed by the sheer volume of song texts.

As Michela Bussotti has noted, the illustrations in late Ming *sanqu* collections resemble those in contemporary printed editions of plays, and they are undifferentiated in modern anthologies of drama illustrations.[43] Nonetheless, the generalized contour of the love affair that the *sanqu* collections help to construct differs sharply from their dramatic counterparts. The southern-style romantic comedies (*chuanqi*) that dominated both in the theater and on the page during the late Ming mandated a happy ending, complete with a wish-fulfilling grand reunion in which the hero marries the heroine (who is not infrequently a courtesan). The illustrations for *Love Lyrics*, by contrast, play out the storyline proper for a collection of sentimental songs, in which parting and separation are understood to be the normal ending to an affair with a courtesan but, most important, furnished the necessary melancholy sentiments of longing, regret, and nostalgia that are the main themes of so many of the songs. In this respect, it is tempting to find parallels between the structure of a *sanqu* song-suite, with its set pattern and temporal arc, its cyclic structure of verse-chorus and repetition of familiar tunes set to new lyrics, and the norms of relationships in the pleasure quarter.[44] This indeed may be a further reason why *sanqu* were perceived as so integral a part of the courtesan entertainment world.

Appendix 2.1: Translation of Gu Zhengyi's "Ode on Singing"

1a. *To the tune "Erlang shen" (The god Erlang)*
Is she grieving for the passing of spring?
I marvel whence comes the oriole's warble into this ornate chamber.
Her soul about to melt, the lady by the lattice window already grown thin and wan.
The twists and turns of these limpid tones divulged at once her springtime feelings.
Each note full of longing, each line full of sadness.
Where the gentle sound wafts, a sweet smell rises from her mouth.
Chorus: How hard this is to bear.
Yes indeed, spring triggers a million romantic feelings
in the human world.

1b. *To the previous tune with opening variation*
Such pellucid singing:
Bright rays of light flash by, sunset-streaked clouds curl up;
Waves come crashing and spray billows out.
I watch the play of her slim ivory fingers on the sandalwood clapper.
I hear the mating calls of paired birds chirping outside the grove.
The spring river keeps flowing on and on.
So mellow and full [her voice], a circle of pearls endlessly rolling back and forth.
Chorus as above

2a. *To the tune "Ji xianbin" (A gathering of good and wise guests)*
New tunes keep on setting old griefs to music,
Stirring up boundless regrets for spring.
Just like gossamer threads (*qing si*) floating in the breeze
entangled with tender willows,
Breaking off but still joined together; trying to halt yet still drifting on.
Behind moonlit windows and cloud-filled casements,

I wonder how many people have been enticed into feelings of love?
   Chorus: Let's call for another round of wine
   And keep company
   Till the water clock drips out in the Han palace.

2b: *To the previous tune*
   Behind the peach blossom fan, her face is soft and warm.
   How many senseless feelings of sorrow she calls forth!
   Slowly light clouds scud across the mountains of Chu.
   The sound suddenly stops, yet still lingers on.
   Motes of dust float 'round the rafters.
   Impossible to count all the flowers and willows in a single spring.
   Chorus as above

3a. *To the tune "Huang ying'er" (Yellow oriole)*
   She softly plays "Little Liangzhou."[45]
   The melody rises and falls in harmony; the tune turns sad and deep.
   Waves rippling on the cold, cold water.
   Orioles weep and swallows lament
   Blossoms falling into the river's current.
   Trailing sleeves in a blizzard of icy flakes.
   Chorus: Her delicate voice trills.
   When Maestro Zhou[46] throws her a glance
   She turns her head, suppressing a smile.

3b. *To the previous tune*
   Her voice sobs as though saddened by autumn
   Spinning out the silkworm's threads (*si*) that never end.[47]
   Just like the playing of reed pipes amid the flowers.
   Her cherry lips slowly part
   And the hidden scent of orchids floats out.
   Let's idle the day away with a cup of wine and "A Song of White Ramie."[48]
   Chorus as above

4a. *To the tune "Hupo mao'er zhui" (The calico cat falls down)*
   She modulates between musical modes
   With such brio and enchanting freshness,
   Dispelling the thousand beakers of last spring's sorrows.
   The bolts of silk I mean to give in recompense will have to wait.
   Chorus: Being so besotted,
   We must repair to the bed curtains embroidered with mandarin ducks
   Inside the lady's bower of green and crimson.

4b. *To the previous tune*
   Her song still echoes softly.
   At the horizon, the night's clouds are receding.

The moon is setting over the bare rafters but is not yet gone.
When will she sing "A Song of Yizhou" again?[49]
Chorus as above

Coda
Do you know Midnight's "Four Seasons"?[50]
I will match them with "White Snow" and "Sunny Spring."[51]
Just don't sing "The Black Colt" and inflict the pain of parting.[52]

Appendix 2.2

Topical Headings for *Love Lyrics of Stylistic Brilliance* (j. = *juan* 卷 [chapter, section])

- j. 1 "Composition Bestowed as a Gift on a Courtesan" (Zeng mei 赠美), part 1
- j. 2 "Composition Bestowed as a Gift on a Courtesan" (Zeng mei 赠美), part 2
- j. 3 "Pleasurable Union" (Hehuan 合欢)
- j. 4 "Modulation and Harmony" [making love] (Tiaohe 调合)
- j. 5 "Exchanging Verse" (Tizeng 题赠)
  "Taking a Courtesan on an Excursion" (Chunxie 春携)
  "Being in Love" (Danlian 耽恋)
- j. 6 "Obstacles" (Jianzu 间阻)
- j. 7 "Parting" (Libie 离别)
- j. 8 "Recalling with Emotion" (Ganhuai 感怀), part 1
- j. 9 "Recalling with Emotion" (Ganhuai 感怀), part 2
  "Meeting Again after Breaking Up" (Fangyu 访遇)
- j. 10 "Longing for Each Other" (Xiangsi 相思), part 1
- j. 11 "Longing for Each Other" (Xiangsi 相思), part 2
  "Teasing and Satire" (Chaoxue 嘲谑)
- j. 12 "Sending Letters" (Jichou 寄酬)
  "Mourning a Courtesan's Death" (Shangshi 伤逝)

Notes

Epigraph: Liang Chenyu (1519–91), "'Xiangbianman: Ji Wang Guifu' xu" from his *sanqu* collection *Jiangdong baining*, in *Liang Chenyu ji*, ed. Wu Shuyin (Shanghai: Shanghai guji chubanshe, 2010), 361. This song suite, minus the preface, was also included in Feng Menglong, ed., *Taixia xinzou*, vol. 15 of *Feng Menglong quanji*, ed. Wei Tongxian (Shanghai: Shanghai guji chubanshe), *juan* 6, 235.

1. Dorothy Ko, "The Written Word and the Bound Foot: A History of the Courtesan's Aura," in *Writing Women in Late Imperial China*, ed. Ellen Widmer and Kang-i Sun Chang (Stanford, CA: Stanford University Press, 1997), 74–100; Ōki Yasushi. *Chūgoku yūri kūkan: Min shin shinwai gijo no sekai* (Tokyo: Seidosha, 2002).

2. Kathryn A. Lowry, *The Tapestry of Popular Songs in 16th- and 17th-Century China: Reading, Imitation, and Desire* (Leiden: Brill, 2005); Ōki Yasushi, *Fū Bōryū "Sanka" no kenkyū: Chūgoku Mindai no tsūzoku kayō* (Tokyo: Keisō Shobō, 2003); Ōki, *Chūgoku yūri*

kūkan; Yuming He, "Productive Space: Performance Texts in the Late Ming," PhD diss., University of California at Berkeley, 2003.

3. Zhou Zhibiao, editor's preface (dated 1615) in *Wuyu cuiya*. Facsimile reprint in *Shanben Xiqu congkan*, ed. Wang Qiugui, series 2, vol. 12–13 (Taipei: Xuesheng shuju, 1984–87), 9. *Shiqu* could also be used to refer to popular songs. Late Ming sources also refer to *sanqu* as *qingqu* (pure arias) because they were destined for *qingchang* (pure singing) recitals alone in contradistinction to *xiqu* (dramatic arias), which could be performed on stage in a full-fledged opera as well as sung separately as part of a recital.

4. Feng Menglong, "Fafan" to *Taixia xinzou*, 1.

5. Hua Wei, "Ma Xianglan yu Mingdai houqi de qutan," *Xiqu Xuebao* 12 (2007): 12.

6. Judith T. Zeitlin, "'Notes of Flesh' and the Courtesan's Song in Seventeenth-Century China," in *The Courtesan's Arts: Cross-Cultural Perspectives*, ed. Martha Feldman and Bonnie Gordon (New York: Oxford University Press, 2006), 75–99; and Zeitlin, "The Gift of Song: Courtesans and Patrons in Late Ming and Early Qing Cultural Production" in *Hsiang Lectures on Chinese Poetry*, ed. Grace S. Fong (Montreal: McGill University Centre for East Asian Research, 2008), 4:1–46.

7. Katherine Carlitz, "Printing as Performance: Literati Playwright-Publishers of the Late Ming," in *Printing and Book Culture in Late Imperial China*, ed. Cynthia J. Brokaw and Kai-wing Chow (Berkeley: University of California Press, 2005), has made a similar argument with regard to late Ming playwrights and publishers.

8. Zeitlin, "'Notes of Flesh'"; and Zeitlin, "Gift of Song."

9. Feng Shike's preface (dated 1600) to Gu Zhengyi's *Gushi shishi*, comp. Tang Ruxun, mentions the earlier publication of Gu Zhengyi's *Yongwu tupu*. See facsimile reprint in *Siku quanshu cunmu congshu* vol. 288 (Ji'nan: Qilu shushe, 1997).

10. Michela Bussotti, *Gravures de Hui: Étude du livre illustré Chinois; Fin du XVI siècle-première moitié du XVIIe siècle* (Paris: École Française d'Extrême-Orient, 2000), 115n55; Zhou Wu, *Zhongguo banhua shi tulu* (Shanghai: Shanghai renmin meishu chubanshe 1988), 425–26n295; Zheng Zhenduo, "Zhongguo gudai banhua shilüe," in *Zheng Zhenduo yishu kaogu wenji* (Beijing: Wenwu chubanshe, 1988), 370.

11. Xie Boyang, ed. *Quanming sanqu* (Ji'nan: Qi Lu shushe 1994), 3:3162.

12. Ronald Egan, "The Controversy over Music and 'Sadness' and Changing Conceptions of the *Qin* in Middle Period China," *Harvard Journal of Asiatic Studies* 57, no. 1 (1997): 7.

13. Ibid.

14. Both *flower* and *willow* are common references for courtesans.

15. Joseph Lam, "The Presence and Absence of Female Musicians and Music in China," in *Women and Confucian Cultures in Premodern China, Korea, and Japan*, ed. Dorothy Ko, JaHyun Kim Haboush, and Joan R. Piggott (Berkeley: University of California Press, 2003), 97.

16. Zeitlin, "'Notes of Flesh.'"

17. For a reproduction and discussion of this image, see Lowry, *Tapestry of Popular Songs*, 284–86.

18. Gu Zhengyi, *Gu Zhongfang xinci tupu*, appended to *Gu Zhongfang baiyong tupu* (ca 1596). Damaged Ming editions in Peking University Library and National Library of China.

19. For a reproduction and discussion of the illustration of singing in *Pinhua jian*, see Zeitlin, "'Notes of Flesh.'" Deng Zhimo, ed., *Sasa pian*, in *Ming Qing shanben xiaoshuo congkan* (Taipei: Tianyi chubanshe, 1985), vol. 113, includes a poor reproduction of the singing party illustration. *Sasa pian* consists of abridgements of *Seductive Beauties of*

Suzhou, Stylish Verse from the Green Bower, and *Songs of the Southeast* along with other amorous or joke-related sections from books I have not yet identified. The prefaces to this compendium are undated, but it cannot have been published before 1617.

20. On the difference between *tu* (picture) and *hua* (painting), see Craig Clunas, *Pictures and Visuality in Early Modern China* (Princeton: Princeton University Press, 1997); Lucille Chia, "Text and *Tu* in Context: Reading the Illustrated Page in Chinese Blockprinted Books," *Bulletin de l'École Française d'Extrême-Orient* 89 (2002): 241–76.

21. All we know is that his style name was Shuzhou and his sobriquet was Mengzi (Dreamer). *Caibi qingci* includes twenty-one of his *sanqu*, seven *xiaoling* (single-stanza songs), and twenty-one *taoshu* (song-suites), the extent of his entire known corpus. See Xie Boliang, ed., *Quan Ming sanqu* (Ji'nan: Qi Lu shushe, 1994), 3:4281–301. All page numbers for *Caibi qingci* in this paper are keyed to the late Ming facsimile reprint in *Shanben xiqu congkan*, ed. Wang Qiugui (Taipei: Xuesheng shuju, 1985–87).

22. Judith Zeitlin, "Between Print, Manuscript, and Performance: Imagining the Musical Text in Seventeenth-Century Songbooks and Plays," in *Text, Performance, and Gender in Chinese Literature and Music: Essays in Honor of Wilt Idema,* ed. Maghiel van Crevel, Tian Yuan Tan and Michel Hockx (Leiden: Brill, 2010), 273–78.

23. Carlitz, "Printing as Performance."

24. Admittedly, this claim comes from Zhang Qi and Zhang Xu, the editors of *Songs of the Southeast, Combined Edition,* the last and largest in the *Songs of the Southeast* series.

25. Zhang Xu's preface ("*Caibi qingci* xu" in *Caibi qingci*) opens by citing the popularity of its predecessor: "A few years ago, Liuguan Hall published *Stylish Verse from the Green Bower* and its reputation and price resounded for a time. Across the country everyone jockeyed to get hold of a copy." Liuguan jushi was one of Zhang Mengzheng's sobriquets; adding the term "hall" (*tang*) is frequent in the name of a publishing house.

26. In both the editions of *Love Lyrics* that I have seen (the Library of Congress microfilm and the *Shanben xiqu congkan* reprint), *juan* 8 includes a page that mistakenly prints *Qinglou yunyu* and the names of that book's compiler and illustrator rather than *Caibi qingci* and the names of its compiler and associate.

27. Although no independent book of this title survives, the identical content circulated almost verbatim in late Ming encyclopedias for daily use under various headings such as "Regulations of the Green Bower" (Qinglou guifan).

28. Zhang, *Caibi qingci*.

29. A minor difference is that the lines of verse being illustrated in *Stylish Verse* are inscribed as part of the illustration, whereas in *Love Lyrics* the line is printed on the page before the illustration with the caption "line selected for illustration" (*huatu zhaiju*).

30. Zhang, *Caibi qingci*, 16.

31. Patricia Sieber, *Theaters of Desire: Authors, Readers, and the Reproduction of Early Chinese Song-Drama, 1300–2000* (New York: Palgrave Macmillian, 2003), 80, argues that, in contradistinction to the earlier genre of *ci* song lyrics, *sanqu* privileged the male point of view in romantic relationships and therefore helped legitimate the direct expression of male longing and desire.

32. Ibid., 67–68.

33. Zhang, *Caibi qingci*, 1–2.

34. The image of the waves recalls depictions of the famous tidal bore of the Qiantang River near Hangzhou, but Liang Chenyu's song suite, which is the source for the illustration's caption, specifies the Gu River in Hunan. See his "Climbing the Tower at the Gu River Courier Station and Recalling with Emotion" (Qiuri deng Gushui yilou ganjiu), in Zhang, *Caibi qingci, juan* 8, 608.

35. Ibid., 585.
36. Ibid.
37. For example, see ibid., *juan* 5, 347, and *juan* 6, 429.
38. For example, see Xie, *Quan Ming sanqu*, 4:4297.
39. Judith T. Zeitlin, "Music and Performance in Hong Sheng's *Palace of Lasting Life*" in *Trauma and Transcendence in Early Qing Literature*, ed. Wilt L. Idema, Wai-yee Li, and Ellen Widmer (Cambridge, MA: Harvard University Asia Center, 2006), 473.
40. On the use of visual metaphors on decorated screens in a picture to represent the inner world of the figure placed before it, see Wu Hung, *The Double Screen: Medium and Representation in Chinese Painting* (London: Reaktion Books), 21–22.
41. Why *do* listeners find interest and pleasure in hearing the same thing over and over? This is the question that Richard Middleton tries to answer for pop music. See his "'Play it Again, Sam': Some Notes on the Productivity of Repetition in Popular Music," *Popular Music* 3 (1983): 235.
42. For similar lists of topical headings used to narrate the stages of an affair, see the captions to the prefatory album of woodblock illustrations in Feng Menglong's *Taixia xinzou*, and the subtitles to a song suite by Liang Chenyu included in the same anthology (*juan* 14, 709–12). In both lists, the affair ends in separation, though not with the death of the beloved.
43. Bussotti, *Gravures de hui*, 114n49.
44. My thanks to Rachel Harris for this insight.
45. "Little Liangzhou" (Xiao Liangzhou) is a Yuan dynasty *qu* tune title.
46. Zhou Yu (175–210), military general and strategist during the Three Kingdoms period, was a proverbial connoisseur of music and uxorious husband of the famed beauty Little Qiao.
47. Common allusion to a famous line from the Tang love poet Li Shangyin (ca. 813–58), with the ubiquitous pun on silk threads and longing: "Only death puts an end to the spring silkworm's threads."
48. "White Ramie" (Baining) is a song-lyric tune title, but it is an especially topical allusion here because *Jiangdong baining* (White ramie of the Jiangdong region) is also the title of an influential sixteenth-century collection of *sanqu* by Liang Chenyu.
49. A famous Tang dynasty tune title, named after the region of Yizhou, which bordered on central Asia, the source of the most popular music in the period.
50. "The Four Seasons" (Ziye wusheng sishige) is a famous collection of Jin dynasty (265–420) lyrics from the Jiangnan region attributed to a female singer named Midnight (Ziye).
51. "White Snow" (Baixue) and "Sunny Spring" (Yangchun), song titles from the ancient state of Chu during the Warring States period, were archetypal elegant music. The allusion, though ubiquitous, is again especially apt here because *Sunny Spring, White Snow* is also the title of an influential fourteenth-century collection of *sanqu*.
52. "The Black Colt" (Liju) is an old Han dynasty song conventionally sung at parting; as an allusion it connotes the heartbreak of saying farewell to a friend or lover.

Chapter Three

From Courtesans to Modern Hostesses

Music and Construction of Gender in the Entertainment Industry in China

Tiantian Zheng

In a dimly lit karaoke bar room, several hostesses were accompanying their clients. To lure clients, these hostesses purred, laughed, screamed, and moaned while singing love songs to seduce clients and convey their "devotion." One hostess chose a contemporary popular song titled "Why Do You Love Other Women behind My Back?" (Weishenmo ni beizhe wo ai bieren).[1] She sang:

> Thinking of your face—your empty face
> Feeling numb, I am walking on the fringe of a nervous breakdown
> I need a garden that can shed tears
> To water this withering promise
> My most beloved lover hurt me the most
> Why do you love other women behind my back?
>
> Women's innocent eyes hid cruel needles
> I cannot see through life but I have an extravagant hope for eternity
> Oh my weak soul has fallen too deep
> Why do you love other women behind my back?
>
> I have hidden our frozen kiss inside my heart to warm it up
> Love is full of cruelty but I have been too sincere
> Love has been torn open, layer by layer
> I have been destroyed by love, layer by layer
> I do not have time to find an exit
> I have been destroyed by love, layer by layer[2]

This is a romantic love song that expresses a woman's devotion and love for her lover and the devastation and anguish caused by her lover's deceit. As the hostess was singing the verses with pouring emotions, she turned to her client and leaned her whole body over him. In the middle of the music, she fondled her client and coquettishly quoted the line in the song to ask her client: "My husband (*laogong*), why do you love other women behind my back?"

Throughout Chinese history, prostitution has been linked to arts and entertainment such as dancing and singing. Early records from China showed the two Chinese characters representing "prostitution" (*ji* 妓 and *chang* 娼) as a "female musician." Prostitution has been inseparable from entertainment, as *listen to prostitutes* meant "listen to music"; *watch prostitutes* meant "watch dancing and singing." Through historicizing the relationships between prostitution and music, this chapter seeks to scrutinize the dynamics of the historical and contemporary mutual construction of gender between music performers (courtesans and hostesses) and music receivers (male elite and clients). More specifically, this chapter will juxtapose the two kinds of masculinities: the refined masculinity judged by the courtesans in imperial China and the entrepreneurial masculinity judged by male peers in postsocialist China. Drawing on my twenty-four-month-long ethnographic fieldwork in northeast China, this chapter will also contrast the kind of freedom and control courtesans enjoyed vis-à-vis the kind of agency and subservience hostesses embraced. This chapter aims to unravel the kinds of masculinity and femininity constructed in karaoke bars, where hostesses accompany men in singing and dancing and, at times, provide sexual services.

Courtesans and Music

The literature relating to courtesans in China, both in English and Chinese, ranging across different historical periods, consistently emphasizes their performance skills. The Chinese term for prostitute, *yi ji*, means "a female artist, performer, or courtesan." The word *ji* is related to words meaning ingenuity, talent, and ability.[3] Courtesans were trained in theatrical, musical, and literary composition and performance. During the Tang dynasty, the definition of prostitute was a female entertainer specialized in singing and dancing skills. The highest-ranking courtesans were those who had outstanding skills in chess, calligraphy, painting, singing, composing poems, and playing a wide array of musical instruments.[4] During the Ming dynasty, courtesans were labeled according to their specializations, including poet courtesans (*shiji*), song courtesans (*geji*), and actresses (*you*).[5]

In order to become suitable concubine candidates, courtesans had to possess literary and artistic talents so that they could serve as supplements to elite men's married lives. Elites visited courtesans to find an interesting diversion from the obligatory sexual life in the family and because of a craving for a variety of female companions. Thus the artistic entertainment offered by courtesans constituted their primary employment, and the sexual services which might flow from these occasions were seen as less important. Exclusive sexual relationships with clients were discouraged because they reduced the frequency of lucrative banquets and blocked out other male visitors.[6] Elite government officials and scholars came to consider courtesans as an indispensable component of their lives.

To satisfy these needs of the elite, courtesans received training since childhood from teachers who were masters of musical knowledge. Their work was to provide social companionship and artistic performances for the elite. In the latter half of the nineteenth century at the top of the rank of courtesans was the *shuyu* (singers and storytellers). They identified themselves as artists whose profession was to entertain customers at festive occasions and banquets in customers' homes, in their own apartments, or in the city's designated places of entertainment. They were renowned as skilled entertainers who only sold their voice and skills, not sex. What they provided was company at banquets, service of wine, and entertainment with their songs.[7]

There were stringent entry rules for this courtesan profession. *Shuyu* had to demonstrate their singing, storytelling, and *pipa*-playing abilities in an annual examination in order to enter the profession or renew their performance credentials. The annual examination was usually chosen on a festival date, and candidates had to sing a song and recite a piece of opera. These songs and operas had to be different each year to illustrate the wide range of each participant's repertory.[8] Those who failed to meet the standards or attend the festival were barred from the traditional music halls. Toward the end of the Qing, when the rules were less strict, two categories coexisted: those who could both sing and perform opera and those who could only sing.

By the 1920s, the *shuyu* had been completely absorbed into the *changsan* (long three) class of courtesans. Throughout the Republican period, *changsan* courtesans replaced *shuyu* and were positioned at the top of the hierarchy of prostitution. Similar to *shuyu*, *changsan* performed classical songs and scenes from opera. The *changsan*'s range of performed pieces was less wide than that of the *shuyu*. Dressed in elaborate costumes, *changsan* courtesans hosted banquets and gambling parties for merchants and high-profile officials. *Changsan* courtesans entertained daily, and they were not expected to conduct sexual relations with customers.[9]

Courtesans and Elite Masculinity

Before the May Fourth movement in 1911, masculine identity had to do with social class and had no reference point outside of China. The courtesan house was a site that produced an elite masculinity of self-control and cool demeanor. Elite masculinities had to be validated by the courtesans, the arbiters of their maleness, as worldly, urbane, knowledgeable, sophisticated, and refined.

Since at least the medieval period, the lives of the courtesans and literati intersected with each other.[10] Patronizing courtesans displayed elite men's social status. Ever since the Zhou dynasty (770–220 BCE) when the princes kept troupes of trained "female entertainers" (*nüyue*), possession of such a troupe had been an indispensable attribute of men's social prominence. Later when this practice was gradually superseded by commercial brothels, courtesans became an indispensable part of elite men's elegant life.[11]

Courtesan houses, or public places where courtesans were summoned as professional entertainers, formed an integral part of the official and business routine where social relations of officials, literati, artists, and merchants were conducted. Customers would call for a courtesan to entertain them at public occasions either inside or outside of the courtesan house. Men's commercial and political contacts were forged and solidified through courtesans' entertainment. Every official entertained his close colleagues—superiors, inferiors, and merchants—to conclude or negotiate deals. An official could ensure his promotion by introducing his superior or an influential politician to a discreetly chosen courtesan, and by the same means a merchant could obtain much-needed credit or an important order.

The courtesan house was a venue where elite men displayed a refined, urbane, and sophisticated masculinity. The most important quality was self-control and cool demeanor in the face of any problem that might arise. These values were so important that there were guidebooks instructing men in appropriate conduct. Customers were avid learners of the business practices of brothels from guidebooks to demonstrate their sophistication. A customer had to study, and then exhibit, the aesthetics and etiquette of frequenting courtesans to obtain respect from other men, avoid ridicule from courtesans, and demonstrate his sophistication. With the inside knowledge of the brothel, he would know how to adhere to the ritualized behaviors required between courtesans and clients, between clients and madam, and between clients and brothel servants, and how to negotiate a complicated financial and social obligation to her and her house in order to appear urbane and knowledgeable.[12] For instance, he would be able to manage the tea ceremony (the best time to build an intimate connection) skillfully and with face. He would spend time establishing a relationship with the house and a courtesan, fulfilling his obligations such as hosting banquets or gambling parties. He could demonstrate his connoisseurship and his membership in the elite through his appreciation of the artifacts decorating the courtesan's body and by describing them eloquently, by his informed admiration of her musical performance, and by his composition of appropriate poetry for her to sing.[13] He would know how to judge whether he was treated by the courtesans with due deference. He would be careful to exhibit not only wealth but good taste in dress. He would go to the courtesan house in the company of powerful male companions so that the courtesans would not dare to play tricks on him. He would not speak of her secrets and would not call on more than one courtesan at a time. A customer who failed in these manners lowered his own status and risked exposure in front of his fellow customers as a "country bumpkin."[14]

The courtesans' role in validating refined masculinity allowed them to enjoy much more freedom and control over their lives than common prostitutes.[15] They not only had the power to select clients but also to humiliate them in front of their friends. Ming courtesans were defiant, independent, and autonomous, defining themselves as the "warriors of love."[16]

As illustrated, because courtesans played active and discerning roles in defining elite masculinity, elite males were avid learners of rules, guides, and rituals on how to act appropriately around them.[17] These rituals and guides were established and promoted by the courtesans to regulate clients and place the courtesans in positions of control.[18] These rituals included the client's access to and meeting with the courtesan, his courtship of her, and her acceptance or rejection of his advances. These rituals also enhanced her "cultural capital of romantic love."[19] The courtesans, through defining masculinity and circumscribing clients' behaviors, articulated their power as independent entertainers and dignified businesswomen.[20]

The Republican era witnessed a decline of the performance-based courtesan culture in tandem with the vanishing future generations of literati when the imperial examination ended and intellectuals called for an end to the association of performers and prostitutes. The Republican era linked prostitution to nationalism and associated it with cultural weakness, national shame, and social, political, and even physical sickness. For the first time, prostitution was treated as a social evil that harmed social order, women's rights, and the progress of the race. The state attempted to regulate the crisis through legislation and the creation of fiscal and public health systems.[21] In 1958, the Maoist regime proudly declared to the world the eradication of prostitution from mainland China, embodying China's transformation into a modern nation. However, these claims were to be short lived.

The Rise of Karaoke Bars, Entrepreneurial Men, and Modern Hostesses

Consonant with the relaxation of state control and the economic reforms of 1978, nightclubs and karaoke bars mushroomed. Karaoke, literally "empty orchestra," is a form of singing to prerecorded music accompaniment without the vocal lead, along with video images and lyrics displayed on TV.[22]

The components of karaoke technology that include audio, video, and laser recording were originally invented in the West and later spread to other parts of the world. It was not until after World War II that Japanese inventors reconfigured these components into a new and hybrid technology form for the purpose of communal singing. The prototype of the karaoke machine emerged in Japan in the early 1970s.[23] The karaoke bar culture radiated from Japan to many countries throughout Asia and around the world and has since become a popular mass entertainment, particularly in Asia.[24]

Karaoke machines were introduced into China in the 1980s. In Shanghai, the first karaoke was established in a hamburger shop owned by a Hong Kong businessman.[25] In the city of Dalian in northeast China, the first karaoke bar, named Tokyo 898, was established by Japanese businessmen in 1988, with karaoke equipment imported from Japan.[26] Since then new karaoke bars have mushroomed throughout the city. The use of prostitutes by businessmen and government officials in these karaoke bars became ubiquitous and was accepted as a legitimate way to conduct business. With the rise in popularity of karaoke bars, red-light districts sprang up where hostesses flourished.

Visitors to these bars comprise middle-aged businessmen, government officials, entrepreneurs, the nouveau riche, policemen, and foreign investors. Entrepreneurs and officials routinely participate in the so-called coordinated sequence (*yitiao long* 一条龙) that includes luxurious banquets in expensive restaurants, singing in karaoke bars, and massages in sauna salons. Engaging in entertainment offered in karaoke bars and hostesses' services has become a common procedure through which entrepreneurs and officials build business networks and negotiate contracts.

These hostesses or companions are addressed in Chinese as *sanpei xiaojie* (three accompaniment girls), young women who accompany men in alcohol consumption, dancing, and singing. These hostesses, generally between the ages of seventeen and twenty-three, act as companions for male clients, providing chatting, flirting, singing, dancing, drinking, and caressing services. Some hostesses provide additional sexual services for an extra fee. Their monthly income oscillates from 6,000 yuan to tens of thousands of yuan. Hostesses' services have become indispensable not only in male recreation at karaoke bars but also in male-centered worlds of business and political networking among male businessmen and local political elites.

A majority of these hostesses are rural migrants who took advantage of the economic reform and flooded into the city. Because of institutional (e.g., household registration policy) and social discrimination, a vast majority of these migrants are forced into the lowest rung of the labor market. Migrants tend to work as construction workers, garbage collectors, restaurant waitresses, domestic maids, factory workers, and bar hostesses.

Modern hostesses, like traditional courtesans, are not just prostitutes but also entertainers and companions. Hostesses express their contempt of women in establishments that involve nothing but sex and consider their own services to be of a much higher caliber. Although erotic services are offered in a plethora of establishments, including hotels, saunas, hair salons, disco, parks, some roadside restaurants, movie houses, video rooms, and other dance halls, karaoke bars are renowned for being most demanding in their requirement for the women's height, facial beauty, figure, and social skills such as singing, dancing, flirting, drinking, and conversation. An important reason for the stringent criteria is that, while sexual intercourse is the exclusive service offered to clients in many other establishments, only a few karaoke bar hostesses consent to strangers' request for intercourse. They also charge twice as much as is charged in many other establishments. Since sex, in general, is not the purpose of clients' visit to karaoke bars, a hostess must possess extraordinary charms to otherwise attract and sustain client's interest, or she will not be able to survive in karaoke bars.

Hostessing as a mode of sexual service is different from prostitution. Prostitutes engage in genital and oral sex with clients, whereas hostesses' sexual services encompass waiting on clients (*zuotai*) and "going out" (*chutai*). The former occurs within the karaoke private rooms and includes a range of behaviors from entertainment such as singing, dancing, and drinking to non-genital-to-genital sexual contact (fondling). A *zuotai* session typically lasts for one to two hours, for which hostesses earn an average tip of 200–400 RMB—the equivalent of, and often more than, other rural migrants' monthly wages and almost half the average monthly wage of an urban worker.

Hostesses can earn even higher incomes by "going out"—performing genital or oral sex with clients. The cost of such services can range anywhere from 300 to 5,000 RMB, depending on numerous factors such as the length of the service session (e.g., some customers contract hostesses for an entire evening) and other idiosyncratic bargaining conditions. Virgins command especially high prices of up to 10,000 RMB. Services occur either in the "sex rooms" (*pao fang*) provided by bars or in outside hotel rooms provided by clients.

Unlike courtesans, with their elite status as professional entertainers and artists in traditional China, modern hostesses share the incommensurately low status of prostitutes, and their musical talents are generally ignored and sex appeal dramatized and amplified. This shift of role definition away from performer and toward prostitute in contemporary China, I argue, derives from the new constructions of entrepreneurial masculinity that depart from the models of elite masculinity based on social class, sophistication, knowledge, and refinement.

Gendered Practice in Karaoke Bars: Karaoke and the Construction of Entrepreneurial Masculinity

Studies of karaoke singing have explored its role in the expression, maintenance, and construction of social, ethnic, class, and gender identities.[27]

In this section, I will discuss the ways in which karaoke singing constitutes a mechanism through which male clients establish social bonding and construct an entrepreneurial masculinity that entails power, wealth, sexual prowess, and rebellion.

Karaoke bars, through offering a mixture of pleasure, power, resistance, and status, have become a site where postsocialist entrepreneurial men regain and reclaim a lost masculinity. Scholars have written profusely about the crisis of masculinity and the search for a true manhood in postsocialist China.[28] During my research, patrons of karaoke bars complained that they felt repressed and emasculated by women's liberation, state feminism, and suppression of human desire. In my 2009 book, I argue that the Maoist regime created a masculine iconic view of women, subjecting men to new forms of competition. Men, still carrying their traditional views, were confronted by icons of women heroically performing male functions, such as working in the fields and defending the country. This impelled men to greater efforts in the struggle to achieve Mao's goals simply to maintain their traditional sense of masculine superiority. Arguably, the Maoist state, by pretending to liberate women, had actually forged a tool to more fully control men. It is not surprising that men remembered the Maoist era as an era of emasculation. Men's feeling of political, economic, and sexual repression by the Maoist state patriarch caused them to search for their lost masculinity in the post-Mao era. The influential contemporary filmmaker Zhang Yimou in *Red Sorghum* met this need by portraying "the outlaws, drunkards, and rebels of Chinese legend" as heroes.[29] The male protagonist, a tough young peasant, demonstrates his manhood by kidnapping, ravishing, and impregnating the wife of a diseased older man whom he has killed. The old man represents the repressive state patriarchy. Zhang shows a set of figures who are defined not by passivity but by heroic action. They are free and liberated in every way, politically, sexually, and even economically. Although he set the film in the 1930s and created an ideal based on the New Culture movement, it served during the postsocialist era as a model for a revitalized masculinity in China.

One could argue that karaoke bars symbolize a shift from the Maoist era bureaucratic culture to the new entrepreneurial culture. The economic reforms that gave rise to the private sector began to create an opening for emerging businessmen to redefine their masculinity. The karaoke bar provides a means whereby they can not only redefine themselves sexually but also contest the importance of the banquet and food as a symbol of state power.[30] In the 1980s, state corruption was characterized by the practice of large banquets. Susan Brownell contends that the 1980s obsession with food derives from vivid memories of hunger during the Maoist era.[31] The ration system reinforced the state's superior position and made its recipients "beholden to and dependent on it." The central position of food as a symbol of state power, represented by the political importance of banquets, was eroded during the 1990s by the end of the food rationing system. However, the basic principle that power is symbolized by one's ability to more than satisfy bodily needs was established by this practice and extended to more varied forms of food consumption and to sex in the 1990s.

The rising importance of karaoke bars marked a rebellion by the emerging Chinese business class: by embracing the karaoke bar, men challenge the monopoly of state power as represented by the banquet. By appropriating the new karaoke bar, they create a new venue within which they can contest the dominance of the old state order and reestablish their masculine identity. Since their initial emergence, karaoke bars have aroused tremendous social curiosity. They feature the latest audiovisual technology, splendid exterior and interior furnishings, neon lights, high prices, and beautiful hostesses. They suit the rising entrepreneurs' desire for "modern" consumption, allowing them to not only display their talents, creativities, and idiosyncrasies in bringing their voices to the songs and making the songs their own but also to evince their power and wealth.

Patrons usually select rough and heroic songs to convey their aspirations, ambitions, freedom, and wildness. Constructions of masculinity not only derive from these masculine songs sung by the men but they also stem from the gentle, sweet, and romantic songs sung by the hostesses and by hostesses' compliments to the men's talents and creativity in singing. In karaoke boxes, patrons experience the thrill of taking the center stage, receiving full attention from colleagues, and plunging briefly into a simulated experience of being a rock star. The instruments provided by karaoke machines not only amplify and purify the voice of the singer, making it sound like that of a singing artist, but also evince a resounding round of applause at the end of the song, offering effusive praise and a final grade on the TV screen.

Karaoke bars not only provide a spotlight for the patrons but also feature beautiful hostesses paid to cosset and flatter customers, whom patrons can choose to be their companions for the evening. They provide a venue for young entrepreneurs to demonstrate their sexual prowess before colleagues, through singing, bragging, and seducing hostesses. It is not surprising that karaoke bars quickly became the site of the most fashionable recreational and commercial activity for men.

Gendered Practice in Karaoke Bars: Karaoke and the Construction of Submissive Femininity

The settings of karaoke helped transform this public entertainment place into an intimate place that resembles the home. A small karaoke box usually features a U-shaped sofa, a TV, and a coffee table. The closed space without windows, the comfortable sofa, the dim lighting, and the soft and melodic music help create a romantic and intimate ambience that allows the inhabitants to not only live out the fantasies in their minds but also experience an intimate setting that is free from worries, conflicts, and pressures from the world. By offering an escape from the potentially perilous outside world, karaoke boxes help solidify and consolidate group bonding through their shared fantasy consumption experiences. This setting enables patrons and hostesses to experience a romantic ambience, an escape, and a sanctuary. In this pseudo-family refuge, patrons and hostesses perform to each other as an intimate couple. Through selection of songs, both patrons and hostesses express their feelings to each other and to other colleagues.

Such modes of intimate self-expression through music were not allowed during the revolutionary period when music was appropriated as a propaganda tool to extol the Communist Party, communist leadership, revolution, and the nation-state.[32] In postsocialist China, in tandem with relaxed state control and the market economy, mainland, Taiwanese, and Hong Kong popular music flourished in CDs, cassettes, radios, televisions, videotapes, karaoke music TVs, discos, and so on. Researchers argue that many of these heterogeneous voices represent a resistance against and an escape from the centralized hegemony of the state.[33]

In karaoke boxes, romantic songs fall into three gendered categories: songs sung by female singers to display femininity, songs sung by male singers to exhibit masculinity, and duets sung by both male and female to express romantic love. There are two microphones in a karaoke box, and sometimes patrons and hostesses sing duets together just like a romantic couple. Hostesses hardly ever sing male singers' songs; likewise, patrons hardly ever sing female singers' songs.

Such musical expressions of gender difference only proliferated during the postsocialist era. The Maoist era promoted gender erasure where women and men wore unisex clothing and traditional modes of femininity were attacked as capitalist and decadent. The celebration of gender difference in the 1990s allowed men to recover their masculine identity by reconstituting a feminine identity for women. Market reform and consumerism produced flourishing images of sexualized and hyperfeminine women, which embodied less a refeminization of women than the recovery of masculinity.

Hostesses' Songs

Hostesses usually purposefully select popular romantic songs that affirm and confirm their submission, devotion, passivity, and faithfulness to men. In the lyrics of the popular romantic songs sung by hostesses, "I" refers to the woman herself, and "you" refers to her male lover. In general, the lyrics of these songs feature the following themes:

1. The woman's life has become meaningless and empty since her male lover left.
2. The woman is still helplessly, painfully in love with her male lover after he abandons her.
3. The woman is an anonymous admirer of a man's singing talents and creativity.
4. The woman wishes that she was her man's only lover, but she is not.
5. The woman's love toward her man is slow-paced, gentle, and patient.
6. The woman suffers in pain because her male lover rejects her love.
7. The woman is heartbroken and devastated after being abandoned by her male lover.
8. The woman tries all means to please her male lover, despite his mistreatment.
9. The woman is still waiting for her male lover to return after he abandons her.
10. The woman is gentle and understanding, hungry and lonely for love.
11. The woman is gentle, quiet, devoted, and faithful to her male lover.

Tears, rain, and snow usually accompany the sentimental lyrics appearing on the TV screen, dramatizing the heartbreak and devastation of the woman. Hostesses sing these songs in a coquettish style with soft, gentle, sweet, and at times whispering voices to convey to their male clients that they exist for their men, they suffer for their men, they are devoted to their men, and they desire to have their men in control. The music scenes are also abundant with women wearing bikinis and assuming suggestive and seductive postures for the enjoyment of the male audience, reinforcing the role of women as sexual objects for men.

One night when I was in the karaoke bar, a hostess was singing a song titled "I Can't Walk out of Your Eyesight" (Zoubuchu ni de muguang):[34]

> Walking out of your eyesight, I feel lonely
> I can only live a natural life with your gaze
> Only when I return to your hands and am held close to you
> Can I feel assured of my love
> Walking out of your story, I feel empty . . .

While singing this song, she coquettishly thrust one of her hands into her client's and made him grasp hers tightly. She cast her tearful yet seductive eyes on her client while singing the song with a fragile and heartbreaking tone. By invoking her powerless outlook and expressing her desire to be controlled and domesticated by her man and to exist for her man, she skillfully helped her male client bolster his sense of masculine power and superiority.

Another song frequently sung by hostesses was titled "A Spiritual Date" (Xinling zhi yue):[35]

> I am waiting for you in my memory
> Only there can I feel your love

> Although the past is far and far away
> I hope nothing has changed
> My love has never changed
> In my heart, you are my only dream

Between the touching lyrics and the sentimental ballad melody, these songs create a romantic ambience that facilitated hostesses' displays of devotion and submission to their male clients. To strengthen their expressions, hostesses also exhibited their affection through physical contact. In the karaoke rooms, a hostess typically gently massaged the man's back and chest, resting her head on the man's shoulders, sang songs when gazing at the man, or shed tears, and, depending on the nature of the intricate relationship between the two, kissed the man's cheeks or lips, sat on the man's lap and embraced his head and shoulders, danced cheek to cheek, embraced the man's waist intimately, and so on. Sometimes the bolder ones would even grasp the man's penis or pull down his pants to invite more sexual intimacy and physical contact, depending on the man's propensities. They also indicated their devotion to their men through serving them food and drinks, peeling fruit or melon seeds for them, and even feeding them their favorite snacks.

Duets

The duets sung by both hostesses and patrons comprise themes such as the celebration of the gendered roles of a traditional couple, gratitude for each other's company, valorization of mutual love, and everlasting love. Among these songs, "Husband and Wife Returning Home" (Fuqi shuangshuang bajia huan) was very popular during my research at karaoke bars. The hostess sings, "You plant the fields and I weave the cloth." The patron sings, "I carry the water and you water the garden." The man's deep voice contrasts against the woman's sweet, soft, slow, and gentle voice. The song champions a gendered division of labor, juxtaposing the man's strong and rough image with the woman's passive and weak image.

Clients' Songs

Clients usually sing masculine songs to express their aspirations, freedom, and individuality and to evince their aggressive and unbridled desires. Frequent references to wine and drinking elicit a rebellious, bold, and active masculinity. One popular song is entitled "Drink Up, My Friend" (Ganbei pengyou):[36]

> My friend, you are embarking on a long journey today
> Please drink up this glass of wine
> Let's forget the sorrows of a lonely journey and get completely drunk
> Maybe you will never have a time to stop in your long journey starting from today

Let us hold up this glass of wine and drink it up, my friend
The sky is such a blue freedom, and you desire to possess it
Let's hope that the uninhibited and unrestrained days will no longer be a luxurious aspiration
Let's hold up this glass of wine again and drink it up, my friend

This song explicitly displays a man's physical power and masculinity through a yearning for freedom, individuality, resistance, and courage. He longs for the "uninhibited and unrestrained days," embodying his desire to break free from the controlling forces of society that deny his masculinity, be it the state or the woman. Male clients usually sing this kind of heroic and masculine song with a coarse, shouting, and deep voice.

Clients in general boost their ego and reclaim their lost masculinity not only through these masculine songs but also through hostesses' admiration. After clients sing each song, hostesses usually applaud and rave in a loud voice: "Wow, that was great! Amazing singing! You are my idol! Let me toast you and I will drink up first!" Hostesses make a concerted effort to compliment men each time after they sing to make them feel like stars. One client told me in an interview: "I always get carried away when my beautiful hostess compliments my singing and my looks. They commented that I looked like a Hong Kong star singer. It gave me a great deal of face in front of my colleagues. We [men] want admiration from beautiful hostesses. It definitely satisfies our psychological needs before our peers."

Female Entertainers and Male Clients, Past and Present

Throughout Chinese history, musical performance and female entertainers have played a significant role in constructing masculinities. Modern hostesses resemble traditional courtesans in two aspects. Both play roles not just as prostitutes but also as entertainers and companions. Both serve as the testing ground for masculinity, respectively for elite masculinity and entrepreneurial masculinity.

Modern hostesses differ from traditional courtesans in that traditional courtesans enjoyed greater autonomy and control over their clients than modern hostesses because of the different natures of elite and entrepreneurial masculinity at two different historical junctures. The courtesan house was a site for the production of refined urban elite masculinity. Men's social relationships made the courtesan house a venue for elite men to display a refined version of masculinity where sexual services were the least significant part of a sophisticated interaction between courtesans and the scholars who sought their services. In the postsocialist era, the new class of entrepreneurial man requires a hypersexualized, provocative trophy woman to monopolize, control, and objectify. A consistent pattern through the two historical stages of the twentieth century (revolution and reform) has been a coarsening of masculine identity. Entrepreneurial masculinity is constructed in tandem with the return of male privilege and female disadvantage. The two are inextricably interwoven.

This chapter has illustrated how this kind of entrepreneurial masculinity is played out in karaoke bar settings. Karaoke bars allow men to experience a fantasy world of wealth, celebrity, prestige, creativity, individuality, pleasure, sexual prowess, and rebellion by singing masculine songs like a rock star, displaying the status symbols of conspicuous consumption offered by karaoke bars, and enjoying the erotic, submissive services of hostesses. Karaoke bars have been appropriated by men to reclaim a lost masculinity and reassert an entrepreneurial masculinity. As demonstrated in the chapter, within the karaoke bars, this masculinity is constructed and bolstered by hostesses who flatter and praise the men's talents and in their own performances utilize romantic, soft, and gentle songs to convey their subjugation and devotion to men. While asserting their agency to perform this ultrafeminine, dutiful, and faithful image to their male clients in exchange for economic benefits and possible opportunities for upward mobility, hostesses paradoxically reproduce and reinscribe their objectification and victimization.

Notes

I would like to thank Rachel Harris and Rowan Pease for their most constructive and helpful comments that have significantly helped improve this chapter.

1. Composer: Zhang Hongliang. Lyricist: Zhang Cuihua. Singer: Li Xiangjun.
2. Translations by the author.
3. Victoria Cass, *Dangerous Women: Warriors, Grannies, and Geishas of the Ming* (Lanham, MD: Rowman and Littlefield, 1999), 28.
4. During the late Tang dynasty, brothels were restricted within special quarters of the cities according to the status of the prostitutes. R. H. Van Gulik, *Sexual Life in Ancient China* (Shanghai: Shanghai People's, 1990).
5. Cass, *Dangerous Women*, 28.
6. Liu, Dalin. *Zhongguo gudai xing wenhua* (Yinchuan: Ningxia Renmin Chubanshe, 1993); Van Gulik, *Sexual Life*.
7. Christian Henriot, *Prostitution and Sexuality in Shanghai: A Social History, 1849–1949* (Cambridge: Cambridge University Press, 2001), 24.
8. Henriot, *Prostitution and Sexuality*, 24.
9. Gail Hershatter, *Dangerous Pleasures: Prostitution and Modernity in Twentieth-Century Shanghai* (Berkeley: University of California Press, 1997), 43–44.
10. Cass, *Dangerous Women*, 27.
11. Hershatter, *Dangerous Pleasures*; Van Gulik, *Sexual Life*.
12. Hershatter, *Dangerous Pleasures*, 69–70.
13. See Zeitlin in this volume.
14. Hershatter, *Dangerous Pleasures*, 69–102.
15. Van Gulik, *Sexual Life*, 238; Hershatter, *Dangerous Pleasures*.

16. Cass, *Dangerous Women*, 35–46.
17. Hershatter, *Dangerous Pleasures*; Henriot, *Prostitution and Sexuality*.
18. The degree of power exercised by courtesans is debated in the literature. See Catherine Vance Yeh, "Reinventing Ritual: Late Qing Handbooks for Proper Customer Behavior in Shanghai Courtesan Houses," *Late Imperial China* 19, no. 2 (1998): 1–63.
19. Yeh, "Reinventing Ritual," 18.
20. However, the lowest-ranking prostitutes lacked control and relied entirely upon sexual services.
21. Fran Martin and Larissa Heinrich, *Embodied Modernities: Corporeality, Representation, and Chinese Cultures* (Honolulu: University of Hawaii Press, 2006).
22. Toru Mitsui and Shūhei Hosokawa eds. *Karaoke around the World: Global Technology, Local Singing* (London: Routledge, 1998), 40.
23. Deborah Wong and Mai Elliot, "I Want the Microphone: Mass Mediation and Agency in Asian-American Popular Music," *Drama Review* 38, no. 3 (1994): 152–67; Mitsui and Hosokawa, *Karaoke around the World*.
24. Casey Man Kong Lum, *In Search of a Voice: Karaoke and the Construction of Identity in Chinese America* (Mahwah, NJ: Lawrence Erlbaum, 1996); Mitsui and Hosokawa, *Karaoke around the World*.
25. Akiko Otake and Shuhei Hosokawa, "Karaoke in East Asia: Modernization, Japanization, or Asianization?" in Mitsui and Hosokawa, *Karaoke around the World*.
26. Zheng Tiantian, *Red Lights: The Lives of Sex Workers in Postsocialist China* (Minneapolis: University of Minnesota Press, 2009).
27. Lum, *In Search of a Voice*; Mitsui and Hosokawa, *Karaoke around the World*.
28. Nimrod Baranovitch, *China's New Voices: Popular Music, Ethnicity, Gender, and Politics, 1978–1997* (Berkeley: University of California Press, 2003); Susan Brownell, "The Body and the Beautiful in Chinese Nationalism: Sportswomen and Fashion Models in the Reform Era," *China Information* 13, no. 2-3 (1998): 36–58; Susan Brownell, "Strong Women and Impotent Men: Sports, Gender, and Nationalism in Chinese Public Culture," in *Spaces of Their Own: Women's Public Sphere in Transnational China*, ed. Mayfair Mei-hui Yang (Minneapolis: University of Minnesota Press, 1999), 207–31; Judith Farquhar, *Appetites: Food and Sex in Post-Socialist China* (Durham, NC: Duke University Press, 2002); Kam Louie, "The Macho Eunuch: The Politics of Masculinity in Jia Pingwa's 'Human Extremities,'" *Modern China* 17, no. 2 (1991):163–87; Kam Louie, "Masculinities and Minorities: Alienation in Strange Tales from Strange Land," *The China Quarterly* 132 (1992): 1119–35; Kam Louie and Louise Edwards, "Chinese Masculinity: Theorizing Wen and Wu," *East Asian History* 8 (1994):135–48; Wang Yuejin, "Mixing Memory and Desire: *Red Sorghum*, a Chinese Version of Masculinity and Femininity," *Public Culture* 2, no. 1 (1989): 31–53; Zhang Yingjin, "Ideology of the Body in *Red Sorghum*: National Allegory, National Roots, and Third Cinema," *East-West Film Journal* 4, no. 2 (1990): 38–53; Zheng, *Red Lights*; Xueping Zhong, "Male Suffering and Male Desire: The Politics of Reading Half of Man Is Woman," in *Engendering China: Women, Culture, and the State*, ed. Christina Gilmartin, Gail Hershatter, Lisa Rofel, and Tyrene White (Cambridge, MA: Harvard University Press, 1994), 175–94; Xueping Zhong, *Masculinity Besieged? Issues of Modernity and Male Subjectivity in Chinese Literature of the Late Twentieth Century* (Durham, NC: Duke University Press, 2000).
29. Susan Brownell, "Gender and Nationalism in China at the Turn of the Millennium," in *China Briefing 2000*, ed. Tyrene White (Armonk, NY: M. E. Sharpe, 2000), 195–232.
30. Zheng, *Red Lights*.

31. Brownell, "Gender and Nationalism."
32. Otake and Hosokawa, "Karaoke in East Asia"; Baranovitch, *China's New Voices*.
33. Baranovitch, *China's New Voices*, 3.
34. Composer, Lyricist, and Singer: Chen Lin.
35. Composer: Tan Jianchang. Lyricist: Xiao Xuan. Singer: Deng Miaohua.
36. Composer and Lyricist: Yang Haichao. Singer: Tian Zhen. Although the original singer of this song was a woman, it was generally sung by men in karaoke bars because of the nature of the lyrics and the low, deep voice of the singer.

Chapter Four

An Interview with Zhang Han, Karaoke Bar Host

Zhang Han (b. 1977, Dongbei) lived and worked in northern China and moved to Singapore in 2009 in the hope of expanding his career in the world of karaoke lounges. He is currently the stage manager of the Miracle Karaoke Lounge in the Balestier District of Singapore and gave this interview to Shzr Ee Tan at Miracle, in Mandarin.

"Never Taken a Single Day Off"

I've been in this business for seventeen years—seventeen years, can you believe it? I've been on stage since I was sixteen. I finished secondary school in Dongbei and didn't know what I was going to do. It just seemed like an option. I've *pao* (跑 run) all over China, and a friend got an introduction for me to come to work in Singapore six months ago. It's been good so far. I've never taken a single day off, not even gone on medical leave. That's dedication for you. Obviously earning in Singapore dollars is better than *renminbi*, but I've found out that the costs here are quite high too.

Most of the singers in karaoke lounges are women, but it's always useful to have a man around. We can rally the crowd, we're the emcees, we introduce people officially, and we oil the machinery. We sing, too. The girls tend to sing the slower, romantic songs. We sing the fast ones so that the mood in the bar won't be too low key. But I'm here also as a stage manager. I plan the song routines and delegate different songs to different girls according to their personality and voice types. We make sure there aren't repeats or similar-sounding songs delivered in succession. We make sure that the program is varied. But I don't actually get to choose the girls the first round before they join the lounge—they have been screened beforehand by my boss, the general manager, probably from photos.

"Singaporean Men Are a Well-behaved Lot"

What I do is make sure that all the music runs smoothly and check that all activity within the lounge during opening hours remains civilized, within the law. Maybe it's easier to do this as a man. Things are strict here in Singapore!

And of course nothing usually happens—Singaporean men are a well-behaved lot; we never get any brawls. What happens after the girls knock off with our clients is their own business. But at least I can keep a lookout on their behalf within the club. I do have good rapport with them and also with patrons. I'm still quite young myself and I'm serious about my work; I don't take advantage of the girls—or patrons. I wouldn't go so far as to call myself a bodyguard, though. The girls are clever enough to look out for themselves. There's a sense of sisterhood rather than rivalry. They're all from China, living in Singapore, after all. The time they spend here is too short to be worth engaging in creating a diva persona or trying to outdo each other on stage. It's just not worth it.

Chinese Girls in Singapore Lounges: "Quieter and More Feminine"

I'm here on a two-year work permit; I hope to stay longer if things go well. Our manager is Singaporean; he uses an English name. Our waiters are from Singapore or Malaysia. But all our singers come from China: Sichuan, Dongbei—everywhere. They stay for six months and they leave. When their contracts end, some move on to other bars or explore other opportunities outside Singapore—Malaysia, Taiwan; it's a circuit. Some return to China. There are tough employment laws here. But also it's important that we have new faces and new talent. In this business, our clients don't want to keep on seeing the same old routines.

We look for fresh blood, but Singaporean girls don't want to dirty their hands with this kind of work—it pays too little by their standards, and it's thought of as a shady, seedy world. Most importantly, Singaporean girls can't sing in Mandarin properly, and they don't know the old songs! Our patrons like singers who know what they're doing. They prefer girls from China because they're quieter, more feminine and charming, better at conversation. They don't like those aggressive *lamei* (辣妹 hot sisters). They're old-fashioned; they like sweet, docile singers. We never ask what our clients do; it's an extremely private affair, but obviously they can afford to come here—some even every night. But, as you can see, they are a primarily Mandarin-speaking crowd, unlike a large part of Singapore. And of course they're all men.

Older, Slower Songs

The scene in Singapore is obviously quite different from China. But it's hard to compare. China is so huge. In Beijing it's a shark's world. Every singer is top rank—I've given up working there because the competition is not worth the salary. But, in the smaller cities, it's a different thing. Still, you can see a difference in the kinds of songs that are sung in Singapore: they're slightly older;

they're slower. In Singapore people somehow are more conservative. Or maybe our patrons expect our singers to be conservative and demure—from somewhere in deep China, not a city like Singapore!

In reality, in China the singers wear hot pants and groove to upbeat songs. Of course they don't go as far as singing the current radio hits—that's for a much younger, active crowd! Can you imagine our clients—in their fifties and sixties—B-Boying to Jay Chou from their plastic lounge seats? The contrast is even more pronounced in Singapore. Over here our singers wear evening gowns and perform the romantic and well-known love songs—Teresa Teng, Phil Chang, Andy Lau. But of course patrons vary; tastes vary; it's always hard to say. In China, the patrons openly honor their favorite singers with wads of cash. The money is presented to the singers directly, fanned out in the patron's palms and delivered individually to each girl in person; it's a big gesture. Over here, you have to "buy" sashes—$50, $100, $200, $300 . . . these are hung around each girl by facilitators like myself. The patrons don't get onstage to interact with the girls directly.

Five Shows a Night, Twenty Songs per Repertoire

On a typical night we have five shows. We start at 9:30 p.m. and end at 2:30 a.m., but of course we never shut on time, and people can adjourn for supper if they want. Sometimes we go to supper as a group, without clients; it builds a sense of solidarity. I go with the girls like a big brother.

Surprisingly, weekends aren't as crowded as weekdays, because our patrons reserve Saturdays and Sundays for their families. Instead, people come and relax after a hard day of work during the week. Some entertain their clients here—it becomes an extension of a work day. So, ironically, Mondays and Tuesdays are actually quite busy.

The girls take turns singing in a medley, together, and then they sing separately, solo. They all have number plaques on their gowns for the patrons to remember them by. They have stage names too—Qianqian; Yoyo; Xiao Huang. I think each of them has a repertoire of about twenty songs, all memorized. We rarely repeat our songs, and most of them sing them in the original key, although we can adjust this with the karaoke machine. Most of our singers don't have professional vocal training but have naturally good voices. Coming to Singapore, a few have learnt to speak Hokkien and sing Hokkien songs.

Bad Singers, Good Conversationalists, and Charming Smiles

It's not always the best singer or the one with the best voice who is the most popular or gets rewarded with the most sashes. Some say the ethnic minority singers have the best voices, because they've grown up singing their folk songs in the village. Personally, I like the voices from Dongbei, where I come from, where there is power combined with femininity. But obviously in this line of the business, the younger, prettier ones hog the limelight. Still, I think it's also very important to smile, to have stage presence, to make conversation, to entertain the patrons. That counts too.

"A Man in a Woman's Place in a Man's World"

Even *I* have to do this as a man, as general host. It's part of the PR package, or regulars will feel slighted. I sing too—obviously the patrons are not going to concentrate on me but rather on the girls! But I sing also to give the girls a bit of a break and to vary the musical content. Men's songs are different from women's songs. It's not just about key but also tempo and character. They're less "soft" and "sweet." I have to make sure that I still sound professional because I'm the stage manager, in charge of the music and dance. My songs sort of frame the entire evening, my interludes pace and give the evening structure. I play a different kind of role as a man in the lounge; obviously I'm different from the male patrons who sit with the girls. But I don't feel out of place, I've been in the industry for so long already. I'm a man in a woman's place in a man's world. I like meeting people. I believe in building old-fashioned relationships based on trust and honor—it's possible even in what people call a shady business like this.

Going out of Tune

I'm on my feet on stage and running around everywhere, every day, making sure there is always some entertainment happening in the lounge and that the patrons are taken care of and not bored. It's very tiring for me and for the girls too. And needless to say that takes the toll on our voices. We do sing out of tune. It happens to everybody, how can you not expect it to happen? We're all human after all. All that drinking, too—it might not affect you on the night itself, but the morning after, when your throat is gone and you can't sing for a few hours, you're done for. How much do I drink per night? We don't measure in pints, *laoban* (老板 boss)! We measure in jugs. That's what the game is.

A Father Who's in Showbiz

People ask me if it's worth coming to Singapore. I'll tell you one phrase: *she* (舌 willing) *de* (得 gain). I'm *willing* to leave behind the good things in China, the slower pace of life, so as to *gain* the good things in Singapore. Of course it comes at a price. I've never worked so hard. A long time ago I was married. I'm actually divorced now, and I have a seven-year-old daughter in Dongbei. I don't see my daughter as much as I'd like to, but I get to buy her more things, give her the education and opportunities she deserves. I do my duty as a man and as a father. You laugh. I look very young! Too young to have a daughter. Perhaps I'll bring her out here, when things at the lounge are more stable. I'm not sure if I'll take her here to the lounge. But definitely Singapore has more opportunities than in China, even for a man in the karaoke lounge industry.

Chapter Five

Impulsive Scholars and Sentimental Heroes

Contemporary Kunqu Discourses of Traditional Chinese Masculinities

Joseph Lam

Since 2001, when UNESCO declared *kunqu* 昆曲 (kun music or kun opera) a Masterpiece of the Oral and Intangible Heritage of Humanity, the genre has attracted many young and college-educated Chinese audiences, providing them a means to engage with their contemporary and traditional culture, history, and identities in national and globalized contexts. One common theme in these negotiations concerns Chinese masculinities,[1] be they traditional or contemporary, practiced or imagined. Chinese masculinities, many scholars have noted,[2] always evolve to cope with changing conditions and needs. To investigate and interpret such evolving masculinities, Kam Louie has proposed the dyad of *wen* 文 (mental or civil) and *wu* 武 (physical or martial) attributes, each of which represents established ideals or generalized understandings in Chinese culture and society.[3] Applying Louie's dyad to specific negotiations of Chinese masculinities, nevertheless, leads to many broad and specific questions. For example, if *wen* and *wu* attributes help define Chinese manhood publicly and privately, how do they function in specific social and personal times and sites? And, if the attributes do not operate in isolation, how do they coexist, conflicting or complementing one another? How do individual Chinese men perform their *wen* and *wu* attributes with their singular bodies?

To probe contemporary negotiations of Chinese masculinities and their theoretical deliberations, this paper examines as case studies two *kunqu* masters' performances of Chinese manhood. The two masters are Yue Meiti 岳美缇 (b. 1941) and Hou Shaokui 侯少奎 (b. 1939), whose biographies and artistry are well known and richly documented.[4] Yue's renditions of *caizi* 才子 (young and talented scholars), an idealized type of man in traditional China, have charmed many *kunqu* audiences, male and female. Hou's enactments of *yingxiong* 英雄 (heroes) have defined for many *kunqu* practitioners what a Chinese he-man is. *Caizi* and *yingxiong* personify the opposite ends in Louie's theoretical dyad of Chinese *wen* and *wu* masculinities.[5]

Kunqu parades a wide variety of traditional Chinese male characters whose staged performances directly inform and connect with contemporary ideals and practices. As a classical, social, and sophisticated form of multimedia performance, *kunqu* showcases a diversity of male acts and thoughts that publicly and privately address critical life problems and situations. Regardless whether these male characters and their acts and represent Chinese manhood positively or negatively, they become cultural, historical, and social references for contemporary Chinese masculinity discourses. References to male characters in specific role types, such as Zhang Junrui 张君瑞 as a *xiaosheng* 小生 (the role type of a young and romantic man who has yet to achieve his career) in the *Romance of the West Chamber* (*Xixiang ji* 西厢记) or Wu Song 武松 as a *wusheng* 武生 (the role type of a martial man) in *All Men Are Brothers* (*Shuihu ji* 水浒记), often appear in Chinese daily conversations and social interactions.

Based on documented evidence as well as personal experiences with the genre,[6] I posit that contemporary *kunqu* performances constitute an aesthetic, cultural, and social discourse of traditional Chinese masculinities as references for contemporary ones.[7] Through virtuosic performances of realistic male characters, *kunqu* projects complex and nuanced masculinities which emotively appeal to *kunqu* practitioners, namely its patrons, producers, performers, critics, and audiences. They manipulate *kunqu* performances, or representations, of Chinese masculinities as objects, sites, and processes to negotiate the manhood that they deem desirable and relevant to their emotional and practical lives in the present. In other words, *kunqu* practitioners negotiate their contemporary gender norms and values with reference to traditional ones. This is particularly the case when the masculinities thus negotiated are neither abstractions nor generalizations but are personified and personalized gender ideals and practices that *kunqu* practitioners emotionally, intellectually, and socially embrace for themselves. Being complex, fluid, and personalized, the negotiated masculinities reflect how contemporary *kunqu* male practitioners learn from their fathers to become their own men in the present. Their discourses are culturally and historically rooted.

Male characters enacted by master *kunqu* artists are always "alive" on stage: they appeal to their audience with their thinking minds and emotional bodies and are rarely simple demonstrations of singular masculine attributes.[8] Their virtuosic acting, dancing, and singing demonstrate diverse male images and voices, ranging from the fragile to the stalwart.

A Historical and Theoretical Overview

This function of *kunqu* is historically rooted. *Kunqu* is a classical genre of performing arts that first blossomed in late sixteenth-century China, and it has since then been continuously performed.[9] One of the earliest fully documented example of *kunqu* performance is Liang Chenyu's 梁辰渔 (1519–91) *Washing Silk* (*Huanshaji* 浣纱记) of the late 1560s.[10] The play is a dramatic negotiation of Chinese manhood, as it tells the historical and masculine struggles among the king of the Wu State (Fu Cha 夫差, ?–473 BCE), the king of the Yue State (Gou Qian 勾践, 520–465 BCE), and their loyal officials. *Washing Silk* is the first libretto specifically written for *kunqu* singing and performance; its popularity helped *kunqu* develop its performance and interpretive tradition. By the late seventeenth century, *kunqu* had already transformed into a Chinese opera *par excellence* that subsequent genres, such as Peking opera in the early nineteenth century China, emulated.

By the mid-nineteenth century, *kunqu* had an established and large repertory of more than seven hundred scenes, many of which dramatically paraded traditional Chinese men and their masculinities.[11] Currently, this classical repertory has shrunk significantly; nevertheless, it still boasts a couple of hundred scenes, offering a comprehensive and revealing reminder about traditional Chinese men and their *wen* or *wu* attributes. For example, young scholars, as represented by Liu Mengmei 柳梦梅 in *Peony Pavilion* (*Mudanting* 牡丹亭) and Pan Bizheng 潘必正 in *Jade Hairpin* (*Yuzanji* 玉簪记), are often talented and romantic; they embody mostly *wen* attributes but are not without some *wu* qualities. Similarly, the mature and heroic man, such as Wu Yuan 伍员 (?–484 BCE) in *Washing Silk*, Guan Yu 关羽 (162–219 CE) in the *Single Sword Meeting* (*Dandaohui* 单刀会) or Lin Chong 林冲 in "Flee by Night" (*Yeben* 夜奔) are models of martial heroes and stalwart men.

Such staged characters embody Chinese men's gendered memories and practices. On- or offstage, men dominated historical Chinese theatre, a reality driven by legal, moral, and social forces. In Qing China, it was illegal for men and women to publicly perform together on the same stage. Such laws allowed men to monopolize public theater, controlling it in their roles as patrons, authors, actors, composers, critics, and audience. In such a theater, female roles were performed by men, in particular by young and often androgynous men, whose artistic and physical charms were idealized as something that biological women could hardly achieve.[12]

Kunqu male characters appeal to a wide range of audiences. Diverse and nuanced, the characters' stories are dramatically complex and intellectually intriguing, and their staged performances expressive and virtuosic. *Kunqu* libretti are based on Ming and Qing *chuanqi* 传奇 dramas, a literary genre that tells extended stories in thirty or more scenes,[13] each of which is a suite of arias and speeches. Many *kunqu chuanqi* dramas, such as the *Jade Hairpin* by

Gao Lian 高濂 (1573–1620) are superficially romantic stories about talented scholars, charming beauties, and their amorous affairs. Upon closer scrutiny, however, many such romantic stories are also unmistakable statements on masculine attributes, conflicts, desires, and practices. These stories, as a matter of fact, discuss loyalty, filial piety, personal sacrifices, and other nominally gender-neutral Chinese virtues from male perspectives. As commented by Wang Jilie 王季烈 (1873–1952), an early-twentieth-century *kunqu* authority, even though many *kunqu* operas highlight heterosexual love, the bulk of its traditional repertory concerns loyal officials, filial sons, stalwart heroes, righteous men, and other archetypical Chinese men and their homosocial realities.[14] That is why Wang and his *kunqu* colleagues promoted the genre as a cultural and moral heritage for their time. They wanted their contemporaries to learn from the genre what real men would do in turbulent times like theirs.

Kunqu audience can learn a lot from their beloved shows. Chinese men displayed on the *kunqu* stage are often historical figures dramatized. All are richly described in numerous historical records and understood and negotiated with reference to institutionalized and hierarchical roles. For instance, classical Chinese records of men, such as the dynastic histories and formal biographies, catalog them as rulers, officials, fathers, sons, brothers, friends, and other institutionalized and negotiated male roles. Each carried socially particularized and sanctioned notions of political and social power, access to material and nonmaterial resources, interpersonal duties and obligations, and personal desires and emotions.

These male categories are positively or negatively assessed. Thus, they are wise sages, nurturing rulers, dutiful officials, courageous heroes, learned scholars, righteous gentlemen, stern fathers, loving brothers, devoted friends, and so forth. They can also be confused and foolish rulers, treacherous officials, evil rascals, despicable cowards, hen-pecked husbands, uneducated brutes, simpleton villagers, and so forth. All demonstrate *wen* and *wu* attributes singularly and collectively, in a diversity of combinations. Only idealized men have proper amounts and combinations of *wen* and *wu* attributes.

To authentically and realistically perform such traditional men on stage, *kunqu* employs multimedia expression to aurally, corporeally, kinetically, and visually perform the masculinities being negotiated. To establish aesthetic and interpretive frameworks and to organize performance practices, *kunqu* performers are divided by role types, namely those of *sheng* (生 young male), *dan* (旦 female), *jing* (净 fainted faces), *mo* (末 old male), *chou* (丑 clowns). Four of five of the above role types are male. Performers acting those male roles distinctively act, dance, dress, sing, and speak to play their parts, projecting the types of men they are constructing and negotiating with their audiences.

Through their communicative and expressive performances, *kunqu* performers persuasively invite their audiences into a dramatic and musical world, where the latter would suspend their sense of disbelief and allow boundaries between the stage and their personal lives be blurred and made penetrable. Whereas the stories *kunqu* performances tell are fiction or fictionalized histories, the emotions and values projected are authentic, intelligible, and timeless in Chinese contexts. This is what *kunqu* connoisseurs would declare with not only analytical words but also enthusiastic applause. Successful performances that unite performers with audiences generate aesthetically and socially integrated communities.

The Chinese practice of overlapping theatrical and actual realities is traditional, a fact that biographies of two *kunqu* actors, one historical and one contemporary, would clearly attest. As described by a celebrated late Ming scholar, Hou Fangyu 侯方域 (1618–54),[15] Actor Ma was a famous *kunqu* performer of the painted face role. Active during the early decades of the seventeenth century, he once competed with another famous actor using performances of Yan Song 严嵩 (1480–1567), a powerful and abusive official of mid-Ming China. Actor Ma lost; his audience deserted his stage and gathered in front of his rival's performances. Actor Ma felt so ashamed that he left the stage for three full years. When he returned, he performed the same role of Yan Song. This time he won with mesmerizing performances, and his audience rushed back to his shows. His former rival also came; acknowledging Actor Ma's supreme portrayal of the official, the rival knelt down, and begged to become Actor Ma's disciple. Then a colleague asked Actor Ma how he acquired the skills to project the powerful but treacherous official so realistically. Actor Ma confided to him: during his three years absence from the stage, he served as a manservant in a high official's house. There he closely observed the official's words and behavior and learned how to act like a powerful official on stage.

Hou's description of Actor Ma's success is anecdotal, but it makes a revealing statement on the interrelationships among traditional Chinese men's actual lives, their operatic representations, and the performers' roles in masculinity negotiations. Actor Ma's story rings with authenticity because it has many contemporary echoes. A noteworthy and current example is the case of Zhang Jun 张军 (b. 1974) of Shanghai, a young but established *kunqu* star. In 2009, he won a Plum Blossom Award (Meihua jiang 梅花奖), a national index of operatic success in China.

In his autobiography, *I Am a Young Male Actor*, Zhang explains how he moves between his real and stage lives and how he communicates with his audience.[16] On the stage, he can become a simple commoner, a poor but talented scholar, a martial and extrovert general, and even an egoistic and powerful emperor, he declares. Offstage, he lives a cosmopolitan "Generation X" life. To perform persuasively on stage, he constructs his male characters for himself and his audience. And to ensure his constructions are appealing and intelligible, he analyzes his own performances like an audience sitting in front of the stage, noting what works and does not work.

Zhang Jun masterfully shows how *kunqu* can be manipulated as an object, a site, and a process to negotiate traditional Chinese masculinities in contemporary China. It is a discourse that can be hypothesized as *musiking*: to *musik* is to negotiate by manipulating music as objects, sites, and processes. When Chinese men musik their masculinities, they manipulate musical objects to negotiate masculinities defined by not only institutionalized practices and ideological theories but also by subjective emotions and situated conflicts. Music, this author posits, is what renders *kunqu* masculinity negotiations emotively appealing and multivalently intelligible; analyses in the latter part of this essay will illustrate.[17]

As musiking, a *kunqu* negotiation of Chinese masculinities theoretically operates as follows: *kunqu* librettists and performers create arias or spoken lines (*bai* 白), which are sonic objects purposefully produced and consumed. The arias and spoken lines are in fact multimedia in nature; to highlight their musical nature, they are heuristically discussed as sonic expressions here. As artistic, intelligible, and meaningful expressions of Chinese masculinities, the arias and spoken lines make *kunqu* objects, evidence, or texts of Chinese masculinities. When performed on stage, such objects demand responses from audiences who would examine, analyze, and interpret what they are witnessing with their own cultural and musical knowledge and from their personal and social positions. This is to say that they would understand and negotiate melody, rhythm, timbre, and other sonic and nonsonic features of *kunqu* in ways that advance their masculine perspectives and agendas. They might, for example, find a performer's voice or singing of a particular aria not masculine enough—the sonic object does not measure up to the critics' notion of what a male voice or aria should be.

As *kunqu* music demands aesthetic and associative responses from its audiences, it generates a musiking site in which sonic and nonsonic meanings are intelligibly and interactively produced, understood, and negotiated. Anchored by dramatic acts, sights, and words, the site operates as a distinctive, discursive, and informative soundscape; it amplifies and clarifies meanings being interactively negotiated there and then. For example, when *kunqu* instrumental music, and in particular those rhythmic and loud sounds of gongs and drums, projects the soundscape of a traditional wedding, practitioners experiencing it have to negotiate whether what they hear matches with what they know about Chinese weddings. They also ask whether and how the music reveals the emotions of the bride and the groom being performed.

As discursive objects and sites, *kunqu* forces its performers and audiences to interactively engage with one another, negotiating meanings and agendas from their individualized positions with reference to the music being performed, heard, and discussed. As they engage with one another, the practitioners' dialectic interactions constitute a dynamic process of negotiation involving sonic and nonsonic entities. Like most traditional Chinese music or performance audiences, practitioners do not hear the performed music as autonomous and self-referential sounds masterfully and meaningfully organized and performed. Subscribing to traditional Chinese theories about music and its political and social functions, the practitioners always produce and consume *kunqu* as artistic and sonic expressions of human desires, emotions, imaginations, memories, and values. They do not separate the sonic or artistic from the nonsonic or humanistic, because they are both uttered through performers' voices, bodily gestures, and seminal words. When such sonic and nonsonic utterances stimulate practitioners to connect, or contrast, traditional and contemporary Chinese masculinities that they know, the utterances evoke strong emotional and intellectual responses and negotiations. The more ideological and emotive the connections and contrasts are, one notes, the more they propel contemporary *kunqu* practitioners to musik.

Yue Meiti's Discourse of the Impulsive Scholar

Such *kunqu* musiking is as aesthetically and culturally expressive as it is intellectually and socially provocative. A revealing illustration is Yue Meiti's performance of Pan Bizheng in the *Jade Hairpin*.[18] Yue, a male impersonator, is currently one of the most senior and respected performers of the *xiaosheng* role. Pan Bizheng is one of the most beloved *kunqu* male characters: young, talented, and romantic, he exemplifies the traditional *caizi* and his many *wen* attributes. As performed and negotiated by Yue, however, Pan Bizheng is also impulsive, a quality that is not usually associated with scholars—at least not with the idealized literati (*wenren* 文人) that many verbal texts have projected. By projecting this impulsiveness, however, Yue nuances Pan Bizheng's *wen* manhood and challenges stereotypical images of the *wen* or fragile scholars.[19]

The *xiaosheng* manhood that Yue performs on stage is traditional, one that contemporary *kunqu* practitioners discuss with the concept of *shuquanqi* 书卷气, a term that has no English equivalent. Literally, the term means "books, fascicles of manuscripts/paper, aura." Discursively, the term evokes the aura of traditional Chinese elite and male scholar-officials who are idealized as having some or all of the representative masculine and *wen* attributes. These include but are not limited to erudition about the classics, grand career ambition; lofty aspiration to serve the country; moral benevolence and integrity; proper and elite progeny; social and material privileges; artistic, expressive, and literary talents; smart and effective administrative and executive skills; youthful physical charm; and romantic and virile sexuality. In short, a man with *shuquanqi* is an idealized elite man of traditional China. *Shuquanqi*, one notes, is gender specific; practitioners do not use the term to describe women performers enacting female characters on or off the stage.

Figure 5.1. Yue Meiti as a *caizi*. Photograph courtesy of Yue Meiti.

The *kunqu* master who defined contemporary understanding of *shuquanqi* was Yu Zhenfei 俞振飞 (1902–93), the legendary and towering *xiaosheng* performer of twentieth-century China.[20] Projecting the much-desired and much-discussed aura of traditional literati onstage with his performances and offstage with his literary works and calligraphy, Yu personified the idealized elite men of traditional China, his biographies claim. As historically documented, these elite men lived emotionally and sexually fulfilled lives, enjoyed material and social privileges, studied the classics, composed poems, created calligraphy and paintings, and wrote books before, during, after, or throughout their service as benevolent, erudite, and responsible public officials. Evoking these historical and idealized men and their gendered lives, Yu canonized a number of male characters, which include, for example, Liu Mengmei of the *Peony Pavilion*, Pan Bizheng of the *Jade Hairpin*, Xu Xian of the *White Snake Saga* (*Baishe chuan* 白蛇传), and Li Bai 李白 (701–62 CE) of "The Drunken Li Bai Writes" (Tai Bai zuixie 太白醉写). Each of Yu's canonized male characters acts out a diversity of male thoughts and acts, ranging from public service to society at large to private utterances of love and sacrifice. As negotiated by Yu and his audiences, traditional men filled with *shuquanqi* are admirable, desirable, and relevant to contemporary Chinese living. They make nostalgic, if not practical, references for contemporary manhood.

Yu Zhenfei passed his *shuquanqi* to Yue Meiti, his female disciple who has become a distinguished artistic successor of his. Being a biological woman and a male impersonator in contemporary China, Yue has not only to excel in her performance skills to impress her audience but also artistically and intellectually justify her performance of Chinese manhood. She has to strategically negotiate with her female self and her audience, male or female.

Yue has most convincingly portrayed traditional Chinese *caizi*, a fact that her performance of Pan Bizheng in the *Jade Hairpin* attests. It is a strategic musiking performance: Yue's deliberations are detailed in her autobiographical treatise on *kunqu* performance, *Handsome and Musical: Yue Meiti's Performance Artistry of the Commoner Young Male Role*.[21] In the book, Yue explains her understanding of Pan Bizheng as a typical young and elite literatus. Such a man, Yue declares, has many talents, knows how to conduct himself in his daily life, and will have a brilliant career in the future. Being young, Yue analyzes, Pan Bizheng nevertheless has not yet completely mastered his manly skills, in particular those concerning his dealings with women. Being single and a bit naïve about the opposite sex and subject to youthful impulses, he would occasionally commit social faux pas, Yue concludes. He would momentarily lose his scholarly demeanor of proper behavior and appear impulsive, if not aggressive, rude, and vulgar. Comparing such a traditional young literatus to young men in contemporary China, Yue describes him as one of those socially somewhat awkward, nerdy, and impulsive youngsters whom contemporary girls like.[22]

The Pan Bizheng of complex masculinities that Yue has constructed vividly appears in the "Zither Seductions" (Qintiao 琴挑) scene in the *Jade Hairpin*. Having failed his national examinations, Pan Bizheng visits his aunt, an abbess, and stays at her nunnery to prepare himself for another round of examinations. There he meets Chen Miaochang 陈妙常, the daughter of a good family that war has put asunder; to survive as a war refugee, she becomes a nun. As soon as they meet, the young man and woman fall in love with one another, but they find few opportunities to meet by themselves and to confirm their intentions. One night, Chen Miaochang plays the *qin* in the garden, sonically expressing her womanly loneliness and yearnings. Pan Bizheng happens to stroll into the garden and hears her musical lament. There and then they meet and take turn playing the *qin*, probing one another's amorous feelings with music and words. Being a woman and a nun, Chen Miaochang tries to hide her desires and resists his advances. Being a young and inexperienced man, Pan Bizheng makes advances in ways that are not expected of elite gentlemen.

The scene makes a delightful drama and a revealing case study of musiking. Its dramatic representation and negotiation of a young Chinese scholar's masculinities are unmistakable, expressive, nuanced, and provocative. When Pan Bizheng first appears in the scene, strolling into the garden, he presents himself as a learned, talented, and sensitive scholar. In his entrance aria, for example, he melodiously sings of how he finds melancholy in the quiet, misty, and moonlit garden scene of fallen leaves and westerly breeze; like Song Yu 宋玉 (fl. third century BCE), the famous author of rhymed prose (*fu* 赋), Pan Bizheng sympathizes with nature. As contextualized by the drama of the *Jade Hairpin*, and as performed on stage by Yue, Pan Bizheng is *shuquanqi* or *wen* Chinese masculinity personified.

As he flirts with Chen Miaochang in the garden scene, however, Pan Bizheng transforms into an impulsive and sexually excited young man. Forgetting his *wen* decorum, he attempts to physically touch her, the object of his desire; traditional Chinese morality dictates that men and women who are not related should not physically touch one another. Underscoring the eroticism of Pan Bizheng's attempts to touch, and its challenge to social norms, the acts are dramatically and musically articulated by isolated gong and drum strikes.[23] As the young couple flirt with one another by playing zither music, their musiking of love intensifies. Responding to Chen Miaochang's affected declaration of her celibate and peaceful life, Pan Bizheng responses with more impulsive and non-*wen* acts and singing. Bawdily, he asks how she could spend lonely nights with no one to share her thoughts, and to warm up the cold pillows and quilt on her bed. To emphasize his words on her being alone and cold, he strikes the zither table twice with his fan, challenging her to reveal her intentions with him.[24] These acts of fan striking and the sounds they produce visually, kinetically, and sonically index Pan Bizheng's sexually charged male persona. The sounds poignantly contrast with the stylized singing by sharply puncturing the theatrical soundscape of balance and refinement.

Few traditional or contemporary Chinese would accept such a dissonant and impulsive assertion of male sexuality as something representative of *wen*. Some might associate it as a *wu* feature, an interpretation that others would challenge. For the convenience of argument here, it will be heuristically labeled as a "non-*wen*" act of musiking. As the title of a book on Kenneth Bai's new production of the *Jade Hairpin*, *"Jade Hairpin": A Drama of a Lust So Extensive That It Can Wrap Up the Sky* (*Sedan baotian yuzanji* 色胆包天玉簪记), attests, some would argue that Pan Bizheng is a bold male who would aggressively and impulsively approach the woman he desires.[25] Yue's performance negotiates a balance with Pan Bizheng's typical *wen* qualities, however, to prevent this "non-*wen*" act from making him a brute. Many mature and informed male audience members would agree with Yue: Pan Bizheng is a young, masculine, and "attractive" (*fengliu* 风流) man; he might be impulsive, but he is not "reckless and promiscuous" (*huangyin* 荒淫). Such a nuanced argument about traditional Chinese manhood is culturally sanctioned and pertinent to contemporary living. Should young and contemporary Chinese men encounter their Chen Miaochang in moonlit gardens, would they impulsively reach out to her? What kind of man they become by attempting to touch? How do they touch?

They would, needless to say, answer the ways they can and want, revealing the masculinities they construct for themselves. As they answer, they engage with a musiking with Yue, a process that would heuristically unfolds as follows. When Yue Meiti performs Pan Bizheng on stage, she manipulates the sounds of fan striking and gong playing to underscore the character's masculine intentions and attributes: the former marks his male desire to physically connect with Chen Miaochang's female body; the latter manifests the psychological force of his male libido. Dramatically, the sounds transform the garden site from a serene setting into a battleground of the sexes, where a nun and a young scholar erotically and musically flirt with one another. Experiencing such a dramatic performance, a critical audience would have to aesthetically and personally respond—as evidenced by comments posted on Chinese and English websites, *kunqu* connoisseurs actively and critically review performances they have experienced. If some would find Yue's rendition artistic and convincing, some would criticize it as too explicit, or even vulgar. Like other *kunqu* masters, Yue herself takes her performances and their reception critically, and that is why she continuously adjusts her performances of Pan Bizheng to assert her artistic voice and agenda, communicating with her audience. This interaction between Yue and her audiences is discursive. Before they can agree or disagree, they have to formulate for themselves what kind of *caizi* Pan Bizheng was, is, or should be. And as contemporary practitioners, they have to decide whether and how traditional Chinese masculinities are or are not relevant to their twenty-first-century globalized practices.

Figure 5.2. Hou Shaokui as Guan Yu. Photograph courtesy of Hou Shaokui.

Hou Shaokui's Discourse of Heroic Chinese Men

To comparatively understand the *wen* and non-*wen* masculinities that Yue's Pan Bizheng negotiates, one needs to contrast him with *wu* characters, such as Guan Yu, a historical hero who frequently appears in Chinese performing arts. As performed on the *kunqu* stage, Guan Yu is not only a bona fide martial hero but also a quintessentially complete man. He is, as a matter of fact, so esteemed by Chinese people that they often respectfully addressed him as Guan Gong (Lord Guan); some would even ritually worship him as a deified person. For instance, some Hong Kong policemen, security guards, and even gangsters have small Guan Gong altars installed in their offices.

Projecting the cultural and social understanding of Guan Gong, Hou Shaokui performs him as a dignified and wise man with an abundance of both *wen* and *wu* attributes.[26] As seen in Hou's *Single Sword Meeting*,[27] Guan Gong oozes a heroic and grand presence, one that dwarfs the manhood of his personal escort, Zhou Cang 周仓, and his host and rival, Lu Su 鲁肃 (172–217 CE). Zhou Cang, a fictive character, personifies the martial man who has more physical force than smarts. On stage, Zhou Cang appears as a physically imposing general; his military armor, facial makeup, and threatening acts theatrically show off his *wu* attributes. His forceful words are, however, hollow because they are not backed by military seniority or manly wisdom. Lu Su, an actual historical person, is a scholar-official who also serves as a military commander; his simultaneous and impressive possession of both *wen* and *wu* attributes is dramatically projected on stage. As told in the *Single Sword Meeting*, Lu Su invites Guan Gong to a meeting, which is really a trap. There and then, Lu Su wants to either force the hero to return a piece of borrowed land or to have him killed when he refuses. Lu Su, however, is no match for Guan Gong. Knowing Lu Su's intention, Guan Gong wisely travels to his host's camp with a minimal entourage, crossing the river between their military camps with a small boat. As Guan Gong talks with his host, he asserts his superior manhood by strategically telling stories of his heroic acts and explains why there is no need to return the borrowed land. As their verbal negotiation breaks down, Lu Su calls in the soldiers he has hidden to subdue Guan Gong. The hero, however, courageously fights back and forcefully takes Lu Su hostage to facilitate his retreat to his boat, which quickly takes him back to the safety of his own camp.

As a musiking discourse, the male homosocial drama of the *Single Sword Meeting* theatrically sounds out how Guan Gong has more *wen* and *wu* qualities than either Lu Su or Zhou Cang. As discussed above, Zhou Cang's visually and kinetically staged manhood is not substantiated by music; he hardly sings or talks during the performance. Lu Su's *wen* and *wu* attributes are clearly staged: he appears on stage dressed as a civil official, but his entrance is accompanied by martial music. The dissonance between the sonic and visual markers of his *wen* and *wu* attributes indexes his nuanced manhood. Guan Gong is, needless to say, the man of the show: he carries his phallic sword, displays with a red face his unquestionable loyalty to his sovereign and sworn brothers, and asserts his own virility with a long beard. Above all, he enunciates authoritative and wise words with stylized speaking and expressive singing.

Hou's musiking of Guan Gong's complex masculinity is most effective. With a deep and rich voice, Hou sings and speaks slowly and solemnly, generating a formidable and intelligible sonic projection of *wu* attributes. The first and last arias Hou sings, for example, feature modal and northern melodies (*beiqu* 北曲) accompanied by the shawm (*suona* 唢呐). This stylized music evokes a cultural and historical association of northern China and its nomadic and martial peoples, who have more than once invaded central and southern China and challenged its Han Chinese men. In the *Single Sword Meeting*, one notes, Hou's Guan Gong is the only character who sings extended arias. Their revealing lyrics, expansive melodies, and solemn rhythms musically assert Guan Gong's *wen*-nuanced *wu* masculinities. These musiking objects and acts sharply contrast with those of the Zhou Cang and Lu Su characters. The former has little voice: thus his martial acts appear superficial; the latter essentially talks, and thus his masculine words have more semantic than emotive persuasion. Neither Zhou Cang nor Lu Su can measure up to Guan Gong.

Hou's musiking of Guan Gong and other Chinese male characters has earned him critical acclaim. His audiences note that Hou's physical presence makes a grand and handsome hero, while his expressive singing with a deep and rich voice sonically reveals a feeling and thinking man. Hou's performances of Chinese heroes often prompt his audience to ask: Who and what makes a consummate Chinese hero? Does he have to be a man with not only an abundance of *wu* attributes but also a critical wealth of *wen* qualities? Performed by Hou, Guan Gong is as martial as he is civil; he fights like a formidable general and thinks like a learned scholar-official. Such a hero is timeless; his traditional manhood shows no sign of becoming obsolete, on and off the contemporary *kunqu* stage.

As much as Guan Gong appeals to Chinese audiences, however, he makes only one among many acclaimed models of negotiated Chinese manhood. This is apparent if one compares Hou's performance of Guan Gong with his rendition of another favorite male character, namely Lin Chong of the "Flee by Night" (see fig. 5.3). A psychological thriller, the show tells how a fallen hero flees in the dark of the night, being chased by his enemies. As he hurries along unfamiliar and winding roads, further and further away from home, he recalls his former successful career as a military commander, worries about his own safety for the time being, asks whether his old mother and young wife are still alive, and determines to join the outlawed heroes and request their help to promptly avenge the wrongs done to him. "Flee by Night" is originally a scene from Li Kaixian's 李开先 (1502–68) *The Precious Sword* (*Baojianji* 宝剑记), a complex *chuanqi* drama about Lin Chong's struggles with his enemies. A

Figure 5.3. Hou Shaokui as Lin Chong. Photograph courtesy of Hou Shaokui.

fictitious man, Lin Chong first appeared as a character in the *All Men Are Brothers* (*Shuihu zhuan*水浒传), a classical Ming novel that constructs the hero as the commander of a large army and then the leader of a group of outlawed heroes gathered at Liangshan.[28]

Whereas Li's *chuanqi* drama has faded into oblivion, "Flee by Night" has become a masterpiece of *kunqu* and is still regularly performed. This is because it is not only a yardstick of male *kunqu* performers' artistic and physical prowess but also a poignant image of the sentimental Chinese he-man caught in impossible situations.[29] The scene demands its performer, a single man, continuously act, dance, sing, and speak on stage, and by himself, for about thirty minutes. Within that theatrical time and space, the performer must project vivid images and complex emotions of a wronged, anxious, but resilient man fleeing in the dark of the night. He is a down but not out male character, one many traditional and contemporary audiences find appealing and pertinent.

The character appeals because it musiks an authentic and nuanced manhood, a fact that analyses of the show's scripts and performances clearly demonstrate. Reading the monologues and lyrics of "Flee by Night," one finds a sad and frightened martial man who remains loyal to his emperor, filial toward his old mother, and devoted to his young wife. The man's *wen* and *wu* attributes and acts seem to be schizophrenically at odds with one another. Witnessing a master actor acrobatically and expressively perform the character, however, one would encounter a Chinese hero simultaneously and alternately exercising his *wen* and *wu* attributes. Listening to the arias Lin Chong sings in "Flee by Night," one hears how his different masculine qualities can flow in and out of one another in split seconds of dramatized time. In other words, as audiences engage with expressive performances of "Flee by Night," they negotiate with the performers a complex manhood that dynamically exercises *wen* and *wu* attributes.

A poignant and representative example of such a performance and negotiation is Hou's rendition of the aria of "Yan'er luo" 雁儿落 (The wild geese descend) in the play. Acting, singing, and dancing, Hou brings Lin Chong alive as a man desperately fleeing and soulfully confessing the deepest worries in his male and sensitive heart. Its lyrics say:

Looking at the road homewards from afar, which winds further and further away, I ask "who would take care of my mother and wife?" Here, I do not know if I would live or die; there, there is no telling whether they are alive or dead. Oh! Alarmed, I am soaked with sweat which burns my body like scalding soup; it also fries my heart like fire. Where is my young wife? My old mother, I am afraid, has passed away. I can no longer thank her for raising me; I can only sadly and loudly cry! I lament and ask how I can quench this manly anger in me?[30]

Reading the lyrics alone, one gets the image of a lamenting and scared man, one who can hardly qualify as a *wu* hero. What affirms Hou's Lin Chong as a genuine and sensitive hero is, however, his portrayal through vigorous dance of the character's *wu* heroism and determination to revenge, along with his soulful singing of the pursued man's *wen* filial piety and matrimonial love. As performed by Hou, Lin's dynamic masculinities are poignantly expressed by distinctive shifts of melodies and rhythms. The dramatic fermatas and repetition of melodic motives in the aria Hou sings underscore the semantic and structural meanings of the lyrics, sounding out Lin Chong's general *wu* masculinities. The rhythmic and tempo shifts between the regular and elastic beats that Hou sings sonically project a heartbroken *wen* hero. Experiencing and expressing conflicting feelings, the Lin Chong Hou performs shuttles among past, present, and future times and spaces.

This is to say that, by its structured and stylized sounds, the aria affords the performer and his audience a means to enter an aesthetic and dramatic soundscape in which they can construct and witness how a hero confronts his physical and emotional limitations, activating his *wen* and *wu* attributes. By manipulating musical objects and ascribing to them associations of Chinese masculinities, the performer and his audiences musik their manly agendas. For instance, a performer might choose to perform Lin Chong as a down-and-out hero by singing aloud his male and sentimental lamenting. Such a Lin Chong, however, might strike some audience as too effeminate. In contrast, if a performer highlights Lin Chong as a he-man with martial acts and rhythmic singing, he might project a *wu* hero, who might, however, appear as more a brute and less a feeling hero. How *kunqu* performers and audiences construct and interpret Lin Chong fleeing in the dark of the night will involve dynamic musiking. Each performance will prompt Chinese men to negotiate their idealized and personal understandings of filial, marital, and social duties with reference to their practical and imagined experiences of manhood. Personifying the resilient and feeling man whom Chinese esteem, Lin Chong appeals to Chinese audiences of all kinds of performing arts, ranging from traditional *kunqu* to experimental theater to populist movies and TV serials.

Negotiating Masculinity through *Kunqu* in Contemporary China

Experienced as multimedia performances and analyzed with the musiking hypothesis, *kunqu* negotiations of traditional Chinese masculinities are aesthetically fascinating and intellectually challenging. Stimulating its audiences' senses, *kunqu* elicits critical and emotional reactions about Chinese masculinities which are being vigorously debated in twenty-first-century globalized China. How contemporary audiences accept, reject, or adjust *kunqu* and traditional masculinities to serve their present needs depends on their relationships with traditional China and on their own masculine performances. If some would embrace traditional Chinese manhood to legitimize their contemporary ones, some would, without doubt, opt to develop new ideals and practices. Traditional masculinities would, however, always serve as positive or negative references. This is particularly true for *kunqu* audiences, who are proud of their beloved masterpiece of oral and intangible heritage of humanity and who are exploring artistic, emotive, and intellectual means to assert their manhood in twenty-first-century globalized China. In *kunqu*, they will always find objects, sites, and processes to negotiate their masculinities.

Notes

1. The negotiations do not approach Chinese masculinities as a hermetically sealed topic; in fact the negotiations can hardly discuss masculinities without references to Chinese femininities, cultural values, and historical-social realities. For convenience of discussion, nevertheless, this essay will focus heuristically on Chinese masculinities as negotiated through *kunqu* performances.

2. See Kam Louie, *Theorizing Chinese Masculinity: Society and Gender in China* (London: Cambridge University Press, 2002), in particular, 140–65. There is a growing literature on Chinese masculinities. See, e.g., Susan Brownell and Jeffrey N. Wasserstrom, eds., *Chinese Femininities, Chinese Masculinities: A Reader* (Berkeley: University of California Press, 2002); Martin Huang, *Negotiating Masculinities in Late Imperial China* (Honolulu: University of Hawaii Press, 2006); and Martin Huang, ed., *Male Friendship in Ming China* (Leiden: Brill, 2007).

3. Louie, *Theorizing Chinese Masculinity*, 11.

4. For Yue Meiti's biography and artistry, see Yue Meiti, *Jinsheng jinshi—Yue Meiti kunqu wushi nian* (Beijing: Wenhua yishu chubanshe, 2008); and Yue Meiti and Yang Hanru, *Linfeng duqu: Yue Meiti kunqu jinsheng biaoyan yishu* (Taipei: Shitou chuban gufen youxian gongsi, 2006). For Hou Shaokui, see Hou Shaokui and Hu Mingming, *Da Wusheng: Hou Shaokui kunqu wushi nian* (Beijing: Wenhua yinshu chubanshe, 2007). For samples of online resources, search with the performer's names and famous *kunqu* play titles, such as *Yuzanji* and *Dandaohui*. See, for example, Hou Shaokui, "Shipin: Dandaohui Hou Shaokui," posted on YouKu by "Suo Linnang," February 15, 2011, http://v.youku.com/v_show/id_XMjQ0MDkwMjMy.html.

5. Louie, *Theorizing Chinese Masculinity*, 1–21.

6. As interest in *kunqu* has greatly expanded in the last fifteen or so years, a wealth of academic as well as journalistic publications on the genre has emerged. Two representative scholarly works are Wu Xinlei, ed., *Zhongguo kunju dacidian* (Nanjing: Nanjing daxue chubanshe, 2002); and Hong Weizhu, *Kunqu cidian* (Taipei: Guoli chuantong yishu zhongxi, 2002). Since 2006, I have been studying *kunqu* as a music historian, an ethnomusicologist, and a fan of the genre.

7. This argument is informed by current studies on music as a cultural-social discourse and practice. For three representative studies on such theoretical approaches, see Michel de Certeau, *The Practice of Everyday Life* (Berkeley: University of California Press, 1984); Tia DeNora, *Music in Everyday Life* (Cambridge: Cambridge University Press, 2000); and Thomas Turino, *Music as Social Life: The Politics of Participation* (Chicago: University of Chicago Press, 2008).

8. To bring a character "alive" on the stage is a *kunqu* aesthetic ideal. *Kunqu* practitioners always assess performances by noting how the characters "laugh from their hearts, and cry with tears and blood." For visual illustrations of the characters and their presence on the stage, see Xiao Li, *Chinese Kunqu Opera* (Shanghai: Shanghai Press, 2005).

9. For an introduction to *kunqu* history in English, see William Dolby, *A History of Chinese Drama* (London: Paul Elek, 1976), in particular, 71–156, 216–31.

10. Liang Chenyu, *Huanshaji*, in *Liushi zhongqu*, 2nd printing (Beijing: Zhonghua shuju, 1982). Liang probably finalized the text of his *Washing Silk* in the late 1560s; soon after that, the play was regularly performed as *kunqu*. See Hu Ji and Liu Zhizhong, *Kunju fazhanshi* (Beijing: Zhongguo xiju chubanshe, 1989), 70.

11. Lu Eting, *Kunju yanchu shigao* (Shanghai: Wenyi chubanshe, 1980), 89–91, 328–40.

12. In China during the last three or four centuries, women performers and audiences of *kunqu* were not unknown, but they operated from marginalized positions. Elite women would enjoy *kunqu* performances from female quarters, sites that were screened off from the main and male halls. Female *kunqu* performers, who were mostly courtesans and entertainers working in the pleasure quarters, conventionally sang as amateurs and inside their studios, restaurants, and other private venues. In early twentieth-century China, the traditional ban on women performing on public stages was gradually removed, and woman performers doing male or female roles on the *kunqu* stage gradually became acceptable. By the 1950s, the tradition of female impersonators (*nandan*) had lost its political and social support; since then women performers have blossomed on the *kunqu* stage. Currently the *kunqu* practice of female impersonators is being revived after being suppressed from the mid 1950s through the mid 1990s. The practice of male impersonators (*nü xiaosheng*) continues.

13. For an insightful introduction to *chuanqi* and its theatrical performances, see Cyril Birch, "Introduction: To the Reader as Fellow Mandarin," in *Scenes for Mandarins: The Elite Theater of the Ming* (New York: Columbia University Press, 1995), in particular, 1–20.

14. Wang Jilie, Xu [preface] in *Zhongguo gudian xiqu xuba huibian*, ed. Cai Yi (Jinan: Qilu shuju, 1989), 203–5.

15. Hou Fangyu, "Maling chuan," May 11, 2001, http://data.jxwmw.cn/index.php?doc-view-64452 (accessed February 7, 2013).

16. Zhang Jun, *Wo shi xiaosheng* (Shanghai: Cishu chubanshe, 2008), in particular 32, 173–79.

17. For another discussion of the author's musiking hypothesis, see Joseph Lam, "Imperial Music Agency in Ming Music Culture," in *Culture, Courtiers and Competition: The Ming Court (1368–1644)*, ed. David Robinson (Cambridge, MA: Harvard University Press), 269–320. For a discussion of music as an emotive and social practice, see DeNora, *Music in Everyday Life*.

18. Yue Meiti has performed many versions of the *Jade Hairpin*. The version analyzed here is a 1992 production of a performance with Zhang Jingxian, a video recording of which is available as vol. 10 of the *Kunqu xuanji* (A selected video collection of *kunqu* performances) (Taipei: Xingzhengyuan wenhua jianshe weiyuanhui, 1992). Video clips of other performances are available on YouTube; see, for example, Yue Meiti and Grace H. Wang, "Kunqu Performance 2007," posted on YouTube by "kunquskai," March 21, 2009, http://www.youtube.com/watch?v=SZCKmpQYpiE; also compare Yue's performance with those by her mentor, Yu Zhengfei, which are available as Yu Zhengfei, "Kunqu Yu Zhengfei yuzanji-'Qintiao,'" posted on YouTube by "ilcibo3," November 16, 2008, http://www.youtube.com/watch?v=_AAqgtn4G4g.

19. For an in-depth discussion of Chinese fragile scholars, see Song Geng, *The Fragile Scholar: Power and Masculinity in Chinese Culture* (Hong Kong: Hong Kong University Press, 2004).

20. For Yu's biography, see Tang Baoxiang, *Yu Zhenfei chuan* (Shanghai: Wenyi chubanshe, 1997). For Yu's aesthetics, see Wang Jiaxi and Xu Yin, eds., *Yu Zhenfei yishu lunji* (Shanghai: Wenyi chubanshe, 1985).

21. Yue Meiti, *Linfeng duqu*; see in particular, 1–34, which details Yue's construction and performance of Pan Bizheng.

22. Yue Meiti, *Linfeng duqu*, 32.

23. As preserved in vol. 10 of the *Kunqu xuanji*, the gong and drum strike referenced here respectively occur at 16'19" and 18'56" of performance time, when the couple change their positions by the zither table and walk pass one another.

24. The hitting of the fan on the *qin* table is performed when Pan Bizheng sings his response to Chen Miaochang, occurring, respectively, at 27'09" and 29'50" of the video recording.

25. Bai Xianyong ed., *Sedan baotian yuzanji* (Taipei: Tianxia yuanjian, 2009).

26. For a detailed analysis of Guan Gong as a Chinese hero, see Louie, *Theorizing Chinese Masculinity*, 22–41.

27. The video recording of the performance analyzed here is *Dajiang dongqu langqiandie*, track 1, DVD 2 (Beijing wenhua yishu yinxiang chubanshe; ISRC: CNC020630700). For Hou's explanations of the performance, see his *Dawusheng*, 193–246. For a video clip of Hou's other performance of the same play, see Hou Shaokui, "Shipin: Dandaohui Hou Shaokui," posted on YouKu by "Suo Linnang," February 15, 2011, http://v.youku.com/v_show/id_XMjQ0MDkwMjMy.html.

28. Luo Guanzhong, *All Men Are Brothers*, trans. Pearl Buck (repr., Kingston, RI: Moyer Bell, 2006), 76–82.

29. The video recording of the performance analyzed here is *Dajiang dongqu langqiandie*, track 2, DVD 4. For Hou's explanations on the performance, see his *Dawu sheng*, 157–92. For video clips of Hou's other performance of the same play, see Hou Shaokui, "Kunqu baojianji yeben Houshaokui," posted on YouTube by "reverdie," May 23, 2010, http://www.youtube.com/watch?v=D0zQSGwg5k8&feature=related. For a *yinbeixiang* (visuals or acting performed to match preserved audio documents of historical performances) recording, see Hou Yongkui and Hou Shaokui, "Kunqu: Lin Chong yeben Hou Yongkui/Hou Xiaohui; Yinpeixiang," posted on YouTube by "krokodiligrai," September 26, 2011, http://www.youtube.com/watch?v=hnwlsYz219A&feature=related.

30. The aria performance appears between 21'35" and 23'20" in track 2, DVD 4, of Hou's *Dajiang dongqu langqiandie*.

Chapter Six

An Interview with Madame Zinnia Kwok, Amateur Opera Singer

Madame Zinnia Kwok (b. 1939, Hong Kong) is a retired schoolteacher and social activist. She is currently a member of an amateur Cantonese opera club in Hong Kong. This interview was given to Shzr Ee Tan over Skype in a mixture of Mandarin, Cantonese, and English, and facilitated by Madame Kwok's daughter, Joanna Lee.

"I Joined to Keep an Eye on My Husband"

I got into Cantonese opera when my husband began singing in an amateur club, and I decided to join him. It was five years ago, something like that. Basically when he joined the club, he was getting a lot of attention from the women in the club—there were a lot of them! I wanted to keep an eye on him; watch out for the other aunties, heh! But since I joined the club, we've all become good friends. We're not really rivals, there's not that much competition; I prefer this kind of relationship. We're all educated people, we're not petty, and I'm very clear as to what kinds of friends I make within this community. It's a friendly and tight-knit one.

We see each other not only during rehearsals and concerts. We *yum cha* (喝茶 lit. drink tea, have an afternoon meal) together. We eat, drink, chat, gossip, and—of course, we go shopping together! Many of the other *taitais* (太太 ladies of leisure; ladies who lunch) play mahjong together, but I don't. Mahjong goes on forever, and it can be a waste of time, you end up gossiping a lot . . . far too much gossip. But we do chat a lot. There's a sense of camaraderie. We talk about anything: husbands, children, clothes, politics. The more dedicated ones among us—we've formed a group to go across to sing in Shenzhen. We sing together there but also shop together, eat, spa, and of course . . . have our manicures and pedicures done. Obviously, it's a *taitai* thing; just the women. There are no men in our midst because they are busy working. The group I hang out with is between forty and sixty years old, so the men have to go to work, except for the retired ones, like my husband. We don't have that many younger women; most of the young ones are here because they have been introduced by their parents or come from a Cantonese-opera-loving background. But things are getting better. Schools in Hong Kong are starting to have Cantonese opera programs. There are competitions, other kinds of activities.

Figure 6.1. Zinnia Kwok. Photograph courtesy of Zinnia Kwok.

"*Wah Wah Wah*" at Rehearsals

A typical rehearsal for us usually consists of light live music—we have a real band accompanying us while we take turns to practice and sing. Sometimes we sing to "minus-one" [backing track only] CDs released by the big stars like Yan Shufang—it's not your ordinary karaoke, definitely not commercial! Sometimes I practice at home, because I have—my husband and I have—a little studio to record ourselves and practice in. I don't have an official *sifu* (师父) or master with whom I train. But I know the different masters, I just accompany them for lunch and dinner, and every time I have a chance, they let me sing, listen to me, give opinions. So, they are male and female. I used to just go to rehearsals with my husband, and *wah wah wah*. But now I spend a lot of time listening to CDs of well-known actors and learn from them. It's very important. After some years of doing that and practicing at home by myself, I pick up a few things. The masters also give me tips when I see them.

Wearing the Pants Onstage

I've sung many different roles over time. At first, I started singing the female voice. It was very high, with lots of falsetto. But, perhaps because of age and the actual quality of my voice, I've switched to the male voice type—I'm able to deliver this in a much more natural way, and I sing it much better. So, most of the time I end up taking male roles because of the male voice type. It's interesting playing a man opposite other women. But it's not awkward; because we're an amateur club, we meet to sing rather than to act. The main thing is to take part in the rehearsals and practice sessions. And, when it comes to the stage, what we do is concert performance, not a full theatrical event. We wear a nice outfit; we don't put on the full makeup. We don't have the full works of acting, moving around on stage, acrobatics, or props. So, because what we do primarily is to sing, the question of "maleness" has to do with how we sing rather than act. It lies in the turn of the melodies, the small ornamentations. On top of that, there are many types of male roles, and the young scholar role that I do doesn't require me to be too macho. One of my favorite roles is Zhu Yingtai of *Butterfly Lovers*, where I am a woman pretending to be a man. I also like Jia Baoyu in *Dream of the Red Chamber*, where I play a frail scholar. Sometimes I play more macho roles, but I don't usually act them out.

Dragon Lady, Cool Scholar

My daughter says I am a bit of a dragon lady; I'm feisty. I'm very active, I'm also a unionist, and I have even more energy than my daughter! Maybe this kind of personality lends itself to interpreting the male roles . . . you do need a dynamic streak, after all, to walk on stage like a handsome chap, all *xiaosa*

(瀟灑 cool) and confidence. If you're a shrinking violet you won't be able to take on the male roles. You need to command authority and look like you are able to conquer the world. The male role I take on is not an old-man role; it's made for a young male, so you have to really sing and enunciate everything. Most of the women in my club are also not the shy types. But if they have to act *jiao didi* (嬌滴滴), like a sweet young thing, they will pretend. They have to pretend anyway at their age, of course, and they will learn to gesture like a pretty little thing with small finger actions and sing with little melodic ornaments.

Flirting with a "Safe" Woman

My husband is definitely very popular among the ladies, because there are not many men in the club and therefore not that many people who can sing the male roles for balance! The men have to go to work; earn their money. It's only their wives, rich *taitais* like us, who have time for this sort of thing. But I have to tell you that I've become quite popular as a "man" myself not only for women who need someone to fill the male role in love duets but also for their husbands in the audience. In general we sing many duets, and some of these duets can be very romantic, very flirty. Some *taitais*—their husbands feel that if they sang in public with another female singer playing a man, it would be safe and okay, because all that flirting and saucy talk would just be play-acting and games. But if they were singing opposite a real man, a real male guy doing a male role, even if it was in an opera, it would be onstage and in public . . . well, there would be a little bit of . . . awkwardness.

Just this afternoon, I did a duet with my husband. It was a fund-raiser for the Sichuan earthquake. It's not a love duet but a piece for friends reunited after the war, between the poet Du Fu and his mate Li Guinian. Is it saucy singing with my husband while I'm in drag? Ah, but we're very dedicated performers. When we're on stage, we play the roles, we *are* the characters. We assume and adopt the persona and everything else disappears. Normally when I perform, I put on a nice outfit. But I require that my costume reflects the role; it somehow approximates the character, so when people see me they will be able to imagine the character. I don't wear the traditional stage costumes. But when I'm playing a monk, I'll wear something of a monk's color with a robe that's of a monk-like cut. It's not as if I am walking on stage *as* a monk, but people can have a good idea of what I am aspiring to when they see me.

Amateur but Not Dilettante

There's a difference between the amateur and professional groups. They have more or less the same audience, but the expectations are different. It's not always about standards, though. You have to understand that, in the Cantonese opera circle, a lot of professionals might be good actors but that doesn't mean that they have the same level of intricate singing and style. These are two different kinds of performance. Some can act very well; some can sing very well; some can do both but some only one. Sometimes people will compare recordings to concerts and theatrical performances. You'll be surprised that some of the amateur singers actually sing better than the professional ones. It depends on the audience—some go for the big opera stars, these are the fans. Then, there are others who know the music very well, who would listen. And they realize that professionals are not always the best, especially the younger crop of mainland Chinese singers who are not actually trained well. It's very interesting because the mainland Chinese singers who do Cantonese opera all sound the same; they have the same kind of shrill, "trained" vocal quality and technique. They don't have the nuances and emotional range of singers in Hong Kong. They're nowhere near as expressive as us. It's a very complicated world, Cantonese opera. So many different communities, different kinds of stars and singers, different kinds of audiences, fans, and supporters.

Chapter Seven

Men Behaving Badly?

Shawm Bands of North China

Stephen Jones

The music of shawm bands—surely by far the most common form of Chinese instrumental music for several centuries, right until today—may seem to embody macho virtues in rural China. These are groups (usually of around five to seven men) performing for life-cycle and calendric rituals, whose core repertoire is played on two shawms (officially called *suona* 唢呐) and percussion.[1] The bands are commonly known as *guyueban* (鼓乐班 drum music bands), *chuigushou* (吹鼓手 blowers and drummers), or *chuishou* (blowers)—here I use the latter term. Most of my material comes from fieldwork in north Shanxi[2] and Shaanbei (north Shaanxi).[3]

Social Aspects

Despite the recent dominance of women in the conservatoires and the consequent urban association of traditional instrumental music with femininity (see the introduction to this volume), in local communities it remains male-dominated. These groups are hereditary and household-based,[4] but, apart from the extended family of male kin, disciples commonly join the group, so shawm bands reflect the rather loose ties of kinship often found in folk society. Some groups have hereditary traditions of five, eight, or more generations, but many can only recall three; their ability to maintain hereditary transmission is as fragile as the survival of the family unit.

Reasons there are so few female *chuishou*[5] are not so much musical or physiological (women are perfectly able to play wind instruments!) as social. Fathers see no point in teaching daughters when they will leave the household unit to belong to another family, traditional morality still discourages them from appearing in public, and to include women in an itinerant performing group (*chuishou* are always on the road) would be "inconvenient." But as I noted in chapter 1 of this volume, one doesn't have to search so hard for such reasons: there are few women in any public roles at all.

In imperial China the literate elite might have despised the *chuishou*, but their music was just as indispensable to their rituals as to those of the common people—below we also observe the folk-elite symbiosis musically. Of course, shawm music is for the outdoors, for public occasions, partly explaining its loudness; public events largely involve men outdoors, and shawm music represents them. However, I don't think peasants associate *chuishou* in particular with masculinity, because the whole society is predicated on male dominance.

Since *chuishou* have been partially assimilated since the 1950s, it needs stressing that, until then, they were virtual outcasts—not only illiterate (like most of the population) but legally disqualified from *wen* civil values: they were not allowed to take part in the imperial state examination system. *Chuishou* were often bachelors, disabled, opium smokers, and beggars, associated with theft and violence.[6] They were despised and feared: they couldn't eat with the other guests, they had to walk to the side of the road, their houses (if they had houses at all) were built lower and on the edge of the village, and they had to wear special costumes.[7]

Indeed, they still perform outside the gate and to one side, unlike the more prestigious lay Daoist ritual specialists, who occupy the central space before the altar inside the courtyard. Whereas the Daoists retire to a specially allocated room to rest between ritual visits, the base of the *chuishou* is outside, huddled round a fire in winter and exposed to the fierce sun in summer. They "march in front of people, eat after them," as the folk saying goes. They still can't eat with the guests at ritual events; and when they finally get to sleep, it is in a poor house, often that of a village bachelor.

Chuishou were less stable than ordinary peasants: often away from home (short-term for weddings, funerals, and temple fairs; long-term when they migrated, as was common), they were less tied to the land, going around in gangs, and fond of opium, liquor, and gambling. Qiao Jian claims that they favored extravagant spending of their earnings, unlike ordinary peasants—a portrayal that can only partly be attributed to a conventional bias against them.[8] Still today, their male camaraderie of drinking and gambling may be less controlled by the stabilizing influence of the family.

Chuishou went begging when there was no work for them[9] and were suspected of theft. Shaanbei cultural cadre Huo Xianggui recalled an incident revealing their own sense of inferiority. One morning in 1974 he invited celebrated *chuishou* Li Daniu to his room and offered to take Li out for breakfast, but he wouldn't go. As Huo was about to go off to get food to bring back, Li wanted to sit outside to wait for him, with the room locked; only half-jokingly, he said, "What am I supposed to say if something in your room goes missing?"[10]

But even before the 1950s, *chuishou* were not an entirely homogeneous group. Some were mainly occupational, some not, and some had families, some didn't. Some (like the shawm players and drummers) were more skilled than others (extra percussionists). The more successful they were as musicians, the less they relied on tilling the fields. If opium was sometimes blamed for their common family disintegration, peasant life generally was not so stable: poor families were smaller and more prone to disintegration.[11] Polyandry (not so rare among the peasantry anyway)[12] was common among *chuishou*. But until at least the 1990s, most worked the fields as well as performing for ceremonies and might be quite hard to distinguish from peasants, despite their supposed outcast status.

Amateur music like the elite *qin* zither or even *sizhu* silk-and-bamboo ensembles is esteemed, whereas professionals like *chuishou* are despised—if indispensable. Even amateur ritual groups (percussion or dance) are not stigmatized; among occupational groups, only lay Daoists have local prestige. Still, since the 1950s, characteristics differentiating *chuishou* from ordinary peasants have become blurred. They have not disappeared entirely, as prejudice remains; but they have bettered their social status to some extent, first when they were forced to assimilate when they were tied more to the land in the 1950s, and then since the 1980s in a "getting-rich-is-glorious" society where private enterprise has become reputable and the stigma of professionalism has been largely removed.[13] Since the 1980s there have been fewer rootless bachelors among their ranks, and fewer blind men. Indeed, the very sound of their traditional music may express the ethos of their former outcast status better than their present condition.

By extension from the peasant virtue of physical strength, *chuishou* pride themselves on endurance. Their myths often boast of *chuishou* "marching for 40 *li* playing in one breath" and of fine *chuishou* who died young from coughing blood while sustaining high notes. Largeness is a general peasant virtue. Peasants (male and female) traditionally seek a large family with male heirs. The most prestigious music was the repertoire of "large suites" (*datao* 大套) played on large shawms. The northeast, source of many tall strong athletes, has some of the largest shawms. Men measure prowess in terms of the quantity of noodles they can eat and *baijiu* they can drink; musically, they pride themselves on a large repertoire.

Opium

Opium, too, was "large smoke" (*dayan* 大烟). Opium smoking was common among all classes throughout China for at least a century before the 1950s. *Chuishou* were commonly linked to opium; in Shaanbei, a major opium production center even under the Communist base-area in the 1940s, we commonly heard (from *chuishou* themselves) that eight out of ten *chuishou* smoked it on the eve of Liberation.

Now that few *chuishou* remember taking opium, it may be hard to get detailed information. The negative effects of opium are trumpeted in Chinese studies: the expense, shortened life expectancy, the destruction of family lines. But once we dismiss tired stereotypes about addiction,[14] there were varying levels of dependency. Opium was a social drug for rich and poor alike, and small—even frequent—doses did not necessarily lead to addiction, serious health problems, or the destruction of the family line. In some cases it may have led to debilitation, poverty, and early death, in others not.

Some more affluent funeral hosts used to supply opium to *chuishou* (perhaps not the higher-quality they smoked themselves but "dross"—and surely not sharing it but supplying it in a separate room); despite our image of its debilitating effects, the host used to give them opium to help them stay awake and play with more energy.[15] Opium was also generally available at temple fairs, the other main venue for *chuishou*. Thus busy bands might take it frequently, though not necessarily in large quantities. Was opium part of their payment? Did they need it much when not performing?

Apart from helping the *chuishou* overcome fatigue, forget their social rejection, deaden physical pain, and kill hunger, opium was thought to enhance their performance—like heroin for jazz musicians, it often became part of their lifestyle. So we should also note the contribution of opium to their image and their playing—as with heroin and jazz, it gave them a solidarity and a buzz; you can surely still hear it in the wild playing of a band like that of Hua Yinshan in north Shanxi.[16] Taking opium was one measure of a "good musician";[17] along with liquor and gambling, such spontaneous consumption and irresponsibility differentiated them from prudent peasants. So opium was one aspect of male solidarity among *chuishou*, but not a defining one.

Violence and Power

In chapter 1 of this volume, I contrast images of the simple industrious peasant with the more violent aspect of society. Rural society never consisted purely of simple industrious peasants, and many of the prejudices against *chuishou* applied to other marginalized rural classes such as barbers and opera performers. No wonder it was hard to find suitable recruits for the "civilized" mission of the state troupes.[18]

Aside from general images of *chuishou* as violent men, economic competition between rival bands of *chuishou* gives rise not only to competitive musical standards but sometimes to violence. Two or more bands often compete at a funeral. Apart from sheer technical quality, the main traditional criteria for excellence are quantitative ("large" again): how large a repertory a band has, how long they can play, and how many scales they can play in. As a Shaanbei shawm player told me: "If you meet a new band, and they're not too friendly, then you can have a bit of a competition to see which pieces they know." Another observed that two bands taking turns to play at a funeral makes for a more "fiery" (*honghuo*) atmosphere. "But there are often conflicts—once two bands couldn't get along [*tanbulai* 谈不来] so while they were competing they started fighting." Violence is common between bands; I have heard several cases of *chuishou* being murdered by their rivals, sometimes even during a ceremony. One got his head smashed in with a hammer.

One enterprising virtuosic young band leader put it frankly: "People in the same business are enemies [*yuanjia* 冤家]. A host often invites two bands, playing at the same time. If we play well, the other band comes over to start a fight [*qihong* 起哄]. After I started my own band, my old boss made a fuss; at the temple fair, just as we got to the best bit, he turned up and played chaotically." It got worse. In 2000 he was beaten up by a gang of thugs hired by his rivals. They broke two of his fingers, slashed his eyebrow, and he had to spend more than a month in hospital. The culprits made a deal with the police and were not punished.

Outside their own ranks too, men from *chuishou* ranks were, and are, imprisoned rather often for violence and sex crimes. We met the son of a *chuishou* who had just been released from prison for his part in a gang rape; the gang leader, son of another *chuishou*, had been executed. A famous Shandong shawm player imprisoned for sex crimes lived in penury after his release, supported only by loyal disciples.

Qiao Jian notes *yiqi* (loyalty among brothers) among shawm bands in southeast Shanxi, with them taking in beggars or other musicians down on their luck.[19] If this recalls the image of the *haohan* righteous outlaw, I cannot see them as tragic heroes.[20] Senior *chuishou* do indeed recognize their masters; hereditary transmission is admired, and, when disciples from another family study with a master, they recognize their fellow students as "brothers." But I find little evidence of long-term solidarity; desperate people may band together for temporary profit, but it is not absolute, and their rivalry counteracts it.

Of course, violence or sex crimes are not unique to the underclasses, in China or elsewhere: the elite that controls the legal system naturally uses its power to deflect accusations better. Yet *chuishou* have, or had until the 1950s, to show a certain care in public to maintain their business and such positive reputation as they have, addressing people respectfully as elders[21] and using their own secret language to avoid others knowing what they are talking about (money, sex, even music)—a language that seems to be rather standard among *chuishou* across north China and has a lot in common with that of opera performers. There are some instances of trade "rules" (*guiju*) for proper behavior—significantly from the days when their status was still lower, as if the more lowly they were, the more they had to preserve what little reputation they had. But I have no recent examples—indeed, some senior *chuishou* now lament their disciples' lack of understanding of correct behavior. Or is it just that, as peasants commonly lament, there is no social order anymore?

Though the Communist Party promoted violence, with many poor and ill-educated "lower peasants" rising to dangerous power, the *chuishou* were never a remotely plausible role model for the tough new peasant ideal. But until the Cultural Revolution at least, they were not attacked personally—"they were wretched enough anyway," as one peasant reminded us. Though they suffered from political restrictions on the ritual contexts on which they relied, and many had to give up, others managed to maintain the tradition. The very outcast status of the *chuishou* was a form of violence perpetrated upon them. If violence is a resort for men otherwise deprived of power, maybe it also expresses itself in the violence, or pride, of their music.

As we saw, shawm music is now played among the folk, but it represents Confucian power just as much as more "refined" genres. Its first use in China may have been in the army,[22] sometime after the fourteenth century, leading troops into battle and denoting military victory on their return—accompanying, encouraging, or legitimizing violence, enhancing morale and solidarity, all on behalf of the ruling elite. In some areas, like north Shanxi, historians link the grandeur of shawm bands with the location of military bases since imperial times. The military connection is still represented in common titles such as *Jiangjun ling* (将军令 "The general's command") and *Desheng ling* (得胜令 "Ode on gaining victory").[23] But the bulk of the repertory, just like those of Daoist or *sizhu* groups, consists of classic "labeled melodies" (*qupai* 曲牌) common to other ensemble types, once derived from literate culture,[24] even if the style is different.

This use of shawm music to legitimize power soon spread to ritual. Shawm bands accompanied the rituals of regional yamens, local elite, and commoners, and their music was as much urban as rural until the 1950s. It is still used for calendric rituals, such as temple fairs, and for life-cycle rituals—mainly mortuary but also weddings, rituals for the well-being of children, and so on. A marker of the excitement and conviviality of "red-hot sociality" (*honghuo*),[25] shawm music denotes the patriarchal victory of the groom leading the bride to her new home, but since mortuary rituals are a major component of their ritual repertoire, most people seem to associate shawm music not with victory but rather with grief. What was being legitimized here was the ideology of a ruling elite. The musicians may be thought immoral, but their music represents not some kind of affront to civilized values but conformity to them, inculcating submission to a rigid social structure, enforcing the *liyue* 礼乐 "rites and music" ideology of Confucianism. Today perhaps this as much as the difficulty of the music for audiences contributes to its decline in an age seeking liberation from old values.

Thus shawm music lies in between the cosmological abstractions of the Confucian state ritual and the mass of entertainment music that Confucians actually favored. If the musical material speaks on behalf of a patriarchal system, the style inevitably reflects a certain peasant toughness, though I would not go so far as to see it as a stylistic subversion of conformist material, like some Chinese prototype for the Sex Pistols' rendition of *God Save the Queen*. While ordinary peasants also contributed to maintaining the rules of a hierarchical society that kept them in poverty, the job of the *chuishou* showed a still more explicit irony, since their program structured the whole ritual event and they had still less of a stake in the society, despised even by their peasant neighbors.

Shawm Music

Behind the stories of sex and violence, there hides magnificent artistry,[26] the product of long imperial traditions. Indeed, far from the demeaned social status of the northern *chuishou*,[27] playing these ancient and complex repertoires demands consummate skill.

First we need to modify our assumptions about the boundaries of art music and folk music. Shawm bands, though outcasts, served the rituals of the elite as much as those of commoners, both based on prescriptions deriving from Confucian values. The musicians adapt musical material largely derived from the elite, adding a rich patina of folk style. In musical detail, it is they who are in control of the "rules": all the rich complexity (scales, repertoire, and so on) lies almost entirely in their hands, not understood by the elite or other commoners.

At the level of style, their core repertoire may seem to reflect a certain peasant toughness, remote from the Confucian ideal: if "proper music" is "calm but not sad; harmonious but not excessive,"[28] and "moderate,"[29] then shawm music is neither calm or moderate but often sad and most excessive. Of course, Confucians favored a whole range of musics that flouted all their prescriptions; and, as I suggested, one might dismiss the whole Confucian theoretical apparatus as mystification. Even so, I still hope to discern aspects of social structure in musical structure.

So, if music is capable of creating affect and reflecting social mores, is shawm music violent, triumphant, exuberant, tragic, laden with suffering, hardship, and bitterness? Or none or all of the above? If we identify violence as a core aspect of Confucian, and Communist, society, then might it be revealed in a genre like this? As Susan McClary convincingly shows the violent submission of the female in the sonata form or in Beethoven's bludgeoning cadential chords,[30] so we might hope to identify a Chinese parallel here. Both the peasants and the *chuishou* are thoroughly downtrodden, but maybe this harsh northern rugged sound does exemplify the archetypal rugged image of the northern peasant; maybe it is a source of pride for musicians whose social realities afford them few others, somewhat akin to the status of jazz for mid-20th-century African American musicians. Violence and opium might not define the sound, but they may contribute to it.

Before moving on to the "notes," we may look at the general performance context. Despite the intrusive nature of the music, the core repertoire attracts no clear audience response in body language: there is no physical response, though people don't stay away.[31] As to the body language of the *chuishou*, in their everyday behavior, like other peasants, they commonly adopt a lowly, submissive posture, squatting or sitting on low stools. When performing their core repertoire seated outside the gate (also usually on low stools), their posture is quite unassuming—by contrast with Hua Yinshan's proud bearing on foreign tours.[32] Some sit square, while others like Hua Yinshan sit cross-legged. However, they do hold the shawm high, the bell in front of the face.[33] While I am as keen as McClary to avoid searching for "unintentional phalluses" and in China the shawm itself hasn't been explicitly described as phallic, in the north the instruments used for the core repertoire are big, as we saw above. Boys can only stretch their fingers enough to cover the holes when in their teens.

Indeed, apart from the core repertoire for two shawms, within the separate entertainment repertoire, the *shuashua* "fooling around" segment is way outside the bounds of Confucian morality. Here the way they thrust the trunk of the shawm in and out of the bell and manipulate the parts of the telescopic *mahao* trumpet surely suggests what I guess the quasi-Confucian etiquette of scholarly discourse obliges me to term "sexual congress." They don't tell us so; maybe they are shy, but I think more likely they are reluctant to give mundane verbal explanations. By contrast to the solemn core repertory, *shuashua* is plainly unrestrained, ribald; and here, at least, the (largely male) audience responds boisterously.

General Musical Features

First, loudness: the very sound of shawm music is intrusive, invasive, almost a "sonic weapon."[34] In extreme contrast with the soft sound of the *qin* zither, wailing, shouting, howling, and the insistent beating of the woodblock in *bangzi* opera are major aspects of rural genres, but shawm music, like the accompanying firecrackers, is at an extreme decibel level. Despite a fairly constant dynamic level (common to many ritual genres,[35] and indeed to *sizhu*), there are degrees, such as (in the Hua band's suite repertoire) the dropping out of the drum in certain parts of some sections or the extreme aural bombardment of the opening of *Jiangjun ling*. Loud music, and percussion in particular, like firecrackers, is not so much macho as associated with exorcism, driving away evil influences. Hua Jinshan (admittedly an impoverished drummer nursing a long-term resentment against his shawm-playing brother, leader of the band) told me the old adage of "70 percent percussion, 30 percent blowing"; although people associate the music with the shawms, the percussion element is considered important, and its common name is "drum music" (*guyue*).

So we might begin by listening to the complex drum rhythms (in contrast with the more staid percussion of the local *shengguan* 笙管 paraliturgical wind ensemble or southern *sizhu*). Syncopation is a prominent feature. The two pairs of cymbals often play funky syncopations in hocket, matching the highly syncopated melodies. Syncopation, of course, is not limited to "folk" music: elite genres like *kunqu* and *qin* use it a lot. Nor is it "chaotic": the slow opening $\frac{8}{4}$ drum pattern is strictly prescribed, and at faster tempi too Hua Jinshan accompanies the melody with a remarkably consistent rhythmic vocabulary.

As to timbre, I know of few articulated ideals. *Chuishou* in Shaanbei around 1980 were so impressed with the "stout" (*zhuang* 壮) timbre of the large shawm in C that it soon became standard. Conversely, in north Shanxi, the Hua band plays ferociously, but Shi Ming, another revered local player, was also admired for his "fine and smooth" (*xini* 细腻) sound. Actually, shawms are sometimes called by names that seem to mean "kid" (*wazi* 娃子, *wawa* 娃娃).

Heterophony is a basic aspect of all Chinese instrumental ensembles; in shawm bands we have only two identical melodic instruments. It is rare to find an explicit link of the two shawms with male and female, as in the *gong-mu* metaphor in Fujian; in north China it might be fanciful to suggest that they represent two men, one dom (*chuijian* 吹尖 blowing shrill), one sub (*lata* 拉塌 dragging out the bass). Many pieces begin and end in unison in the low register, and players anchor themselves around the lowest note of the shawm, constantly returning there. In all three main scales, the two parts often "rub up against each other,"[36] grinding around in the low register.[37] Might we read this as the expression of their lowly status through an emphasis on the scalar basis?

By contrast with the basic alternation of playing in unison and in octaves, two of the most distinctive techniques of the upper player may suggest erection and ejaculation. The sustained high G# (*mi* in the basic scale) serves structurally as punctuation, a rallying point, but may sound brash, flamboyant, defiant.[38] And does the ejaculatory "blowing shrill" technique, shooting off right up to the very top register (used consistently, not randomly, at certain points in the melody) afford the player a temporary relief before returning submissively to his allotted status? For both techniques, the player priapically raises the bell high in the air, even waving it around.

Structures

In ritual performance, the shawm bands observe plenty of prescriptions (choice of repertoire, scales for the time of day, and so on), but they are rarely of any obvious significance, not distinguishing between types of guest or the gender of the deceased. A large repertoire is desirable for long rituals; though short processional pieces are repeated many times, repetition within the lengthy melodies of the seated repertoire is remarkably scarce. Shawm players

Figure 7.1. Funeral, Zhuanlou village, Yanggao, Shanxi, August 1992. The oldest son of the deceased leads the procession to the well for the Fetching Water ritual, followed by shawm band and household Daoists. Photograph by author.

pride themselves on being able to "march for forty *li* playing in one breath," and though suites have been abbreviated (along with rituals) in recent years, the complexity of long through-composed melodies crafted into suites and the sheer stamina required, is a notable feature. For a 1990 funeral[39] the Hua band had to accompany the report to the temple ritual on the first evening for five hours. The next evening, with Hua Yinshan now fuelled by opium, it took more than seven hours; and then, after only a few minutes' rest, they had to go straight into the transferring offerings ritual for a further hour and a half, deep into the night before accompanying the early-morning burial rituals.

One aspect of suites that does highlight motivic repetition is the ostinato sections (called by terms like *chudui* 出队, *chugu* 出鼓, *guogu* 过鼓), linking movements or serving as climactic finales, using short, simple building blocks (as opposed to the preceding complex "rational" melodic argument), revolving around different cadential pitches, accelerating, building up—again it is easy to plunge into a sexual metaphor with this music.

Scales, Phrases

In a civilization with such an ancient and verbose history of *yin-yang* cosmology, it seems disappointing if we cannot identify gendered aspects of scale. The scale systems of shawm music (and other instrumental genres) seem to have no such links, though each has a distinctive affect. Shawm music is not just a suitable random loud noise announcing a public ritual. The musicians use sad scales for funerals (though far from exclusively), happy pieces for weddings, and their playing may reflect the mood of the mournful nocturnal procession to the edge of the village[40] or the hasty turbulent taking out of the coffin.

Apart from the musicians' behavior and the thick patina of style, the core repertoire is cut from the same cloth as melodies from a more evidently *wen* literate background. As to detailed use of pitches within phrases, the actual melodic argument—if romantic Western art music is driven by what McClary would call a male-centered harmonic ethos of tension and release, then might we identify an ethos for linear, nonharmonic Chinese shawm music? Drama—the creation of suspense, surprise, tension, and release—is a major feature of Chinese expressive culture. Whether we call it drama, tension, or logic, a series of notes can be expressive.

One might, theoretically speaking, devise a static music, placid, uneventful: that might even be a valid style for ritual music, like the piped music of elevators and shopping malls. But the way pitches and rhythms are deployed here is anything but static. In my 2010 analysis, I tried to show these shawm melodies as full of dramatic incident in their organized deployment of pitches, rhythms, and phrases. Local audiences, or even the musicians themselves, may not get as excited as I do by the melodic detail, like the crazy scalar lurch at the end of section two of *Da Yanluo*.[41] But when shawm players sustain a rasping high *mi*, it is deliberately intimidating; when they stutter on the *fa* in *Shuilongyin*, they are making a dramatic point, highlighting the surprise of sustaining a note on a main beat that doesn't belong in the main scale. My analysis of *Shuilongyin* eventually shows that after early competition between phrases on *do* and *so* scales, the *do* phrases emerge triumphant, just as in sonata form. I have no Chinese evidence that the *do* scale is considered masculine or the *so* feminine to complete the analogy with McClary's analysis, but the element of competition, of battle, is clear.

Since the 1980s

As we have seen, this music belonged not just to the peasants but to the imperial elite too. Now that modern elites don't want it, it belongs largely to the peasants, though they are also turning to new fashions inspired by TV and media culture. Of course, music, its reception, and the status of performers, may change over time. At least since the 1950s, the outcast status of the *chuishou* has become less obvious, and the reception of the music has perhaps been dulled, first by political disapproval and then by a loss of confidence in tradition derived from the new capitalist ethos. Since the dismantling of the commune system, social and musical changes have been evident among the *chuishou*, the ground for both of which was partly laid during the Maoist era.

First, *chuishou* have become ever more assimilated with the wider peasant population. Education is more available (and more attractive) to them, and furthermore people are increasingly able to seek an escape from peasant life, even if only to work as laborers in town. Thus senior *chuishou* do not want their sons to follow them, and hereditary traditions are in decline. Some bands have sought to dress more smartly to do business; riding motorbikes, with mobile phones, wearing shades, they are now the epitome of rural cool, a far cry from the status of their forebears. While the new sanctioning of the money-making petty-capitalist household leaves new room for occupational musicians, in practice, the *chuishou* are merely grudgingly accepted. Prejudice remains: people still won't let their children play with the children of *chuishou*.

So if able-bodied men are leaving for the towns, who are the men that remain to perform instrumental music for rituals? Temple committees can still be made up of older men, but what of *chuishou?* Since *chuishou* now rarely encourage their sons to continue the family tradition, new recruits often consist of young men with no *chuishou* family background, those not even able to make it to find work in the towns, a rootless pool of restless men.

Even if boys do follow their *chuishou* fathers into the trade, now the demand is mainly for pop music. Musically, this is a radical revolution of the reform period, affecting the countryside as much as the cities. Does this recent replacement of imperial tradition for urban-derived pop have implications for changing ideals of gender? In the rural taste for pop, might one detect a peasant sensibility distinct from urban taste? Is pop music emasculating them and their audiences? If the traditional rural ethos is so macho, why does no one like rock and roll or the rugged "Northwest wind" style? Audiences and *chuishou* alike prefer romantic sentimental pieces. Does this suggest a change in gender values? Rather, perhaps they look to pop music to provide something they lack—romance; perhaps they don't need a pop style that chimes in only too well with their own uncouth background. Whether traditional shawm music reflects Confucian power, patriarchal violence, or the whole toughness of rural life, maybe they no longer need to be reminded of those, now that there is an alternative on offer.

The gradual replacement of the large shawm by the small shawm might seem to suggest feminization, emasculation—the small shawm was always preferred in the urban conservatoires. There is regional variation, but there seems to be a clear trend toward higher (more feminine?) sounds. The adoption of trumpet and saxophone adds glistening Western phalluses to the group. In *chuishou* versions of pop music, the subtle heterophony of tradition has been replaced by unison—shawms, trumpets, and saxes playing mostly in octave unison. By contrast to the "large" suites of tradition, pop pieces are short, repeated like the old processional pieces, and their melodic structure is simple, built on answering four-square phrases. But if rural patrons no longer want the old pieces, they still need loud sounds, with the amplification of a sound system. There is a certain camp flamboyance in their playing of pop, unlike the male bravado of the traditional repertoire; but then we might see this whole pop repertoire as a continuation of the subsidiary popular vocal repertoire of the *chuishou*, expanding to occupy most of the ritual event.

Some bands now employ a young female singer. This is partly related to competition from the pop bands coming out of the opera troupes, which use young female singers, but casts doubt on the traditional taboo against taking women on the road. I have not pressed for details on sleeping arrangements, but I surmise that the women still stay rather separate from the men, even if they are partners of male *chuishou*; perhaps also, not being required constantly throughout the ritual, they appear only for a shorter time, or for bookings in town, allowing them to return home, facilitated by improved transport.

The adoption of pop music by the shawm bands accompanies their own belated liberation from outcast status. They are no longer dangerous but are leading the way to modernity. The abandonment of old shawm music may be partly due to its associations of outcast status; indeed, the Daoists aren't abandoning their old music—but then their music is prestigious (and conservative) through its connection with the gods, not merely a worldly social structure.

All this sex and violence may appear to make strange bedfellows with the harmonious image of Confucian structuring, but it may highlight the fault lines within society that such an image conceals. Still, perspectives based on gender, or indeed class, will not explain everything. *Chuishou* did not hold a monopoly on violence, opium, or unstable families, yet such negative images accompanied their low status. Until recently they served the elite as much as they served commoners, bolstering the patriarchal system. Even if it is hard to relate precisely to gender issues, their music—in which *wen* virtues are well concealed beneath a thick patina of male folk bravado—shows immense artistry.

Notes

1. Stephen Jones, *Folk Music of China: Living Instrumental Traditions* (Oxford: Oxford University Press, 1998, with CD), chap. 10.

2. Stephen Jones, *Walking Shrill: The Hua Family Shawm Band*, CD (Pan Records, 2004); *Ritual and Music of North China*, vol. 1, *Shawm Bands in Shanxi* (Aldershot, UK: Ashgate, 2007, with DVD); "Living Early Composition: An Appreciation of Chinese Shawm Melody," in *Analysing East Asian Music: Patterns of Rhythm and Melody*, ed. Simon Mills, Musiké 4 (The Hague: Semar, 2010).

3. Jones, *Ritual and Music of North China*, vol. 2, *Shaanbei* (Aldershot: Ashgate, 2009, with DVD).

4. Compare Adam Yuet Chau, "'Superstition Specialist Households'? The Household Idiom in Chinese Religious Practices," *Minsu Quyi* 153 (2006): 157–202.

5. Reasons for local exceptions, as in parts of Shandong (forthcoming work from Jan Chlemarcik) and Henan, may make an interesting study. For north Shanxi, Wu Fan's documentation of exceptions in *Yinyang gujiang: zaizhixu kongjianzhong* (Beijing: Wenhua yishu chubanshe, 2007), 235–76, only confirms the rule.

6. Cf. Matthew H. Sommer, "Dangerous Males, Vulnerable Males, and Polluted Males: The Regulation of Masculinity in Qing Dynasty Law," in *Chinese Femininities, Chinese Masculinities: A Reader*, ed. Susan Brownell and Jeffrey N. Wasserstrom (Berkeley: University of California Press, 2002), 67–88.

7. Xiang Yang, *Shanxi yuehu yanjiu* (Beijing: Wenwu chubanshe, 2001), 117–30; Qiao Jian, Liu Guanwen, and Li Tiansheng, *Yuehu: Tianye diaocha yu lishi zhuizong* (Nanchang: Jiangxi renmin chubanshe, 2002), 346–50.

8. Qiao et al., *Yuehu*, 8, 49, 103.

9. For begging in China, see, e.g., Leila Fernandez-Sternbridge and Richard P. Madsen, "Beggars in the Socialist Market Economy," in *Popular China: Unofficial Culture in a Globalizing Society*, ed. Perry Link, Richard P. Madsen, and Paul G. Pickowicz (Lanham, MD: Rowman and Littlefield, 2002), 207–30.

10. Jones, *Ritual and Music*, Vol. 2:105.

11. William Hinton, *Fanshen: A Documentary of Revolution in a Chinese Village* (New York: Vintage, 1966); for harrowing tales of desperation among families suffering disability, see Liu Hongqing, *Xiang tian er ge: Taihang mangyiren de gushi* (Beijing: Beijing chubanshe, 2004, with VCD).

12. Matthew H. Sommer, "Making Sex Work: Polyandry as a Survival Strategy in Qing Dynasty China," in *Gender in Motion: Divisions of Labour and Cultural Change in Late Imperial and Modern China*, ed. Bryna Goodman and Wendy Larson (Lanham, MD: Rowman and Littlefield, 2005).

13. Compare Qiao et al., *Yuehu*.

14. Compare Frank Dikötter, Lars Laamann, and Xun Zhou, *Narcotic Culture: A History of Drugs in China* (Hong Kong: Hurst and Co, 2004).

15. Compare Ibid., 69.

16. Jones, *Walking Shrill*; Jones, *Ritual and Music*, 94–101, and DVD.

17. Qiao et al., *Yuehu*, 8.

18. Jones, *Ritual and Music*, vol. 2.

19. Qiao et al., *Yuehu*, 7–8.

20. Compare David Ownby, "Approximations of Chinese Bandits: Perverse Rebels, Romantic Heroes, or Frustrated Bachelors?" in *Chinese Femininities, Chinese Masculinities: A Reader*, ed. Susan Brownell and Jeffrey N. Wasserstrom (Berkeley: University of California Press, 2002), 226–50.

21. Qiao et al., *Yuehu*, 345.

22. On military bands and violence in Europe and elsewhere, cf. Bruce Johnson and Martin Cloonan, *Dark Side of the Tune: Popular Music and Violence* (Aldershot: Ashgate, 2009), 32–33.

23. Jones, *Folk Music of China*, 138–40; for the Hua band version of *Jiangjun ling*, see Jones, "Living Early Composition," 93–97.

24. Jones, *Folk Music of China*, chap. 8.

25. Adam Yuet Chau, *Miraculous Response: Doing Popular Religion in Contemporary China* (Palo Alto, CA: Stanford University Press, 2006), chap. 8.

26. This section is based on Jones, "Living Early Composition," a detailed analysis of the Hua band's core repertoire; the musical features discussed here may be heard on the CD *Walking Shrill*.

27. And far from shawm players in Hong Kong, where "playing a funeral pipe does not require a great deal of skill" and "the appropriate range of notes [sic] can be learnt in one or two afternoons of practice," James Watson, "Funeral Specialists in Cantonese Society: Pollution, Performance, and Social Hierarchy," in *Death Ritual in Late Imperial and Modern China*, ed. James Watson and Evelyn S. Rawski (Berkeley: University of California Press, 1988), 123.

28. Joseph S. C. Lam, "The Presence and Absence of Female Musicians and Music in China," in *Women and Confucian Cultures in Premodern China, Korea, and Japan*, ed. Dorothy Ko, JaHyun Kim Haboush, and Joan R. Piggott (Berkeley: University of California Press, 2003), 110, citing the sixteenth-century Zhu Zaiyu.

29. Alan Thrasher, *Sizhu Instrumental Music of South China: Ethos, Theory and Practice* (Leiden: Brill, 2009), 39–41.

30. For example, Susan McClary, *Feminine Endings: Music, Gender, and Sexuality* (Minneapolis: University of Minnesota Press, 1991), 127–31.

31. Jones, *Ritual and Music*, DVD §C. Of course, it is hard for me to assess the body language of audiences when I'm there, precisely because I'm there: their very presence may be partly due to mine.

32. Jones, *Ritual and Music*, 51–54.

33. One thinks of the *pipa* lute, which, although not phallic, was once held at a benign horizontal angle, gradually achieving its present upright position in the hands of (latterly largely female) players over a millennium—perhaps the most gradual sustained erection in world music history.

34. Johnson and Cloonan, *Dark Side of the Tune*, 147–60, again recalling McClary on Beethoven.

35. Bell Yung, "The Nature of Chinese Ritual Sound," in *Harmony and Counterpoint: Ritual Music in Chinese Context*, ed. Bell Yung, Evelyn S. Rawski, and Rubie S. Watson (Palo Alto, CA: Stanford University Press, 1996), 18.

36. McClary, *Feminine Endings*, 37, on seventeenth-century trio sonatas.

37. See, e.g., sections 3–4 of *Da Yanluo*, Jones, *Ritual and Music*, DVD §C; and Jones, "Living Early Composition," 82–84.

38. Less often today, *chuishou* use a menacing unstable pitch precisely to announce a challenge to another band, to intimidate them (cf. the rasping *pogong* technique in the northeast; Jones, *Folk Music of China*, CD track 4). Though two bands are invited less often these days, competition remains intense and can still lead to violence, as we saw above.

39. Jones, *Ritual and Music*, 29.

40. Jones, *Ritual and Music*, vol. 2, DVD §B4.

41. Jones, "Living Early Composition," 81–82.

Chapter Eight

An Interview with Coco Zhao, Shanghai Jazz Singer

Coco Zhao (b. 1977, Hunan) is a prominent jazz vocalist based in Shanghai. This interview was conducted in Shanghai in both Mandarin and English by Ruard Absaroka.

"I'm a Bit of Everything"

I was from the countryside, Hunan, a really small place, a village. My grandmother's still there, my auntie, my uncle, my cousins are all there. So, that's what I miss. But the town? Not really. Did my parents support me? Spiritually, emotionally, not financially. They're musicians. My dad's a Chinese opera composer, my mum used to be a Chinese opera singer, but not anymore. Local opera, in Hunan. I grew up with that. Sometimes it comes out in what I do. Especially in my own compositions. My mother moved to Shanghai. 2002. My dad's still in Hunan. Still working. But soon he'll move here as well. He retires. Yeah, I get on with them. Pretty harmonious, *hexie minzhu* (和谐民主 democratic) . . . I forget the words I want to say, but it's like they're my friends. They don't really behave like . . . well, they *do* behave like my parents, but most of the time they behave like my friends. It's not very common. Not in China. They know I'm gay, they know I live a wild and fun life, live a different life, and they're okay with that. They've always been supportive. They say, "As long as you are a good person, as long as you are happy, as long as you don't hurt other people, as long as you don't do stupid things, then *be* . . ."

As well as being a Chinese opera singer, my mother sold tickets at a movie theater, then she became an accountant, and then she retired and came to Shanghai. Done a lot of things. And she sang opera during the Cultural Revolution. A lot of it. A lot of propaganda. Jia Zhangke's *Platform* (*Zhantai* 站台) . . . I think my mum also did similar things. They don't really talk about the past. No. Well, they do, they say, "Back then, people had different values about life and love. Friendship and family and money. Now they've become so decadent and *de de de dumdi da* . . ." But at the same time they say that life is so much better nowadays and so much easier, and there's so much more happening and it's exciting. You know, just contradicting themselves. Making money, all big cities have the same . . . sickness. Shanghai is a strange city. It's not China. It's not the

West. It's Shanghai. But it has a little bit of China, a little bit of the West. I'm a bit of everything, Chinese, Hunanese, Shanghaiese. I am who I am from growing up, from the past. Wherever I went I took a little bit and made it part of me.

A Learning Experience...

I remember, when I started to do Chinese songs with jazz, not every Chinese person liked it, because usually a lot of the older generation in China have a particular frame of mind, a set "ideal" about how Chinese songs are supposed to sound. If you change a little bit, it's wrong. It's almost like classical music. People were coming up and telling me, "I don't like what you did. Look at what you did to those beautiful Chinese songs!" I'm like, "What did I do?" People even booed me off in the concert hall, in 1998 at the Shanghai Jazz festival. They went, "Go! Go!" But back then, I have to say, I myself wasn't polished enough, the music wasn't good enough, but, secondly, the audience wasn't educated enough to be more open-minded back then, as well. So I got booed off stage! But I stood up. I told them—when they booed it was almost the last song—I said, "Just give us a second, we have one more song." And we did the one song, and I told them, you know, "Thank you so much for giving us this opportunity to play for you guys in this Shanghai Concert Hall, and you are so kind to us, and maybe we haven't brought you as beautiful a sound as you wanted, but just please keep this in mind: always give people a chance, because you never know what they are going to become."

My mum was crying. She ran backstage and held me and cried, and said, "God!" You know, she didn't know how I could face all this. I said, "It's OK, Mum, I choose what I want to do, and I have to take what I have to take." A learning experience. I'm glad that they booed me off. It's, like, a slap on my ass, it makes me become better. I always think that people should take the best from the worst.

But it was definitely a reaction to my sexuality as well. They were not ready, back then, to see a feminine gay guy, you know, wearing see-through clothes on a stage. A see-through shirt and see-through pants even. I guess I'm just me. It's changed. People are better. More open-minded. You know, homosexuality has been acknowledged. Eight years ago already actually. 2001. Meaning it's no longer a crime or an illness. But I've never found this hard, I was just being myself, you know. I mean people booing me off, even that, I didn't give a shit. I just thought, "They don't like me because they don't like me!" I didn't even think it's because of... I mean, I know it's because of my sexuality as well, but I wouldn't make it an issue. So, you don't like me behaving as a gay man, well, I don't like you behaving as a closed-minded person. So we can dislike each other for different reasons. So what? You can still be yourself, and I can still be myself. You can keep being closed-minded, and I'll keep being Coco! Well,

I've got good friends, but, most of all, I think I am a person who knows—most of the time—who I am, what I want, and what I'm doing. Most of the time. Sometimes I can get lost too. But I think you shouldn't be afraid of any surroundings. Well, it's a challenge, of course.

Working Jazz, Shanghai-Style

So, after Wuhan Music Conservatory from the age of nine, I went to the Shanghai Conservatory of Music. I was sixteen. I think I was the youngest kid in the whole Conservatory. I was good, yeah! Ha ha ha! I guess I still am! But I dropped out of doing oboe in the second year. I'm just too lazy, I think. And also not only lazy but my family is rather poor, so I had to make money. I started to make my own living when I was in Wuhan, the last year, when I was about fifteen. At seventeen I started again, in Shanghai. Playing the keyboard. Chinese pop songs and English pop songs. I used to make forty *kuai* one night for three hours, and they took five kuai out of me as an introduction fee. So I made thirty-five *kuai*. And then one day there's a guy called Mathew Harding who came to the bar. He asked, "Can I play a song?" I said, "Yeah, sure," and he came up with a guitar and played "Misty," and I thought, "Wow what a beautiful song!" and I asked him for the song's charts and that's how I started to sing jazz, end of 1995. Back then, the jazz scene was just reviving. People helped me lots, but I'm basically self-taught.

I did meet the old guys in the Peace Hotel. But I lost contact with them. I played with them once, actually. For a party. They were lovely people, lovely gentlemen. They're really old. They must be dead! There was a gap when they weren't playing [1950s–1970s]. Well, they couldn't. They would have been killed! I've been so lucky! If I'd been living twenty years earlier, I'd be dead. I definitely would be. I would have killed myself before they could do anything to me. Very hard. Back then. Now, I can live anywhere. If I were to find somewhere to live for the rest of my life, I would want to go somewhere in nature. I've traveled a lot. I have to get up tomorrow to apply for my Malaysian visa, and then afterward I have to go to Wuxi for a gig. With Zhou Xia, this friend of mine, he used to play in my band, The Possicobilities, as a keyboard player, and he opened a bar in Wuxi, so he wanted me and the band to go to play in his club. Festivals: Beijing, Shenzhen, Guangzhou mostly, and then sometimes Sichuan, Qingdao. And Hangzhou, Suzhou I've done too. I think Shanghai is the best place for jazz in China.

I've also worked with female vocalists. Well, me and Erica (Li Yuejun), we did quite a lot together, performed together in Hong Kong. I was the male singer, she was the female singer. And then we've collaborated a few times afterward as well on different projects. She and I, and Heidi Krenn as well. We did some experimental pieces together. There aren't that many jazz vocalists in Shanghai. But yeah, it's fun to play with different people.

Then, for local TV, the regular jazz program. Good program, but the production and organization. . . . They actually asked me, before the program was even born, asked me to be the presenter. But it turns out someone said, "No, you're too gay, you can't do this. This is a governmental TV station, they wouldn't let you do it." Yeah, sure. Well, they didn't tell me straight. I did one or two shows, actually. I don't think it was the producer's prejudices, maybe his boss, or something. He has no problem with me. He just . . . I mean he has to listen to what his bosses say.

"I Consider Myself an International Musician as Well"

Yeah, so that's how it happened. I can compose songs, I can write lyrics, but I'm not a good arranger, though I'm trying to learn now, to do everything by myself. I will go buy loop machines, software. Maybe in America, this trip will do something to me. I have a scholarship. Asian Cultural Council, Rockefeller Foundation. I'm going to spend most of my time in New York. I have some people I want to go to study with or do some projects with, these avant-garde, experimental vocalists and musicians. Very out. Very cutting edge, which I love. I don't want to do standards. . . . I mean I do standards in Shanghai to make money, but no, I don't want to do them anymore. In Shanghai I'm so caught up with all these commercial gigs and also just the vibe. I don't know, daily life can just be messy. I find myself terribly busy in Shanghai, and I don't know what I am busy with sometimes. Most of the time it's making money. And promising to go places. People bumping in to me and saying, "Can you come to this exhibition? Can you come to this concert, this party?" and they're my friends. Running around. You know, I want to just be myself, without anybody asking me to do this and that. And then I can chill out and do some music that I really want.

America will be perfect. Someone is going to pay me the money, and all I have to do is just sit there and do my own stuff and absorb different elements. Five months. I'm really happy. So next year, look, it's going to be a very exciting year for me. I'm going to be in New York from February to April, and then at the beginning of April I go to San Francisco. I'm going to be there for two weeks to perform for the Asian Art Museum. And then I fly down to New Orleans to see the Jazz Festival, and maybe I might actually go to Hamburg in May for a festival. There's a project I did there with a German band. And June back to New York. July back to Shanghai. August to Heidelberg, September to Australia. October to Frankfurt and some other cities in Germany. November: Switzerland. And then London?

Cocolicious

I have a lot of straight guy friends. Yeah, really close friends. They always talk to me about their own love lives, and when they have a problem they always come to me, because they know I understand women the most. I guess I have more "bloke" friends. And more . . . actually I'm a pretty straight man myself, I just like sexual activities with men! Besides that I'm a straight man! Ha ha! I'm not a sissy, I would say. I mean [puts on camp accent] I can play cute and queen, but. . . . It's an act. Then there's Cocolicious [alter ego character in drag], my twin sister! Doing it Fridays at the Cabaret bar on the Bund in Shanghai wasn't the first time. No, I've done it before. In Shanghai. Even in Zurich. I performed in a gay club in Zurich, in drag. I got booed off. They said, "We wanted a drag show!" I'm like, "I *am a* man!" They thought I was a woman at the beginning. After that they really laughed. Well, I was thinner back then, and I had a corset that really made my waist small.

Of course in Shanghai they don't cover this in the [Chinese] press. They're not allowed. I don't work for the government. You're asking the wrong person. I don't know why. They should *promote* homosexuality! Exactly. I mean, *then* they wouldn't need the one-child policy anymore, right? I'm speaking the truth. Anybody who has a brain can work it out. Right? It's perfect for China. Why do you need a one-child policy? Just have a lot of gay people! That's best. I think it's from the Cultural Revolution. Or when Communism in China started. Maybe, I mean the most recent eighty, ninety years. Before that, you know, there were eunuchs all over China—they were mostly gay—in important positions of government. It was pretty open. There was even a story about this king.

You know, in China we call homosexuality the "cutting sleeve hobby" (*duanxiu zhipi* 断袖之癖). It's a very beautiful story. Basically, there was this king [Western Han dynasty], who loved one of his eunuchs so much—I shouldn't say eunuch—he loved one of his male concubines. One morning he woke up and realized his lover was sleeping on his sleeve, and he was so beautiful, sleeping there, that he didn't want to wake him up. So he took a pair of scissors and cut the sleeve. Then he went to work [to attend a court audience]. Beautiful isn't it. Come on. That's true love. That's the term used for homosexuality. I just think it's a beautiful story. Back then, in China, homosexuality was not dirty, it wasn't dodgy, or bad. It was something pure. Love. I mean nowadays not even straight people do that. Would you cut your sleeve off for a woman sleeping on your sleeve, because you love her so much? No, you wouldn't, you'd be, like, "Hey, bitch! Wake up!" Well, maybe you wouldn't say "bitch," but . . . now things may open up. Change. Like wearing see-through clothes.

Chapter Nine

New Chinese Masculinities on the Piano

Lang Lang and Li Yundi

Shzr Ee Tan

New Piano Darlings of China

The story of the pianist Lang Lang begins with his parents and their obsessive dreams for him. When his mother was pregnant, she listened to countless hours of Western classical music—a rare practice in China—hoping to transmit the rhythms to the fetus. Before he turned two, his mother and father spent half of their yearly income to buy him a piano. "I have wanted Lang Lang to go beyond the boundaries of Asia and enter the global stage as an artist since he was a little boy," said his father, Guoren Lang.[1]

Today Lang is a superstar, playing piano on television for the 2008 Macy's Thanksgiving Day Parade, appearing in concerts throughout the United States, and, of course, having *People* magazine name him one of the year's sexiest men.

The artist formerly known as Yundi Li has dropped his family name and is now styled merely Yundi. He has also changed record companies, having been let go by Deutsche Grammophon and picked up by EMI, who plan to record a complete Chopin edition with him. His all-Chopin recital was a sell-out, with his fanbase out in droves. As China's second best-known pianist after Lang Lang, the handsome 27-year-old is a force to be reckoned with in the classical world.[2]

Born in 1982 within four months of each other at the start of the Asian economic boom, pianists Lang Lang and Li Yundi have emerged as household names within China and, more recently, the international classical circuit. Beyond talent and training, the rise of both soloists has also hinged upon the market-savvy cultivation of personality cults riding on complementary notions of new Chinese masculinities. In this chapter, I analyze the performative and politico-cultural contexts behind Lang and Li's articulations of such gendered personas. I present them as neotraditional projections of the *wen* (文 literary) versus *wu* (武 martial) dichotomy found in Chinese aesthetics. A consideration of their careers as well as performance styles will first be made on aesthetic and kinesthetic levels, particularly in reference to two well-known video excerpts of their piano playing. This will be the basis for further discussion on contemporary reception of Lang and Li, against historically influenced projections of Chinese pianism. In so doing, I suggest that both pianists, in their polarized and ethnicized performances of gender, resist as well as reify existing tropes in certain public imaginations about the "robotic, emotionless" pitfalls of Chinese musicianship. At the same time, they also thrive on commodifications of newer and, ultimately, essentialized Chinese male identities.

Lang was born in Shenyang, northern China, to musical parents. Raised in a musical hothouse at home and in studios from age three, he was placed by his parents on child competition circuits, winning prizes along the way. Notwithstanding an early glitch that saw the prodigy disowned by a tutor for recalcitrance, Lang was eventually admitted to the Beijing Conservatory to study with a well-known pedagogue, Zhao Pingguo. Exposure here took him to nationwide fame as he made an appearance on state television in front of Jiang Zemin at the restructured China National Symphony Orchestra's inaugural concert of 1996. A turning point came in 1997, when the teenager began winning youth competitions overseas, attracting the attention of Gary Graffman, piano teacher and director at the Curtis Institute in the United States. At fifteen, Lang left Beijing for Philadelphia, creating a trail that led quickly from the comfort of a quiet new life in an American conservatory to an international career nurtured among New York's philanthropists and big-league classical music artists and managers.

A last-minute replacement for the pianist Andre Watts in a Tchaikovsky concerto appearance with the Chicago Symphony Orchestra in 1999, Lang has since turned into a major media figure. Both favored and castigated by critics for his extravagant performing style, he remains a larger-than-life presence. To date, Lang has started an international foundation for young musicians, played at the Beijing Olympics, recorded for Hollywood soundtracks, written an autobiography, appeared on the *Oprah Winfrey Show*, and launched his own website hawking everything from the "Lang Lang scarf in regal blue"[3] to podcasts on the "Lang Lang Effect"[4] (a self-coined word describing his influence on millions of children across China reportedly learning the piano), all on top of playing two hundred concerts a year.

In contrast to the media presence of Lang, Li has enjoyed a different brand of fame, drawing fans into a strategically marketed cult rather than dazzling audiences everywhere with musical exhibitionism. His initial career-making stunt, however, was no less a media event. At the age of eighteen in 2000, Li became the first winner in fifteen years to be awarded the top prize at the International Chopin Piano Competition in Warsaw. For the relatively unknown son of steel workers, this was a major step. Like Lang, Li had been put through rigorous training with another well-known teacher of competition winners, Dan Zhaoyi, in Shenzhen. Upon claiming the Chopin prize, Li appeared to be in no hurry to make an international career, retreating instead to Germany to study with Israeli pianist Arie Vardi. This did not stop record company Deutsche Grammophon (which had also signed up Lang) from approaching Li for a deal. The result was a glossy album packed with shots of the Chopin laureate in a new hairdo and sporting a Byronic image, primarily marketed to Asian audiences.

My own personal contact with Li in the course of my former career as a journalist showed him to be polite, gawky, and reserved, if also wryly humorous. In 2002, he appeared more interested in sending (private) joke text messages to friends on his new mobile phone than conversing at length about music, his career, or his female fans. At the piano, during rehearsals and while testing keyboards backstage, Li appeared professional and in control of his craft, articulating exact requirements for instrument voicing to concert hall piano regulators.

Since 2000, Li has gone on to front advertisements for the multinational sports brand Nike. He has also acquired citizenship in Hong Kong, where he is currently based. While Li has not undertaken as many public performances overseas or spin-off projects as Lang—prompting the latter to comment in 2002 that Li was "not yet a professional pianist . . . he's still studying in Germany"[5]—the pianist remains, in the words of a music critic from *The Guardian* in 2010, "a handsome 27-year-old . . . with his fanbase out in droves."[6]

This potted history of the two young pianists' lives to date sets the backdrop for my reading of Lang and Li as performers of new Chinese masculinities. If these accounts are couched in journalistic style, then the effect is intentional: Lang and Li's masculinities are as much products of media, hype, and context as they are of musical style and content, and they have to be analyzed on these grounds. What can be discerned is that emerging constructions situate both performers opposite each other not only as career rivals but also as manifestations of two distinct personality types understood in terms of the classical Chinese dichotomous attributes of *wen* versus *wu*.

This dichotomy, which dates back to the Tang dynasty in philosophy and art, is not unproblematic in its stereotypical positioning of male character types as binary and oppositional. Complex and changing applications of this bipartite model have existed over evolving political climates and social mores in China, thus periodically privileging one archetype over the other[7] or symbiotically renegotiating their seemingly rival relationships.[8] This chapter is concerned with the contemporary pop-cultural reappropriation of these two archetypes manifested and represented in the public images of the two pianists.

On the subject of *wen-wu*, Kam Louie[9] has produced extensive research, positing culturally and biologically inscribed constructions of this dyad as an alternative to the better known *yin-yang* (阴一阳 light-dark) dichotomy. The *wen-wu* dyad is applicable to both male and female genders, as well as beyond the spheres of gendered embodiment in music and dance performance styles. Drawing largely from literary references to masculine attributes, Louie describes *wu* as exemplified in the Chinese general Guan Yu for physical power and drive.[10] *Wen*, instead, can be found in appreciation of the classical sage and gentleman-poet, incarnated—as Louie describes—in Confucius.[11] The interplay of both attributes within the same entity, however, is also emphasized. Louie writes, "Chinese masculinity can be theorized as comprising both *wen* and *wu* so that a scholar is considered to be no less masculine than a soldier. Indeed at certain points in history an ideal man would be expected to embody a balance of *wen* and *wu*."[12] On one level, Louie's depiction of this dyad as attained dually in a single person or in two distinct personality archetypes finds root in fictional and historical heroes, including modern globalized icons such as Bruce Lee and Chow Yuen Fatt.[13] However, in the larger canons of artistic and aesthetic pursuits, *wen-wu* subattributes can also be articulated through stylization of complementary performance codes and dramatic characterizations. This can be seen in correspondingly cataloged attributes of costume, affectations, gesture, and vocal style found in different classifications of *wen-wu* Chinese opera roles. Elsewhere, *wen* versus *wu* can be observed in dichotomous repertories and performing techniques of instrumental music genres such as the four-stringed lute, the *pipa*.[14] For the purposes of this essay, two further elements intersecting with the *wen-wu* dyad can also be brought into discussion. The first is that of the *chou* (丑 clown) persona. Described by Ashley Thorpe as a character type in Beijing opera existing for the sake of entertaining audiences through joking, *chou* has also been historically linked to the origins of Chinese acting.[15] As Thorpe writes, there are both *wen chou* and *wu chou*, the latter of which I will use as scheme to describe Lang's style. The second dimension to consider is that of the *caizi* (才子 fragile scholar) versus *junzi* (君子 gentleman) dialectic described by Song Geng.[16] Situating the superficially effeminate and sexualized gendering of the former as a yet-to-be-realized manifestation of the emotionally restrained and morally uncorrupted latter, he highlights the role of class and power perspectives in determining relative difference and the privileging of *wen* characteristics.

Lang Lang: Kung Fu Exponent or Made-in-China Robot?

A preliminary glance at Lang's family background, career, pianism, and media image situates him comfortably within the *wu* scheme. In person, during press conferences, and in interviews with me in 2002, he appeared vocally exuberant and physically demonstrative. Still chaperoned by his father then and proudly wearing a music note-embellished necktie, he described both musical interpretations of the works he was to play that season, as well as day-to-day life in the United States, with large gestures. Generously sharing anecdotes about the fruitful outcome of a harsh childhood-turned-international career, he moved excitedly about a room full of reporters, agents, music colleagues, minders, and fans, not unlike one might expect of a Beijing opera fighter caught off duty.

As Louie has pointed out, the personification of *wu* is often found in quasi-mythical military heroes such as Zhang Fei and Guan Yu. Their leadership capabilities and aggressive attributes are celebrated throughout Chinese history, literature, and the performing arts. Lang's proactive stance in conquering new markets and audiences can be read in a similar light, as can his youthful male ambition for forging successes on the competition circuit and tackling virtuosic repertoire.[17] Beyond career-making moves, performative embodiments of machismo and drive have often also been flagged in contemporary media reports of Lang's concerts, if in conjunction with his pursuit of these attributes to willful and aesthetically offensive ends.[18]

Taken in association with the *wu* aesthetic of the "outlaw space of *jianghu*—familiar to martial arts movie fans," Lang's unorthodox antics can be read as transgressions of orderly behavior.[19] While the pianist has not exactly led an army to war in the manner of the best-loved *wu* generals, he has unabashedly professed his need to be always "number one."[20] His capacity for mobilizing followers can be detected in his relentless touring around the world, commanding legions of fans through spirited displays and tactical dissemination of "Lang Lang Effect" video podcasts. More recently, Lang's nascent leadership skills have been honed in attempts to cultivate his own school of piano learning. Taking on young disciples in the United States and establishing a private piano foundation, he has begun styling himself as a guru.

To be sure, Lang's exploits are not an exclusive practice within the classical music world. Indeed, they have to different extents been employed by fellow superstars such as MTV-appearing cellist Yo Yo Ma, violin "goddess" Anne-Sophie Mutter, and save-the-wolf campaigner pianist Helene Grimaud, described for example by Mari Yoshihara[21] and Norman Lebrecht.[22] Within China, the pre- and posthumous construction of cults around the lives of songstress Zhou Xuan[23] and, more recently, Faye Wong,[24] has also been closely connected with harnessing dramatic personal stories to their full commercial potential.

What distinguishes Lang from the fold is how he has consciously put forward his own agenda, speaking directly to audiences about his artistic intentions over press interviews, TV appearances, documentaries, blogs, and YouTube videos.[25] Visual representations of Lang, who cuts a dashing figure at a taller-than-average Chinese height, frame him within dramatically extravagant poses.

Leather-cloaked and spiky-haired, images of the pianist show his giant palms sprawling either toward the viewer or at the piano.

Lang Lang's "Dragon Ball Z" Music Video

At the heart of these representations is the notion that, beyond the packaging, Lang is ultimately a pianist whose warrior proclivities are manifested through his chief weapon: musicianship. This is exemplified in a video of the performer that has circulated widely within online classical music communities.[26] Recorded when Lang was in his early twenties, the pianist is shown playing an excerpt from the third movement of Prokofiev's Piano Concerto no. 3 while providing simultaneous commentary on his interpretation of the work. Throwing his punches literally at the piano, he breaks off from a chain of agitated vocalizations in tempo with his own thumping ("Ta! Ta! Tada Da! Ta!") to jump off the instrument and continue his boxing match standing up, against an imaginary opponent. The result is a comic display of martial-arts-meets-keyboard technique, climaxing in a flushed and grimacing Lang roaring out kung fu-inspired whoops ("Like two hands fighting," 0′32″). At the peak moment, Lang manipulates his arms and palms in imitation of a superhero power move referred to as "you know . . . the cartoon," understood among insiders as a signature of the pianist's favorite Japanese *anime*, Dragon Ball Z.

Kinesthetically, Lang Lang uses gesture, in the words of Robert Hatten, to biologically and culturally "synthesize the energetic shaping of motion through time into significant events with unique expressive force . . . negotiated within the conventions of a musical style, whose elements include both the discrete (pitch, rhythm, meter) and the analog (dynamics, articulation, temporal pacing)."[27] As Hatten might say, Lang conveys "affective motion, emotion, and agency by fusing otherwise separate elements into continuities of shape and force."

But what, one might ask, constitute the "conventions of musical style," and *whose* style are we talking about? Can Lang's authenticity of expression be measured as hailing from a deep place of emotive sincerity, as opposed to *affect* brought about by the surface excitement of a young man playing hard and fast?

On one level, Lang's weight-levered punches are clearly both sound-production related movements that stem from rehearsed, tactile muscle memories, as well as strong programmatic responses to the music. On the other hand, their largesse—functioning beyond sound production—reeks of showmanship. Lang's detractors lament that such gestures hint of exaggerated piano technique; they launch the performer (and listener) into overdrive. Lang's supporters might describe this state as "flow," where—in the words of psychologist Mihaly Csikszentmihalyi, theorizing on the technical ability of a performer and optimal emotional experience—"concentration is so intense that there is no attention left over to think about anything irrelevant, or to worry about problems. Self-consciousness disappears, and the sense of time becomes distorted."[28]

A commonly discussed gauge of whether Lang has entered overdrive or flow or whether his expressions derive from gravitas or sentimentality has often focused on the notion of "pure sound." While the Dragon Ball Z video does not offer good recording quality, the sound Lang creates can be percussive and harsh. Removing the visual element from Lang's performances, in his discography, radio broadcasts, and live performances (a number of which I have attended), it can be argued that the pianist often overemphasizes accents, creating surface sonic contrasts at the expense of deeper musical structures. Another frequent trait is Lang's unorthodox manipulation of tempo, taking fast passages to maximum velocity while slowing down quieter passages to a standstill. Often, he combines erratic speeds within the same subsections, playing against conventional interpretations of repertoire. Finally, while Lang is in possession of a formidable technique, this is not always put to discerning use in a subtle tonal palette. The pianist has often been described as having a powerful but also hard-edged tone, gradated in variations of volume but less molded or sculpted according to the needs of repertoire. Where musical molding and sculpting is concerned, he appears to rely more heavily on visual, and sometimes vocal, gestures.

One reconciliation of multiple readings of Lang's sound and gestural articulations can be achieved by understanding that the multimodal nature of musiking includes consideration of cultural context and individual style. As Bell Yung writes of *qin* performance practice, the "visual and kinesthetic components play a significant role in the total musical experience."[29] He makes a persuasive case against sound-only focused studies of Chinese music, arguing instead for holistic analyses of the dance space and notation-coded prescriptive movements. These, in turn, are intellectually embedded within larger literary and philosophical metaphors reflected in, for example, enigmatic *qin* music titles such as *Meihua sannong* (Three variations of plum blossoms).

Lang Lang's extramusical expressions around Prokofiev's Third Concerto can be similarly understood, although his programmatic references originate from pop culture: Japanese manga artist Akira Toriyama's martial arts cartoon series, Dragon Ball Z. Imported into China in the fast-globalizing post–Deng Xiaoping economy, the cartoon and associated video games proved a hit with technologically savvy male teenagers. Lang's appropriation of this character is significant in that it is an updated representation of the Chinese classical *wu* masculinity. Dragon Ball Z is inspired by the Ming dynasty Chinese novel *Journey to the West* (*Xiyouji*), which has in turn been the subject of countless Chinese opera, folk theatrical productions, and TV dramas operating along *wen-wu* dualities. Lang's channeling of techno-kung fu reflects his upbringing as a transnational consumer-producer within China's outward-looking economy, even as his gestures hark back toward age-old notions of classical Chinese masculinity embedded within historical references.

Performing Monkeys and Cultural Stereotyping

It is tempting to superimpose attributes of martial aggression upon Lang's cult today. However, subtler appreciations of the pianist within his formative years during the 1980s—growing up a privileged single child under the hopeful eyes of anxious parents—chime with newer stereotypes about the spoiled "Chinese princelings" of the elite in post–Cultural Revolution China.[30] Still drawing on gendered metaphors in classical Chinese culture, Lang's manifestation of *wu* masculinity can be filtered through the less kingly and more willful *chou* character, for which *wu* versions (in addition to *wen*) exist. *Chou* can be found in theatrical archetypes such as the Monkey King Sun Wukong (on whom the Dragon Ball Z character is based). This view has been proposed by academic Yu Siu-Wah. Critics have also frequently written about Lang's "monkey antics," which range from his manhandling of phrase lines, exaggeration of dynamics, to—in another online video—playing Chopin with an orange.[31]

Such interpretations of Lang as a grotesque curiosity may situate him within the gender-neutral category of a freak-show animal. However, his relative youth at the time of these videos' making, as well as stories about a pampered childhood, may have reinforced his early reputation as a hothouse enfant terrible. Similar notions of Chinese child performers often emerge from historically and politically-based suppositions about the robotic and desexed nature of East Asian musicianship today. Most often heard in whispers in European and North American conservatories where Chinese, Japanese, and Korean students have become sizeable communities,[32] such sentiments have also surfaced frequently in mass media.[33] Such projections recall James Doyle's observation of the American stereotypification of Asian Americans as "inscrutable,"[34] as well as Louie's identification of problematic projections of alleged Asian sexual conservatism against hegemonic benchmarks.[35] The image thus imposed upon Asian musicians—together with false assumptions of the Suzuki method's reach across an imagined East Asian "bloc"—creates an ethnically and politically tinged stereotype of the performer as machine. This image has more recently been underpinned by fears over the gradual rise of an economically expanding and politically active China.

Also interesting are the comparisons made with another cult of over-the-top pianism, American camp pianist Liberace. Critics have drawn parallels between their shared "moony gyrations," "crazy outfits" (Lang has been known to adopt kung fu dress onstage), and "piano-bench histrionics."[36] The comparisons take further root in demonstrations of self-confidence and self-entitlement perceived in both artists as personality traits born of their show business profiles.

In terms of gendered performance, the implications of such a comparison are worth considering: while Lang's sexual orientation has been assumed to be heterosexual and male, references to the gay Liberace allow the contextual masculinities exhibited by the former to be understood within more fluid, gender-amorphous, and cross-cultural contexts. Lang's personality and artistic makeup as a China-born, ethnically coded Chinese performer dabbling in the "international" playing field of classical music has been regarded with both suspicion and glee in the West: indeed, Chopin and Rachmaninov are not composers of languages as universal as cultural diplomats might like to think. The range of appreciations for Lang say as much about the pianist's fans and detractors and their expectations of spectacle as they do about culture and gender construction in the Chinese world.

Li Yundi: Scholar-Poet or Emotionally Embarrassed?

Not too far away from Lang's displays of keyboard prowess, Li has been slowly building up his own audiences through a different brand of new masculinity delineated by the *wen* archetype, denoted by Louie and Song as the *caizi* (gifted young scholar).[37] Exemplified through fictional Chinese icons such as the impoverished scholar Liang Shanbo (from the classic tale, *The Butterfly Lovers*) and erudite dandy Jia Baoyu (in Cao Xueqin's *Dream of the Red Mansion*), Li's *wen* model espouses learnedness, quietude, and stoicism wrapped up in a more androgynous masculinity.

These attributes are discernible in Li's career path, which has been carefully paced and guarded by agents, producers, and teachers. Notwithstanding his ambitious Chopin win in 2000, Li has eschewed the bigger repertoire and late romantic concertos favored by Lang. Instead he has concentrated on solo recitals and developed a recording profile built on, not surprisingly, Chopin. Taking time away from a relentless round of postconcert activity to work in the relative seclusion of Hanover, the pianist has since emerged and (re)styled himself as a "young romantic"[38] and "prince of the piano." On the beige and earth-toned interface of his trilingual website, portraits present him as pensive and inert, gazing sideways through a windowpane in the half-shaded sunlight. While critics have been cautious in their praise, they have consistently compared Li against Lang as aesthetic opposites, hailing Li's "cooler, more straightforward and elegantly restrained" approach.[39]

Behind the elegance of this image, however, is a high-wattage industry seeing Li endorse multimillion-dollar sports and telecom industries. In a much-publicized advertisement for Hong Kong mobile network 1010, he wears a flowing jacket and cravat modeled on popular images of nineteenth-century

Chopin, while his fingers skate nonchalantly through the composer's *Fantasie impromptu* on a piano in a palatial courtyard. Around him, people of an unnamed European city swoon to his playing.[40] In another advertisement for Nike (opposite Lang's endorsement of Adidas), Li is lean, helmeted and willowy in a white biker's suit, pedaling madly through the Beijing streets to make time for an imaginary engagement at the Forbidden City. A soundtrack of Grieg's Piano Concerto runs in the background.[41]

Li Yundi's *La Campanella* Music Video

While the above two romanticized expressions were made for commercial interests, a third well-known video of the pianist, created in the name of building his own cult, serves as an example for analysis of his gendered performance. In this slick, three-and-a-half-minute presentation, Li is first pictured as a solitary artist quietly playing Liszt's *La campanella* Etude on a grand piano.[42] Both pianist and instrument are situated as lonely protagonists in a large, dimly lit loft apartment. Within seconds, the camera pans across the room's window to a scene in an apartment opposite, where a long-haired sylph of indeterminable ethnicity lounges on a sofa in a dressing gown. Her interest is piqued by Li, and she heads over to the window to look. Li, meanwhile, appears oblivious to her presence. He makes his way through the entire piece before finally departing the instrument in a cascade of octaves. Upon completion he rises to survey the street from his own window. By then, the girl has disappeared.

The video merges Li's pianism with a painstakingly constructed public image, where diegetic sounds (music coming directly from Li's piano shown in the video) are fused seamlessly with nondiegetic elements (music used to "narrate" the girl's story but not presented as direct a sound source). The presence of the sylph says as much about Li's suave, female-targeted appeal as it does of his performing style. At the keyboard, dynamic contrasts brought out by Li are frequent but never stylized to the point of Lang's extravagance, even as phrase lines are neatly articulated, sometimes to the fault of bland predictability, as critics have accused the pianist. Kinesthetically, his individual movements describe discrete musical gestures in accordance with Hatten's notions of affective motion, but not to the extent of Lang's affectations.[43] Endothermic in his seduction of listeners *inward* rather than playing out *at* viewers, Li manipulates energy in a contained fashion, seeking equilibrium rather than exuberance.

Where these movements find their resolution in actual musical sound, opinions vary. Li has been hailed for possessing a "smooth and flowing" touch by critics and fans in Asia, and to some extent he is celebrated by American and European reviewers for a sensitive tone lending itself to poetic expression.[44] And yet, the pianist has also been castigated by piano communities in Europe and the United States (in personal communications to myself and on various

Internet forums) for employing a tone not so much "hard-edged" like Lang's but cold or "unimaginative."[45]

As far as *La campanella* shows, Li is physically more economical than Lang. He engineers precision-weighted movements chiefly originating from the lower arms and lower torso. While the video quality leaves something to be desired, the tone colors he extracts from the piano appear to be varied. At a turning point of the video (1'40"), Li conveys an emotionally ecstatic (if hackneyed) moment by half-opening his mouth while shutting his eyes in unbearable bliss. Such a gesture—employed not only by Li but also by other contemporaries—can be read as the musical containment of an orgasmic climax.

The covert performance of sexuality here may be understood in the words of Richard Leppert on musical gesture, where "musicians literally played out, in sight and sound, the exotic, sensual, and dramatic fantasies of those seated before them."[46] Li's ecstasy is released safely through the prophylactic conduit of music. Like the Romantic artist that Richard Sennett describes, Li becomes a "person who can really express himself and be free. Spontaneous expression is idealized in ordinary life but [only] realized in the domain of art."[47]

Li's sensuality can also be interpreted within the articulation of his own brand of a new *wen*-inspired masculinity. His moment of emotional containment within a physiological climax described above, for example, can be seen in the eyes of Geng Song as referencing the dramatic shift of the pianist's video persona from effeminate and emotionally excitable *caizi* to a more Confucian and restrained *junzi*, largely through the channeling of controlled, *wen* attributes.[48] This subtle affectation of *wen* characteristics in delicately layered guises of historical Chinese masculinity closely reflects his rise in the contemporary Asian cultural industry, ironically involving emulations of non-Chinese models of gendered behavior and images. Rebranding himself under the single name Yundi in 2010, the pianist has since chosen to sport a loose and wavy haircut and don tailored jackets over designer trousers. This new image is uncannily reminiscent of androgynous Japanese TV idol and pop singer Kimura Takuya and allows Li Yundi to exude glamour underneath his quiet appeal.

As with Lang's neotraditional *wu* and *chou* references, Li's channeling of Japanese pop culture can be understood in the context of an increasingly networked East Asian cultural industry that, from the Chinese perspective, reinforces Chinese identity within East Asian cosmopolitanism. In the parallel world of Korean pop and its huge success with Chinese communities, Kai Khiun Liew and Kelly Su depict non-Chinese but distinctly East Asian idols as cultural alternatives to the "West," thus ironically consolidating Chineseness as a result.[49] A related argument can be made for Li's appropriation of Takuya: he markets his Chineseness based on a Japanese idol image already popular within the female Chinese community. This has been adeptly layered over the Western Byronic references. The two layers of masculine identity dovetail into the androgynous *wen* aesthetic. This is not so much Li as a traditional Chinese persona as it is Li as a contemporary and cosmopolitan artist, recently relocated to Hong Kong.

Sublimating *Wen* and *Wu:* Ethnicity, Gender, and the "Artist"

One factor to consider within a larger discussion of the *wen-wu* dyad is that the final maintenance of aesthetic and emotional equilibrium (seen in Li's comparatively "contained" performances, for example) has often come to be an overriding force in representing the classical dichotomy. Here, the *wen-wu* scheme ultimately privileges the *wen* aspect. Chris Berry argues that "an ideal balance of *wen* and *wu* emphasizes the skill and strategy that comes with learning as a means of avoiding descending to the use of violence. A world in which *wen* masculinity does not dominate is a world of disorder and chaos."[50]

One might also point out that the *wen-wu* dyad's existence itself is largely situated within the *wen*-prioritizing literary medium. Louie has been critiqued for restricting his analyses to examples found only within artistic and philosophical realms, shying away from the flesh-and-blood factory workers, farmers, and businessmen of China. In his discussion of the *caizi*, Song himself writes of the importance of reunderstanding concepts and positive representations of *wen* attributes as historically filtered through the perspectives of the elite and educated classes.[51] Likewise, as musicians, both Lang and Li are effectively bound by *wen* prescriptions. To what extent can the literary spheres of Chinese cultural practice be mapped onto the Western milieu of classical pianism? If Lang and Li are to be appreciated as products of the literary realm, where does this leave their flesh-and-blood selves? And how might a *wen*-prioritized schema accord with the apparent dominance of Lang's *wu*-reflective career over Li's *wen*-reflective one?

Tentative answers may be found in that the *wen-wu* dyad of masculinity, as Louie illustrates, is fast becoming globalized and inscribed into contemporary Western culture. This has been achieved through the increased export of Chinese martial arts, kung fu movies, *fengshui*, teahouse traditions, and other cultural practices.[52] I have already highlighted interplays of multiple masculinities in the articulation of Lang and Li's transnational and cosmopolitan identities. We can also consider the effective impact of Lang and Li as agents in the realms of reception, trend making, and cultural diplomacy in global markets.

In this respect Li appears to have made an initially bigger splash in his entry into the international world with his dramatic win at the 2000 Chopin competition. Such an achievement had been long awaited in China, since the legendary appearance (and subsequent defection) of Fou Ts'ong as a prizewinner at the same competition of 1955. Fou himself was eventually presented to European audiences, and retrospectively in China, as a romantic artist in exile. Looking across the wider arc of history, Li's twenty-first-century win had many political implications. It provided a validation of China as a global cultural force, alongside its economic rise. It also harkened the arrival of a new, rehabilitated breed of Chinese pianist, following earlier, problematic models personified by the likes of Yin Chengzong and Liu Shikun, whose reputations, personal tragedies, and career comebacks were intertwined with Maoist cultural politics.[53]

While Li's sudden underdog rise appeared to take the world by storm, Lang was cultivating his connections and reputation among Philadelphia's and New York's powerful philanthropic and artistic circles. He soon overtook Li in terms of international exposure. In 2001, Lang elbowed out "a recent [unnamed] prizewinner" for a solo spot with the Philadelphia Orchestra at their prestigious inaugural performance in Beijing.[54] By 2008, Lang's fame was such that Chinese authorities could not but invite him as a guest performer in a coveted slot at the Beijing Olympics opening ceremony. Here, the question was not how Lang had managed to nail the gig but how the Olympic Committee had managed to secure Lang, on account of his international superstardom. Play-synching on a white piano off a prerecorded track with a five-year-old pianist, Li Muzi, Lang's performance was a political flourish, with the pianist galvanizing his personal cult as a vehicle of international cultural exchange. In the following section I examine how respective national and international fan groups and audiences (no doubt separate communities) for Lang and Li differ in demographics and agency.

The Politics of Reception

Preliminary observations of audience attendance at sell-out concerts around the world show both Li and Lang to enjoy a large number of international as well as Chinese and Chinese diaspora fans. Audiences in the latter category may turn up to the pianists' recitals as a matter of ethnic or nationalist pride. Frequent salutations of "*Hao! Hao!*" in lieu of *bravo* or *encore* are heard in the wake of their performances. I suspect that a substantial fraction of these audiences do not necessarily belong to established communities of regular classical music concerts but have instead been attracted by the cults surrounding the names.

Closer inspection of audience catchment shows that Li has consistently drawn a good proportion of young female Chinese fans. They demonstrate their loyalty in squealing and rapturously applauding at his concerts and collecting autographed CDs, posters, key chains, and other Li paraphernalia. This is not surprising since Li's carefully managed image is modeled after J-pop idols who target a similar demographic. The fact that Li is now based in metropolitan Hong Kong instead of his hometown of Shenzhen—or yet further afield in Europe or North America—speaks for his transnational Chinese outlook. Li has positioned himself in the middle ground staked by a cosmopolitan East, while looking outward at a romanticized West. By the same token, his ethnicity is also negotiated and received differently within and without Chinese communities: not surprisingly he is less celebrated among non-Chinese audiences.

Li's Chineseness is not simply a matter of nationality or ethnicity. His dashing embodiment of the cravat-wearing male is paradoxically East Asian. This faux-European image is a product of East Asia's reverse exoticization of the West, where Japanese animators such as Hayao Miyazaki envisage Old Europe through fairy tale, and Korean restaurants are modeled on romantic templates of French cafés. Similar instances are found within and without China.[55]

Li has staked his transnational masculinity, wooing primarily female audiences in the Chinese world and a potentially mixed group beyond. Just as in the West, while the most successful Chinese pianists are male, actual piano enrollment in keyboard classes and private lessons throughout Chinese and East Asian communities appears to privilege female over male piano students.[56] The implication is that entrenched forms of Chinese paternalism encourage female musical dilettantism in the name of the "virtuous, well-rounded Asian female," but not superstar professionalism. This pattern may be challenged by emerging female performers like the Hanover-rooted Chen Sa and New York-based Wang Yuja. Like Li, Chen was a young prizewinner at a major British competition; Wang was a pupil of Lang's teacher, Gary Graffman. However, such mappings are premature. As female performers of the subtler Chinese variety, they often appear together, rather than being presented separately in macho oppostion, as Lang and Li are.

Lang's courting of audience demographics functions through a completely different paradigm from Li's. Operating from New York, his manipulation of transnational Chineseness moves in bigger terms of scale and physical distance. Lang traverses four continents for more than two hundred concerts in the course of a single year. His playing field is larger in audience catchment and repertoire, even as he consciously ramps up his Chinese identity for both Western audiences and supporters within China. Lang's 2007 CD of flashy Chinese encore pieces, *Dragon Songs*, is a testament to one brand of ethnic self-stereotyping, alongside his frequent appearances onstage (in contrast to Li's high-collared tuxes) in a traditional Chinese suit.

On this subject of Chinese pianism, Eric Hung has examined Lang's performance of ethnic identity in his deliberate choice of recording repertoire, dress sense, showmanship, technique, grooming of new students, and, finally, words to the press.[57] Hung writes, "[Lang's] 'Chineseness' is based to a considerable extent on a sense of nostalgia and loss that many first-generation immigrants experience. . . . Lang is a 'superstar' and needs to be marketed as such. In the current market, orientalism sells, and Lang and his marketing team have exoticized him throughout his career to ensure that he maximizes his stardom."[58] Unlike Li's projected image as an object of Asian female fantasy, Lang's appeal is more universal, and—if press gossip is to be believed—partly the result of industry power play. To be sure, in the early days of his career, Lang had garnered enough teenage female fans. On the strength of his wild-child exuberance, however, the pianist has come to win accolades not only within the transnational Chinese circuit but also among America's exclusive arts circles and powerful record companies. Lang's masculinity—puck-like and mercurial, even punk—was not so much packaged for young females as for everyone—Western, Asian, male or female. Mark Swed observed in the *Los Angeles Times*: "He is a poet. But he is an immature poet with a nuclear arsenal, and that makes him a very dangerous poet. The nuclear part of the weaponry is a killer technique. The threat is in the delivery system. He has the charisma to hold an audience in his power. Responsibility, though, is another matter."[59] Tales of Lang's rise over Li have been recounted in detail by Internet conspiracy theorists. Here, Li's embodiment of a comparatively nonmercenary artist in the *caizi* "scholar-poet" schema appears to have won him some sympathy, even if in reality he is still extensively commercially marketed. Norman Lebrecht specifically situates Lang's alleged enmity for Li in lurid stories, such as Lang's reported refusal to play with orchestras that had engaged Li within the same year.[60] Lebrecht tells of a deal orchestrated by Lang to force his then-record label, Deutsche Grammophon, to drop coartist Li in 2009.[61] While Li has since been picked up by EMI, Lang himself was bought over from Deutsche Grammophon by Sony in 2010, in a highly publicized $3 million deal.[62] Bereft of both Lang and Li, Deutsche Grammophon has gone on to sign twenty-three-year-old female talent Wang Yuja, whose "astonishing percussive power" and "innate musicality" have been as celebrated by classical music bloggers as her "tiny and gorgeous" frame.[63]

Chinese Musicianship as an Industry

The emerging picture of deal cutting is one of a classical-music record industry leveraging the market influence of gender and ethnicity in addition to talent. Lebrecht hints at a larger master plan of Sony in accumulating Chinese artists, such as recent international prize-winning violinist Ray Chen alongside established artists including Yo Yo Ma.[64] His observations suggest industry interest in tapping into new markets within China's burgeoning cities, as well as discovering emerging talents in Chinese conservatories. This trend raises another issue of gender: the question of Chinese femininity and Chinese masculinity in the classical music industry.

Taking Li, Lang, and their predecessors as a whole, a larger emerging issue is that notions of Chinese pianism have come to be received as male-centric phenomena. Notable protagonists of the scene, Yin Chengzong, Fou Ts'ong, Liu Shikun, and, more recently, Kong Xiangdong, are heroes and villains (or martyrs), not heroines. Female performers such as Chen Sa, Wang Yuja, and Chen Jie have very recently been introduced to the market, packaged, and mediated as "hot" or "gorgeous." These performers may constitute a future trend, but for now the realm of Asian musical orientalization seems to belong to the world of violinists, as seen in the superstar careers of Kyung-Wha Chung, Midori, and Vanessa Mae.

Multiple Chinese Masculinities Embodied in the Artist as Individual

In writing this article, I have so far projected *wen-wu* gendered readings of Lang and Li in terms of traditional Chinese, transnational, contemporary, and globalized aesthetics. I have also reassessed the same dyad in a bid to reposition cultural projections from the exclusive literary realm into the gendered and ethnicized world of politico-economics. The analyses show that, just as there are multiple masculinities in different embodiments of the *wen* and *wu*, Chineseness is also multifarious in its manifestation. Rey Chow writes:

> Chineseness can no longer be held as a monolithic given tied to the mythic homeland but must rather be understood as a provisional, "open signifier" . . . from now on [we] simply speak of Chineseness in the plural—as so many kinds of Chineseness-es, so many Chinese identities? Should Chineseness from now on be understood not as traceable origin but rather in terms of an ongoing history of dispersal, its reality always already displaced from what are imaginary, fantasmatic roots?[65]

I have described the co-option of different foreign strands from Japanese anime to TV idol-hood and Byronic heroism in the image making of Lang and Li as distinctly Sino-centric mappings of cosmopolitan identity. A return to Lang and Li's fundamental *non*-Chineseness is worth consideration: To what extent are both "European" or "American" in their cultural makeup? Important concerns here are that while both pianists were born in and underwent early training in China, they have also spent considerable amounts of time overseas as students and continue to tour internationally. As representatives of that nebulous concept called new Chinese pianism, they are complex and layered subjects, notwithstanding the fact that at only thirty years old in 2013, a few more decades of development as performers await. The different masculinities expressed by Lang and Li lie not only in talent and ethnicity but also in the third, crucial factor of youth. Ultimately, necessary to ongoing research into new Chinese pianism is a study of how the two musicians' diametrically projected masculinities will change over time as the two men age, playing the piano (or not) in a future China and a future classical music world.

For now, both Lang and Li have spoken forthrightly about bringing glory to China through their work. They have also traced their beginnings to the amorphous idea of a "Chinese piano school," even as they choose to be appreciated as international artists.[66] Alongside projections of their masculinities in performance, Lang and Li have been hailed for their nonmasculine attributes. The former is often seen as asexual in his childlike penchant for willful precocity. The latter has been androgynized—even feminized—in his demonstration of scholarly fragility. Together, these layered and intersecting negotiations of identity come together in two separate packages of personality that are imagined, produced, and marketed in the name of the artist as individual. By the same token, Lang and Li's audiences cannot be thought of as demographically homogeneous or delineated purely by divides between East and West or male and female. Indeed, just as the two pianists express transnational and distinctly compounded individual identities, the same can be said of their audiences.

The superficially oppositional *wen-wu* dualisms surfacing in my discussion of Lang and Li, as well their fan cults, have to be understood as constructed models against which multiple psychological, political, and sociological realities exist. In a contemporary China, where the humanity of the single person is so often perceived to be drowned out by the country's millions of factory workers, farmers, victims, single-child families, dissidents, and, of course, pianists—the paradox lies in how multifaceted iconoclasts like Lang and Li continue to be appreciated as beacons of individualism.

Notes

1. Yilu Zhao, "A Prodigy, A Piano, Hardship, Stardom; Dreams Comes True for Lang Lang," *New York Times*, September 2, 2003.

2. George Hall "Yundi: Classical Review," *Guardian*, March 18, 2010.

3. "Lang Lang's Scarf Now Available in the Store," October 20, 2009, accessed February 7, 2013, www.langlang.com/us/news/lang-lang039s-scarf-now-available-store.

4. "Lang Lang Effect," accessed July 1, 2010, www.langlang.com/langlangeffect.

5. Interview by Shzr Ee Tan with Lang Lang, October 2002, Singapore, on behalf of the *Straits Times*.

6. Hall, "Yundi: Classical Review."

7. Kam Louie, *Theorizing Chinese Masculinity: Society and Gender in China* (Cambridge: Cambridge University Press, 2002); Chris Berry, review of *Theorizing Chinese Masculinity: Society and Gender in China* by Kam Louie, *Intersections: Gender, History and Culture in the Asian Context* 8 (2002); Song Geng, *The Fragile Scholar: Power and Masculinity in Chinese Culture* (Hong Kong: Hong Kong University Press, 2004).

8. Ronald Egan, *The Problem of Beauty: Aesthetic Thought and Pursuits in Northern Song Dynasty China* (Cambridge, MA: Harvard University Asia Center, 2006), 372–74.

9. Louie, *Theorizing Chinese Masculinity*.

10. Ibid., 22–42.

11. Ibid., 43–58. Louie's in-depth citing of Confucius as a *wen* icon has to be understood in the context of Confucius' own writings (also quoted by Louie in his same book) on the importance of aspiring toward both *wen* and *wu* attributes, vis-à-vis contemporary and post-Confucian appropriations of his iconic aura.

12. Ibid., 11.
13. Ibid., 140–66.
14. John E. Myers, *The Way of the Pipa: Structure and Imagery in Chinese Lute Music* (Kent, OH: Kent State University Press, 1992).
15. Ashley Thorpe, "Only Joking? The Role of the Clown and Percussion in *Jingju*," *Asian Theatre Journal* 22, no. 2 (2005): 269.
16. Song, *Fragile Scholar*.
17. Lang Lang and David Ritz, *Journey of a Thousand Miles: My Story* (New York: Spiegel and Grau, 2008).
18. Rian Evans, review of concert performance by Lang Lang (piano), Symphony Hall Birmingham, *Guardian*, February 10, 2010; Nick Kimberley, "There's Something About Lang Lang," review of concert performance by Lang Lang (piano), Royal Albert Hall, London, *London Evening Standard*, May 24, 2010; Anthony Tomasini, "Lang Lang: His Life So Far," *New York Times*, November 27, 2008, .
19. Berry, review of *Theorizing Chinese Masculinity*.
20. Lang and Ritz, *Journey of a Thousand Miles*, 36–41.
21. Mari Yoshihara, *Musicians from a Different Shore: Asians and Asian Americans in Classical Music* (Philadelphia: Temple University Press, 2007), 118.
22. Norman Lebrecht, "The Piano Man," *La Scene Musicale*, July 26, 2006, http://www.scena.org/columns/lebrecht/060726-NL-pianoman.html.
23. Jonathan Stock, "Reconsidering the Past: Zhou Xuan and the Rehabilitation of Early Twentieth-Century Popular Music," *Asian Music* 26, no. 2 (1995):119–35.
24. Anthony Fung and Michael Curtin, "The Anomalies of Being Faye (Wong): Gender Politics in Chinese Popular Music," *International Journal of Cultural Studies* 5, no. 3 (2002): 263–90.
25. Lang Lang (blog), accessed July 1, 2010, http://www.langlang.com/blog.
26. Lang Lang, "Lang Lang Gone Mad," posted on YouTube by "Jeff Barnes," April 8, 2006, http://www.youtube.com/watch?v=b85hn8rJvgw.
27. Robert Hatten, "Musical Gesture: Theory and Interpretation" [introduction to lecture notes, University of Indiana], 2004, accessed July 1, 2010, http://www.indiana.edu/~deanfac/blfal03/mus/mus_t561_9824.html.
28. Mihaly Csikszentmihalyi, *Flow: The Classic Work on How to Achieve Happiness* (London: Random House, 2002), 71.
29. Bell Yung, "Choreographic and Kinesthetic Elements in Performance on the Chinese Seven-String Zither," *Ethnomusicology* 28, no. 3 (1984): 505.
30. Tim Collard, "Chinese Princelings—the Cover-Up Gets More Difficult," *Telegraph*, August 10, 2000; Howard W. French, "In China, Children of the Rich Learn Class, Minus Struggle," *New York Times*, September 22, 2006.
31. Lang Lang, "Lang Lang Plays Chopin with Orange," posted on YouTube by "pogface," January 27, 2007, http://www.youtube.com/watch?v=oiziGLe1jBw.
32. Yoshihara, *Musicians from a Different Shore*, 61, 82, 108, 145.
33. Detlef Schneider, "Music Moves Him and, Coupled with His Extrovert Personality, He Can't Help Reaching Out," *Classic FM Magazine*, August 2009, 24–27; Nancy Pellegrini, "From Mao to Mozart," *International Piano* March/April 2009, 24–31; Andrew Stewart, "Lang Lang: Artist? Showman?" *International Piano* July/August 2006; 14–18; Nancy Pellegrini, "Chamber Music to the Rescue?," *International Piano* September/October 2009, 18.
34. James Doyle, *The Male Experience* (Dubuque, IA: Wm. C. Brown, 1989), 290–91.
35. Louie, *Theorizing Chinese Masculinity*, 2.

36. David Remnick, "David Remnick Profiles the Pianist Who Will Liberace Up the Olympics," *New York Magazine*, July 28, 2008.
37. Louie, *Theorizing Chinese Masculinity*, 6; Song, *Fragile Scholar*.
38. This was the title of a 2008 documentary made about Li by director Barbara Willis Sweete.
39. Anthony Tomasini, "A Little Sturm and Drang Leavens the Usual Pianism," *New York Times* October 12, 2008.
40. Li Yundi, "*Fantasie impromptu*: Yundi Li," posted on YouTube by "simusic120," April 1, 2009, http://www.youtube.com/watch?v=z_ZPsmR46C0.
41. Li Yundi, "Nike Commercial," posted on YouTube by "xxsnow," July 26, 2006, http://www.youtube.com/watch?v=ptIVOPYifRg.
42. Li Yundi, "*La campanella*," posted on YouTube by "dogdens," April 21, 2006, http://www.youtube.com/watch?v=4ziWUDr0DkE.
43. Hatten, *Musical Gesture*.
44. "Li Yundi's Bangkok debut," *Bangkok Post*, Outlook, November 17, 2010; Bernard Holland, "Yundi Li: Living Large with Schumann and Liszt," *New York Times*, April 5, 2006.
45. Lance G. Hill, "Yundi Li: Disappointing New DG of Chopin/Liszt PCs1," *Classical Music Guide* Forums, March 18, 2007, http://www.classicalmusicguide.com/viewtopic.php?f=10&t=16143&view=next.
46. Richard Leppert, "Music, Gesture and the Embodiment of the Utopian Imagination," paper presented at the IMR Conference, The Musical Body: Gesture, Representation and Ergonomics in Performance, London, 2009, 26.
47. Richard Sennett, *The Fall of Public Man: On the Social Psychology of Capitalism* (New York: Vintage, 1978), 191.
48. Song, *Fragile Scholar*, 87–124.
49. Kai Khiun Liew and Kelly Su, "Hallyu in Singapore: Korean Cosmopolitanism or the Consumption of Chineseness?" *Korea Journal* 45, no. 4 (2005): 206–32.
50. Berry, review of *Theorizing Chinese Masculinity*.
51. Song, *Fragile Scholar*, 8–17.
52. Louie, *Theorizing Chinese Masculinity*, 10–66.
53. Richard Kraus, *Pianos and Politics in China: Middle-Class Ambitions and the Struggle over Western Music.* (Oxford: Oxford University Press, 1989); Sue Tuohy, "The Sonic Dimensions of Nationalism in Modern China: Musical Representation and Transformation," *Ethnomusicology* 45 no. 1 (2001): 107–31; Sheila Melvin and Jindong Cai, *Rhapsody in Red: How Western Classical Music Became Chinese* (New York, Algora, 2004).
54. Lang and Ritz, *Journey of a Thousand Miles*, 212.
55. Susan Napier, "Confronting Master Narratives: History as Vision in Miyazaki Hayao's Cinema of De-assurance," *Positions* 9, no. 2 (2002): 467–93.
56. Yoshihara, *Musicians from a Different Shore*, 101–16.
57. Eric Hung, "Performing 'Chineseness' on the Western Concert Stage: The Case of Lang Lang," *Asian Music* Winter/Spring (2009): 131–48.
58. Ibid., 135, 143.
59. Mark Swed, "So Much Talent, So Much to Learn," *Los Angeles Times*, March 6, 2008.
60. Norman Lebrecht, "The Rise of an Orchestral Superpower," *La Scena Musicale* November 12, 2008, http://www.scena.org/columns/lebrecht/081112-NL-power.html.
61. Ibid.

62. Norman Lebrecht, "Sony Pays $3 Million to Win Pianist Lang Lang," *Bloomberg*, February 1 2010.

63. Michael Strickland, "Yuja Wang Plays Vintage Modern at the Symphony," June 21, 2010, http://sfciviccenter.blogspot.com/2010/06/yuja-wang-plays-vintage-modern-at.html.

64. Norman Lebrecht, "Lang Lang Gets a Partner," *Slipped Disc*, March 22, 2010, http://www.artsjournal.com/slippeddisc/2010/03/lang_lang_gets_a_partner.html.

65. Rey Chow, "On Chineseness as a Theoretical Problem," *Boundary* 2, vol. 25, no. 3 (1998): 24.

66. Shzr Ee Tan, "Chopin's Right on His Liszt," *Straits Times* (Singapore), February 11, 2003; Shzr Ee Tan, "From China with Verve," *Straits Times* (Singapore), November 15, 2002.

Chapter Ten

An Interview with Aloysius Lee, Fan of Singer Faye Wong

Aloysius Lee (not his real name; b. 1980, Singapore) is a bank officer and self-styled "fashion aesthete" who also calls himself a fan of Mandopop and Cantopop singers Faye Wong and Sammi Cheng. He considers the two women his personal heroines and has been tracking their careers since the 1990s. Aloysius gave this interview in a café in Singapore to Shzr Ee Tan in English and Mandarin.

I'm gay—not openly to everyone and anyone, but to the gay community in Singapore. I'm also a big fan of Faye Wong, Sammi Cheng, Nicole Kidman, and Madonna. As far as I know, these women are gay icons among all my friends—among gay Singaporeans, if you like. These women—they're all beautiful in their special ways, and somehow they mean something extra magical to us. If you went to a Sammi or Faye concert, there'd be straight men as well as women, but all their gay fans would be there too, sitting in groups, banding together and holding up flowers, posters, torches, and glowsticks. When we've decided on our icons, we go all the way to love them.

Tragic Asian Heroines, Sad Lyrics

A gay icon doesn't have to be conventionally pretty. But she has to be perfect—big, over-the-top, glamorous "perfect" or simple and classy "perfect." They're immaculate: their hair, makeup, costumes . . . they all have great fashion sense. Usually they have sad stories; tragic love lives. Google Faye or Sammi, and you'll find out straightaway about their horrible boyfriends, their disastrous love affairs. Faye's difficult relationship with Dou Wei, who was unfaithful and treated her like shit. Or Sammi—with her on-off-on-off-on-off lover and how she had that terrible lymphatic-whatever disease. And then there's Anita—although she's not an icon from *my* generation—I'm *much* younger—but she has a ginormous number of older fans. Anyway, Anita never married; she gave up her life to try to have a baby even though it caused her to delay her treatment for cervical cancer. She's a survivor . . . well, no not really, since she died so tragically—but her spirit is *big*, her courage is *big*.

As gay men we empathize with their stories and all their sad, sentimental love songs. The lyrics say something about their lives and *our* lives. Gay men—

Figure 10.1. Aloysius Lee. Photograph courtesy of Aloysius Lee.

you know that stereotype about [how we tend to have] affair after affair and so on. It's endless. I have to say there's a bit of truth to that stereotype, because the scene is really cruel and relentless. It's like, how . . . marginalized as we are, we also end up being hard on ourselves. We don't trust the love we find and we don't trust ourselves to keep it. It's so hard to find stability, and the gay scene is a scene that cares so much about looks, about perfection. All the little tragedies of that scene can be found in the lives and songs of our heroines, our icons. Faye's angelic voice and its fragility remind us of our own difficult walks through life as gay men—gay men who have to cope with unrequited love, rejection, bad boyfriends. . . .

Maybe it's something about their voices. I have to say Faye's voice is really quite special, she does all these high octaves, but she's also like Björk and can be breathy and childish. She's a complete diva—her tantrums, her willfulness—we love her for it! Sammi—she's not such a good singer as Faye, but her voice is distinctive in its own way. She's got a few good dance songs, and her beat is just great to move along to and lose yourself in, lose all your worries and sadness in. Sammi's not so much of a diva like Faye but people think of her as Faye's rival, Faye's competitor.

White and Black Divas

The *real* divas, however, are the white women, or rather the black women! They're gay icons too. But they're slightly different, you gotta judge them slightly differently because they come from another culture. It's like the Asian, feminine types are like Faye, who wallow in their own cool and tragic way, but the white divas are the "I-Will-Survive"-Gloria-Gaynor type. Like Madonna and her conical bras. Or Lady Gaga and her huge, *huge* voice. Or Kylie—whose voice is so-so only. But, *man*, she can dance and is she *sexy* or *what*? I mean, I can appreciate her sexiness even though I don't like women. It's a kind of perfection-perfection glamorous-glamorous sexiness. Or at least, flawed as they began, they aspired toward and eventually attained perfection. When Kylie and Lady Gaga sing, it's like their voices are smooth and complete and just . . . powerful. They're over the top, and they strut over their men and their fans and their lives in this perfect-but-flawed way. We aspire to be like them, and of course their songs come as part of the whole package. Their songs are like anthems, they get us going, they get our mojo up when we're down and out. We lip-synch their songs all the time—sometimes we hum and sing them out loud when we're partying. They inspire us to survive in the straight-dominated world and to live the big, honest lives we want and are entitled to live.

I'm not sure we really think about the split between the Chinese singers and the non-Chinese ones. Actually, I haven't thought about this question until you've asked it. It's like, everybody speaks English here—or some kind of

English anyway—so we know all the big Western artists, even those I wouldn't consider gay icons. But because Faye and Sammi are so big in Asia anyway, you just can't help but notice them. And you know what, they're *cool*, and Asian-*cool*. I like to think that as a gay community Singapore's pretty eclectic; we appreciate the best of all worlds—whether it's mainstream American pop, Indie rock, Cantopop, or Mandopop. I think cultural difference and cultural variety is something we've come to deal with and to celebrate. That's because we ourselves have so often been marginalized as a "different" kind of people. For us, the gay icons are a sort of slightly symbolic thing.

Chapter Eleven

"I Prefer a Man Who Is Fresh like a Jumping Fish"

Gender Issues in Shan'ge, Chinese Popular Rural Songs

Frank Kouwenhoven and Antoinet Schimmelpenninck

Only one century ago, rural popular songs were sung widely, almost daily, in the fields and mountains of China. Today, singing in the countryside continues on a more modest level, albeit still as a part of outdoor work and in ritual contexts. While music making in rural China is predominantly a male activity, the key repertoire of *shan'ge* (mountain songs), the most widespread and best-known form of oral poetry, is sung and shared by men and women. Other rural song repertoires—none of which have as wide a currency as *shan'ge*—sometimes belong exclusively to one gender group, and these gender-specific repertoires point at distinct perceptions about the roles of men and women in rural society: songs associated primarily with women include bridal laments (sung by female performers mainly to members of their own sex), funeral laments, ritual chants sung by female monastic orders, and work songs sung during activities such as spinning, weaving, and embroidery. Equivalent male repertoires are the ritual song traditions of male monastic communities, work songs associated with fishing, construction work, and carrying heavy loads, and some other song types predominantly—though not exclusively—sung by men, such as drinking songs.

In the mixed-gender genres—including not only *shan'ge* but also certain types of work songs and domestic songs—the number of men involved in performances often outweighs the number of female performers. This may be ascribed to the general predominance of men in the Chinese population, but the often provocative, sometimes blatantly sexual content of *shan'ge* has led many people to view them as basically unsuitable for female performers; if women want to sing mountain songs they may face opposition from people in their environment.

Shan'ge are often love songs, but they can be about almost any topic. They are not as context constricted or imbued with moral principles as most other rural song genres in China. They can (with a few notable exceptions) be sung nearly anywhere, at any time, and they have an overarching repertoire, in that they incidentally take over the functions of other genres: *shan'ge* are often performed as working songs and occasionally as bridal laments or as ritual songs in temples; they may be addressed to gods or to mortals.

The lyrics of the vast majority of rural songs—whether *shan'ge* or not—tend to confirm the underdog position of women in traditional China. However, *shan'ge*, perhaps uniquely among rural song genres, go a good deal further than passive complaints about the hardships of womanhood: they may serve as active vehicles of protest and as a demonstration of relative independence on the part of women; they provide female singers with tools to express themselves—eloquently and in personal ways, if they like—about crucial matters, including sexuality and relations with men. As we show, the songs even offer women space to give personal direction to their lives, if they accept the challenge. No wonder there has always been social resistance against the idea of women singing *shan'ge*. In fact, the genre is ridden with taboos:

> I used to sing *shan'ge* as a child, but my parents were against me doing it after I had married. They thought it would bring shame on the family. I was so sad about it that I decided to attend *hua'er hui* [song festivals] secretly. My parents, when they discovered it, turned their backs on me. So I would just go out in the woods to cut firewood and sing softly.[1]

> The imam and religious people all opposed those who sang *hua'er* [a type of *shan'ge*], especially women: in the old days, they would beat them with a whip.[2]

> Wang is one of the best singers of her village. Her family is well-off middle class and her husband is an official in the local county government. . . . She said that her entire family objected to her singing *hua'er*. "I was beaten for singing, I was afraid of them using the stick. . . . And my son, who is twelve, doesn't like it because he feels that it makes him lose his face. He says: mama, please, don't sing.[3]

China's oral mythology is rife with heroines who nevertheless decided to sing *shan'ge*. And indeed we interviewed many defiant women who became practitioners of the genre, regardless of local disapproval:

I wanted to travel to Lianhua mountain for the temple festival, and quarreled about it with my husband. "You are ill," he said, "you're hardly fit enough to do your work at home, so how can you think of going to Lianhua mountain?" "Going to the festival will cure me!" I said. "Try if you dare!" he said. I said: "I'll go anyway!" . . . If I get back home and my husband keeps quiet about the whole thing, I won't even tell him that I've been singing *shan'ge* at the festival. But if he starts bullying me, I will tell him that I've sung *all day*. Not only that, I'll tell him I sang loud, long and beautifully![4]

Drawing on fieldwork in China from 1986 to 2007, particularly our excursions to Jiangsu (eastern coastal China) and to Qinghai and Gansu, the heartland of the famous *hua'er* (flower songs) tradition, this chapter examines the world of female *shan'ge* singing and addresses some basic questions: How do women learn to sing this most "liberating" but also most "taboo" of all Chinese song genres? How do the myths of bold, outspoken singers relate to the realities of rural female life? When and where do women perform such songs? And what—beyond mere entertainment—is at stake for the singers and their audiences? We first position *shan'ge* among other forms of female rural singing.

Weeping and Singing: *Shan'ge* versus Other Repertoires

In China's economically more developed coastal and urban regions, life may offer better prospects for many Chinese women today than at any time in the past, through increased educational and career opportunities, but in many respects their lives continue to be beset by difficulties peculiar to their gender. This is even more true in the country's rural interior—in large portions of Gansu, Ningxia, Qinghai, Shaanxi, and other provinces where we carried out fieldwork and where rigid traditional social customs prevail. Women in rural China are widely viewed as inferior, even expendable, beings. Their social rights are few or none, their duties many, and their mobility limited. Traditionally, women were mostly kept indoors, and they could be sold and bought as commodities if necessary and betrothed to children or to old men if this was thought to be profitable or meritorious. Female songs, such as bridal laments, ritual wailing for funerals, and lay Buddhist songs, continue to refer to such circumstances, unfortunately not just as reminders of the past. In bridal laments—a widespread custom until the late 1960s—young women can pour out their grief and express all their fury and disappointment about life, parents, and matchmakers. These songs, though, are fairly stylized forms of lamenting, offering very limited room for negotiation or resistance. With few exceptions,[5] they pay lip service to existing structures of social inequality, without fear of reprisals.[6] Ritual wailing is a more widespread, more resilient tradition, performed by groups of mourners or by professional wailing women, hired to cry at a funeral in order to comfort the spirit in the afterworld. These songs can turn from formal acts of grief into very personal complaints or heated debates about almost any issue, even in the solemn context of funerals. The majority of laments are cast in rigid structures and formulaic patterns, and they are governed by firm moral principles. In this respect, they resemble another genre mainly (but again not exclusively) sung by women: the lay Buddhist songs performed at temple festivals or in private ceremonies. The lyrics borrow material from Buddhist sutras and rely strongly on formulas and stock phrases, allowing singers to improvise and to pour out their personal grievances in music. Their words strictly adhere to a Buddhist moral framework, and the singers frequently remind one another of the correct rules of Buddhist behavior. These songs tend to share common goals with funeral laments, extending into the realm of metaphysics: they are meant to soothe and to console but also to establish contact with the spirit world and secure divine protection. Female singers of lay Buddhist ceremonial songs in Weixing in Jiangsu Province told us that some of their religious tunes were also used for singing (secular) *shan'ge* texts.[7] The lyrics of the lay Buddhist songs we recorded at Bingling in Gansu feature a great many textual formulas and phrases shared with local *shan'ge*, as do laments of Nanhui in Jiangsu and the *shan'ge* of the Wu dialect area.[8] *Shan'ge* are sometimes used for prayers or as weeping songs. All these song types are part of the emotive expressive continuum of praying, weeping, and chanting.But what sets *shan'ge* apart from these other genres? They are not as imbued with moral and religious principles as the lay Buddhist chants and laments. The term *shan'ge* is almost a container notion—some villagers would even equate the term *shan'ge* with "songs"—in the sense that they provide room for the widest possible range of topics and emotions and can be sung in all kinds of situations. Their musical form matches their topical and functional flexibility: the songs have no fixed meter, very elastic rhythms, and melodies that tend to climb high, frequently into the falsetto register. They are performed in a loud and unabashed manner, often at the top of one's voice. This is different from the more resigned (and less controlled) ways in which laments or temple chants are sung. But perhaps a more substantial difference is that *shan'ge* are essentially life embracing rather than death embracing. They appear to be overwhelmingly geared toward subjects like sexuality, courting, fertility of soil and mankind, the growth of the crops, food, health, and procreation: basic concerns of life on earth. The songs tend to underpin the exceptional powers, defiant character, and sexual boldness often ascribed or allotted to Chinese women in literary and religious myths.

Myths and Reality of *Shan'ge*

Chinese folklorists and anthropologists who operate in a framework of Marxist thinking may be happy to detect evidence that women in traditional

China offer resistance to feudal hierarchy and oppression.[9] Critical researchers have warned against romanticizing female folk genres: there is no use in projecting protofeminist norms onto lyrics that in reality harbor mainly conventional notions and formulas; the songs may be standard fare within the boundaries of specific ritual contexts but inconsequential as "voices of protest."[10] However, romantics and skeptics alike face the difficulty that most specialized female repertoires in China have disappeared, or have survived only on paper, in the form of printed texts or scattered memoirs. This is true for the famous women's script of Jiangnanxian in Hunan Province[11] and for many regional traditions of female laments and temple chants. It is hard to judge what meanings traditional lyrics, metaphors, and poetic notions acquired for a new generation of women in the early twentieth century in such genres. No such difficulties exist with respect to *shan'ge*, since the living performance practice can be studied firsthand in a number of regions. A major task, then, is to compare the lyrics, existing mythologies, and discourse on *shan'ge* with the realities of everyday performance.

Large temple festivals in China—important occasions for singing *shan'ge*—will often bring together hundreds of male and female performers. The female singers we recorded in several regions were anything but docile or passive reciters of standard lyrics. Many adopted a bold, provocative tone, humorous, bawdy, often slightly over the top, in any event keen to trigger responses from others. On first encounter, it may seem difficult to reconcile the bleak prospects of arranged marriages and domestic slavery with a radiant and provocative text like this:

> I prefer a man who is fresh like a jumping fish.
> Don't be afraid that mum and dad will lift the lid of our cooking-pan!
> But mind you, if a claret lobster jumps into a pot of boiling water
> It turns pretty red when it gets cooked.[12]

The fact is that *shan'ge* may be sung at any time "in the wild,"[13] in the presence of few people or none, or at temple festivals, in the midst of vast crowds of people or in quiet corners. They may be sung at day but also at night, when singers remain largely invisible to the public and to each other. They may be entertainment, but they can also serve to establish sexual contacts. The above-quoted text would seem to fit the bill for an occasion of flirting and challenging potential male partners.

How common is flirting in rural China? Fei Hsiao-tung, in his landmark study, *Peasant Life in China* (1939), wrote that the children of Kaixiangong village (southeast of Lake Tai, Jiangsu) always gave their parents a free hand in arranging their marriage affairs, that it was considered improper and shameful to talk about one's own marriage, and that "there was no such thing as courtship."[14] But the vast majority of the seven hundred *shan'ge* we collected near

"I PREFER A MAN WHO IS FRESH LIKE A JUMPING FISH"   161

Figure 11.1. *Hua'er* singers near Majiaji village, Southern Gansu. Photograph courtesy of authors.

Lake Tai in the late 1980s and early 1990s are in dialogue form and are love songs, many of them frank and outspoken in content, much like the bawdy *shan'ge* which were collected and published by Feng Menglong in the same region four centuries ago.[15]

Fei Hsiao-tung probably knew what went on in his own native region, but like other scholars he could not write about it, at least not without triggering devastating criticism. In the Maoist years, Chinese peasanthood—the ideal societal model for Mao—was better not associated with immoral behavior or sexual "decadence." Before 1949, southern Jiangsu featured a lively tradition of temple fairs, in which *shan'ge* singing played an important role.[16] These festivals are long gone, but elsewhere in China they continue to flourish. Some of them feature lively traditions of musical courting and flirting.[17] Among the best-known regional traditions are the *hua'er* gatherings of Gansu and Qinghai, where humorous exchanges on all kinds of topics (not just love) take place in musical form. *Hua'er* are a regional type of *shan'ge* from the northwest. At *hua'er* gatherings, people of all ages participate in the spontaneous singing of *hua'er*, especially during crowded temple gatherings in late spring and early summer, in between the periods of planting and harvesting.

Traditionally, for young people there might be more at stake than cozy get-togethers. The songs are most commonly cast in dialogue or polylogue form and often assume the aspect of a battle: Who can outwit the other party in improvised texts? The adversaries may be two individual singers or two groups of singers. They alternate stanzas and are expected to pick up each other's formulas and twist them in unexpected and funny ways. Much of it is harmless entertainment, but the songs can also become a form of sexual education or flirtation, which may culminate in short-term sexual contacts. Young married women sometimes attempt to get pregnant from strangers if their marriages remain childless. Women often have to take the blame for childless marriages, and they may risk public derision. One possible solution we were told of—especially if a marriage has not been consummated—is resorting to temporary flirtation with strangers. Ideally, this takes place under the protective umbrella of gods presiding over a temple festival. A husband, if pragmatic, will remain silent about such unorthodox efforts to extend the family line, and others are unlikely to raise questions, as the following stanzas suggest:

> The girl is on the threshing floor
> In her arms she holds a little child
> People know the hen has laid her egg
> They'll never know a wild cock fathered it![18]

During seven years of extensive interviews with singers, festival visitors, and scholars in Gansu and Qinghai, it became clear to us that these are the basic premises of *shan'ge* dialogues sung at temple festivals. For obvious reasons, the songs are a sensitive issue. Young girls in rural Gansu and Qinghai are usually forbidden to attend festivals, not so much to avoid exposure to erotic texts—many will know such lyrics well before they are teenagers—but to elude confrontations with pushy men and the risk and humiliation of a premarital pregnancy. As a rule, only married women in Gansu and Qinghai are allowed to attend the festivals in which *hua'er* are sung. All the same, a woman's marital state can be problematic for different reasons: it may give her an excuse to freewheel at festivals and to maintain short-term sexual contacts. Hence the many stories about newlywed women who are told by their husbands to stop singing *hua'er*. Men may also try to keep their partners away from festivals to forestall interruptions of domestic work or child care. Conscientious husbands may act as babysitters, or women can take their children along to festivals: "I attended those festivals ... for many years. I went there when I was pregnant, and the next year with my baby in my arms. ... I took my daughter along on my back, and sang at the festival all night. I couldn't give her to anyone else, for then she would cry."[19] The taboos surrounding *shan'ge* are similar everywhere in China: *shan'ge* ought not to be sung in front of one's relatives and not inside people's homes, temples, or on village grounds, only "in the wild," and then there may be objections to women performing such songs. But there is also widespread trespassing of these rules, which primarily seem to reflect the functions of *shan'ge* as songs of dissent, flirtation, and sexual experimentation.

One might argue that *shan'ge* only confirm conventional views—they underpin the supposed "duties" of women in the realm of procreation—but singers' tendencies to flout social conventions position the songs in the realm of carnival: the temple festivals are a social space in which normal modes of behavior may be turned upside down, and the *shan'ge* are the ideal vehicle to take action. Importantly, such action may be authorized, and perhaps even actively encouraged by, the presence of the gods. The rich mythology of *shan'ge* emphasizes the special position of women and the "sacred" roots as well as the dissident qualities of *shan'ge* singing. This merits closer investigation, especially the fantastic stories about "first" *shan'ge* singers, which shed revealing light on the role of the temple festival as the main performing arena for this genre.

Women as Learners, "Founders," and Sacred Guardians of *Shan'ge*

In Chinese lore, tales about hunters and fairies singing *shan'ge* exist alongside quasi-factual reports about recent "famous" performers and their miraculous talents. Past and present blend in these tales to produce a fluid yet consistent picture of *shan'ge* as a liberating medium and a precious gift from the gods—a difficult and potentially harmful gift that requires careful handling.

Intriguingly, most *shan'ge* heroes and "founders" of *shan'ge* in the folk-song mythology of southern Jiangsu are men, and they are either saints or incorrigible pleasure seekers: "Zhang Liang is the one who began our *shan'ge*. He is a demi-god [*banxian*]. He was imprisoned by Lady Guanyin because he sang dirty songs."[20] Zhang Liang was a statesman of the early Han dynasty who, like other leaders, has found his way into Chinese mythology. He is venerated as a demi-god and founder of *shan'ge* but is also held in awe as a fabled adventurer who caused havoc in the Land of Women (*nürenguo*) and, upon returning home, notoriously tried to seduce his own daughter via *shan'ge*. According to one story, Zhang Liang was unaware that he was singing his illicit songs to such a close relative. Once he discovered his error, he was deeply ashamed and turned to the goddess Guanyin for help. Guanyin scolded him for behaving like a pig and imprisoned him "until such time when no one in the world will sing *shan'ge* for at least two hours." This amounted to eternal damnation for Zhang because "there is always someone at work in the field singing *shan'ge*, at any time of the day."[21] The story, told or sung with minor variations by several singers in our fieldwork, establishes the potentially illicit nature of *shan'ge* as well as their inevitable presence in popular culture; the basic idea is that the songs may cause harm ("*shan'ge* singers die with rotten teeth"), but they are something that all share and relish.

By contrast, founders of *shan'ge* in the folklore of Gansu and Qinghai tend to be women. They, too, are strong characters, sometimes real-life persons, remembered for behaving courageously and expanding social frontiers via their songs. More commonly, they are divine beings of an imagined past, fairies who have brought these songs as a gift for the mortals. Several tales about the founding of local temples refer to the sudden appearance of female deities who begin to sing *hua'er*.

In one version, about the completion of the Yuhuang temple—located on Lianhua mountain, the site of the biggest temple festival in Gansu—a workman notes that the main beam holding the roof is still missing. During the night the Jade Emperor (the god of the Yuhuang temple) arranges for cattle to carry the missing building materials up to the top. When the temple is finished, people argue about how they can best inaugurate the new shrine: "The Han people wanted to sing opera, the Tibetans wanted to recite scriptures, the Muslims wanted to have horse races." As they are quarreling about this, three beautiful fairies (*san xiao niangniang*) appear, floating on colored clouds. They hold colorful fans and umbrellas made of lotus leaves and begin to sing, finishing together on the words "*hua-a, lianye-er*" (flowers, lotus leaves; the refrain of the most common type of *hua'er* heard at Lianhua mountain).[22] The spectators conclude that these three celestial ladies urge them to sing *shan'ge* on this important occasion. "This marked the beginning of *hua'er* singing at Lianhua mountain."[23]

This tale not only connects the founding of a major regional temple with the birth of the *hua'er* tradition but also hints at negotiations among ethnic groups who have been fighting one another in this area for centuries. The myth recognizes the fact that these songs are shared by all ethnic groups in the region and can help to bridge cultural differences. Interethnic flirting in the area via *shan'ge* (sung in Han Chinese) is quite common. Ethnic groups blend freely during temple festivals, and singing among individuals from different ethnic backgrounds frequently develops spontaneously.[24]

A different tale links the birth of a temple with a mysterious woman singing *shan'ge* near a river, overheard by a young hunter. He memorizes some of the songs, but the girl disappears. Upon his return to inhabited places, he starts singing and spreading the songs, manifestly *hua'er*. The tale concludes: "Since that time they built the temple at Songmingyan and held annual gatherings there on the 28th of the 4th month."[25] Still other stories in Gansu and Qinghai point at women as the inventors of *hua'er*—or at least *hua'er* tunes:

> It is said that the *Bai mudan* tune was first sung by a young and beautiful widow named Bai mudan who lived in Ledu county in Qinghai.[26]

> The *Da yanling* tune was made by a young woman of the Hui minority who waited in vain for a lover to return.[27]

It is unclear what these attributions mean, but, in the case of the deities who launch the *hua'er* tradition at Lianhuashan and Songmingyan, the connections among the songs, their inventors, and the temples are more easy to grasp. The *san xiao niangniang* are a well-known trinity, who work wonders in shrines dedicated specifically to them through much of China. They carry different individual names in different regions but have in common the promotion of fertility and protection of childbirth. Shrines devoted to these goddesses—particularly to *Songzi niangniang* or *Hua'er niangniang*—are found widely in Gansu and Qinghai and are frequented by country women who come to sing and pray for offspring, bringing branches of the *pipa* plant.[28] They often sing *hua'er* in front of the shrines and deposit sacrifices near the altar. If a temple guard is present, they will pay him to cast his divination bones or blocks. Folklorists sometimes define the "praying-for-a-child songs" (*qiuzi hua'er*) as a subcategory of the "bitter heart songs" (*kuxin qu'er*).[29] If women are desperate for children, they can sing about their miserable lives in the hope of mollifying the gods. But most of the young women whom we observed singing *hua'er* in front of fertility shrines looked resigned or relaxed, perhaps a sign that times are changing. Some of their praying-for-sons *hua'er* were dark in tone, but most sounded like a gleeful preparation for motherhood:

> Oh, mighty Goddess, you are truly great.
> This year, I've come to ask for a little one.
> Next year, I'll bring that baby on my arm.
> How sweetly will it smile! How sweet
> The dangling little willie in his pants.[30]

The name *hua'er niangniang* for one of the fertility goddesses apparently links her directly to the singing of *hua'er*—and this is the usual interpretation—but there are reports that it initially referred to the homonym *hua'er*, meaning "measles."[31] The lady presumably also offered protection against child diseases. Her glorious role as the bringer of new life is manifest in the way she is depicted in most temples: as a woman with many babies on her arms and on her back.

The *hua'er* tradition is thus connected in a variety of ways with fertility cults and goddesses, and the shrines of these deities are a meeting place for young women aspiring to be mothers. There is one such spot at Lianhua mountain, and Xi Huimin has signaled the presence of other sacred spots there that supposedly promote fertility; for example, cavities in a rock surface near the top: if people manage to throw stones inside these caves they will have a baby.[32]

The courtship dialogues sung by men and women "in the wild" seem a practical extension of the prayers for offspring addressed in *hua'er* form to the gods. Chinese scholars are divided about the idea of connections between *hua'er* and temple festivals.[33] We do not need to subscribe to the idea that *hua'er* sprang from religious ceremonies in order to recognize their relevance in religious contexts. The temple festivals are a convergence of the religious and the secular, two inseparably intertwined realms. The elder generation of festival-goers, leading prayers for offspring, fertility, and general well-being inside the temples, and the younger generations, flirting and courting outside, seem to honor a logical division of tasks. They may hardly meet, but the flow of events facilitates this differentiation of roles, and there is a common interest in fertility and the continuation of life. Festivals are not merely places to pray for offspring or to copulate. They are major social events, combining markets, opera plays, disco dancing, kung fu movies, soothsaying ceremonies, acrobat shows, ritual processions, prayer sessions, and a great deal more. Nevertheless, the central position of *shan'ge* in hundreds of temple festivals in the area (of which we attended twenty) is uncontested. The connections of these songs with religion are apparent not only in prayers for offspring or tales about singing goddesses but also in other ritually applied *shan'ge* and *shan'ge* singing contexts, such as processional songs,[34] prayers for rain, and exorcist chants.[35]

These songs could never function if the only opportunity to sing and to learn them were the temple festivals, held once a year for the duration of a few days. Female informants in Gansu and Qinghai told us that they picked up their knowledge of *hua'er* as children aged seven to ten, while herding cattle, gathering medicinal plants in the mountains, working in the fields, or staying at home, listening to elderly women singing such songs. Long-term exposure to performances is necessary to internalize the genre's idioms, formulaic expressions, and structural rules. Women who join the dialogues sung in the fields take a major step in gaining practice in the art of singing; for many it may be the first opportunity to sing with men.[36]

Most female singers in Gansu and Qinghai picked up their first songs in the fields or home, but they all agree that the festivals are the most important occasions for *hua'er* singing. And festivals are the ideal settings for observing female singers in action.

Bold Female Singers

Ma Xiaojun narrates the life story of a girl called Qiong Gamei, who in 1935–36 ignored her family's prohibition and went off to Lianhua mountain to sing *hua'er*, although "it was forbidden for women to do so" at that time.

> Qiong Gamei was one of Lianhua mountain's shining, eye-catching stars. She became famous by singing *hua'er* at the age of 20. Right until she died in 1981, her fame prospered all over Lianhua mountain. She was a top singer of her generation, the crowds craved for her. Among singers and visiting crowds, the story of how Qiong Gamei came galloping to the festival in those years is still on everyone's lips. This beautiful and romantic story resounds over the three districts and six counties.[37]

"I PREFER A MAN WHO IS FRESH LIKE A JUMPING FISH" 167

In her youth, Gamei followed her mother into the mountains to collect firewood and learned the *hua'er* that her mother used to hum, "the songs of us, poor people." She dreamed of becoming a "master singer," of joining other singers at Lianhua mountain. Her mother nodded approvingly when Gamei told her about her aspirations, but then she frowned and responded with the following sad lines: "Don't be presumptuous, sweet girl of mine / Lianhua mountain does not invite women to sing." After her marriage, Qiong Gamei's parents-in-law and husband disapproved of her interest in *hua'er* and simply forbade her to sing. She was treated "like dirt" and frequently beaten, but she did not give up singing. When it was time for the annual temple festival at Lianhua mountain, she joined other women in blocking the entrance to her native village with hemp rope, a traditional custom still practiced near Lianhua mountain: visitors on the road to the top may be required to sing a few lines before they can be allowed to pass. "At first, Qiong Gamei only listened to the people who turned up, but her throat itched like mad. After a while she couldn't contain herself anymore and burst out in song: 'Visitors, please open your mouths, let me hear your songs!'"[38] A lively musical dialogue now arose with people arriving on the scene, and Qiong Gamei sung to a rapidly growing crowd about what kind of life she was leading:

> An axe is used to chop the red birch.
> My mother-in-law's family strikes fear in people's hearts:
> The men beat me, the mother shouts abuse at me.
> My niece tears out my hair, Grandfather howls that he will kill me.[39]

Bystanders felt pity and encouraged her in songs to take her fate in her own hands. Some years later, in the summer of 1936, Qiong Gamei obtained permission from her parents-in-law to visit Lianhua mountain, albeit on the condition that she would not sing *hua'er* while there. She was sixteen, and her husband was sent along to keep an eye on the unruly girl. Riding a donkey, she arrived at the foot of the mountain and was immersed in the festive crowds. The surrounding landscape was awash with songs and merriment. She could not contain herself for very long and began to sing. At first, her husband got angry, but others defended her; they explained to the husband that this whole business of singing was a mere game. But others who overheard Gamei's chanting were less positive. They complained that she offended the gods with her songs. A local landlord accused her of undermining public morals: "You don't know any shame!" She replied to him in song: "Well, I haven't sung at your front door, have I? I'm singing out in the open. I haven't sung into your throat!"

> The whole mountain was now noisy with excitement. In the old society, women suffered heavy oppression from the feudal customs. Every summer, women at Lianhua mountain were free only to burn incense to ask the gods

favours, and to beg for sons and ask for daughters. They did not have the right to openly sing *hua'er* dialogues. . . . Qiong Gamei . . . was the first to stand up and to sing her own *hua'er*. She challenged the feudal beliefs. . . . People roaming on the mountain leapt up and ran to meet the first female singer. Women and girls drew courage from Qiong Gamei.[40]

Later in the story, Gamei loses her husband. She is married off to a new one, who again maltreats her, and eventually is sold to a third husband. At this point her life takes a more positive turn. Her new partner is good-looking, supportive of her art, and in fact eager to sing *hua'er* with her. Qiong Gamei makes an impressive reentry at the festival on Lianhua mountain, on horseback, and she and her husband visit all the singing spots of the mountain and stir people's hearts with their songs. "They became well-known personalities. The good-natured mountain people gave them red ribbons, and often invited them to be guests in their houses."

Ma Xiaojun, the author, claims that Qiong Gamei contributed in unique ways to the *hua'er* tradition at Lianhuashan not just by breaking the monopoly of male singers but also by enriching the content of the songs.

Before Qiong Gamei, men sang *hua'er* mostly about gods, buddhist virtues, feudal etiquette, historical tales, farming activities and everyday life. Not many *hua'er* about love could be heard, although there were some dirty songs (*hun'ge*), and most of the love songs were descriptions of female beauty or of unrequited love from the male perspective. There were few exchanges of genuine feelings. After Qiong Gamei appeared, a great many *hua'er* about love began to be heard, and these songs described the psychology and the inner feelings of women.[41]

Undoubtedly this tale—committed to paper shortly after the singer's death—is based in part on Qiong Gamei's own memories or the memories of people who had known her, but the tale was adapted by the author to create a heroic role model. Qiong Gamei here becomes a feminist, a woman of refined taste who breaks loose from the fetters of feudalism and singlehandedly raises a trivial genre of folk verse to the level of romantic and meaningful feminine poetry. She convinces other women to follow her and to pour out their true feelings in new and effective ways. All this is highly unlikely. A formulaic tradition dependent on oral transmission, shared by countless singers in a vast region, cannot be completely rewritten by a single person. With its mixture of prose and song lines, its abundant praise for the central heroine, and references to the old "feudal society," the story reads like a propaganda text. It is not difficult to see how this took shape. After the traumatic Cultural Revolution, many folklorists continued to present their research in a Marxist framework, from conviction or habit or to protect the sources or the genre they were studying. Depicting

Qiong Gamei as a female liberator and champion of social equality could help to make politically palatable a genre that, only a few years earlier, had been prohibited and denounced in a nationwide violent revolution. Lianhua mountain had been the scene of bloody skirmishes between Red Guards and local singers, its temples had been destroyed, and most festivals came to a standstill. But we are less concerned here with the meaning of Qiong Gamei's life story as an ideological construct as with the reality of *hua'er* singing behind it.

"Famous" singers in the *hua'er* lore of Gansu and Qinghai frequently happen to be women. But, if certain details in Qiong Gamei story sound trustworthy, it is because they also turn up in the biographies of ordinary singers, rural women whom we interviewed and who showed no intention of romanticizing their past. Thus we can assume that Qiong Gamei really put up a fight with her family in order to become a public singer. She was of course not *the* first female singer at Lianhua mountain. There is evidence from our own interviews and from travelers' reports that women participated in *hua'er* singing at Lianhua mountain and at other temple festivals by the end of the nineteenth century or much earlier.[42] But portraying her as a pioneer could be an effective device to stress her great courage or to exaggerate the impact she made when she first sang in public.

What the story shows is that in Qiong Gamei's youth women did know how to sing *hua'er* and presumably sang them among themselves, but only a limited number of women dared to perform *hua'er* in public. And only by adopting a defiant stance and taking considerable risks could they appropriate these songs as tools for public self-expression. This fact probably lies at the heart of Qiong Gamei's tale, and it is probably true for women of her generation all over China. We recorded similar tales about gutsy female singers in Jiangsu. Whatever the romantic appeal of such stories, they ring true when it comes to the ability of the women to resist social pressures, and they obviously stood out by their intelligence: the stories brim with sung dialogues illustrating how the women beat their adversaries in song (particularly men) with quick and spirited replies. There is no room here to quote lengthy examples, but one telling case is that of Lu Qiaoying (b. 1895), a fisherman's daughter from Changqing (Jiangsu Province). At the age of twelve she hid in her father's boat while he went out fishing on Lake Tai:

> The fishermen were singing *shan'ge*. But nobody could defeat the man in the little boat who was known as the King of *Shan'ge* [*shan'ge dawang*]. He was just lighting a pipe to celebrate another victory when Lu Qiaoying, who had been hiding under a blanket, sprang forward and sang:

> 'Hey you! Sleepy fellow with drooping eyes—having a smoke?
> Take care not to set your lips afire!
> If you're awake you can smoke what you like.

> If not, don't light that deadly pipe: you might never pipe up again!

> Everyone burst into laughter. Lu Qiaoying became a *shan'ge* celebrity among the fishermen. Her father no longer tried to stop her from going out and learning *shan'ge*. The great singer Shen Baoquan taught her numerous songs. Later in life, she often participated in local festivities and was greatly respected as a person and as a performer.[43]

Tales about strong-willed women derive much of their appeal from the contrast they offer with conventional images of women. Features often associated with "traditional" women, such as shyness, subservience, an inclination to withdraw, and unobtrusive behavior, may be much in evidence in rural China, but they are nevertheless stereotypes, no less an imagined ideal than the supposed merits of "strong women." Villagers in Jiangsu who cared to comment on the qualities of female singers often made statements about their "soft" voices and "elegant" songs—qualifications which were demonstrably untrue.[44] Women may—as is often claimed—"sing softer than men," but the fact is that many of them sing quite loud. Falsetto singing is not practiced only by men or accessible only to men. In many parts of China, from northern Zhejiang to Shaanxi, we recorded skilled female falsetto singers, some with rough and rowdy voices. The presumed "shy" nature of women and a tendency to conceal personal feelings may be evident in the delicate metaphors of love songs we collected in Jiangsu, but we encountered as many bold lyrics and provocative stances on the part of female performers. Opinions on the daring and effectiveness of female singers among male singers tend to be divided:

> Women don't sing dirty songs. It is something for men. Women can never get the upper hand in dialogue songs. They don't understand as much as the men do.[45]

> Women are ripe at an earlier age than men. Hence they are also bolder or more imperious in the dialogue songs.[46]

Most certainly, women can be as explicit or as provocative as men. The folklorist Ke Yang relates the story of a group of Han women in Zhuoni who were bold enough to challenge a Tibetan monk, singing *hua'er* to him.[47] Contrary to their expectations, the monk served them with a sharp reply in song, so the women felt defeated. At Lianhua mountain we witnessed a group of women preying on a Hui singer like a pack of wolves. He had very little breath left to respond, but they jumped on him again, with yet another stanza faking their "affection" for him:

Figure 11.2. A tense nightly bout of *hua'er* singing near Majiaji village, Southern Gansu. Photograph courtesy of authors.

> Dear patron, listen, you can use a sickle to cut weeds.
> If I die, let me change into a little flea.
> You know what I'll do? Bite your body from top to toe.
> When finished, I'll take a sweet nap on top of your belly.

Song sessions between men and women can also get quite tense. We won't easily forget the flushed faces of a group of girls near Majiaji in Lintao, Gansu, who hardly looked like a flirting party, but it may have been their first opportunity to test their strengths against a group of (drunk) men. In a festival near Bingling, it was the women who took the main initiative: they went up a steep rock surface to start singing *hua'er*. The mountain, dotted with small caves, seemed an ideal place for different parties to exchange songs. The women went into the caves in small groups and remained hidden from one another as they sang. *Hua'er* singing is not much of a visual experience: performers generally tend to avoid eye contact, and all communication depends on the ear. The young men down in the valley seemed reluctant to follow the women. They lazily strolled about, sang pop songs or cracked jokes as if they wanted to sabotage the *hua'er* ritual or thought of it as a silly exercise. But after a while they did go up to the caves, and soon their chanting began to blend in with the female voices, in a chaotic barrage of sounds. At times, surprisingly, hundreds of voices suddenly fell silent, and one particularly energetic dialogue rang out in the clear mountain air, audible to everyone.

The lyrics of female singers may refer only cautiously to sex or not at all, but occasionally one comes across verses like this one:

> With my whole body of white flesh I want to do it.
> I am gasping, I've got only one breath left . . .
> I feel hurt as if a knife has been stuck into my heart:
> Oh, this bad unscrupulous man who turned his back on me . . . ![48]

We overheard female singers pushing toward more explicit content in dialogues with men. At Lianhuashan we recorded a group of six male Hui singers who sang vague lines in turn about a boy missing his girl or about somebody being addicted to foreign cigarettes. Then a woman jumped in, and immediately contributed four lines about a boy who was ill and who needed to eat some "medicine," namely "the round and shiny nipples of his girl's boobs."

Songs of Rebellion

Ultimately, what can women gain from singing *shan'ge*? We have pointed at the importance of this repertoire for sexual education and for helping desperate women toward sexual contacts or pregnancies. According to several informants, singing for sex occurs less often today than in the past. Increased social mobility, migration of young people from rural to urban centers, and the rise of karaoke bars and dance halls have altered the picture. It is not just that young people explore alternative opportunities for encounters but that their whole outlook on life has undergone a major transformation. Many still go to temple festivals, but the views and customs of their native region may no longer be the sole yardstick in life. There may also be practical obstacles to continuing certain aspects of the *shan'ge* tradition: widespread deforestation in many parts of China has probably contributed to a decline in outdoor sexual activities. The implementation of China's one-child policy has drastically reduced the size of families, and because of this praying-for-children activities at fertility shrines have become less frequent, as many villagers in Gansu and Qinghai told us. The entertainment aspect of *shan'ge* has meanwhile gained prominence, making the participation of women in sung dialogues less problematic: "In the old days, men and women usually had sex after singing *hua'er*, but nowadays it does not happen so often any more. So we don't have a problem now with women singing those songs."[49] So is *shan'ge* singing today becoming an outdated custom—like bridal lamenting—which can do little to improve the social position or personal prospects of Chinese women? Thousands of villagers will probably feel unaffected by *shan'ge*, because they don't sing them and may not even take an interest in hearing them. Others, who do sing these songs, may be triggered mainly by the entertainment aspect of *shan'ge*. This should not obscure the fact that there is more at stake in *shan'ge* performances than diversion and laughter: the songs are still an open realm in which relationships between genders are tested and subjected to public scrutiny. They still constitute a social learning process for both men and women, and the lyrics, no matter how much they borrow from tradition, are sufficiently flexible and open to absorb new modes of public thinking and behavior. In brief, the songs are a continued platform for self-reflection and social discourse, and not just in the context of festivals. They buzz in the air at marketplaces and pop up in daily conversations, in the columns of gazetteers, in chance encounters in the fields, even in people's bedrooms: "If my mother and family are not at home my husband and I will sometimes sing together in the house. We may even sing when we are already in bed."[50] Singers' lives *can* be affected by *shan'ge* as much as *shan'ge* traditions are affected by singers. Women play an active role in protecting or giving a new lease of life to *shan'ge*: women in Lu dong jia, a village in Lintao County (Gansu) reportedly stipulated the right to sing *hua'er* both before and after marriage: if their future husband's family attempts to stop them from singing, they have the right to break off their engagements.[51] Women in Kanputa village (Min County, Gansu) hold secret *hua'er* sessions at a local temple, with support from the temple's supervisor,[52] and so break the strict rule that (nonritual) *hua'er* ought not to be sung *within* temple walls. The women chant about their lives and personal concerns and may wish to share this with the temple gods. The meetings are kept secret, but they remain another example of rebellion against convention and (in this case) religious etiquette. In folk tales we frequently encounter such a spirit of rebellion, exemplified in its more hyperbolical form by the singer-heroes and heroines who—bigger than life perhaps—live on in collective memory.

To conclude, *shan'ge* are not all-powerful weapons to bring about fundamental societal change or to rewrite the fate of Chinese womanhood, as some ideologists would have it, but they do play a role in subtle and surprising ways not just as an outlet for grief or anger, not just as sexual provocation or playfully subversive or ironic commentary or acts of consolation, but also as active pleas for more openness, more compassion, more balanced views on the position and concerns of women. The messages are mostly personal and illustrative, rather than ideological or polemical. The songs contribute a touch of humor to the lives of many and have brought fame and—in spite of all comments to the contrary—admiration for a number of regional female singers. Perhaps, in the end, not such a bad harvest.

Notes

We would like to thank Professor Emeritus Ke Yang of Lanzhou University (Chinese folklore studies) and Huang Fei of the History Department of Sun Yat-sen University, Guangzhou, for their generous support and assistance during our research and preparation of this article.

1. Female singer Kong Aiping, Yongjing County, quoted in Yan Guofang, "Xiangtu shehui shiyu xia de hua'er yanjiu" (PhD diss., Xibei minzu daxue, 2007), 95.

2. Male singer Ma Jinshan, quoted in Ma Li, "Dangdai renleixue shiye xia de 'hua'er' jiqi yanjiu" (master's thesis, Zhongyang minzu daxue, Beijing, 2009), 26.

3. Qi Xiaoping, "Taomin nanlu hua'er xianzhuan diaocha baogao—yi kanputa wei zhongxin," *Xibei Minzu Yanjiu*, 56, no. 1 (2008): 187.

4. Female singer Qing Gaishun, interview Lianhuashan, July 4, 2000.

5. Liu Fei-wen, "Women who De-silence Themselves: Male-Illegible Literature (*Nüshu*) And Female-Specific Songs (*Nüge*) in Jiangyong County, Hunan Province, China" (PhD Diss., Syracuse University, 1997): 272–96.

6. *Fred* C. Blake, "Death and Abuse in Chinese Marriage *Laments*: The Curse of Chinese Brides," *Asian Folklore Studies* 37 (1978): 17; Elizabeth L. Johnson, "Grieving for the Dead, Grieving for the Living: Funeral Laments of Hakka Women," in *Death Ritual in Late Imperial China*, ed. James L. Watson and Evelyn Rawski (Berkeley: University of California Press, 1988), 157–60; Elizabeth L. Johnson, "Singing of Separation, Lamenting Loss: Hakka Women's Expressions of Separation and Reunion," in *Living with Separation in China: Anthropological Accounts*, ed. Charles Stafford (London: Routledge Curzon, 2003), 30.

7. Antoinet Schimmelpenninck, *Chinese Folk Song and Folk Singers: Shan'ge Traditions in Southern Jiangsu* (Leiden: CHIME Foundation, 1997), 319.

8. Anne E. McLaren, *Performing Grief: Bridal Laments in Rural China* (Honolulu, University of Hawaii Press, 2008), 9, 97.

9. Tan Daxian, *Zhongguo hunjia yishi geyao yanjiu* (Taipei: Shangwu yinshuguan, 1990), 121; Jiang Bin, *Wu yue minjian xinyang minsu* (Shanghai: Shanghai wenyi chubanshe, 1992), 240–41.

10. Cathy Silber, "From Daughter to Daughter-in-Law in the Women's Script of Southern Hunan," in *Engendering China: Women, Culture and the State*, ed. Christina K. Gilmartin, Gail Hershhatter, Lisa Rofel, and Tyrene White (Cambridge, MA: Harvard University Press, 1994), 59.

11. Ibid.

12. Ren Mei, *Taihu yuge de yishu tese* (Wuxi, mimeograph, 1987), 12.

13. *Shan'ge* singers all over a China normally refer to "the wild" (*yewai*) as the established arena for *shan'ge* singing.

14. Fei Hsiao-tung, *Peasant Life in China* (London: Routledge, 1939), 40.

15. Feng Menglong, "Shan'ge," in *Ming Qing min'ge shidiao jiI* (Shanghai: Shanghai guji chubanshe, 1984).

16. Schimmelpenninck, *Chinese Folk Song*, 95–99.

17. For a survey, see Yang Mu, "Erotic Musical Activity in Multiethnic China," *Ethnomusicology* 42, no. 2 (1998): 199–264.

18. Schimmelpenninck, *Chinese Folk Song*, 113.

19. Du Yulan, interview, Lianhuashan, July 4, 2000.

20. Singer Qian Afu, quoted in Schimmelpenninck, *Chinese Folk Song*, 103.

21. Schimmelpenninck, *Chinese Folk Song*, 103–4.

22. Lotus-leaf umbrellas are associated with divine beings. This refrain explicitly refers to the flowers and the name of the mountain (Lianhua: "lotus"). Umbrellas are used as a prop in performances of *hua'er* as well as lay Buddhist songs in northwest China.

23. Anon., "Lianhuashan de chuanshuo," in *Kangle xianzhi* (Kangle: Kanglexian chuban, 1985), 463–64. Variants of the story have the fairies themselves arranging for a tiger

to transport wood up the mountain: "Bie kai sheng mian de min'ge yanchanghui: Gansu sheng Lianhuashan hua'erhui diaocha baogao." *Hua'er lunji 1* (Lanzhou: Zhongguo minjian wenyi yanjiuhui, Gansu fenhui, 1983), 73–75. A comparable story is told about the temple at Songmingyan, the site of another festival. Here, the three ladies rescue a man from being devoured by a leopard. In gratitude he orders that a temple be built at Songmingyan. Upon its completion thousands of people gather on the mountain to sing *hua'er*. Yan, "Xiangtu shehui," 81.

24. Sometime interethnic marriages occur, in which the household patrimony remains intact, daughters-in-law moving to their husband's village: Muslim men usually marry Han Chinese women only on the condition that they convert to Islam. Muslim women marrying non-Muslim men are more rare, in line with an age-old rule that forbids Muslims to "lose" their daughters to outsiders. Jonathan N. Lipman, *Familiar Strangers: A History of Muslims in Northwest China* (Seattle: University of Washington Press, 1997), 45. Tibetan women who marry Han Chinese men usually live in (or move to) Han Chinese territory and adopt a Han Chinese lifestyle. Relatively few Han Chinese women in these rural areas marry Tibetan men, but if they do they usually move into the Tibetan community and adopt a Tibetan lifestyle (we've seen some instances of this).

25. Yan, "Xiangtu shehui," 80–81.

26. Ibid., 59.

27. Ibid., 61.

28. Zhongyuan Lüzi, excerpts from "Hua'er' zhong minjian chuanzong jiedai de xinyang," *Xibei minzu daxue xuebao*, trans. Bao Fumin (Lanzhou: Xibei minzu daxue chubanshe, 1989), 74–75; He Jiaguo, "Lianhuashan hua'er hui 'chuanbashi' jiqi chuangzuo yanjiu" (master's thesis, Lanzhou University, 2008), 13–14.

29. Ke Yang, "Taomin hua'er zhong de jisixing," in Ke Yang, *Shi yu ge de kuanghuanjie—"hua'er" yu "hua'erhui" zhi minsuxue yanjiu* (Lanzhou: Gansu renmin chubanshe, 2002), 41–45.

30. Sung by an unidentified singer at the big temple of Liushunchuan (upper village), Zhuoni, Gansu, collected by the authors, June 16, 2000.

31. Ke Yang, interview, Lanzhou, June 11, 2000.

32. Xi Huimin, *Xibei hua'er xue* (Lanzhou: Lanzhou daxue chubanshe, 1989), 108.

33. Zhao Zongfu, *Hua'er tonglun* (Xining: Qinghai renmin chubanshe, 1989), 248; Du Yaxiong, "Taomin hua'er," *Longyuan wenhua* 2 (1997): 14–20; Xi Huimin, *Hua'er xue tonglun* (Lanzhou: Lanzhou daxue chubanshe. 1989).

34. Qi, "Taomin nanlu hua'er,"184.

35. See Xi Huimin for an exorcism and rain-prayer ritual using *hua'er* and exclusively involving female performers. Xi, *Xibei hua'er*, 111.

36. Compare Cheng Qin, "Hua'er zhong de nüxing he nüxing de Hua'er" (master's thesis, Xibei minzu daxue, 2005), 21–22. The practice of foot binding may have made it difficult for Chinese women in the past to contribute extensively to outdoor work, but they often joined field labor during the critical times of planting and harvest. Joseph Trippner saw women in Qinghai in the 1930s singing *shaonian* (a regional type of *shan'ge*) while weeding. Joseph Trippner, "Die *Shaonien* in Ch'inghai," *Folklore Studies*, 1 (1952): 264–305. Field labor data collected in 1921–25 indicate that approximately one-third of all hired and family labor on Chinese farms in east central China was carried out by women in that period. In northern China it was only 11.8 percent, presumably because foot binding was more prevalent there. John L. Buck, *Chinese Farm Economy* (Chicago: University of Chicago Press, 1930): 235.

37. Ma Xiaojun, "Yidai gekui: Qiong Gamei," in *Lianhuashan geshou zhuanji (yi)* (Gansu sheng di er zhou hua'er xueshu taolunhui cailiao, mimeograph, 1982), 1.
38. Ibid., 2.
39. Ibid.
40. Ibid.
41. Ibid., 6.
42. See for instance Ke, "Taomin hua'er," 36; Trippner, "Die *Shaonien*," 268; L. Schramm, *The Monguors of the Kansu-Tibetan Frontier, Part I: Their Origin, History and Social Organization*, Transactions of the American Philosophical Society, n.s., 44, 1954, 112; Tan Shijie, "Minzhou fosi jiqi youguan wenti de tantao," *Xibei minzu xueyuan xuebao (Zhexue shehui kexue ban)* 3 (1990): 62; Ke Yang, "Hua'er Suyuan" in *Hua'er lunji* (Lanzhou: Xibei minzu daxue chubanshe, 1983): 98; "Hua'er suyuan," in Ke Yang, *Shi yu ge de kuanghuanjie—"hua'er" yu "hua'erhui" zhi minsuxue yanjiu* (Lanzhou: Gansu renmin chubanshe, 2002), 97.
43. Related to the authors by Qian Xingzhen, folk song collector in Suzhou, April 19, 1990. See also Qian Xingzhen, "Houji," in *Changpian xushi wu ge zhao shengguan (julugao)*, sung by Lu Qiaoying, edited by Li Lin (Beijing, Zhongguo minjian wenyi chubanshe, 1986), 123–24.
44. Schimmelpenninck, *Chinese Folk Song*, 92.
45. Male singer Jin Wenyin, interview, near Suzhou, May 11, 1990.
46. Male singer, quoted in Ren, *Taihu yuge*, 11.
47. Ke, *Shi yu ge*, 18.
48. Yan, "Xiangtu shehui," 102.
49. Qi, "Taomin nanlu hua'er," 187–88.
50. Qing Gaishun, interview, Lianhuashan, July 4, 2000.
51. Anon., *Geshou* (Lanzhou, mimeograph, 1981), 9.
52. Qi, "Taomin nanlu hua'er," 185.

Chapter Twelve

An Interview with Liu Sola, Composer, Singer, Visual Artist, and Novelist

Liu Sola (b. 1955, Beijing) is a composer, singer, visual artist, and novelist currently based in Beijing. She has traveled to and lived in Europe and the United States and counts the genres of reggae, folk, psychedelic rock, and blues among her musical influences. To date, she has published eight novels, one play and two chamber operas and has released eight solo albums. This interview was conducted by Shzr Ee Tan in English and Mandarin, over the phone and email from Beijing.

Being "Chinese"

I was born into a political and intellectual family, and, like many others, my parents went through a lot of political troubles. This has made me very sensitive about what being Chinese means and what position we hold in the world. The differences, similarities, and clashes between Chinese culture and other world cultures have been the inspiration behind my creations. At the same time, while I acknowledge a lot of Chinese influences in my music, it's not the main drive of my art—certainly I don't compose or sing to promote Chinese culture for its own sake! But the influences are there; it's just another part of me and my background. It's a capacity that I can draw on and use.

It's the same with what you might call foreign influences. I certainly don't reject learning new things; discovering things from beyond Chinese culture—in fact I actively seek it. I've spent quite a bit of time learning how to sing in the *yuanshengtai* (原生态 original ecological) vocal styles of many folksingers—styles that don't employ the bel canto style of vocalization. And it's not just the "original" styles of Chinese folksingers I've gone out to learn—I've learned the blues, the songs of Native Americans, people in India, and people of minority nationalities. I've learnt from Japanese people and Korean people. I've learnt *Henan bangzi* (河南梆子) and *Shaanxi bangzi* (陕西梆子). It's interesting how my experiences in musics of other cultures have led me to understand Chinese music better. For example—learning the music of black communities—I've come

Figure 12.1. Liu Sola. Photograph courtesy of Liu Sola.

to think about things that might have been taken for granted in Chinese music. I listen to singers of the older generation differently. I think about how Chinese singers use their voices from a comparative or a more objective manner.

Women's Voices, Animal Cries, and "Pure Vibration"

Sensuality and sexuality are very important in my work. I am female, I have a woman's voice. But what I am interested in is not only the sensuality of human beings. I am also interested in the transfer and transformation of energy between women and animals. You can hear examples of these in my albums *Hauntings* and *Appearances*, especially in the piece "Drunk on Images." There is a better live recording version of this piece, released in an album included in my book of essays, *Liu Sola on the Move*. This was scored music but with a lot of improvisation. The freer we get, the more sensual the music becomes.

Freedom is important. Sometimes you can say that my voice is simply pure vibration: ethnicity and gender become secondary issues. Often, I think beyond the fact that I am a woman or even that I am human; I think about how my voice can be used to create animal cries, nonhuman sounds—just noises and pure sound. Where my gender comes in is perhaps in the physicality of it all: it's a capacity and constraint I have to work with—in terms of how low or how high in pitch and volume I can go. Sometimes I don't sound like a woman because I've lowered my natural voice, because I'm deliberately working in a specific range. It doesn't fit listeners' expectations of a woman's voice. But that's only because I think of my voice as a sound-production device; I'm moving beyond male and female, beyond being human.

My music and performances obey not only "light" energy but also express "dark" energy. Always change; never stay the same; always listen to the unknown. What kind of category my music belongs to, that is not my concern; that is marketing. What I am concerned with is to always find new sounds for my ears. Female I am, Chinese I am, and these labels naturally describe me. I don't need to deny them or try to fit in. The individuality of my music is the challenge I set up for myself—how much I can do for a human voice—without relying only on language or only on singing or on improvising. Rather, I want to make the voice as sensitive, flexible, and powerful as an instrument, at the same time expressing the complication of being female; that is, of being between light and darkness. You can hear these vocal qualities in my works, such as *Flying Shadows* and *Celebration of the Darkness and Light*. Some of my old works also reflect my intentions, like in the album *China Collage*. When I write for Chinese instruments, I try very carefully to preserve the old sound by using many old Chinese materials. Thus, the wild vocal part grows from the old sound, and, thus, even the crazy vocal sounds do not really depart from tradition. It is in this way that my music develops its complex multiplicity.

From Stories to Screams and Revolutionary Songs

My vocal style depends on the musical style required and the stories involved. For example, when I sing in *The Chicken in the Country Fair*, I use a kind of pure folk style. But when I sing "Drunk on Images," I use a Chinese theatrical vocal style mixed with jazz and art-song vocal styles. When I sing my opera character in *Fantasy of the Red Queen*, I use pop, Chinese theater, jazz, revolutionary songs, screams, and anything I can think of to create the character. Very often I switch vocal styles in the middle of a sentence. Sometimes a single sentence can contain three different styles.

When I compose for film soundtracks, I don't refer to my cultural background first; rather, the story provides the direction. For example, when I composed the soundtrack to Le Yue's film *Thirteen Princess Trees*, I used a Muslim-inspired musical style for the main theme.

"I Don't Want to Blame the World"

Whether as a Chinese person or an African person; a man or a woman; a local or an immigrant, you still have to face different difficulties in life. I don't want to be caught in the position of always blaming the world. If difficulties presented by [ethnic and gender] stereotypes are imposed on me—which happens enough—I try not to make myself become bitter by thinking about them. I am a workaholic, which means I can always find something to work on. How people find something in common does not depend on where they come from. I actively seek out fellow artists and learn from them. I travel within China and go abroad, around the world, to learn how to sing. You can always collaborate with the same kind of people, but that does not mean they have to be of the same race. I don't divide people by race. The differences between cultures excite me to learn; to keep going. My many and varied life experiences make my personal history richer; they make my singing and my music more interesting. Any creator can always find something to make her work unique. Most of the time, what makes a composer unique is the subject and the angle of approach, not the ethnic or gender card.

Chapter Thirteen

Broken Voices

Ethnic Singing and Gender

Rowan Pease

The voice was the first thing that struck me about the song. In a cavernous room, mirrored disco balls hung over a dance area encircled by round tables. At the end, the singer wore a frothy ball gown, only slightly less bouffant than her hair, which was swept back high. Her backing band was overamplified and reverberant. She kindly dedicated a song to me, thinking I was a visitor from nearby Russia. It was a scene familiar in small-town nightclubs throughout China in the early 1990s. But the singing was unexpected: a direct, powerful, and husky voice that I found instantly appealing.

It was five years before I returned to Yanji,[1] capital of the Yanbian Korean autonomous prefecture in Jilin Province in northeast China, to investigate the teaching and performance of songs, professional and amateur. By then I was more familiar with South Korean styles, far more husky and emotional, so it was tempting to be snobbish about the apparent local dilution of style. Yet despite the (to me) jarring modernizations—the dogged I–V harmonies, MIDI backing, disco beat—and my resistance to the conservatories, the state institutions and media that support it, it is still a vocal sound that I viscerally enjoy and want to sing along with.

My own response to this voice was surely (but unconsciously) conditioned by a set of associations from my own musical background: its strength appealed to a feminist desire to hear women use their voices directly and powerfully.[2] Its huskiness and emotion perhaps carried the associations of authenticity that use of the so-called black voice brings to rock music.[3] Even the relatively low pitch range appealed to the prevailing vocal tastes of my peer group.[4] I had lived in Xiamen in southeast China, which was dominated by the nasal quality of *Minnan* dialect pop[5] or more mainstream Hong Kong and Taiwan pop ballads (too breathy for me), and the timbre of Yanji singing was more in line with my own preferences.

In this chapter I explore how changing notions of appropriate female vocal behavior are reflected in the professionalized "ethnic singing method" (*minzu changfa*)[6] of Korean singers working in Yanbian. After a brief introduction to the local songscape, I outline how the genres covered by ethnic singing methods have become feminized and how new demands for authenticity are reintroducing elements of apparently masculine vocality to this state-supported singing style. I focus on three generations of professional Korean folk-song and *p'ansori* (a narrative performance art combining speech, singing, and gesture and accompanied by a single drummer) performers who have passed through the Yanbian University Arts School and describe their changing use of pitch range, timbre, ornaments, and dramatic gesture. This chapter is not concerned with the Koreans as *minority* musicians in China; the exoticization of minority divas is well explored elsewhere.[7] Historical and political circumstances mean that China, North Korea, and South Korea have inevitably had varying cultural influence in the area and shaped vocal styles. The interaction of transnational, national, and local tastes is an important factor in this chapter, but this is not unique to minority musicians.

The focus on women in this chapter is due to the fact that, in Yanbian at least, professional ethnic singing is a gendered activity largely confined to women. The 215 Chinese Korean entries in the *Biographical Dictionary of Korean Musicians*[8] reflect a familiar hierarchy: only 15 percent of entries are women, and two-thirds of those women are singers.[9] Male entries are predominantly composers, and the majority of their output is songs.[10] The eleven male singers or vocal teachers that *are* listed are all bel canto singers, with the exception of long-deceased "folk artists" (*minjian yiren*) who provided much material for the anthologists of the 1950s and 1980s, including the repertories that are now performed only by women. The *Biographical Dictionary* is based mainly on membership in the musicians association and state-run cultural organs.

Outside professional circles there is greater variety. At village parties during my fieldwork, men and women all sang, the men rather more than the women, who were occupied with organizing and cooking. In parks, though, I often came across groups of picnicking women who had abandoned domestic chores for the day and would inevitably have brought a *puk* barrel drum to accompany their singing. Their repertoire was certainly not limited to "folksong" (K. *minyo*, more commonly called *t'aryŏng*); it ranged from 1930s pop and new folk songs through revolutionary songs, mass songs, North Korean songs, and South Korean "trot" pop songs. But the style of their singing was what united these songs. It owed little to the folk-song singing on television, and, when I asked what they might call their singing style, I was told, "it's the way *amae* [aunties or grannies] sing": a singing style, therefore, defined by the age, likely family role, and biological sex of the singers with which it is associated. Many of the women spoke about these songs as a release from life's difficulties, which included alcoholic and abusive husbands, errant sons, or conflicts with mothers-in-law.[11]

One "amae-style" singer, Kim Insuk, became famous and released cassettes under the nickname "Granny Swallow" (K. *Chaebi amae* or *Chaebi halmŏni*); she was famed as much for her past sufferings as a wife as for her distinctive voice. She was immensely popular but not highly regarded by the conservatory teachers, nor was she considered an exponent of ethnic singing style, although her vocal production owed far less to Western singing techniques than the folksong cassettes produced by those teachers. The conservatory's ethnic singing style likewise appeared to have little impact on these amateurs.

In contrast to folksong, pop singing in Yanbian was increasingly a male arena, according to the local Popular Singers' Association and private music schools, perhaps because of the global male dominance of rock (popular in the 1990s) and hip hop (dominant from 2000). On the state media, where more mainstream forms of pop music were promoted, men and women were equally visible. In karaoke bars most customers were men, their entertainers women (see Zheng in this volume), but karaoke singing was a universally popular activity, with TVs set up on street corners, in parks, and at many parties and restaurants. Here men and women used the *t'aryŏng* style for popular folk songs and "golden oldies" of the 1930s and 1940s (K. *hŭllogan norae*), their style partly determined by the backing tracks.

So while singing as recreation was equally popular among men and women, in the media and in professional circles, men were more likely to be associated with modern and creative domains of music, such as Western and popular music, while women represented tradition and skill as interpreters. Rather than revisit a gendering of musical domains found throughout much of the industrialized world, this essay will now turn to the question of women's voices as embodied sound.

I focus in particular in this chapter on vocal quality for several reasons: first, song is the dominant musical form in Yanbian; this was true throughout the People's Republic of China and neighboring North Korea, where the principles of socialist realism required composed music to have a recognizable ideological "content." Even as such political constraints have relaxed, song remains the principal form of global popular music: "the fact that most popular music is vocal music means that we must take account of the voice rather closely."[12] Frith furthermore reminds us that it is the *way* singers sing rather than *what* they sing that is central to their appeal: "in pop music we hear singers as *personally* expressive."[13] My previous research on pop music consumption in China indicates that it is vocal quality that most attracts fans to particular idols, before dance, physical attractiveness, image, or lyrics, despite a commonly held assumption to the contrary.[14] Vocal timbre, Barthe's "grain of the voice," is unique to each person and instantly recognizable. Yet despite individual variations, vocal timbre is often the most distinctive and recognizable characteristic of a music type. Hence, there is a discomfort when crossover artists use inappropriate vocal style (timbre, articulation, pronunciation) even if all other musical elements are correctly reproduced.[15] Vocal style is recognized as being closely allied to expressions of identity and resistant to change.[16] This is borne out by the persistence of the "auntie" vocal style used by the Yanji park singers across genres such as hymns, pop songs, revolutionary songs, and folk songs alike.

The complex interaction of biological and cultural elements in our vocal production is one key for understanding the performance of gender and sex.[17] Our voices carry information about class, race, age, gender, and indeed physical characteristics, which we wield and interpret with instantaneous and generally unconscious sophistication.[18] The physical makeup of the larynx, the vocal folds (cords), and cavities (chest, the tracheal tree, the larynx itself, the pharynx, the oral cavity, the nasal cavity, and the sinuses) that produce the voice inevitably shape its sound, yet much of what we consider to come naturally is learned. In song, this natural skill in vocal manipulation becomes a physical pleasure and performance. Through this chapter I decode the messages about gender that professional singers in Yanbian might communicate, even before the sound is shaped into words.

Vocal Quality and Gender

Despite an agreement that gender is performed, voice is one of those aspects that seem instinctively to be biologically determined: "In our common sense, we believe the voice is the body, its very breath and interior shape projected outward into the world as a way others might know us," standing "for all the imperatives we might imagine to be already implicit in a sexed body, before culture has its way with it."[19] Evidence suggests our voices are as "constructed" as any other aspect of our performed gender: even for the most oft-cited biologically determined distinctions, volume and pitch. There is no simple equivalence between register of voice and gender or even body size. Although the adult male on average has longer vocal folds and the potential for a deeper voice, the pitch range of boys is restricted long before they develop any physical differences from their sisters; even after puberty they are physically capable of speaking at the same range but choose to emphasize the lower ranges.[20] In the United Kingdom, the average pitch range for women has become similarly restricted to lower ranges; as higher voices are pejoratively assessed to be hysterical, shrill, or just stupid, women have adopted the more authoritative registers associated with the male voice.[21]

This mesh of physical and cultural attributes is reflected in the diverse vocabulary used to discuss the voice: the word itself ranges in meaning from sound through text, literary style, expression to political agency. Descriptions of diaphragms, formants, and vocal folds give us little idea of sound, while analogies such as "smoky" are vague and culture specific. The terminology used in Western singing classes, such as "head" or "chest" voices reflect where resonances may be felt but are no more scientific. I use the Chinese, and occasionally Korean, vocabulary of local singers, teachers, and researchers, who frequently draw on Western theory. This is frustrating, given the rich vocabulary of vocal styles in *p'ansori* literature in Korea, which differentiates among techniques such as "straight" voice, "head" voice, "jaw" voice, and "teeth" voice, and timbres such as "husky," "iron," "tough," "bright," "simple," "naked," "quivering," or "full-flavored."[22]

Simon Frith's 1987 discussion of voice as musical *instrument*, as direct expression of the *body*, as the sound of a *person* and of the *character* performed in song,[23] is based on Western singing idols but could be adopted to discuss the more anonymous "ethnic-style" singer. However, his discussion of the use of the effeminate male voice to convey youth is more closely linked to rock and pop.[24] Allan Moore, a musicologist who pays close attention to voice, notes that "informal discussion suggests that there are distinct differences between female and male vocal production" but declines to write about female voices. He discusses established paradigms such as "black" voice (demonstrative and communicates directly using a wide variety of intonational and embellishing techniques) and "white" voice (restrained, gesturally restricted, and *apparently* uninvolved), or "trained" (even tone, in tune, vibrato, limited embellishments) and "untrained," or "natural," voices. Again, there is space to discuss the gesturally rich and emotional performance of Korean ethnic-style singers as occupying a similar space in Chinese majority–minority relations. The untrained voice, Moore writes, signifies authenticity in rock music.[25] Also associated with authenticity is the "straining" high voice of "cock rock": the audible effort to produce this sound produced overwhelmingly in the voice and mouth, with a minimum of recourse to the resonating chambers of the chest and head, indicates naturalness.[26] Shepherd contrasts the constricted harsh voice (which he reads as reproducing the tensions encountered as males engage with the public world) with that used in pop: the "typical vocal sound of woman-as-nurturer: soft and warm, based on much more relaxed use of the vocal chords and using the resonating chambers of the chest."[27] The male head voice, however, is associated with the "'vulnerable male' who appeals for emotional nurturance" without abandoning the supremacy of traditional rationality.[28] Suzanne Cusick, by contrast, hears in rock's harsh, forced timbre a reinvention of masculinity in a new androgynous space, "closing the borders" of the body to culture.[29] She reads women's singing and men's "nonsinging" voices as audible traces of submission to or rejection of penetration of the body by culture, and she reads song as the medium to "perform the borders" where body and extraterritorial culture meet.[30] However provocative, such speculative interpretations cannot be transferred across cultures. In many aspects of its sound, the straining natural voice of a *p'ansori* singer resembles that of the rock male, but it would be facile to read it as a rejection of cultural penetration (however tempting it might be to read it as South Korea's postcolonial rejection of Japanese culture).

The general characterizations of US rock-and-pop singing style match those of Chinese mainstream popular (*tongsu* or *liuxing*) music as described by Andrew Jones, who contrasts the feminine crooning style of lyrical (*shuqing*) songs with the "'masculine,' rough tone" of energetic or hard northwest wind (*xibeifeng*) songs.[31] Jones describes the feminization of the singer, being the focus of gaze and a passive mouthpiece for texts written by others, be they political or romantic.[32] The singer is not without control, though, since such messages are undermined simply by a change of vocal timbre, as Su Zheng suggests in her discussion of rock singer Cui Jian's performance of a revolutionary ballad using a "rough, boorish voice in low range," subversive to ears accustomed to the high-pitched, hyperfeminine original.[33] Like Jones, Nimrod Baranovitch contrasts *tongsu* and rock styles, the former sung "with a sweet voice, in a restrained, soft singing style, which often includes a whisper-like delivery, and sometimes a falsetto voice," which he quotes one Chinese musicologist describing as "sissyish" (*niangniang*), the latter singing style associating "sonic roughness and high volume, and by extension also uninhibitedness, with masculinity."[34]

Jones and Baranovitch do not go into further detail about vocal styles, and perhaps it is not necessary, since the sounds they describe are familiar to anyone with a passing knowledge of contemporary popular music. The sounds of ethnic style singing are less readily open to Western interpretations. For my discussion of the singing styles variously adopted by Yanbian professionals, I consider the parameters proposed by Allan Moore for analyzing vocal style in contemporary pop music: register and range, degree of resonance, and the singer's treatment of pitch and rhythm.[35] *P'ansori* demands considerable manipulation of pitch and rhythm for expressiveness, which are central to the "way of singing." They are less open to gendered readings, although under conservatory training Western tuning has been adopted as "scientific" and hence might be considered masculine in the realm of Chinese professional music (if not rock music, *pace* Cusick).

The Sound of Namdo *Minyo* and *P'ansori*

The range of pitch,[36] timbre, and emotion in *p'ansori* and associated Namdo (southern) folk songs[37] is by any standard astonishing. The voice is supposed to resonate with energy in the lower abdomen with increased pressure on the larynx creating pharyngeal tension that characterizes the voice as hard pressed and husky.[38] *P'ansori*'s most famous chronicler, Shin Chaehyo 申在孝, in the nineteenth-century poem "Song of the *Kwangdae*"[39] ("Kwangdae ga") describes its twists and turns:

The singing voice in high register is like a boat floating with a fair wind.
Gradually changing, it's curious [like a stream], and turns around the peak and changes its way.
The lifting voice is like a lofty peak soaring.
The rolling down voice like the sound of a waterfall
Long and short, high and low, endless changes.[40]

The *p'ansori* narrator-singer gives voice to all characters and expresses a wide range of emotions in stories that range from animal fables through romances to battles and that both challenge and reinforce Confucian hierarchies, including gender hierarchies. Until the late nineteenth century, the *kwangdae* performers of *p'ansori* were all men, but throughout the twentieth century women have mastered this genre. They sing with both men's and women's voices, performing both genders and the range of vocal behaviors appropriate to them. In so doing, Park Chan suggests, they threaten male aesthetics. The idealized Korean female voice, according to Park, should sound clear and high like "a jade ball rolling on a crystal tray," as opposed to the deeply resonant ideal masculine voice that rings metallically to prove leadership and strength. A *p'ansori* singer, however, spends many years developing a husky voice that is otherwise socially unacceptable. It is a voice associated with shamans, who were stigmatized in Korean society. The female *p'ansori* singer's raspy voice is "degendered" and also "unacceptable for a 'decent' woman."[41] The rapid switching between extreme sorrow and humorous asides challenges acceptable ideas of female emotion, as do the sexual jokes that male counterparts include. Female singers find shame in opening their mouths so wide.[42] Apart from their voices, female professional vocalists were often trained in institutes called *kwŏnbŏn* as *kisaeng* (a blanket term for female entertainers for men), and so were not considered respectable.

P'ansori, Ch'anggŭk 唱据, and Korean Ethnic Singing Style in China

How was such a voice to fit into the aesthetics of China following 1949, as the state embarked on the recruitment and training of musicians to create and perform music that blended national form with socialist content? In South Korea, *p'ansori*, its staged cousin *ch'anggŭk*,[43] and associated folksong are said to express the aesthetic of *han* bitterness or suffering, and as such they have come to symbolize the nation's colonial experience. The five traditional stories that are regularly performed are Confucian fables built on traditional social hierarchies. The singing is often deeply emotional, particularly sorrowful, and audibly effortful,[44] but interspersed with humor. In North Korea such emotions were incompatible with socialist realism and were eradicated from performances, as was the timbre, as Kim Il Sung declared "it is offensive to the ears to hear a lovely girl speak in a husky voice."[45] Modern performances of folk songs and traditional opera in North Korea use a falsetto "metallic" style with an even sustained vibrato that Yanbian people described to me as bright and shiny. The use of this voice gives the impression of high pitch, even where the fundamental is not particularly high.

The musicians of Yanbian have trained in both North and South Korea, as well as in China, and in the following section I draw on interviews in which the principal vocal teachers speak of their own "middle" way that draws on influences of both. The creation of this local style began in the 1950s, with the search for local folk artists who embodied "ethnic" style. The *Jilin Annals of Chinese Narrative Singing*[46] lists the professional names of many singing *kisaeng* said to be active in Manchuria prior to liberation, but many may have returned to Korea or retired after 1945, concealing their "shameful" past. Only a few found employment as singers in the PRC. After Mao's 1956 *Talks with Music Workers*, there was a drive to "nationalize" (*minzuhua*) music throughout China: the Yanbian School of Arts, established in 1957, started a *minzu shengyue* (ethnic vocal music) course, and the Song and Dance Troupe (*gewutuan*) required all its performers to learn a Korean instrument or ethnic vocal music.[47] They recruited female singers from several areas of northeast China, all of whom had studied in Korean *kwŏnbon* training institutes for female entertainers. The three singers associated with *p'ansori* and *ch'anggŭk* were Ri Kŭmdŏk 李锦德 (b. 1918), Pak Chŏngnyŏl 朴贞烈 (1920–89) and Shin Okhwa 申玉花 (b. 1919). There was one male *p'ansori* singer, Cho Chungjo 赵钟周 (1914–93) and one *kwŏnbon*-trained singer of classical vocal genres, such as *kagok* and *sijo*, and northern (Sŏdo) folk songs, Kim Munja 金文子 (1908–67). In addition to these Chinese-Korean singers, the city government invited a singer from the North Korean *ch'anggŭk* troupe, Pang Ongnan 方玉兰. Pang stayed in Yanbian from 1959–60, teaching *ch'anggŭk*, Kyŏnggi (central) region folk songs and new folk songs (K. *shin minyo*) before returning to Pyŏngyang.

So what of the vocal qualities of the folk recruits? Ri Kŭmdŏk underwent the harrowing vocal training described by South Korean accounts,[48] to the extent of spitting up blood and using medicine made from dried dog excrement to improve the voice. She was brought to China in 1943 by her husband to join the Korean anti-Japanese revolutionaries in the Chinese Communist base area of Taihangshan 太行山, Shanxi Province. There she engaged in propaganda work but found there was little demand for her specialist repertoire: new folk songs and army songs were the vogue. In post-1949 China again she found little work in state cultural organs: "they said I had broken my voice."[49] The *Anthology of Narrative Singing—Jilin Volume*[50] is more polite, but it is clear where her voice sits in the gender divide. It describes her tone as rough and sonorous (*cuguang hongliang*), her singing breath vigorous (*baoman*), and her *yunqiang* (pitch cavity) as forceful and robust (*tingba xiongjian*) and says she is good at singing melodies in the heroic (*haomai*) Yu mode (K. *ujo*).[51] The same terms are used to describe the male singer Cho Chungjo.[52] Li was taken on as a teacher at the Yanbian Arts School, founded in 1957, but as a teacher of male performers. She only had one female singing student, Kang Shinja (see below) and did not perform with the *ch'anggŭk* troupe. I have no earlier recordings of her than the one I made myself, when she was already in poor health: in my recording her voice was certainly deeper than any of the other singers I heard, and husky but, given her age, hard to assess.

Pak Chŏngnyŏl, who had trained in Korea's eastern city of Wŏnsan from the age of eleven and who was also recruited by the Arts School, in contrast is described by the *Anthology of Narrative Singing* as having a voice that was broad and gentle, the timbre "pure and unadulterated" (*chunzheng*), with clear enunciation, her breathing full and smooth, and her use of microtones and ornaments polished, performing in a "classical Namdo province *p'ansori* flavor."[53] The recordings I have of Pak dating from the 1960s reveal a husky but not particularly raspy voice; the range was deep (C3 to C4, rising at one point to E4). Pak's melody doesn't conform to Western tuning—using the more usual microtonal lowering of the characteristic *kyemyonjo* mode. Although male and female roles, young and old, were in a similar register for singing, during passages of narration she spoke as a women in the range of A♭3 to C4, as a man, a fifth lower and with greater volume.[54]

Shin Okhwa, in contrast, had a voice that recordings reveal to be lighter than Pak's, higher in range, less timbrally varied and less ornamented. In recordings that the two made together, she plays the younger heroines (notably Ch'unhyang) to Pak's male or older female roles. The *Anthology* describes Shin's voice as bright and sweet (*mingliang tianmei*), with smooth breathing and clear diction.[55] The *Annals of Chinese Opera in Yanbian* single out her performance style in the 1950s: "Her excerpts . . . were enunciated clearly, her tone quality was sweet, her voice tender and rich, her dance movements pretty, drawing a warm response."[56] Shin was not a principal source for the folk song collectors of the *Anthology*, if only because her renditions were said to be erratic and more difficult to record.[57] Neither was she a teacher. However, she was well regarded as a beauty and an expressive performer.[58]

The contrasting careers of Ri and Shin perhaps reveal a preference for the more feminine singing style over questions of fidelity to tradition. Working together with the folk recruits, the Song and Dance Troupe embarked on a fully staged *ch'anggŭk* performance of the traditional story *Tale of Hungbo* in 1959, which led to the founding of a dedicated *ch'anggŭk* troupe in 1960, the Yanji City New Ch'anggŭk Troupe (later renamed the Yanji City New Experimental Ch'anggŭk Troupe; *Yanjishi xin changju shiyan jutuan*). Sin Okhwa was its vocal director and star performer, along with Pak. This state-supported troupe experimented with performing *ch'anggŭk* versions of new socialist Chinese operas such as *Red sisters* (*Hong jiemei* / K. *Pulgŭn chamae*), as well as the ever-popular *Song of Ch'unhyang.* Despite such revolutionary experiments, it was disbanded in 1962, and its members were reincorporated into the Quyi troupe, the Song and Dance Troupe, or back to the arts school where a *ch'anggŭk* research team was set up until 1964. This indicates an official ambivalence about supporting *p'ansori* and *ch'anggŭk,* and indeed later in the 1960s those art forms and the leaders who had supported them, were criticized for promoting ethnic nationalism through "national culture blood lineage theory" (*minzu wenhua xuetong lun*).[59]

While folk songs continued to constitute a core aspect of the Song and Dance Troupe's repertory, annals published in 1988 mention only two further *ch'anggŭk* performances, one new historical drama by the Quyi troupe in 1979 and one of the traditional Korean tale *Song of Ch'unhyang* by the Song and Dance Troupe in 1983.[60] Among the "improvements" the *Anthology of Chinese Narrative Singing* record are the introduction and increase in accompanying ensemble, incorporating Western instruments, the introduction of an offstage chorus to comment on action (removing the role of narrator) and of dance interludes. The authors state that "instead of a husky, deep and thick sound (*shaya de chongyin*), in accordance with changes in aesthetic tastes, singers now pay more attention to using a fusion of oral and head cavities for resonance, in order to raise the pitch range and create a brighter and gentler sound (*mingliang roumei*)."[61] In the following section, I introduce two important teachers of Korean ethnic style singing and compare their range and vocal timbres with those of their teachers who were from the earlier generation of traditionally trained "folk" recruits, and with those of their students.

Chŏn Hwaja 全花子 (b. 1943)

Chŏn studied at the newly formed school of arts from 1959 to 1963 and on graduating joined the staff there as a singing teacher. She made her name shortly before the Cultural Revolution as a singer of great range and versatility who could perform in either local Han Chinese or Korean ethnic styles. In 1999 she told me that she had consciously refused to "break" her voice, saying that it would limit her future performing opportunities and recalling that radio audiences of the time would praise her "voice" (lit. throat, *sangzi*) as "pretty" (*piaoliang*), "bright" (*minglang*), and "sweet" (*tian*).[62]

Chŏn's principal teacher had been Kim Munja, with whom she studied the classical sung poetic genre *sijo* and Sŏdo folk song. She also took lessons with Pang Ongnan, the North Korean *ch'anggŭk* performer, and Pak Chŏngnyŏl (of whom more below), with whom she studied *p'ansori* and Namdo folk song. Recordings and even transcriptions of Kim Munja's classical repertoire are no longer available, reportedly destroyed in the Cultural Revolution, yet Chŏn can still sing from the annotated texts she made at the time. Her rendition of Kim's *sijo* shows sophisticated timbral manipulation: holding a C4 still for twelve seconds, slowly altering its frequencies, and then introducing a wide throaty vibrato, almost like a downward yodel of a fourth that she holds for a further twelve seconds. When singing from these scores, Chŏn's range was almost entirely between C3 and D4, as it was when she recalled the singing of her mother and aunt and when she imitated contemporary South Korean traditional singers. She was rarely called upon to perform publicly in such styles and used them principally when assisting local scholars and anthologists or when studying at the South Korean National Centre for Korean Traditional Performing Arts from 1990 to 1992.

Despite this training, Chŏn became popular as a singer using a different style and register. When recalling for me her folk song performances of the 1960s, she instinctively sang a fifth higher for the Yanbian ethnic folk song style (G3 to G4) and a further fourth higher for Han Chinese folk songs and for North Korean songs (D4 to E5). Her renditions of Han Chinese folk songs use the same range as her North Korean songs but instantly sound more feminine: the diaphragm pressure supported the voice but the phonation was breathy rather than pressed, with nasal resonances and characteristic smooth bending of the notes. There was no breathiness in the North Korean style but a bel canto style with sustained ringing quality characteristic of that country's reformed folk songs.[63]

Chŏn became locally and even, briefly, nationally famous for the higher ranges of her voice. In 1975 she traveled to Beijing to perform and record as the heroine Jiang Shuiying in the Korean ethnic-style adaptation of the new revolutionary model opera *Ode to Dragon River* (*Longjiang song*).[64] Listening now, the use of Korean traditional elements seems cautious: the language, compound rhythms, *changgo* drum and twelve-stringed zither *kayagŭm*, all of which were daring coming so soon after the recent persecution of so-called blood lineage theory culture. Certainly Chŏn's singing seems to owe little to her teachers' vocal qualities. In the process of creating "model operas" (*yangbanxi*), singers of the female *dan* role of Beijing opera adapted elements of male *sheng* singing to create a more fitting and robust heroic vocal style, while maintaining a gender contrast. This included using natural rather than falsetto voice for lower and middle registers, a vocal quality that had hitherto only been acceptable for old or "treacherous" *dan*.[65] For Chŏn a reverse process took place, whereby the masculinities in her voice were ironed out to convey the vigor and fighting qualities (*zhandao xing*) of the young woman cadre. Chŏn did not belong to the Song and Dance Troupe at the time when the *Ode to Dragon River* was taken to Beijing, but since she was the only ethnic-style singer who could perform in the higher range, she was seconded to the troupe. In fact the range is not very high—it goes only up to A♭5, but Chŏn's timbre emphasizes the higher frequencies, and it rarely falls below A4. Chŏn sings at a loud volume above the orchestra, with a steady vibrato throughout, rather than using the varied ornamentations described in the *Anthology*.

Chŏn's 1984 article "A Brief Discussion of Korean Vocal Music Characteristics" starts by telling us that the Korean females are "especially soft and yielding, valuing manners and hygiene," and that their vocal sound is characterized as "clear and melodious, soft and gentle, and lovely." Such idealized images dispensed with (see Kouwenhoven and Schimmelpenninck in this volume), she continues, "Korean vocal cords' contraction tension is greater and tighter than traditional Western singing,"[66] which leads to a more pressed sound. Chŏn told me at our first meeting that she and her audiences found the timbre or "vocal color" (*yinse*) used in traditional South Korean singing ugly and unscientific, and her students were afraid it would damage their throats. However, she characterized North Korean sound as "reworked" (*jiagong*). Traditional timbre made her students unemployable within China, and so she first worked on creating a "pretty" (*piaoliang*) sound, extending their range with scales, and on producing a technique that fused the "natural" voice (*zhensheng*, sometimes called the chest register) with bel canto "head" voice techniques. She eliminated some of the raspiness of South Korean singing but maintained the diaphragm pressure, vocal tension, and ornamentation that would differentiate it from bel canto or *tongsu* (popular) singing. When teaching, she always accompanied her students, following the melody in octaves on the piano with chords (she herself learned by imitation with only a *puk* drum for rhythmic support). In the small teaching rooms, I sympathized with her pupils' efforts to be heard over Chŏn's accompaniment but realize that they thus increased their volume, maintaining the pressure of their voices.

They also learned a range of specialist vocal techniques used in traditional songs, such as falsetto for "Sae t'aryŏng," and "cloudy" singing, for long *chapka*; deep breathing for more emotional singing, such as *p'ansori*, and shallow for lyrical and new folk songs; and a wide variety of vibrato and glottal techniques.[67] It was not clear at the time whether they expected to put these to future use. Chŏn had a handful of male students who became well-known performers and teachers, including Sin Kwangho and Ch'oe Sŏngryŏng. It is worth noting that they sang with a similar timbre and in the same range as their teacher, much higher and clearer than the original folk artists recruited to the school, U Chegang and Cho Chungjo.

Kang Shinja 姜信子

It was her ability to mimic Pak Chŏngnyŏl and Shin Okhwa that won the seventeen-year-old Kang Shinja a place at the Yanbian Arts School in 1958, but much to her frustration she was assigned to the ethnic vocal department, rather than the bel canto school that she wished to join: "I basically had no idea about folk songs, and no interest in them. . . . I was jealous of the bel canto students."[68] It was only in 1984 that Kang got her wish and was sent to the Central Conservatory of Music to study bel canto for two years with Ye Peiying, which she then fused

Example 13.1. "Wŏlmae's Lament," sung by Pak Chŏngnyŏl and Kang Sinja. Transcription by author.

with ethnic singing style in her own teaching. In Yanbian, her principal teacher was Pak, although she also had lessons with Ri Kŭmdŏk, who otherwise only taught male students. Although she could imitate the sound, Kang resisted making her voice "raspy" (*ya sangzi*), instead aiming for a "bright" (*liang*) sound. The *Quyi Anthology* describes it as "thoroughly sweet, agreeable and moving," and comments approvingly on her skilled use of vibrato and other vocal ornamentation.[69] Example 13.1 contrasts the performances of Pak and

Kang of "Wŏlmae's Lament," from *The Song of Ch'unhyang*. This is a passage where Ch'unhyang's mother, a former *kisaeng* courtesan, comments on the passing of time and her own faded youth. Kang's rendition is four tones higher than Pak's, closer to equal temperament pitch, and also nearly 50 percent faster. This raising of pitch and elimination of certain microtonal vocal gestures and half-voiced notes (marked with cross-head notes) is also borne out in more extended analyses of the two singers.[70]

When we spoke, Kang's career had suffered through the neglect of *p'ansori* and the preference for modern vocal styles. Despite official support for minority nationality arts, since the onset of the Cultural Revolution she had had no chance to perform except for the collectors of the anthologies of folksong, narrative song and opera, but she continued teaching at the school of arts. Interest further decreased after opening and reform introduced pop and Western music in the 1980s and South Korean pop from 1992. In 1999 she told me, "I cry. I feel so lonely. I teach them this music. If we don't continue it, who will? The students who start at 12 or 13 can take on this attitude. Those who come in later just want to do pop and bel canto."[71] In fact, it was increased cultural exchange with South Korea that led to sporadic performances of traditional music at the end of the 1990s. In 1998 Kang arranged a performance by five of her students of *Tale of Shimch'ŏng*, a classic *p'ansori* tale about a girl who sacrifices herself so that her blind father might regain his sight. It was recorded and broadcast once on television. Rather than use her teacher's recordings. Kang chose to base this performance on a recording made by the famous South Korean singer Kim Sŏhŭi (1917–95; designated in 1964 a Human Treasure of *p'ansori*). She chose Kim because her voice, by South Korean standards and in comparison to the recordings of Pak Chŏngnyŏl, was relatively "bright" (*liang*). While Kang had learned with Pak by rote, her students were accustomed to staff notation, and so Kang transcribed the recording, using Western notation that she said was ill suited to the tonal and timbral subtleties of *p'ansori*.[72]

This performance signaled a renewed interest in more traditional styles of singing, stimulated in part by the increasing educational and cultural exchange with South Korea and by new trends within China as a whole. In the following section I discuss gendered aspects of this renewed interest.

Yuanshengtai and the Rehabilitation of Rasp

Two of Kang's students who took part in the recorded performance of the complete *Tale of Shimch'ŏng* benefited from their teacher's perseverance, as a new fashion for "primordial" voices (*yuanshengtai*, literally "original ecology" singing)[73] and increased interest in intangible cultural heritage, has encouraged the reincorporation of rasp into the Korean ethnic singing style. Pyŏn Yŏnghwa (卞英花) has become a national star in China. I saw Pyŏn several times over the years of my fieldwork, in classes and in traditional music performances for visiting South Koreans, including *Shimch'ŏng*. Like other art school students, she stretched the range of her natural voice, taking it up to E5, and in her last year at the art school she secured a job with the Central Nationalities Song and Dance Troupe (Zhongyang minzu gewutuan). From there she was selected as an entrant for the CCTV's popular Thirteenth Youth Singing Competition (*Qingnian geshou dianshi da jiangsai*) in its *yuanshengtai* category, where she eventually won the silver prize. *Yuanshengtai* was a new category of singing in twenty-first-century talent contests, designed to satisfy new demands for greater authenticity that the established, highly professionalized ethnic singing method was not meeting. Instead, the category privileged unusual vocal techniques, whether minority or Han, some of which also challenge now-established norms of gendered performance.[74]

Fans of this style seek authenticity and exoticism and frequently debate whether performers count as *yuanshengtai* rather than "conservatory style" (*xueyuan pai*), based on their perceived level of training or urbanization. The nature of the selection process alone means that many *yuanshengtai* singers have trained in conservatories and are employed by Ministry of Culture song and dance troupes. This is acknowledged by one of the show's leading judges, Tian Qing, who is director of the Intangible Culture Heritage Research Center of China and of the Music Research Institute in Beijing. In an article addressing this question, Tian is quoted that he requests only that such singers had gone to their "original source" of the music to find the "original essence of the singing" (*yuanzhi yuanwei de changfa*) and that, while adapting their performance for stage, there was no alteration in the flavor of the sound of the vocal quality itself and no adoption of Western elements.[75]

Pyŏn's vocal technique was that of the extended "natural" voice range, heavily ornamented; her performance gestures were those of the professional minority diva: gracious movements, a steady smile, the outstretched arm, and to end each piece, a slowing down, a pause, and an ending an octave higher. Although she used a microphone, the voice was forcefully projected throughout. Pyŏn performed a range of well-known folk songs, an excerpt from *Shimch'ŏng*, and, most cannily, the faux-folk theme song of the smash hit Korean historical drama *The Jewel in the Palace* (*Da zhangjin*). For the folk songs she made extensive use of a throaty vibrato, to the extent that one listener commented online about being reminded of a "multi-cylinder engine" constantly vibrating. Published reviews and online discussion often appreciatively contrasted Pyŏn's feminine appearance (often along the lines of "Korean girls are really beautiful") with the power and range of her voice:

> What was unforeseeable, and amazing, was this gentle and beautiful Korean girl, Bian Yinghua. During one song ("New Arirang"), her voice was at one moment low and deep, another moment high and sonorous, at once rough

and unrestrained, the next shrill and fine, one moment a drum, the next a bell, one moment leisurely, the next urgent, relaxed then tight, shallow then deep, blunt then brittle. Her vocal style was completely free; from the corners of her eyes to the tips of her eyebrows, her hair pin to her skirt flew out this golden voice. People said "This Bian Yinghua, her vocal range is really broad, full of unpredictable changes, with rich and varied emotions."[76]

Pyŏn's performance of the passage in *The Tale of Shimch'ŏng* contained both remorse and rejoicing, as the filial daughter Shimch'ŏng and her blind father are reunited and he recovers his sight. It includes a wide range of traditional techniques including "shouting voice style" (*hanyin changfa*)[77] and falsetto. Pyŏn was accompanied by her teacher Kang Shinja on the Korean *puk* drum and with Korean flute (*tanso*) and zither (*kayagŭm*) following the melody heterophonically. In later performances, to celebrate intangible cultural heritage, she used the slow ornamented style of *sijo* in a performance entitled "Chinyangjo" (after the name of the slow $\frac{18}{8}$ rhythmic mode used), which further emphasizes traditional vocal timbre and ornamentation and eschews ethnic singing style gestures.

Pyŏn's former classmate, Ch'oe Ryŏryŏng 崔麗玲 reached the final stages of the Fourteenth CCTV Youth Singing Competition (2010), singing in the style she had learned at the Seoul Korean National University of the Arts (Hanguk yesul chunghap hakkyo) where she obtained a master's degree in *p'ansori*. According to her competition biography, her teacher there was Ahn Sukson, the successor to Kim Sŏhŭi, upon whose performances Kang had reconstructed *The Tale of Shimch'ŏng*. Ch'oe sang excerpts from the *Song of Hungbo*, a fable about two brothers, and *Song of the Red Cliff* (*Chŏkbyŏk ka*), a military saga. Was gender in part to blame for her failure to win over audiences, even as the judges' marks were respectable? Where Pyŏn had chosen songs about loyal wives and daughters, birds and flowers, Ch'oe's themes were masculine: military strategy, fraternity, and the pursuit of wealth. Ch'oe made fewer concessions to Chinese television performing convention, addressing the drummer as much as the audience. She did not smile but was as direct with her expression as with her voice, mouth often wide open. There was more narration in her excerpt and more guttural singing. Although a finalist, she did not become a star, perhaps because audiences simply found the narration too hard to understand, as some commented afterward. Others put her failure down to keeping *too much* original flavor: however appropriate for South Korea, "she shouldn't sing like this, it's too *minzu* for people to appreciate. She should do it like Bian Yinghua last year, sing adapted style."[78]

Changing Meanings of Broken Voices

The manipulation of timbre is one of the defining characteristics of Korean traditional music, as evidenced in the raspiness of Southern Korean folk songs and *p'ansori*, the overtone-rich resonance of classical *sijo*, or elaborate ornamentation of northern region folk songs. Scholars such as Frith and Moore remind us also that in the modern world song is the dominant musical form and it is the *way* of singing that most instantly defines genre and star. It is perhaps because of this link to identity that the modernization of Korean ethnic singing in China required a drastic modification of such timbres. This modification takes on a distinctly gendered aspect, as evidenced in the terms used to describe professional singers as from the 1950s they restricted the expressive powers of their voices. There was a gradual raising of pitch and an eradication of the huskiest vocal qualities—the "broken" sound that ended Ri Kŭmdŏk's career—which were incompatible with idealized notions of feminine vocalization. The high-pressured chest voice and ornamentation, particularly glottal articulation, remain important sonic markers of Korean ethnic singing style, one that is audibly "bodied," while fused through Western vocal exercises into the falsetto range. This was further feminized in gesture and performance conventions, most obviously through the increasing rarity of professional male ethnic-style singers.

Many of the Yanbian Arts School Teachers now hold postgraduate qualifications from South Korean universities. This, alongside the growing importance of intangible cultural heritage in China, seems to indicate a growing acceptance of traditional styles of singing by professional singers on the local and national stage. While *yuanshengtai* fans nationally have embraced the more raspy style, there are clearly limits to this tolerance, linked to norms of acceptable female performing style. Locally, while pride is expressed in the achievements of *yuanshengtai* stars like Pyŏn Yŏnghwa, professional ethnic singing style is unlikely to challenge the popularity of South Korean pop styles nor impact on the amateur "aunty" style that prevails in local singing parties in Yanbian itself.

Notes

1. For Chinese-Korean personal names, I give the McCune-Reischauer romanization of the local Korean pronunciation as well as Chinese characters. I indicate Korean terms with a K. Local place names are given in pinyin only.

2. Donna Buchanan, *Performing Democracy: Bulgarian Music and Musicians in Transition* (Chicago: University of Chicago Press, 2006), 370, describes how US campus women found similar appeal in *Les voix mysteres de Bulgares*.

3. Allan Moore, *Rock: The Primary Text; Developing a Musicology of Rock* (Basingstoke, UK: Ashgate, 2001), 45.

4. Anne Karpf, *The Human Voice: The Story of a Remarkable Talent* (London: Bloomsbury, 2006).

5. Blandina Brösicke, "The Ideal of Sound in Fujian Nanyin," *Chime* 14/15 (1999/2000), 82–88, describes her difficulty in learning to sing using nasal resonance in the context of Xiamen's more classical *nanyin* genre.

6. The term *minzu* is used for minority nationality and majority Han music and might also be translated as "national." Here I use "ethnic" in order to distinguish it from *guoyue* state national music.

7. Louisa Schein, *Minority Rules: The Miao and the Feminine in China's Cultural Politics* (Durham, NC: Duke University Press, 2000); see also Kraef in this volume.

8. Kim Tŏkkyun and Kim Tŭkch'ŏng, *Chosŏn minjok ŭmakka sajŏn* (Yanji: Yŏnbyŏn taehak ch'ulp'ansa, 1998).

9. The remainder are instrumentalists and teachers, with only one listed female composer.

10. Followed by lyricists, theorists, instrumentalists, conductors, and teachers.

11. Although most songs I heard were sung by both men and women, for the beggar's song "Kaksori t'aryŏng," the women tucked their skirts into their long johns and swaggered comically like men, indicating that this song family, at least, was associated with *male* beggars. Generally men and women shared songs; in songs where people took turns singing verses (such as "Ch'um norae" or "Ŏrang t'aryŏng") the pitch stayed the same for men and women.

12. Moore, *Rock*, 44.

13. Simon Frith, *Performing Rites: Evaluating Popular Music* (Oxford: Oxford University Press, 1998), 186.

14. Rowan Pease, "Yanbian Songs: Musical Expressions of Identity amongst Chinese Koreans" (PhD diss., University of London, 2001).

15. As of 2009, attempts to produce synthesized "soul" voices, encoding race, age, and gender, has been found unsatisfactory by users. Nina Eidsheim, "Synthesizing Race: Towards an Analysis of the Performativity of Vocal Timbre," *TRANS-Transcultural Music Review* 13, no. 7 (2009).

16. Ali Jihad Racy, "Musical Aesthetics in Present-Day Cairo," *Ethnomusicology* 26, no. 3 (1982): 394, 406.

17. Judith Butler, *Gender Trouble: Feminism and the Subversion of Identity* (London: Routledge, 1990).

18. Studies by evolutionary biologists reveal that listeners could accurately assess bodily symmetry (Susan M. Hughes, Franco Dispenza and Gordon G. Gallup Jr., "Ratings of Voice Attractiveness Predict Sexual Behaviour and Body Configuration," *Evolution and Human Behaviour* 25 [2004], 295–304) and physical strength (Aaron Sell, Gregory A. Bryant, Leda Cosmides, John Tooby, Daniel Sznycer, Christopher von Rueden, Andre Krauss, and Michael Gurven, "Adaptations in Humans for Assessing Physical Strength and Fighting Ability from the Voice," *Proceedings of the Royal Society* 277, no. 1699 [2010], 3509–18) by listening to and rating vocal recordings. Sell's research was cross-cultural, worked across languages, and took account of speaker's own self-assessments of strength. Although listeners could accurately predict strength or attractiveness through vocal recordings, there were no simple correlations with vocal fold vibration rates or vocal tract length (pitch or timbre).

19. Suzanne G. Cusick, "On Musical Performances of Gender and Sex," in *Audible Traces: Gender, Identity and Music*, ed. Elaine Barkin and Lydia Hamessley (Zurich: Carciofoli verlagshaus, 1999), 29.

20. David Graddol and Joan Swann, *Gender Voices* (Oxford: Blackwell, 1989), 16–21.

21. Ibid., 38.

22. Hae-Kyung Um, "Professional Music: Vocal," in *Music of Korea*, ed. Byong Won Lee and Yong-Shik Lee (Seoul: National Centre for Korean Traditional Performing Arts, 2007), 219, 221.

23. Simon Frith, *The Sociology of Rock* (Oxford: Oxford University Press, 1987).
24. Frith, *Performing Rites*, 195.
25. Moore, *Rock*, 45–46.
26. John Shepherd, "Music and Male Hegemony," in *Music and Society: The Politics of Composition, Performance and Reception*, ed. Richard Leppert and Susan McClary (Cambridge: Cambridge University Press, 1987), 166.
27. Ibid., 167.
28. Ibid.
29. Cusick, "On Musical Performances," 35.
30. Ibid.," 30.
31. Andrew Jones, *Like a Knife: Ideology and Genre in Contemporary Chinese Music* (New York: Cornell University Press, 1992), 23.
32. Ibid., 76.
33. Su Zheng, "Redefining Yin and Yang: Transformation of Gender/Sexual Politics in Chinese Music," in *Audible Traces: Gender, Identity and Music*, ed. Elaine Barkin and Lydia Hamessley (Zurich: Carciofoli Verlagshaus, 1999), 163. To my ears, Cui's voice here is fairly melodious and in a midrange by rock standards, even compared with his contemporaries such as He Yong. Cui's performance starts on D4, Guo Lanying's on C5. For pitch names, I use the Western letter and number system, where middle C is C4, the octave below it C3, the octave above it C5. In this system 440 hz is A4.
34. Nimrod Baranovitch, *China's New Voices: Popular Music, Ethnicity, Gender, and Politics, 1978–1997* (Berkeley: University of California Press, 2003), 126.
35. Moore, *Rock*, 45.
36. Um, "Professional Music," 118, puts the range at $4\frac{1}{2}$ octaves (inc. falsetto and breathing voice, D#2 to C6) for men and $3\frac{1}{2}$ octaves for women performers.
37. These genres originated in southern Korean provinces but are now widespread. Much of the Korean population of China has its origins in the south of the peninsula, because of Japanese colonial migration programs. This music is no less indigenous to the northeastern provinces of China than music from the northern Korean provinces.
38. Chan E. Park, *Voices from the Straw Mat: Toward an Ethnography of Korean Story Singing* (Honolulu: University of Hawaii Press, 2003).
39. Kwangdae was the name given to the professional entertainers (men) who performed *p'ansori*.
40. Translated by Richard Rutt, quoted in Song Bang-song, "*Kwangdae Ka:* A Source Material for the Pánsori Tradition," *Korea Journal* 16, no. 8 (1976): 26.
41. Park, *Voices*, 228.
42. Ibid., 229.
43. A twentieth-century offshoot of *p'ansori* that uses multiple performers, stage, and props borrowed from non-Korean theater, including Chinese opera and Western drama. Its origins date back to 1902. Andrew Killick, *In Search of Korean Traditional Opera: Discourses of Ch'anggŭk* (Honolulu: University of Hawaii Press, 2010), 30.
44. Heather Willoughby, "The Sound of *Han: P'ansori*, Timbre and a Korean Ethos of Pain and Suffering," *Yearbook for Traditional Music* 32 (2000): 17.
45. Kim Il Sung, "Speech to Arts Workers: On Creating Revolutionary Literature and Arts," In *Kim Il Sung on Revolutionary Literature and Arts* (London: Africa, 1972), 167.
46. *Zhongguo quyi zhi—jilin juan* (Beijing: Xinhua, no date).
47. Pease, "Yanbian Songs," 151–57.
48. Park, *Voices*, 162–63.
49. Interview, Yanji, July 3, 1999.

50. *Zhongguo quyi yinyue jicheng—jilin juan* (Beijing: Xinhua, 2000), 1003.
51. Ibid., 1002.
52. Ibid., 1001.
53. Ibid., 1002.
54. For more on Pak, see Ning Ying, "Yanbian Chaoxianzu namdo minyo, pansuoli chuanji moshi diaocha," *Hundred Schools in Art* 5 (2008): 38–43.
55. *Zhongguo quyi yinyue*, 1001.
56. *Zhongguo quyi zhi*, 722.
57. Anonymous comments to author, 1999 and 2011.
58. Interview, Shenyang, August 21, 1999.
59. "Blood lineage theory" was used in debates about class background during the Cultural Revolution but in Yanbian at least also applied to culture that was felt to promote ethnic over state affiliation. Pease, "Yanbian Songs," 166.
60. *Zhongguo quyi zhi*, 722.
61. *Zhongguo quyi yinyue*, 871.
62. Interview, Yanji, March 28, 1997.
63. Interview, Yanji, July 21, 1999.
64. Originally a play performed in Fujian in 1964 about a drought-stricken commune diverting a river, it was developed over seven years as a model Beijing opera, given a female hero, and presented under Jiang Qing's aegis in 1971. It was then "transplanted" into various minority and regional opera forms, including Henan *Yuju*, Uyghur Opera, and northern Chinese *Pingju*. Paul Clark, *The Chinese Cultural Revolution: A History* (London: Cambridge University Press, 2008), 62–70, 75, 108. It was the last version from which the Korean language version was adapted. See also Bell Yung, "From Shajiabang to Sagabong," in *Popular Literature and the Performing Arts in the PRC 1949–1979*, ed. Bonnie MacDougall (Berkeley: University of California Press, 1984).
65. Rosemary A. Roberts, *Maoist Model Theatre: The Semiotics of Gender and Sexuality in the Chinese Cultural Revolution (1966–1976)* (Leiden: Brill, 2010), 68.
66. Chŏn Hwaja [Quan Huazi], "Jiantan Chaoxianzu minzu shengyue de tedian," *Renmin Yinyue* 10 (1984): 36.
67. Quan, *Jiantan*, 38–39.
68. Interview, Yanji, August 20, 1999.
69. *Zhongguo quyi yinyue*, 1003.
70. See, for instance Cui Liling, "Yŏnbyŏn chiyŏk p'ansori ŭi hyŏngsŏng mit chŏnsŭng kwajŏng e daehan ŭmakchŏk yŏngu" (master's thesis, Korea National University of the Arts, 2010).
71. Interview, Yanji, August 20, 1999.
72. Ibid.
73. Helen Rees, "Use and Ownership: Folk Music in the People's Republic of China," in *Music and Cultural Rights*, ed. Andrew N. Weintraub and Bell Yung (Champaign: University of Illinois Press, 2009), 58–62.
74. "Tian Qing: Yuanshengtai qianwan bu neng bianwei," *Dongfang zaobao*, June 25, 2010.
75. "Geshou jieshao: Chaoxian minyao gehou Bian Yinghua" January 30, 2007, http://yule.sohu.com/20070130/n247939862.shtml.
76. Chŏn 1984, 38.
77. Anonymous comment posted on the CCTV competition bulletin board, April 2010 (no longer available).

Chapter Fourteen

An Interview with Li Sisong, Producer and Songwriter

Li Sisong (b. 1966, Singapore) is one half of a producer-songwriter duo with his brother, Li Weisong. Together, the Lis run a talent agency in Singapore specializing in grooming pop idols. The Lis have also carved out a reputation locally as composers of hit Mandopop and Cantopop tunes. This interview was held in Li's office in Singapore and conducted by Shzr Ee Tan in Mandarin.

I've been in the music business for more than thirty years. I guess you could say some of my songs have been hits—Stefanie Sun's "Tian hei hei" (天黑黑 Dark sky), for example. The song definitely helped her launch her career, but Stefanie is somebody with a special voice, and she caught the market when it was ready for her "look"—that waif, feminine look. The song has been sung and revisited many times by both men and women. It's got lots of potential. And that's what it is—the Mandopop industry—a scene and an industry that still has a lot to go for. That's why I'm still here. Still, if you really want to be honest about it, of course I started out in this job because I wanted to pursue music, and this really is what drives me today. It hasn't always been easy, especially in the beginning. Some things change; other things don't change. The thing that never changes is that you need a lot of talent and luck—that's nothing new. These days, however, if you want to be a famous singer, you can't just rely on singing alone. You have to do everything; everything else.

A Good Voice Will Only Get You So Far

First, you need to have a good voice and be able to stay in tune! These are the basics of basics. Better still if you are an all-rounded musician—no, all-rounded *yiren* (艺人 artiste). My best artistes happen to be good songwriters too. They compose their own tunes; we help arrange and produce their music. When they write their own songs, they sing with more confidence and passion; they have their own stake in the song. It's not just about originality. And even that's not enough: you have to be able to dance well, strike poses. All this is very vital, because you have to promote yourself in an age where

MP3s are downloaded for free and in an industry where CDs are pirated in cheap markets all the time. You have to give our buyers that something "extra." You have to present yourself properly; you have to know how to talk, to come across well on TV, answer questions eloquently, know how to host an event. You have to know how to model too—that's actually a course available in our school; this is something we ask all the artistes we sign on to learn; how to walk, to move, to preen.

We opened our school in the 1990s as part of our larger portfolio of music production-related activities. It's a school for grooming new pop stars. We get a lot of teenagers—boys and girls. There are surprisingly equal numbers of boys and girls. About 30 percent come here because it's just a hobby; it's something fun to do. They come with friends and want to just sing better. But about 60 percent actually come here hoping to become a Mandopop star. They want to be the next Stefanie Sun; they want to sing a hit song that we have written for them. To be honest, it's very difficult to be a star today. About 5–10 percent of our students actually make it as professional singers or minor celebrities. Some drop out. Others still remain in the industry in some way—as production assistants or as producers. It depends.

"Sunshine" Bopper versus "Manly" Crooner

The boys who come to us mostly want to be like *that* Korean boy, Rain. Others want to be in boy bands, although it's not as fashionable these days to be in one as before, back in the days of that Taiwanese group F4. The Rain-inspired boys go for a very distinct kind of image, and it's a more recent one. It's a sunny, *yangguangxing* (阳光形) image. You sing upbeat, boppy songs, you need a voice that's easy on the ear. It's a slightly androgynous look and performance style, but at the same time it's masculine in a pretty-boy-next-door or a surfer-dude kind of way. Nothing too aggressive, but it's gentlemanly in a cool, unaffected way. These are boys who sing happy songs. They don't growl; maybe they might croon a little, but largely they're easy and light.

I suppose Rain's not the only model for our wannabe stars. There's also the manly, macho type. I'd say Andy Lau and some of the hunky Korean actors are of the latter variety. You don't have to be a bodybuilder, but you have to convey manliness in your attitude, your voice—Andy's is not that smooth, for example. You sing certain kinds of song—sentimental ballads that are more husky or songs that are more aggressive. It depends on how the artiste wants to channel his energy.

These two types have overlapping but slightly different audiences. The girls all go for the Rain type: he has access to a huge market of teenagers and also for young gay men. He's cute. But straight men don't really like him, unless they're aspirants in the Mandopop industry themselves and want to be like him. The straight men would go for the Andy Lau old-school types.

"Cutesy" Girl versus "Cool" Woman

When it comes to women, there are also different types of pop idols. It's not so much the "girly" versus the "sexy," but more of a "cutesy" versus "cool"—and slightly androgynous. Take Jolin Tsai, for example, that's the kind of image a lot of our students and artistes go for. She started off "cute-cute," in that Britney Spears way but has come into her own lately, sort of a less teenagerish version of "cute-cute." In a way it's like a female counterpart to Rain's sunny image: you sing upbeat songs, your voice is usually higher-pitched, like J-pop or Britney, and you dress cute. But while Rain is more androgynous, the Jolin Tsais are more girly.

Another type of female singer is more androgynous. I'm referring to the cool, *shuai jie* (帅姐 "handsome" sisters). I'm thinking of people like Karen Mok, Sandy Lam, even China's Super Girl winner Li Yuchun. They're a bit more androgynous but still sexy in their own way. And to be honest they're all different individually; it's hard to put them all in the same category simply because they're not the cutesy type. They dress differently; they're less "bouncy." They have distinct voices—sometimes it's very low and sexy, like Karen. Sometimes it's just manly or boyish. And the songs they sing have very distinct, otherworldly styles. These are not the kinds of women ordinary men go for.

No Sex (Bomb) Please, We're Chinese

Personally, I don't think the sex-bomb type of female really works in Mandopop. Asian audiences don't like Asian females to be too outwardly sexy; they want it to come across as less direct and more "natural." There are people like the husky-voiced Tsai Chin, but she's from a different era. The only one who gets away with the sex-bomb look and sex-bomb voice is CoCo Lee. And that's because she's from America; people here know that and make an exception for her. They let her sing according to a different standard. It's like how it's okay and even good to be like Lady Gaga if you're a white singer—a lot of our students and even I myself listen to her. But it's not okay if you're Chinese-born—it's sad, but that's the prejudice of the Mandopop industry.

Having said all this, you have to admit that in many ways, Lady Gaga is a good model to emulate. Not in terms of sexuality or the kinds of songs she sings but *how* she produces and markets herself. She's well-rounded; she writes her own songs and plays the piano even. She has a big say in how she presents herself, her clothes, the kinds of songs she sings: it's a very distinct look and style. She's also a great dancer and knows how to handle the press. That's the kind of ideal artist, no matter the style or genre. That's what I would like to find in my students and my artistes, whether they are the next Jolin Tsai or Rain.

At the end of the day, this is what counts: that all-around dedication and talent. It doesn't matter whether you are a man or woman: the same criteria for what makes a good or successful artiste apply to anyone. Of course, you have to work very hard too. If you have that and if you are a multifaceted person, you can go a long way. That's the way the Mandopop industry works—or any kind of music industry anywhere.

Mandopop in New China

Of course, Mandopop has its own quirks. It used to be a Taiwan-dominated scene, but it's expanded toward Singapore, Hong Kong, and—our biggest market potential today—China. I'm not just talking about Teresa Teng fans. I'm talking about the new crop of children and richer, younger twentysomethings in China. And China's not just a market; China today is producing newer, more interesting talents—it *is* a huge country after all. To be honest, mainland China is a special world: it used to be that listeners valued vocal quality and singing talent more than looks or dancing or presentation. But these things are changing. And we, as record producers, are also changing. There's also that huge problem of illegal downloading and piracy within China. So we have to fight back by creating something extra, whether it's fantastic dancing at a concert or a very conceptualized package and image. Luckily, China has a talent pool that matches its consumer market. In fact, we've been very busy signing on the next Rain—a boy from the north who's going to be acting and singing in China's version of *High School Musical*. We're also busy signing on the next Chinese—China—version of Jolin Tsai. And we're setting up offices in Shanghai in addition to our school in Beijing, which is already taking in students.

Chapter Fifteen

"Mother's Daughter"

Gender Narratives in Nuosu-Yi Women's Musical Expressive Forms

Olivia Kraef

> Stars in the sky, though sometimes bright and sometimes dim, always turn around the moon. Young girls on earth, though sometimes happy and sometimes sad, always think of their mothers. (Mouth-harp piece "Mother's Daughter")
>
> —Jigu Futie, *Love Song of the Yi Nationality*

Questions of Gender in Nuosu-Yi Music

In this essay I discuss issues of gender and narrative in traditional and contemporary Nuosu-Yi music. The Nuosu-Yi (hereafter, Nuosu) constitute a subgroup of the Yi ethnic group, which spreads out over Sichuan, Yunnan, Guizhou, and Guangxi Provinces. Today, around two million Nuosu live in what has become known as Liangshan Yi Autonomous Prefecture, a mountainous area in southwest Sichuan Province, and increasingly in translocal urban contexts such as Chengdu and Beijing. Until Communist takeover of the area in 1956, the Nuosu were organized in a rigid caste-clan system, branded by official ideology and Han Chinese scholars as the only slave society in feudalistic China. For centuries they were considered an unruly people with great disputes between clans over land, weapons, women, and power. Geographical seclusion and the long history of opposition toward outside influences helped to maintain a distinct people, identity, and cultural heritage.

As with other minority nationalities, traditional and "modern" Nuosu music has witnessed a national and local revival since the beginning of China's reform and opening policy in the late 1970s and early 1980s. Over the past ten years in particular, this revival has gained in momentum, as mass media, the performance industry, and local government efforts to instigate economic development in the area by means of (cultural) tourism have joined hands in promoting "Nuosu culture" both locally and nationwide. This development has not been without substantial repercussions for local Nuosu music culture and for the way local artists, and those doing research on them, reflect on their art in its dimensions of cultural meaning and transmission.

Dru Gladney and Louisa Schein have elaborated on the utilization of gendered displays of minority culture as part of China's project to reimagine itself as a nation after Maoism.[1] Especially in regards to (Miao) minority women and music, Schein has demonstrated how eroticized images of minority women on local and national stages serve as a projection screen for the satisfaction of national and mainstream culture's "orientalist-eroticist" needs.[2] These "top-down" approaches to minority culture argue that romanticized portrayals of minorities are utilized for the construction of a majority discourse and have little to do with the minorities themselves. Yet they have not provided a sufficient answer as to why minority men and women, especially at the local level, actively engage in "exotic" and "erotic" representations of themselves, nor have they provided the reasons for the persistence and perpetuation of these representations.[3] Rather than promoting orientalization and eroticization as a top-down process with minority women at its receiving end then, I follow Litzinger's argument that ethnic minorities, both "common people" as well as local and translocal elites, are actively engaging in a reappropriation and gendered representation of their own culture.

Nuosu women's music can be read as a platform for the contestation of the (often) conflicting images and narratives of gender as promoted, and created, from both within and without the Nuosu. In this chapter I describe and discuss two main genres of Nuosu music—the mouth harp and singing—which I selected on the basis of their proliferation among Nuosu women, as well as their visibility in the media and in academic research. In this discussion I look at why and how gender and, particularly, women are constructed within Nuosu music. I furthermore attempt to approach issues of aesthetics and gender taboos in traditional Nuosu music, especially in their complex relationship to academic renarration, tourist portrayals of Nuosu beauties playing the mouth harp in full attire against the background of photoshopped pastoral idylls, and "modern" Nuosu woman singers.

Nuosu Society and Gender

According to Martin Stokes, "gender boundaries cannot be separated from other social and political boundaries."[4] Yet an adequate assessment of gender in traditional societies is hard to come by since, as with the Nuosu in China, "gender roles in pre-revolutionary society were sometimes fluid."[5] This becomes more apparent when juxtaposing social phenomena such as the distinct gender differentiation and homosociality in Nuosu socializing, dress, and adornment, arranged marriage, and the persistent low schooling and literacy rates for girls and women with instances of women's elaborated social status,[6] men's and women's equal indulgence in drinking and heavy smoking, and modern-day career choices.[7]

Historical sources such as early travel diaries of Han Chinese and foreign visitors[8] to Liangshan occasionally reveal insights into gender roles and relations. Hedwig Weiss appears to have been the first woman foreigner to comment on the elevated social status of women among the Nuosu gentry she and her husband Fritz encountered in 1912.[9] Foreign researchers have made similar observations of contemporary Nuosu society, and both Western and preliberation Chinese sources note a combination of discrimination and reverence for women within traditional and contemporary Nuosu society, as epitomized by the role of the mother (mother cult).[10] Generally speaking, the status of a Nuosu woman born, raised, and married off within the rigid patriarchal social system increased in correlation to whether she bore sons, to the number of sons (and if they survived), and how much honor these sons bestowed upon the family when they reached manhood.[11] Reverence is still measurable today by the "gender-fluid" roles a woman can play in society, by the respect with which she is treated by her social environment, and in song and instrumental music.

Traits, Themes, and Transmission of Women's Music in Liangshan

As with the assessment of gender and gender relations in Nuosu society before 1956, state-led efforts at the reconstruction of traditions of women's singing and instrumental music making have proven to be quite complex and remain a work in progress. One reason is that, as with most other ethnic minority groups in China, all folk literature and musical traditions are essentially oral traditions.[12] Oral here refers to both the means of transmission and to the fact that singing and instruments are considered to fulfill "language" functions. As a popular Nuosu saying goes, "The mouth harp can speak, the moon lute can sing."[13] Oral traditions and their transmission, weakened by social and political changes in the last sixty years, such as the fierce repression of local cultures during the Cultural Revolution (1966–76),[14] have been further eroded by the influx of mass media as well as an increased academic and ideological overlayering. Beginning in the late 1970s, national attempts to alleviate the lost years instigated a string of (local) government-induced activities to reestablish and revive local folklore by means of local stagings of instrumental and sung folk music, such as in Liangshan Prefecture in 1982. This trend was also reflected in a revival of academic research[15] that dealt with different aspects of Nuosu music traditions. Since the 1990s this body of music and existing academic literature has been enjoying increased reappraisal by local government bodies and mass media productions, especially in regard to their potential for tourism and economic development in Liangshan.

Published sources often portray the mouth harp, or *hxohxo* (the common Nuosu language term)[16] as the "preferred," "traditional," and even "indispensable" instrument of (young) women.[17] A highly romanticized interpretation of this "relationship" by Bamo reads:

> Adults and children, men and women—all love the mouth-harp, and expertise with it is especially valued by Nuosu women. They often wear a mouth-harp container around their neck, so that wherever they go they can bring the sound that gladdens the heart. In the memory of every Nuosu woman, the sound curling upward from the mouth-harp, the gentle breeze ruffling the white buckwheat flowers, waving like a soft song and an easy dance in fields among endless mountains, is the magnificent image that accompanies her through life.[18]

Here the *hxohxo* is primarily portrayed as the instrument of women and clearly associated with (the bringing of) feelings of happiness. Bamo establishes a "natural" connection between women and *hxohxo* not only as expressed by the metaphoric use of nature but also by contesting that the *hxohxo* is especially valued by Nuosu women for very practical reasons: ornamentation (the harp comes in intricately crafted bamboo containers and is often attached to clothing or worn around the neck) and easy handling and transport that allowed for a ready pastime to vent matters of the heart, both in privacy and in public.[19]

Yet this cannot explain the scope and persistence of women's association with the *hxohxo*, nor does it justify the *hxohxo*'s gendering as "traditionally female."[20] While trying to find the roots of this recurrent image, I came across the saying, "When one misses one's mother one plays the mouth-harp, when missing one's father one plays the *juhlur*."[21] The mouth harp[22] and the *juhlur* (end-blown flute) are considered the oldest Nuosu instruments with a history of supposedly eight thousand years. The Nuosu language text *Gguxho*, which tells the story of the migration of the Nuosu ancestors into Liangshan,[23] states that "they carried the flute in their belt and the mouth-harp in their hands."[24] Folklore juxtaposes the tonal qualities of the *hxohxo* and the *juhlur* as resembling (and therefore symbolizing) the "voice of the mother" versus the "voice of the father."[25] This narrative eventually gendered the mouth harp as female *by nature*, and the flute as male,[26] and also supports the *hxohxo*'s association with the mother, as well as with the mother cult phenomenon.[27]

Ma relates a beautiful *hxohxo* origin myth, which highlights the instrument's significance for the mother-daughter relationship.[28] An old mother had two very gifted, virtuous daughters, whom she loved dearly. But the heavens had no mercy and both daughters died. The old mother was heartbroken, missing the girls day and night. To express her sorrow, she went and found one thick and one thin piece of bamboo, which she crafted into leaves in the shapes of the tongues and faces of her daughters. By tenderly holding them to her mouth and plucking them, she made her daughters' singing voices come back to life whenever she missed them, and they would speak to and comfort her. People soon heard of the mystical instrument and learned how to craft and play it themselves. Ma gives no reference as to the origin of this story but asserts that it explains why to this day the mouth harp is played in Liangshan when missing one's relatives or lovers.[29]

Rather than standing exclusively for feelings of happiness, as Bamo's above quote would suggest, the mouth harp in Ma's story underlines its frequent association with feelings of sadness and regret. One of my interview partners in the field, Hailai Azuo, then aged sixty, confirmed that she plays her two-leafed bamboo mouth harp when she misses her mother, whereas sadness here becomes synonymous with missing one's mother, even if not directly related to her.[30] Playing the mouth harp turns into a conversation between the player and her "mother," now symbolically represented by the mouth harp as a type of confidante,[31] which helps the player relieve pain or loneliness.[32] The two-leafed harp should not be overplayed, though, as a common belief among Nuosu women *hxohxo* players states that the energy generated by frequent playing will result in leprosy.[33] Here, the mother and music become connected to the taboo of severe illness, which may be influenced by Nuosu religious belief (animism and ancestor worship).[34]

The designation of the mouth harp as "female" or gendered via its reference to the mother is therefore limited and exclusive to tunes or feelings of regret. In this function it is equally appreciated and played by both genders. This was confirmed to me by both men and women instrumentalists in Liangshan. While doing fieldwork in Meigu County, I came across the first instance of a complete reversal of the portrayal of Nuosu women as the central virtuosos of the mouth harp. Apei Luoge contested that men used to be the primary players of the harp until the social and property reforms that began in the 1950s kept men away from home for work.[35] The male genealogy of mouth-harp players in Lama Lada (Madunaida) Village, which is considered to be the origin and hotbed of mouth-harp art in Meigu County, further supports the notion of a primarily "male" past for the *hxohxo*.[36] Hedwig Weiss's account from 1912 mentions only male players, with Weiss noting how she and her husband Fritz were "strangely moved each time one of the fierce men squats down in the circle of attentive listeners and plays a small, melodious piece on the delicate-sounding mouth harp or bamboo flute."[37] While doing field interviews and recordings with mouth-harp players in Liangshan in 1984, musicologist Zeng Suijin met more women than men players, but he considers the virtuosity of the male players to be far more distinct since men's themes were more eloquent than women's based on their broader social experience.[38] In light of the above, claims by the most famous contemporary male Nuosu mouth-harp player, Edi Rihuo, that he was ridiculed by his family and fellow villagers for playing "a woman's instrument" strike one as strange, especially considering that his initial teacher was a man.[39] My own interviews with players in Liangshan revealed that the only instance in which gender actually mattered for the mouth harp was and is in the process of its crafting: only men may make mouth harps,[40] often giving them as presents to the lady of their heart.[41]

The making and the giving both underline the mouth harp's potential for mediating gender boundaries, as in the case of communicating romantic love.[42] The instrument's "talking ability" creates a forum for young lovers to communicate their feelings for each other. Lovers are said to literally understand the personal message inherent in the other's playing of the *hxohxo*.[43] While the technical and (soft but insistent) sonic qualities of the *hxohxo* as well as its ability to speak in place of a human voice[44] can be interpreted as adhering to notions of virtue and taboo, which regulated and often limit(ed) women's verbal (and bodily) emissions, they also possess(ed) the ability to transcend cultural and gender taboos. In the latter sense, the *hxohxo* becomes a platform for the mediation of "unspeakable emotions" (love) between men and women. Perhaps the gift of the (male) crafter to the woman player is already symbolic, the making in itself being an act of giving voice, love, and ultimately life to the instrument,[45] as is the act of the woman wearing her sweetheart's present around the neck. The three (or more) leafed *hxohxo* is commonly used in courting. Contrary to the two-leafed "mother" harp, the three-leafed harp is considered to bless its player with happiness[46] and protection from evil spirits, and it may be played as often as desired. Yet mouth-harp love songs have a relatively short memory life: women *hxohxo* players I interviewed admitted that they could not remember how to play the many fancy love tunes of their youth—let alone how these had sounded—for youth had passed together with these particular feelings of love and affection, and thus had the tunes.[47]

Apart from the traditionally anchored gesture of giving (man to woman), the ways of the actual transmission of the mouth harp are not explicitly gendered. Animistic belief may account for a custom in some areas of Liangshan that entailed the cremation of a mouth harp together with its owner after death, thus preventing its inauspicious transmission. This was based on the conviction that the *hxohxo* is "possessed by demons and ghosts" (*guguai caichan*) and that one may therefore not accept it as a gift from a stranger or keep a *hxohxo* one happened to find somewhere—these actions were considered harbingers of misfortune.[48] This custom might account for the fact that so few two-leafed bamboo *hxohxo* remain in Liangshan today; they are not preserved by being passed down within a family.[49] A closer look at the ruptures in narration this custom creates by ending the life of the instrument before it can be passed down to the younger generation might open new insights into the mother-daughter-*hxohxo* relationship.

Generally, children do not learn to play the instrument before age eleven, which implies that it requires not only technical aptitude but a certain maturity of emotions (love), which is in turn connected to a sexual coming of age (puberty). Girls usually learn from their mothers, but this is not a necessary line of transmission. Hailai Bibi (also Hailai Bibimo), a popular woman *hxohxo* player from Yuexi County and now starring, like Edi Rihuo, in a (yet unfinished) documentary on the instrument,[50] claims to have learned to play the *hxohxo* from male members of the People's Liberation Army at age fifteen.[51] In an interview with the author in 2009, Didi Shiyi, male, aged thirty-eight, stated that he learned to play the harp from an older male relative. The male prerogative of making *hxohxo* is passed down from father to son or elder relative to younger descendants in a family.[52] Both older women and men players often lament that their children are unwilling or unable to learn how to play or make the instrument from them. They attribute this trend to the influx of popular music and media[53] in both rural and semirural contexts.[54] State schooling is also considered detrimental to transmission, as it requires children old enough to learn the instrument to spend most of their time in school, leaving no space for them to acquire virtuosity on the mouth harp[55] through methods such as sitting for hours next to a river trying to emulate, musically, the sound of its flow.[56]

Mother and Song: From *Amonire* to *Duhuo*

Singing is another very popular form of musical entertainment among Nuosu women. For Harrell folk songs and folk tales bear further evidence for the "affection [Nuosu] people have for their mothers."[57] The mother-daughter relationship is most apparent in two genres of traditional Nuosu songs, which were identified by early Han Chinese scholars of Nuosu music starting in the 1950s.[58] The first genre is what Chinese scholars have come to categorize as *kujiage* (wedding laments), or, in their Nuosu language expression, *lire'er*.[59] The *lire'er* are usually sung at weddings. Just before the bride is (literally) carried away by the groom's relatives in the wee hours of the wedding day, her female entourage gathers around her for a day and a night of singing. In the *lire'er* the singer vents her feelings of remorse at arranged marriage and the prospect of having to leave mother (as well as relatives and friends)—and thus "home"—to lead a harsh life with her husband's family (and her mother-in-law). Other topics of this genre include a reflection on the bride's happy childhood and the expression of gratitude and love for her parents.[60] Among the extensive repertoire of *lire'er* songs, the *amonire*[61] and the *reda*[62] are considered to be the most popular *lire'er*.

The *lire'er* are part of Liangshan's oral tradition and were passed down over generations, regardless of the specific family and social (clan) and local background of the women. They are learned by spending hours listening to one's mother and women in the immediate social environment sing and recite, and by attending weddings (before coming of age).[63] The sociocultural interpretation of these pieces varies greatly, with authors such as Ma interpreting them as testimony to the harsh married lives of Nuosu women in traditional society.[64] Others shift the emphasis from the contents to the ritual character, which these songs have achieved as part of ritual spaces (weddings).[65]

Another song tradition, whose narration bears a distinct connection to the mother figure are the *duhuo* (fire songs/singing).[66] *Duhuo* are only sung at the Torch Festival,[67] a major event among Yi groups of China,[68] and they are performed exclusively by groups of young women. The women form a circle[69] of friends and family or neighbours and select a lead singer[70] according to clarity of voice and knowledge of song lyrics. Holding onto embroidered handkerchiefs with one hand each and carrying a rattle stick in the other,[71] the women walk in a circular motion, with the lead singer singing a phrase that is recapitulated by the chorus with minor deviations (much like in a call-and-response format).[72]

The gender specificity of the *duhuo* could be linked to the aforementioned mother cult via orally transmitted festival origin myths.[73] The most popular of these honors the wit of women, in the story of how the (nameless) mother of Nuosu hero Heiti Laba saves her son's life, so that he can then save mankind from evil forces with the help of fire.[74] Zhou Bingqi and Cheng Li consider the *duhuo*, specifically the rattle stick "dance" formation and song themes, to be remnants of religious and shamanistic witch rituals, which they root in an "ancient matriarchal social order."[75] Yang Xifan offers two different gendered readings of *duhuo* origins. The first tells the story of how in ancient times the men brought home kill for the women to cook. The women gathered around the fireplace in circular fashion and then, once the food was ready, would dancingly offer it to the men. In a second version, which casts a very different light on the alleged ritual character of the rattle stick, women would dance in circular formation in the midst of a group of men. A man could touch the woman he liked, and she would beat him with the rattle stick in return. The number of times a woman was touched determined her beauty and (social) status.[76] Yang interprets the circular, female formation and accompanying display of beauty (as an aesthetic combination of virtue and physique) to have developed into modern-day versions of beauty contests, which are held as an indispensable part of (staged) Torch Festival celebrations. Ali Sega emphasizes that wedding laments have also found their way into the very broad scope of themes and contents in the *duhuo* repertoire and regularly make contemporary audiences—and himself—cry with empathy for the young woman leaving mother and home for a bitter life.[77]

While Zhou and Cheng's interpretations appear to be unfounded,[78] Yang's questionable renditions of *duhuo* origins run the risk of presenting a potentially eroticist image of Nuosu women in their relationship to music and men without taking into consideration issues of moral codex and taboo. Perhaps one factor that would speak for Yang's theory of an only recent gendering of *duhuo* is the fact that the transmission of *duhuo* is not limited to mother-daughter. Ali notes that (elderly) men and boys often know all tunes and lyrics through annual exposure to them.[79] In probably the most sincere of all sources consulted, Zeng Lingshi states that his early and extensive fieldwork has not been able to clarify the gender specificity of the *duhuo*.[80]

Love and Song: Singing the Unspeakable

Some authors counter that men suffered just as much from the custom of arranged marriage and the threat of exclusion from the clan (social death) if they dared transgress the norms.[81] The long poem or ballad *asaniu* (translated into Chinese as *wo de yaobiaomei* or, in English, "my [beloved] cousin"), which features the hopeless love of a man for the woman he may not marry, is considered an expression of this suffering. *Asaniu* is sometimes classified as part of the very diffuse category of Nuosu *shan'ge* (mountain songs) but should in fact be recognized as a separate genre.[82] Tian groups *asaniu* (or, as he transliterates it, *aran-niu*) as a discrete category of Nuosu love songs (*qing'ge*).[83] Although these are generally the domain of men, there are allegedly instances in which women may sing love songs to a man. The *qumu midi* (white Yi men), a set of tunes native to Liangshan's northern Ganluo County is sung by unmarried Nuosu women belonging to the "white Yi" or upper serf caste to the unmarried man of their heart.[84] According to Zeng this genre could only exist because Ganluo did not belong to the Nuosu heartland (Meigu County, where such songs would be unthinkable), and the local serf caste therefore enjoyed a comparatively liberal lifestyle.[85]

As a rule, both sexes can sing *asaniu* or love songs in the presence of the person their feelings are directed toward, but never in the presence of either party's elders or siblings.[86] Today, performances of *asaniu* in translocal settings, on physical stages and in the mass media, generate the curious phenomenon of elderly Nuosu women holding their ears in horror. A recent feature by *Minge Zhongguo*, Central Chinese Television's tribute to "ethnic" music in China, introduced *asaniu* songs from Leibo County in Liangshan as a love duet between a man and a woman similar to *duige*-style love songs in other Yi areas of China (Yunnan).[87] More ironically yet, while the male singer (Shen'er Apei) in this feature actually performs an *asaniu* tune popular in Meigu and Leibo counties, the tune sung by the woman (Emu Guoguo) is not at all a Nuosu love song but in fact part of the Torch Festival *duhuo* genre (as described above).

As in preliberation Nuosu society, love and marriage continue to be quite conservative today. Parents still regulate their children's (love) lives, sometimes even promising their children to each other at or before birth. In the past, deviations from arranged marriage, including love relationships between persons from different clan backgrounds, were severely punished by exclusion from a clan and even death of one or both lovers. As in other Asian languages, the Nuosu language(s) knows no word for love. Romantic love and the taboo of direct expression of emotions were often a source of great distress for both genders, who had to resort to an extensive repertoire of love tunes both sung and played (*hxohxo*) to express this sorrow or, at least metaphorically, breach the communication gap that separated them. Although the performance (and therefore transmission) of love tunes was socially exclusive, the younger generation learned these songs by (secretly) listening in on and memorizing the emotional expressions of the older. Also, weddings provided a (ritual) platform for gender mediation, as they allowed unmarried men and women to sing drinking songs to each other. In recent times such traditional spaces for mediation and transmission have been taken over and filled with different possibilities by the genre of "modern" songs and young Nuosu women stage performers.

"Modern" Nuosu Songs, Gender, and Women Performers

In many ways, Nuosu woman singer Qubi Awu and her repertoire of so-called modern ethnic songs[88] have revolutionized Yi gender taboos in Liangshan and beyond. These "orthodox minority songs"[89] usually consist of notions of romantic love but may also describe minority festivities and other customs such as drinking. The origin of "modern" songs goes back to the founding of the People's Republic of China, when a small group of Han Chinese male researchers and composers set out to map and develop the musical landscape of China. Like their colleagues in other (minority) parts of China at the time, early modern Yi song composers Guo Wanchun and Zeng Lingshi conducted extensive musical fieldwork in the area that later became designated as Liangshan Prefecture. Their compositions consisted of adaptations and reworkings of traditional songs, themes, and genres, some of which still exist in rural contexts today. They were later joined by Nuosu composers from among male propaganda personnel (Bamo Erha, Jigu Futie). Modern Yi songs formed the basis of the Liangshan Song and Dance Troupe's[90] early repertoire and of related cultural work in Liangshan.[91] During the Cultural Revolution, modern songs were generally unacceptable, as they contained merely implicit state ideology; this characteristic in turn also determined their revival with "renewed vigor" after the reform and opening policies.[92] Over the past ten years Nuosu modern[93] and traditional songs have increasingly overlapped, with the former fundamentally impacting on the latter to the extent that distinctions between them are increasingly difficult to make.

The aesthetics created by the fathers of modern Yi song added a different and visually stimulating narrative format to that of the original mother-daughter mode of musical transmission. Especially with the reform and opening policies in the early 1980s, the Liangshan Song and Dance Troupe became a route for young talented women performers out of semirural socialization. Their parents were liberated peasants and early-day academics (*zhishi fenzi*), who had been among the first to receive state or military schooling and who came to constitute the first generation of government officials in Liangshan after 1956. They raised their children in almost exclusively Chinese-speaking environments and with minimal exposure to traditional (rural) culture. Born in 1959, singer Qubi Awu was one of these children. She developed a love for singing at an early age while listening to her father(!) playing the moon lute and attained his support of her talent and early career.[94] In 1980 she joined the troupe to pursue a career on China's and international stages. She benefited directly from the new policies and directions of the local minority cultural industry and became representative of a type of new Nuosu stage presence. As part of the wave of Nuosu cultural personnel's migration to China's large city centers, Qubi Awu graduated from Tianjin Conservatory of Music in 1982. She then began a career with the Central Ethnic Song and Dance Ensemble in Beijing, with which she has been affiliated ever since.

Qubi Awu, ever young and ever smiling and always clad in glittery stage versions of Yi women's attire, has achieved nationwide fame with her performances of popular songs such as "Guest from Afar, Please Stay a While."[95] This new image of (the young) Nuosu woman as the hospitable girl offering glasses of goodness to rare visitors completely overturned the conservative image of a, literally, buttoned-down Nuosu femininity. The immense popularity it generated among both the Chinese public and Yi groups ironically earned Qubi Awu a collection of "a thousand different Yi women's outfits."[96] Interpreted in light of this custom, she is regarded as both the continuation of a (traditional) line of transmission, as well as a means to maintain and promote Nuosu identity to China, Liangshan, and beyond.

The medium of modern song, its themes and performance space, substantially facilitated the process of revolutionizing the notion of Nuosu women performers such as Qubi Awu. The compositions of Guo Wanchun and others moved women solo performers to center stage and thus lastingly shifted the boundaries of the socially and culturally acceptable. Instrumental and choral accompaniment, atypical in traditional Nuosu music, highlighted the break with former taboos and customs inherent in traditional song aesthetics. For many Nuosu today—performers, mass-media consumers and Karaoke-goers alike—the allure of modern songs lies in their comparative simplicity and their lightheartedness but certainly also in the charisma of their performers and the fact that they have built a bridge back to their original cultural environment. In this sense Qubi Awu can be considered the "mother" of Nuosu modern song, a role that explains her growing entourage of Nuosu female singers. Sudu Aluo and more recently Jimu Xi'er,[97] Emu Guoguo, and also Guizhou Yi songstress Alu Azhuo have emulated and adapted Qubi Awu's light, enticing style and even parts of her repertoire. Qubi Awu's mothering of Nuosu music also entails a recent appearance in a joint piece with Nuosu (pop) singers. Written by renowned Nuosu singer-songwriter Qubi Habu of the boy group Yiren Zhizao (E Maker) and first recorded for a promotional, government-sponsored CD of Yunnan's Ninglang County (2009), "Yi Hometown Ballad" (Yixiangyao) features a strikingly beautiful mother figure, Qubi Awu, as she engages in a moving Nuosu language dialogue with her fictitious little daughter in an ode to the education of children in Liangshan.[98]

Such mothering of Nuosu (and Yi) pop is as much a product of Qubi Awu's success and popularity as it signifies the conjunction with Nuosu men's artistic reverence for their mothers. In the early 1990s Jike Qubu, one of the "fathers" of Nuosu pop and later frontman of boy group Shanying Zuhe (Mountain Eagle), acquired Liangshan-wide fame with his solo hit "Missing Mother" (Xiang Mama). Yiren Zhizao's hit "Mother" (Mama) (2000), a "pop song about missing mother," not only brought "tears to the eyes of educated or village Nuosu who hear it on boom boxes or play it on car and bus tape decks,"[99] but in fact to an entire host of CCTV personnel and nationwide audiences. For Harrell, songs like "Mama" are evidence of the persistence of a mother cult.[100] It could also be argued, though, that as far as Qubi Awu's mother appearance in "Yixiangyao" is concerned, the image of the Nuosu mother has become tainted, and denatured, by its reappropriation for ideological purposes, namely nine-year compulsory education in Liangshan.

Arguably the downside of this new, positive image of the young Nuosu woman singer is that of a woman who encourages her audience to employ her as a projection screen for sexual and cultural fantasies. Yet this "new tradition" of Qubi Awu-style solo women singers has managed to further expand the possibilities for transcending gender taboos in Nuosu music making and music appreciation, both televised and karaoke. It is because of the efforts of singers like Jimu Xi'er that *asaniu*, formerly a private and almost exclusively male prerogative, has become a tremendously popular karaoke female-male duet in and beyond Liangshan.[101] Much like the *hxohxo*, such reworked songs become "an arena for pushing back boundaries, exploring the border zones that separate male from female."[102] According to my own observations in the field, and in light of feelings of relief and release that explain the enormous popularity of karaoke in China today, collective singing and dancing to *asaniu*, or the belting out of its duet karaoke version, can act as a type of emotional emancipation in the context of quotidian Nuosu life, regardless of semirural or urban contexts.

A Mother Lost, a Mother Found?

Based on my field interviews and sources cited, I argue that Nuosu women's music, past and present, sung and played, neither represents a type of monolithic oeuvre reflecting female experience nor bears a one-to-one correlation between gender and music, such as in specific categories, instruments, or performance modes. Rather, it accommodates ambiguities as they exist within gender relations in traditional and contemporary Nuosu society. These ambiguities in turn offer spaces of meaning that allow for a transcending of social boundaries and taboos, which are irreconcilable in daily life, and thus enhance communication of feelings and a type of gender equality in artistic expression.

As part of local tourist and economic development, not to mention the drive for the inclusion of local heritage in China's list of intangible cultural heritage items, the reappropriation of traditional Nuosu music has been increasingly subject to a gendered renarration by cultural elites. This renarration goes hand in hand with measures and projects designed to "protect" (*baohu*) and "develop" (*wajue, fazhan*) the musical genre at stake. Ironically, these measures often contribute to eroding local music culture and lines of transmission as they are being reflected back into rural and semirural Nuosu settings, where they join forces with the influx of mass media and migration. Efforts to utilize the *duhuo* for the development of local tourism have thus led to an emphasis on their (disputed) gender specificity and thence to eroticised beauty competitions.[103] The *hxohxo*, too, has been undergoing rapid reinterpretation for public purposes, a trend perhaps best illustrated by an unfinished documentary *Lost Mouth Chord*, by Jike Qubu. According to Qubu the aim is to keep the instrumental spirit and tradition of the *hxohxo* alive.[104] So far, though, related materials tell a metanarrative, which reproduces rather than questions stereotypical representations of the mouth harp as the instrument of Nuosu women, and thus supports a silencing of the instrument through a shift in emphasis from voice to accessory.[105]

Similarly, narratives, mass media, and economic development work together in the interruption of modes of musical transmission. Young Nuosu women find themselves (s)exposed to conflicting notions of virtue (beauty) and gender as they are caught between the mother as the institutionalized keeper of a gendered musical narrative and the influx of tourist and mass media images, such as karaoke's favorite, Britney Spears, and commercial beauty contests. The dominance of the transmission of music and female virtue as personified by the mother are thus increasingly contested in relation to professional female role models and cultural figureheads promoted through the media, which are triggering a process that might be termed a de-mothering of traditional Nuosu women's music. Singers like Qubi Awu have developed a public platform on which state and Han Chinese eroticism[105] merge with (new) intraethnic narratives of music, gender, and culture, entailing the construction of a new type of essentially positive Nuosu female aesthetic, albeit an increasingly verbal and visually salacious one.

Yet despite the ambivalence of gendered images and messages promoted by modern songs, postreform Nuosu women solo performers and mass-media images have also advanced a further loosening of gender taboos in Nuosu society. The secret of their success lies not only, as they superficially suggest, in their eroticist-orientalist appeal to national and Yi audiences but in the ways they connect (back) into traditional concepts of gender and music in a Nuosu (Yi) socio-cultural context. Rather than viewing the current state of affairs as the beginning of the end to women's musical transmission in Liangshan, a new type of gendered musical lore as the sum of media images, narratives, and traditional genres could—its sexist, ideological, and artificial aspects notwithstanding—possibly bear the potential of weaving Nuosu women's semirural and urban musical expressions into more sustainable life patterns, precisely because this lore is increasingly translocal and transmedial by nature.

Notes

Epigraph: Jigu Futie, *Love Song of the Yi Nationality*, performed by the Song and Dance Troupe of the Yi Nationality, Liangshan Autonomous Prefecture, HUGO Productions (HK) Ltd., HRP 7178-2, 1998, CD.

1. Dru Gladney, "Representing Nationality in China: Refiguring Majority/Minority Identities," *Journal of Asian Studies* 53, no. 1 (1994): 92–123; Louisa Schein, "Gender and Internal Orientalism in China," *Modern China*, 23, no. 1 (1997): 69–98; Schein, *Minority Rules: The Miao and the Feminine in China's Cultural Politics* (Durham, NC: Duke University Press, 2000); and Ralph Litzinger, "Tradition and the Gender of Civility," in *Chinese Femininities, Chinese Masculinities: A Reader*, ed. Susan Brownell and Wasserstrom (Berkeley: University of California Press, 2002), 415.

2. Schein, "Gender and Internal Orientalism," 69–98; Schein, *Minority Rules*.

3. Litzinger, "Tradition and the Gender of Civility," 416.

4. Martin Stokes, "Introduction: Ethnicity, Identity and Music," in *Ethnicity, Identity and Music: The Musical Construction of Place*, ed. Martin Stokes (Oxford: Berg, 1994), 22.

5. Stevan Harrell, *Ways of Being Ethnic in Southwest China* (Seattle: University of Washington Press, 2001), 99.

6. Certain offices of high social status, such as *ndeggu* (judge or mediator) and *ssakuo* (brave warrior), were often held by women. Harrell, *Ways of Being Ethnic in Southwest China*, 96–97, 99. Yet this may only apply to women who have given birth to sons. Moreover, women can act as spiritual mediums (*moni*).

7. See Harrell, *Ways of Being Ethnic in Southwest China*, on Nuosu women with PhDs. On Yi (Nuosu) women's intellectual migration, see Olivia Kraef, "Yi Frauen in Peking— Zu Problemen Ethnischer und Weiblicher Identität im Kontext der chinesischen Reformpolitik" (master's thesis, Freie Universität Berlin, 2003).

8. Hedwig Weiss, "Von O Pien Ting nach Ma Pien Ting durchs Lololand," in *Chinas Volk der grossen kühlen Berge—Die Yi gestern und heute*, ed. Thomas Heberer and Anja-Desirée Senz (Duisburg, Germany: Kultur- und Stadthistorisches Museum Duisburg, 2006), 20–33. Also mentioned in Harrell, *Ways of Being Ethnic in Southwest China*, 99.

9. Weiss, "Von O Pien Ting," 20–33.

10. Harrell, *Ways of Being Ethnic in Southwest China*, 99. Ma Linying, *Yizu funü wenhua* (Chengdu: Sichuan Minzu Chubanshe, 1995), 23; Kraef, "Yi Frauen in Peking," 106–7.

11. If a woman conceived only daughters, the husband was entitled to divorce or marry a second wife. Ma, *Yizu funü wenhua*, 22.

12. The first Chinese musical notations for the Nuosu were produced around the mid-1950s, primarily by Zeng Lingshi and other Han Chinese music researchers in the area. Zeng Lingshi, interview, December 2009, Chengdu. The Nuosu possess their own ancient complex character writing system, but this was used primarily for religious purposes (*Bimo* priest scriptures).

13. "Kouxian hui shuohua; yueqin hui changge." See, e.g., Luo Qu and Li Wenhua, *Yizu minjian wenyi gailun* (Chengdu: Bashu Shushe Chubanshe, 2001), 383; Bamo Qubumo, "Musical Instruments," in *Mountain Patterns: The Survival of Nuosu Culture*, ed. Stevan Harrell, Bamo Qubumo, and Ma Erzi (Seattle: University of Washington Press, 2000), 47; Lu Xue, "Qiantan Yizu kouxian," in *Liangshan Yizu wenhua yishu yanjiu*, ed. Wei Anduo (Chengdu: Sichuan Minzu Chubanshe, 2004), 645; cf. Zeng Suijin, "Liangshan Yizu kouxian yinyue de fenlei jiqi tedian," *Zhongyang Yinyue Xueyuan Xuebao*, no. 3 (1987): 20–25.

14. Field evidence suggests that the Cultural Revolution impacted the transmission and narration of folk arts, but some contest this theory: Dajiu Shibu, interview, October 2009, Xichang; Zeng Lingshi, interview, December 2009, Chengdu.

15. See, e.g., Zeng, "Liangshan Yizu kouxian yinyue de fenlei jiqi tedian"; and Zeng Suijin, "Kouxian de kexue jiazhi," *Yinyue Yanjiu*, no. 1 (1987): 101–3.

16. *Hxohxo* is the traditional name in the Ynuo and Shynra dialects of the Nuosu of Liangshan. In contrast, the mouth harp of Butuo County in southern Liangshan bears a different name, which is unique to the Adu dialect of the Nuosu.

17. Bamo, "Musical Instruments," 46–50; Ma, *Yizu funü wenhua*, 155–57; Zeng Ming, Luo Qu, Aniu Shiri and Jilang Wuye, *Da Liangshan Meigu Yizu minjian yishu yanjiu* (Chengdu; Sichuan Minzu Chubanshe, 2004): 366; Jike Qubu interview, February 2010, Xichang.

18. Bamo, "Musical Instruments," 47.

19. Ibid.

20. Ibid.

21. Zeng Lingshi, interview, December 2009, Chengdu. For a complete reversal of the usual order, see Bamo, "Musical Instruments," 46. See also Lu, "Qiantan Yizu kouxian,"645: "The mouth-harp is the voice of the girl's heart; the flute is the companion of the young man."

22. Also known around the world as Jew's or jaw harp, Ozark harp, trump.

23. *Nimu*, or *nuosu muddi* (land of the Nuosu), in local languages; Stevan Harrell, "Introduction," in *Mountain Patterns*, ed. Harrell, Bawo, and Ma, 3.

24. Bamo, "Musical Instruments," 48; confirmed by Zeng Lingshi, interview, December 2009, Chengdu.

25. Zeng Lingshi, interview, December 2009, Chengdu.

26. Zeng Lingshi, interview, December 2009, Chengdu, my emphasis. Bamo, "Musical Instruments," 48.

27. Harrell, *Ways of Being Ethnic*, 99.
28. Ma, *Yizu funü wenhua*, 158.
29. Ibid., 158.
30. Hailai Azuo and Qumu Mama, interview, March 2010, Bapu Town, Meigu County.
31. Compare Ma, *Yizu funü wenhua*, 156–57.
32. Qumu Mama, interview, March 2010, Bapu Town, Meigu County. I have not heard this theory from the male instrumentalists and experts interviewed so far, although male musician Edi Rihuo indirectly confirms this view through the "mother" tunes on his first album, which he plays on the two-leafed harp (bamboo and copper). Edi Rihuo, *Feiyang de kouxian: Lingting laizi wode xinxuan jidang* (Sichuan Wenyi Yinxiang Chubanshe, 2004).
33. Hailai Azuo, interview, March 2010, Bapu Town, Meigu County. Ma, *Yizu funü wenhua*, 157, refers to the connection between "overplaying" and leprosy but merely states that this is a belief common to Jinyang County, which borders on Meigu.
34. Despite the fact that leprosy is curable now, it remains a taboo and irreversible social stigma in Nuosu society.
35. Apei Luoge with Hailai Azuo and Qumu Mama, interview, March 2010, Bapu Town, Meigu County. A similar development can be traced with a "newer" instrument in Liangshan, the moon lute (*yueqin*), which used to be exclusively played by men. It was "revolutionized" by Shama Wuzhi, who (as part of the Liangshan Song and Dance Troupe) became the first professional Nuosu woman moon lute player on Chinese and international stages in the 1950s. See Bamo, "Musical Instruments," 46.
36. Jiniu Muguo, "Qiantan Liangshan meiguxian de gulao minge yueqi yuequ," in *Liangshan Yizu wenhua yishu yanjiu*, ed. Wei Anduo (Chengdu: Sichuan Minzu Chubanshe, 2004), 623; Didi Shiyi, interview, December 2009, Bapu Town, Meigu County.
37. Author's translation from the German in Weiss, "Von O Pien Ting," 30.
38. Zeng Suijin, interview, September 2010, Beijing.
39. Longyue Wenhua, *Lost Mouth Chord*, media booklet.
40. Apei Luoge, interview, March 2010, Bapu Town, Meigu County. Dajiu Shibu, interview, October 2009, Xichang.
41. Lu, "Qiantan Yizu kouxian," 644.
42. For example, Ma, *Yizu funü wenhua*, 156; Jiniu, "Qiantan Liangshan meiguxian de gulao minge yueqi yuequ," 623. This custom is similar to Hmong courting in southwest China and Vietnam, as well as in Indonesia. See Marcy Paulson, "Vietnamese Mouth Harps versus European Jew's Harps," February 27, 2010, http://suite101.com/article/vietnamese-mouth-harps-vs-european-jews-harps-a207279; Michael Wright, "The Jews Harp, the Fool of Instruments: A Personal View," *The Living Tradition*, accessed June 25, 2012, www.folkmusic.net/htmfiles/inart545.htm.
43. Dajiu Shibu, interview, October 2009, Xichang; Zeng Suijin, interview, September 2010, Beijing.
44. Angela Impey, "Sounding Place in the Western Maputa Borderlands," *Journal of the Musical Arts in Africa* 3 (2006): 55–79. Also Paulson, "Vietnamese Mouth Harps."
45. For the act of giving the mouth harp from men to women in Swaziland, compare Impey, "Sounding Place," 65.
46. Didi Shiyi, interview, December 2009, Bapu Town, Meigu County; Hailai Azuo and Qumu Mama, interview, March 2010, Bapu Town, Meigu County.
47. Hailai Azuo and Qumu Mama, interview, March 2010, Bapu Town, Meigu County.
48. Ma, *Yizu funü wenhua*, 157.
49. Hailai Azuo (and Qumu Mama), interview, March 2010, Bapu Town, Meigu County.

50. Jike Qubu, *The Lost Mouth Chord*, unfinished documentary. Preparatory interviews, which were conducted by Jike Qubu and Luohong Muguo for the documentary, can be found online at http://www.56.com/w51/play_album-aid-5764659_vid-MzI2NTk4NDc.html (posted April 12, 2008, by www.56.com user Zhongguo Yizu MTV Wang).
51. Longyue Wenhua, *Lost Mouth Chord*.
52. Jike Qubu, interview, February 2010, Xichang; affirmed by Didi Shiyi, mouth-harp player from Lama Lada Village, Meigu County, interview, December 2009, Bapu Town, Meigu County.
53. Bum Tsering and Gerald Roche, "The Plateau Music Project: Grass-Roots Cultural Preservation on the Tibetan Plateau," www.scribd.com/doc/37276498/Plateau-Music-Project-English. On the ambivalence of the impact of mass media, see Oskar Elschek, "The Dual Role of Mass Media in Traditional Music Cultures," in *World Music, Musics of the World: Aspects of Documentation, Mass Media and Acculturation*, ed. Max Peter Baumann (Wilhelmshaven: Noetzel, 1992), 37–54. On language loss and modernity as major factors in the loss of Sibe musical traditions, see Rachel Harris, *Singing the Village: Music, Memory and Ritual among the Sibe of Xinjiang* (Oxford: Oxford University Press, 2004), 173–74.
54. Impey, "Sounding Place," 65, attributes the loss of popularity of the mouth harp in southern Africa to the popularization of radio and cassette players.
55. Hailai Azuo and Qumu Mama, interview, March 2010, Bapu Town, Meigu County; Didi Shiyi, interview, December 2009, Bapu Town, Meigu County; Dajiu Shibu, interview, October 2009, Xichang.
56. Maji Shizi, interview, December 2009, Meigu County. Compare notions in other cultures that rivers relate to a spiritual mapping of physical space: Impey, "Sounding Place"; Carole Pegg, *Mongolian Music, Dance and Oral Narrative: Performing Diverse Identities* (Seattle: University of Washington Press, 2001), 97–98; and discussion of the timbral and spiritual qualities of the Jew's harp: Theodore Levin and Valentina Süzükei, *Where Rivers and Mountains Sing: Sound, Music and Nomadism in Tuva and Beyond* (Bloomington: Indiana University Press, 2006).
57. Harrell, *Ways of Being Ethnic*, 99.
58. Note that neither the criteria for these categorizations nor their use is standardized in Chinese and Nuosu research. For a critical appraisal of issues in Chinese music categorization and classification, see, e.g., Yang Mu, "Academic Ignorance or Political Taboo? Some Issues in China's Study of Its Folk Song Culture," *Ethnomusicology*, 38, no. 2 (1994): 303–20.
59. See Zeng Lingshi, "Sichuan Yizu minjian gequ shulüe," in *Sichuan sheng minzu minjian yinyue yanjiu wenji*, ed. Zhu Jiaqi (Beijing: Dazhong Wenyi Chubanshe, 2008), 305–10; Tian Liantao, ed., *Zhongguo shaoshu minzu chuantong yinyue* (Beijing: Zhongyang Minzu Daxue Chubanshe, 2001), volume 2, 777. Zeng and Tian conceive the *lire'er* as part of the broader category of weddings songs.
60. Zeng, "Sichuan Yizu," 306.
61. Luo and Li, *Yizu minjian wenyi gailun*, 341–42. These songs are also transliterated as *amolire*; see Zeng, "Sichuan Yizu," 306; and Tian, *Zhongguo shaoshu minzu chuantong yinyue*, 777. Tian, 784, and Ma, *Yizu funü wenhua*, 154, also mention *ayi-azhi* songs (transliterated as *ayou-azhi* in Tian), which, as Ma states, are not as old as the *amonire* songs and broach women's (often imaginary) escape from arranged marriage and the trials and sad end (death) this deviation from social norms often entailed.
62. The Chinese translation generally offered for both types of songs is *mama de nü'er* (mother's daughter). According to Zeng, "Sichuan Yizu," 306, the most pertinent

difference between *amonire* and *reda* is that the latter are limited to weddings, whereas the former can also be sung in other unspecified social contexts.

63. Qumu Mama, interview, March 2010, Bapu Town, Meigu County.

64. Ma, *Yizu funü wenhua*, 154.

65. Luo and Li, *Yizu minjian wenyi gailun*, 311.

66. Zeng Lingshi, "Yizu 'duhuo' ge de wenhua he yinyue tezheng," in *Sichuansheng minzu minjian yinyue yanjiu wenji*, ed. Sichuansheng Yinyuejia Xiehui (Chengdu: Dazhong Wenyi Chubanshe, 2008), 385–92; Zhu Wenxu, *Yizu huobajie* (Chengdu: Sichuan Minzu Chubanshe, 1999), 240, 247. See also Ali Sega and Emu Shama, "Duoluohe he zehe," in *Huowu liangshan*, ed. Shen Luqing and Gan Jianrong (Xichang: Liangshan Tourist Bureau & Liangshan Television, 2006), 86; Zeng, "Sichuan Yizu," 307–8. On the question of misleading terminology, see Zeng Lingshi, "Liangshan butuoba Yizu 'duhuo' de gaishu," *Zhongguo Yinyue Nianjian* (1991): 227.

67. See also Pu Yongguang, *Sichuan Liangshan Yizu chuantong wudao yanjiu* (Beijing: Minzu Chubanshe, 2005), 71.

68. See Ali and Emu, "Duoluohe he zehe," 85–89. In Liangshan the festival is only celebrated in Suondi- and Adu-speaking areas. Research in the early 1990s showed that the larger part of these songs now exist only in written or recorded form.

69. Usually comprising twenty to thirty but sometimes up to several hundred women. Many such circles may be ongoing simultaneously. Zeng, "Liangshan butuoba," 227.

70. Or *hemu* in Nuosu vernacular. See Zeng, "Sichuan Yizu," 307.

71. Zeng, "Liangshan butuoba," 227. In the early nineteenth century, it was permanently replaced by a yellow umbrella. See also Zeng, "Yizu 'duhuo' ge," 386–87; Pu, *Sichuan Liangshan Yizu*, 73–74.

72. This type of antiphonal singing is as extraordinary in Nuosu music as choral singing, as both are generally taboo; see Luo Muge, "Liangshan Yizu minjian gequ chusuo," in *Liangshan Yizu wenhua yishu yanjiu*, ed. Wei Anduo (Chengdu: Sichuan Minzu Chubanshe, 2004), 606.

73. The origins of the festival remain unclear. See for example Zhu, *Yizu huobajie*, 2.

74. See Shen and Gan, *Huowu Liangshan*, 48, for a complete version.

75. Zhou Bingqi and Cheng Li, "'Zang Yi Zoulang' minzu yinyue yichan jiqi baohu yanjiu," *Yunnan Shehui Kexue*, no. 2 (2007): 109–12.

76. Yang Xifan, *Zang Yi Zoulang de yuewu wenhua yanjiu* (Beijing: Minzu Chubanshe, 2009), 183. Yang contests the supposition that these stories originate from a "folk" background, but without offering references.

77. Ali and Emu, "Duoluohe he zehe," 88. Cf. Zeng, "Yizu 'duhuo' ge," 388.

78. Zhou and Cheng, "Zang Yi Zoulang."

79. Ali and Emu, "Duoluohe he zehe," 85.

80. Zeng, "Liangshan butuoba," 227. Compare also Zeng, "Yizu 'duhuo' ge," 386–87.

81. Luo and Li, *Yizu minjian wenyi gailun*, 311.

82. Zeng Lingshi, telephone interview, April 2010, China. Its popularity with experts of Nuosu songs notwithstanding, the s*han'ge* category remains contested.

83. Tian, *Zhongguo shaoshu minzu chuantong yinyue*, 786. *Asa* or *aran* is the Nuosu term for "female cousin." Tian notes that the term *asaniu* has come to signify a whole genre of Nuosu love songs, thus commonly replacing the Nuosu umbrella term for "love songs," *guzhuhe*.

84. Zeng Lingshi, interview, December 2009, Chengdu.

85. Zeng Lingshi, interview, December 2009, Chengdu. Nuosu male pop singer Aojie Age, interview, April 2010, Beijing, confirmed the existence (of a separate category) of

love songs sung by Nuosu women but said that these constituted a much smaller number than those generally sung by men.

86. Tian, *Zhongguo shaoshu minzu chuantong yinyue*, 786. Zeng Lingshi, telephone interview, April 2010, China, notes that issues of gender in Nuosu love songs remain difficult to assess as research on these remains at best sketchy: Luo and Li, *Yizu minjian wenyi gailun*, 274.

87. "Fenghua Guoyue. HD. Areniu. Yizu Gaoqiang Minge Qinge," posted by Tudou user Wasiqu on March 4, 2011, http://www.tudou.com/programs/view/TV0PdSI9Bpw/. Original video by China Central Television, "Fenghua Guoyue" program: http://cctv.cntv.cn/lm/fenghuaguoyue/, accessed February 7, 2013.

88. Nimrod Baranovitch, "Between Alterity and Identity: New Voices of Minority People in China," *Modern China* 27, no. 3 (2001): 366.

89. Ibid.

90. Established in 1956.

91. Tian Liantao, interview, November 2009, Beijing; Zeng Lingshi, interview, December 2009, Chengdu; Guo Wanchun, interview, December 2009, Chengdu.

92. Baranovitch, "Between Alterity and Identity," 366.

93. Now increasingly by younger, ethnically Nuosu male composers with a background in propaganda work, such as Bamo Erha and Jigu Futie.

94. Qubi Awu, interview, March 2002, Beijing. See also "Qubi Awu: Yueliang de nü'er," posted November 30, 2006, by Yixuewang (lit. Yi studies net) of Southwest University for Nationalities (original post in Zhongguo Wenhua Bao/CN11-0089), http://222.210.17.136/mzwz/news/11/z_11_4603.html

95. "*Yuanfang de keren qing ni liu xia lai*" is an adaptation of a Sani song but now commonly referred to as a "Yi song"; see "Qubi Awu: Yueliang de nü'er."

96. Local Yi women would come up on stage or backstage and present her with self-made or inherited Yi women's attire. Qubi Awu, interview, March 2002, Beijing.

97. Jimu Xi'er, born in Leibo County in the 1970s, is an acclaimed Nuosu singer. The former housemaid of Liangshan Song and Dance Troupe's famous moon lute player Shama Wuzhi, she joined the same troupe in 1991 and has since enjoyed a remarkable solo career.

98. "Yixiang Yao—Yiren Zhizao, Qubi Awu," posted April 7, 2010, by 56.com user "zhongguo yizu mtv wang," http://www.56.com/u12/v_NTA3NTQyNjU.html.

99. Harrell, *Ways of Being Ethnic*, 99.

100. Ibid.

101. Arrangement by Risha Erti and Song Xiaochun, for instance "Areniu—Jimu Xi'er," MTV by Duan Yongsheng, posted November 29, 2007, by 56.com user "zhongguo yizu mtv wang," http://www.56.com/u18/v_MjM5NTY5NTE.html.

102. Stokes, "Introduction: Ethnicity, Identity and Music," 22.

103. With Yi groups in Yunnan, Torch Festival songs are more often performed *duige*-style: as antiphonal singing between a male and a female singer. Luo and Li, *Yizu minjian wenyi gailun*, 289; Zhu, *Yizu huobajie*, 263.

104. Jike Qubu, interview, February 2010, Xichang.

105. Compare Impey, "Sounding Place," 20. I provide a detailed overview of Jike Qubu's project as part of a larger discussion of questions of Nuosu mouth harp preservation in Olivia Kraef, "Strumming the 'Lost Mouth Chord'—Discourses of Preserving the Nuosu-Yi Mouth Harp," in *Music as Intangible Cultural Heritage: Policy, Ideology and Practice in the Preservation of East Asian Traditions*, ed. Keith Howard (Farnham, UK: Ashgate Press, 2012), 77–98.

106. Schein, "Gender and Internal Orientalism."

Chapter Sixteen

An Interview with Xiao Mei, Ethnomusicologist

Xiao Mei (b. 1956, Beijing) is a professor at the musicology department of the Shanghai Conservatory of Music and vice president and secretary general of the Institute for Traditional Music in China. She has been collecting and studying the traditional, folk, and ritual musics of Han and other ethnic groups in China. Her publications include "Echoes from the Field: Notes on the Anthropology of Music" (2001) and "The Musical Arts of Ancient China" (2004). This interview was given to Shzr Ee Tan in Mandarin at a conference on traditional music in Vienna.

"It's a Man's World" in Chinese Academia

From personal experience, I have the impression that there are very few women in our field in China. It's a man's world—at least when I first started out. What's interesting is that the next, younger generation has produced quite a few female scholars—Yang Xiao and Qi Kun, for example. Some of them are still students, and they take their research very seriously. For them, it's not just a pursuit of any academic discipline for the sake of attaining a doctoral degree. That's where I see myself as coming from as well: ethnomusicology is my calling and my life; it's not just a job. Given all that I had to give up on a personal level, choosing ethnomusicology was a conscious decision: you had to *want* to do it. Maybe this is true for ethnomusicology as a field at large, but, in many ways, for my generation at least in China, I had to give up a lot more, being a woman. I think it's easier for younger generations of women in China now.

"Male Logic" and "Female Subjectivities"

When I first started out, the field was full of men—many of them eminent scholars—who approached research with what I think of as "male logic." I did not get the feeling that, for these colleagues, choosing ethnomusicology was about pursuing an "ideal" or a "calling," but about making a career. Work for them was not "life" like it was for me. Maybe this is reflected in how they tend to take more objective, "outsider" and "etic" approaches to the discipline, in

Figure 16.1. Xiao Mei. Photograph courtesy of Xiao Mei.

the name of professional objectivity, if you like. As a woman, I feel that I am more conscious of the "insider" and "emic" dimension or that I am trying to move between the "insider" and "outsider" statuses. Why? Because as a woman you have family, you have children, and at the same time you want to work in society—you are always negotiating between different spheres of personal and professional relationships. Things are slightly different today, but that was the situation in my earlier years. Nowadays, a lot of things are done in a combination of these two approaches, via the Chinese system of professional-personal *guanxi* (关系) relationships.

Fieldwork: Cooking and Sewing Together

When I first started out, male ethnomusicologists felt that female researchers were not "logical" enough. But female ethnomusicologists felt that male researchers were stiff, that they lacked certain social skills. I'll give you an example: When I was doing fieldwork sometime back with minority nationalities, the men and women took totally different approaches. The men were very organized, appearing on the site with focused questions, and they knew exactly what they wanted to ask and how they could go about finding answers to their questions. It was very businesslike. They conducted formal interviews; they were very efficient. Their relationships with their informants were professional, like those of a superior to a subordinate. The women, however, just "hung out" with their informants. We cooked and sewed together; we didn't ask outright questions but learned through listening. Our informants became our good friends; we learned to read into subtle, unsaid things; we empathized with each other and shared girly jokes. I remember having to give some unofficial advice to my informants on prophylactics, general hygiene, and basic medicine! These close relationships allowed us into certain socio-ritual spheres—the world of shamans, for example—that were secret and less accessible to men. That's not to say that having such close emotional attachments to your informant was always ideal; there were also conflicts of interest.

Pretending to Be a Monk or Japanese Tourist

There is the idea that communism in China brought about greater equality between the sexes, a professionalization of men's and women's roles. Everyone had to work and contribute. To a certain extent this is true, but in practice a lot of gender stereotypes still persisted. Everyone looks at you differently if you're a man. For example, it was difficult and potentially unsafe for me to conduct fieldwork as a single woman when I was in Yunnan in 1991. There was some occasional sexual harassment—sometimes this was not direct; you could just be made to feel uncomfortable when a group of men got together to share off-color jokes. Of course there's always a cultural context to off-color jokes, but that's another story. More importantly, it was frowned upon for a lone Chinese woman to be running around by herself, conducting an "investigation" in the remote regions. It might have been different if I was foreign. My students get around this today by asking their boyfriends to come on their field trips. Back in Yunnan, whenever I was traveling between villages, I shaved my head, wore loose clothes and lowered my voice to sound gruff. I tried to adopt the androgynous look of a monk. Five years later when I returned to the region with my hair regrown, some locals were surprised to see me as a woman: they had either assumed that I was a man or a traveler from Japan!

Male-Centric and Female-Centric Scholarship

Is there a "male-centrism" to the canon of ethnomusicological scholarship and writing in China? I think so. Looking back at the historical documentation of Chinese music, many of these record the passing of edicts, the changing of policies, the movements of officials; these were all the activities *of* men, recorded *by* men, and reanalysed and discussed decades or centuries later by *more* men. Women, it seemed, functioned in the realm of oral history. As a contemporary scholar working with ancient annals, there's nothing you can do about the inherent male-centric leanings of primary sources. But in more recent historical documents I think you can look at gender differentiations more carefully.

This was one of the subjects of my PhD research. I looked at the development of the field of ethnomusicology within China from 1900 to 1966. In the recorded minutes of an important annual meeting held in Hunan in the 1950s in which Yang Yinliu and Cao Anhe attended, I came across references to rebuilding a paradigm for a new national music and the initiation of subsequent research movements on regional and minority musics. There are straight accounts of this meeting given by male scholars, but I looked more carefully at the original notes. It's a small thing to mention here, but a tiny detail such as how one particular director was actively clipping his nails while another was speaking shows you the relative importance that was accorded to what was being discussed and what was going behind the scenes in intellectual circles. Male scholars today wouldn't bother with such apparently insignificant details. I don't know whether this was just an individual quirk of mine, or a particularly "feminine" way of conducting research. But think of the alternative Chinese music histories we could rediscover if we looked at nonofficial records and the small details revolving around big developments such as the Cultural Revolution! Of course, everyone's experience is different then as compared to now, and I don't think I would like to gender things unnecessarily, but it will be good to just take a step back from the "official" view—male-centric or not—once in a while.

A Female Ethnomusicologist's Challenges

One of the main reasons I've managed to lead a fairly balanced life as a female ethnomusicologist in China is that I have a supportive husband and family. My husband is a medical doctor who later became a lawyer. I'm very fortunate in that I can rely on his financial support if need be, but more importantly—on his moral and emotional encouragement. It's very hard to find a husband who will let his wife wander around in the wilderness for three months doing fieldwork or attend conferences overseas. He's done his good share of housework and looking after our daughter. In this respect I am a very fortunate person—but then again, you could always say it was *I* who chose wisely!

That's not to say that it's always been easy balancing everything. There's tremendous stress being a working woman in China—I say this not just as an ethnomusicologist. I'm also a daughter in addition to a mother and a wife. I remember only recently having to rush back and forth between Hangzhou and Beijing for urgent meetings, somehow trying to find time to run home to look in on my daughter practicing her piano, then hopping onto a plane and almost missing it, and finally arriving at my maternal home—only to be confronted by my parents who were seated at the dining table. Not quite understanding my job and roles in Beijing, they were waiting for me to cook dinner for them, only because this was what all filial daughters of their generation were expected to do—whether you're an academic working in the city or based at home. It was a particularly stressful day. I remember crying real tears into the vegetables I was frying in the wok and thinking: Could I have chosen an easier way out if I had not pursued ethnomusicology or academia? Would it have been different with a different kind of job? Perhaps not. My story is in many ways every woman's story, and I chose this profession myself, so I can't complain now.

New Female Blood

What's interesting is how the next generation of female ethnomusicologists in China will pan out. I'm very encouraged by what I've seen and sometimes envious of the opportunities they enjoy today. Maybe communism has finally, effectively bequeathed its legacy of equality between sexes. In a very strange way, it's also come to develop a sense of individual moral responsibility—and by extension, a sense of *individualism*—among the younger scholars. There is a—not untraditionally Chinese—idea that you have to save yourself first before you can save the world. So the next generations of women researchers are out there, carving out their little, individual niches with a view to contributing to a larger cause. For them, ethnomusicology has grown out of the universal quest for learning but also from a deeply personal curiosity to find out about the different peoples of the world and about the paradoxes of life on earth. For these women, ethnomusicology is not charity work; it's about discovery, and it's a lifestyle choice.

Chapter Seventeen

"Doing Satan's Business"

Negotiating Gendered Concepts of Music and Ritual in Rural Xinjiang

Rachel Harris

This chapter represents the preliminary stages of a research project that focuses on the ritual practices of rural Uyghur women within a broader framework of the analysis of gendered emotional expression. Here I develop a rationale for the musical analysis of ritual performance, discussing various models from the literature in ethnomusicology and folklore studies. I draw on fieldwork experiences to explore the links and contradictions between musical and ritual performance in the Islamic world and the gendered nature of this nexus. In particular I focus on the roles and status of female Uyghur performers, here broadly and perhaps controversially defined to include both singers and ritualists, suggesting that the role of ritualist offers Uyghur women in traditional village society a socially sanctioned outlet for emotional, and what in other contexts might be termed artistic, expression through religious practice.

I spent the first ten years of my research in Xinjiang studying the masculine world of Uyghur music as it is conventionally understood. In this mode I wrote on the "classical" *muqam* suites and the Uyghur pop industry.[1] I problematized the now somewhat well-worn issues of ethnicity and nationalism and the politics of representation, but I rarely concerned myself with the politics of gender. I associated with male scholars, Han and Uyghur. The wives of my urban Uyghur colleagues were reticent figures, appearing from the kitchen with food, rarely sitting down at table with us to eat. In the villages, I worked with the male musicians who sing at *mäshräp* celebrations or term themselves *muqamchi* (masters of the Muqam); among the professional troupes I was most interested in the older generation of men, instrumentalists and singers, and bearers of the tradition. I had a lot of fun traveling with my male colleagues around the countryside, openly smoking and drinking (I now find it hard to admit to such behavior in print), translating the scatological humor of male village musicians, enjoying my outsider status, which enabled me, if not to be entirely gender neutral, at least to flout some of the rules. Sabine Trebinjac writes in similar vein of her fieldwork in the early 1990s in the Uyghur region, where she possessed a "faculté de mutation . . . refusé aux hommes." Most difficult was for her to be accepted by women as a woman: difference equated to masculinity.[2]

Then I got married to a Uyghur man, and my view of Uyghur culture and society was turned inside out. In my fieldwork I moved from an urban base to a rural one and replaced my male associates with women. In 2006, we spent a long summer in my mother-in-law's village in central Xinjiang. I took my place in the heart of the women's sphere, certainly not as a normal daughter-in-law but as a female guest of the family women, with my own small child in tow, observing and attempting to participate in the work of housekeeping and hospitality: fetching the water from the well and lighting the fire for tea, looking after babies, feeding animals, baking bread in the *tonur* brick ovens, preparing dough for noodles and dumplings. Now it was the men who appeared as shadowy and inconsequential figures on the periphery of a world that was woman-centric.

In summer 2009 we returned to the Uyghur region to begin a long-term research project on the topic of Uyghur women and the expression of emotion. Years earlier, as a student in the Uyghur region, I had been struck by the frequent appearance in Uyghur pop music videos of weeping women, primarily weeping mothers. I thought that there was an element of nationalism in it: tears for the motherland, but there was more to it than that. Weeping was also a regular public act for women off-screen, an accepted part of daily life. Once I went on a field trip with my colleague and mentor, Yasin Muhpul, and his wife, Gulbahar, and we arranged to stay with some of their relatives in southern Xinjiang. As we approached their door, four women came running to meet us. They formally embraced Gulbahar, and then all five women began to sob. Yasin Muhpul caught my expression and laughed, clearly not partaking in any way of this emotional outpouring. "Are you wondering what's going on?" he asked. "Someone in the family died a while back, and they haven't seen each other since it happened." Of course, such ways of being are common among women across the globe, and the pairings of emotionality-female and rationality-male are naturalized across many cultures,[3] but they were sufficiently strange to my own reticent English upbringing, and indeed to my experience of living among educated Han Chinese in Beijing, to catch my attention.

When we (my husband, I, and our two small children) arrived in the regional capital of Ürümchi in late June 2009, political events swiftly gave the research theme stark relevance. Ürümchi was seething with rumors of an incident in Guangzhou where several Uyghur migrant workers had been beaten to death by their Han Chinese fellow workers. An initially peaceful demonstration on July 5 gave way to rioting and interethnic violence. State media stressed Uyghur violence against Han victims but did not report on the use of police violence against the protestors nor the retaliatory attacks by Han against Uyghurs.[4] The authorities brought in a group of foreign journalists to witness the aftermath of the violence. They were waylaid by a demonstration by a group of Uyghur mothers, who stood weeping before the journalists, surrounded by Chinese riot troops, demanding the return of their children, victims of the mass arrests of young Uyghurs that followed the violence. These images upended the perception of victimhood in international media reports and highlighted the social and political force of Uyghur women's emotional display.

Village Women's Rituals

Alongside many other Uyghur residents of Ürümchi, we fled the city and made for the family village, which was also the main focus of my research. This entailed working with a group of women addressed variously in different parts of the Uyghur region as *büwi, ayäm* or *qushnach*: women highly respected in the community, who can recite the Qur'an and whose role it is to wash the bodies of dead women, act as mourners in funeral ritual, and conduct various rituals for expulsion or cleansing as well as to mark points on the Islamic calendar, primarily during the month of Barat.[5]

One of our relatives was a regular participant in the women's ritual meetings, and she was enthusiastic about my project. She introduced me to Aygul,[6] who she said was already a büwi of considerable power. Aygul was a young mother, unusually tall and with a manner of exceptional authority. She spoke to us at length of her background and training in the art of Qur'anic recitation and offered to teach me this art. This was a generous offer, made at some personal risk: religious teaching for girls was then banned in the Uyghur region, and Aygul, like several other *büwi* I interviewed, had been arrested several times and imprisoned for a short period for teaching the Qur'an to local girls.

Aygul invited me to attend a large *khätmä* ritual that they planned to hold in the locality to mark the month of Barat.[7] Although such gatherings were not explicitly banned, in the political circumstances (armed troops patrolled the local town, the weekly bazaar was canceled until further notice, and there were checkpoints on all the major roads), the women decided to invite a small group of around twenty pious women, led by three acknowledged *büwi*, and, in a departure from usual practice, to hold the ritual in the daytime in a secluded household, so as not to attract undue attention through nighttime comings and goings and noise. In the event, not at all deterred by the security situation but on the contrary attracted by the news that a foreign scholar wanted to film their activities, some sixty women turned up. They arrived in small groups, on donkey carts or on foot, impeccably dressed,

Figure 17.1. Pious women in southern Xinjiang gather in a family home before a ritual. Photograph by author.

some with their faces covered by a large embroidered veil, others with their headscarves pinned below the chin, marking them as women of social standing and religious merit. The following brief description of this *khätmä* drawn from my field notes gives a flavor of their activities.

We all squeezed into our host's large guest room in the baking midday heat. The ritual lasted nearly three hours and was divided into two roughly equal halves with a short break in between. The first stage consisted of Qur'anic recitation, which they term *hät oqup* (reading); longer solo sections were interspersed with periods of short, rhythmic, repeated phrases sung together by all the women. The ritual was led and conducted (in the sense of an orchestral conductor) by the most senior and respected *büwi* in the locality, a diminutive, vibrant woman whom I will call Maryam. Seated in the place of honor at the center of the back wall, she controlled not only the order of events, leading off a new group chant, pointing to various women at other times to perform solo recitation, but also the emotional intensity of the meeting, which grew gradually through peaks and troughs to a climax. Maryam's opening solo recitation was in every sense "performed": beautifully voiced and pitched and full of emotion. Shortly into this recitation, Aygul began to weep, and as the intensity grew other women joined her. Around an hour into the ritual, Maryam gestured urgently to the women to form a tighter circle around her. At this signal the intensity and weeping reached their peak, and one woman began to jerk her body and cry out. The women nearest to her comforted her while the chanting continued. At its conclusion all the women rose, still weeping, and moved around the room, embracing each other.

The second stage, termed *hikmät*, consisted of melodic prayers recited (or perhaps sung) in Uyghur and the classic *dhikr*, "*Allah hu*," which accompanied dancing, first by Maryam's pupils, later joined by a few of the other younger women. Maryam sang a melody over the chant in the manner of *hapiz* (reciters) in the male Sufi meeting houses.[8] Again, many of the women began to weep, and another woman fell into a trancelike affective state. Then Maryam rose to dance while the younger *büwi* led the chanting. When this chant concluded, Maryam called on different women to recite individual *hikmät*; then she and her main disciples moved outside while another woman took up the central role and gave a long prayer in Uyghur to conclude the proceedings. Outside in the courtyard the women ate rice and mutton *polo* and watermelon, watched the video, and posed for endless photographs. This was the first time I had seen fully veiled women pose for photographs, a fascinating phenomenon deserving of an article in its own right. The host family women were exhausted but impressed. "When we die they won't come with so many women," they said, "we'll be lucky if one or two turn up."

When discussing their activities, in particular their emotional response to the ritual, the participants themselves emphasize the notions of religious duty and merit. They perform these rituals as a service for the wider community, both the dead and the living. Several of the *büwi* answered my question, "Why did they cry?" explaining, "We cry for the sins of the world." Ildikó Bellér-Hann provides historical underpinnings for this statement in her exploration of early twentieth-century Uyghur ritual practices relating to the month of Barat: the period during which the *büwi* today perform their largest and most significant rituals. In popular belief, the night of the fourteenth of the month is when the tree of life is shaken. Each person has his or her name written on a leaf of this tree, and the leaves of those who are going to die in the coming year fall to the ground. The fourteenth was also termed the Night of Forgiveness. This reflected the belief that two angels sit on every person's shoulders; the angel on the right shoulder recording good deeds, and the angel on the left recording sins. On the Night of Forgiveness, the angels enter into the individual's book the amount of merit that person has accumulated during the year. Bellér-Hann draws together several historical accounts of vigils and prayer for the forgiveness of sin held on and around the night of the fourteenth across the Uyghur region. She emphasizes the domestic and female aspect of Barat rituals and notes that "Barat had a very important spiritual dimension rooted in local definitions of the moral person and in notions of sin and punishment, meritorious deed and reward."[9] Further fieldwork is needed to explore how these beliefs still resonate in contemporary Uyghur society.

In terms of ritual practice, the women's *khätmä* bears many similarities to the rituals of Uyghur male Sufi groups,[10] with the key difference that men's rituals are conducted in the specially constructed ritual space of the *khaniqa* or Sufi lodge, whereas the women's rituals, as with most of Uyghur women's religious practice, are usually home based.[11] It also has close similarities in its structure and content to accounts of women's rituals, sometimes explicitly termed Sufi rituals, across the Islamic world.[12]

Many of the existing studies of women's ritual practice in the Islamic world have focused on the social and psychological needs they meet for the participants in terms of creation of community and the cathartic experience of the ritual itself. They emphasize the gendered division of space and unequal access to religious authority as key to their interpretation. Judith Hoch-Smith and Anita Spring argue that ritual validates bonds between women. Relationships built on the healer-patient relationship and the ritual expert-novice bond crosscut ties based on kinship, friendship, and residence. Women benefit from the community and prestige offered by participation in ritual groups.[13] In her overview of Islamic women's ritual practices, Eleanor Doumato notes the particular value for women of becoming part of a spiritual community under circumstances where women are excluded or marginalized by the power structures of orthodox tradition.[14] This interpretation has clear relevance to women's religious practice in Uyghur culture. In her studies of Uyghur women's ritual and healing, Bellér-Hann also argues that Uyghur women's practices are regarded as superstition and devalued both by the state and by reformist Islam.[15] Doumato draws on a wide array of sources on women's religious practices across the Islamic world, including ritual healing groups and group visits to shrines where women go to pray to the saint to intercede in health problems or childbirth. She cites Fatima Mernissi's argument that shrine visitation is "critical to the mental health and well-being of otherwise powerless women by providing a chance to share common grievances ritually, to feel the blessing of the saint, and to come away with hope."[16]

Moving beyond the body of literature on Islamic women's ritual practice, we might also find relevant studies in Han Chinese culture. Marginalization is also key to interpretations of women's emotional expression in the context of Chinese marriage ritual, usually termed in English *bridal laments*. As Rubie Watson argues, in (Han) Chinese culture, marriage for men means harmony and hierarchy; for women it means alienation and possibly death (in childbirth or potentially through suicide if maltreatment by the new family is severe). Laments express the tensions and contradictions (fears, longing, and anger) of those who must live in the periphery of two worlds but belong fully to neither. Watson argues that "laments give expression to an individual experience that is momentarily externalized through public performance, they do not resolve contradictions but celebrate them . . . the power of laments lies in their conflation of cultural form and personal style."[17] Through Mernissi's reading of the psychological impact of shrine visitation and via Watson's perception of bridal laments as the culturally prescribed performance of individually experienced emotions, we can now move toward a focus on the emotional experience of the Uyghur ritual described above. This brings us more firmly within the sphere of ethnomusicology and introduces the possibility of a reading of the ritual as (musical) performance, improvised within a flexible structure and imbued with affective power. Approaching the ritual from this perspective, studies from the ethnomusicology literature with less obvious relevance to the immediate ritual context can offer useful insights. Take, for example, Ali Jihad Racy's study of the affective state of *tarab* (ecstasy) and its production in the context of *takht* musical ensemble performances in twentieth-century Eygpt. Racy describes how the feeling of a "true *sama*" event (note the borrowing of Sufi vocabulary) rises and descends in an arc. The "singer" (*mutrib*) is a psychologist who gauges and plays with the mood of the audience. Light "signal" pieces, or "musical aphrodisiacs," throw the audience into an instant "participatory frenzy."[18] There is much to link Maryam's role in the ritual and her relationship to the other participants to Racy's description of the *mutrib*'s role as musician and his relationship with his audience. It is also striking to compare the strength of the terminology employed by Racy to describe affective states with that employed by some writers dealing directly with Sufi women's ritual who shy away from "exoticizing" the participants through a focus on altered emotional states.[19]

Moving beyond the sphere of Muslim cultures, an unlikely yet fruitful source of inspiration is Christine Yano's study of Japanese popular *enka* song.[20] Yano develops the notion of *kata* (a term borrowed from traditional Japanese arts) to denote culturally patterned formulas through which singers communicate emotion, distinguishing specific musical, performative, and bodily *kata*. Steven Feld's analysis of form and performance codes in song and weeping among the Kaluli of Papua New Guinea is similarly relevant.[21] Feld draws on local concepts like the "hardening" of a song and the aestheticized perception of birdsong as expression of loss and nostalgia. Both of these authors find continuity in singing and weeping; both are performed and embodied with intent to connect with the audience. For Yano, a singer's crying is counted among her list of bodily performative formulas; the "most effective and primal *kata*[,] . . . tears, and the suffering they display, become an irresistible link between singer and audience. . . . Embodiment becomes engenderment . . . the body parades emotion even as it evokes emotion: it becomes the medium through which pain, longing, and resignation are conveyed, eliciting in turn an empathetic, cathartic response in audience members.[22] These performance contexts are worlds apart, yet it seems to me that Yano's careful delineation of the culturally patterned display of emotion in *enka* has much in common with the work of Feld and Watson on weeping or laments. In each of these analyses weeping is no less "authentic" because it is formalized, performed, and culturally codified.

Indeed, in Feld's discussion of the Kaluli mourning rituals, in Yano's analysis of Japanese popular song, and in the Uyghur *khätmä*, the weeping and singing are deliberately constructed and rehearsed, carefully calibrated to exert emotional impact on listeners, and appreciated for their ability to do so.

Ritual or Music?

There is considerable artistry in Maryam's performance, but can it be termed singing? In the field of ethnomusicology, there is a rich literature on the subject of music in the ritual context (often the term *music* is not applied by the practitioners themselves) and its relationship to affective states or trance.[23] In the sphere of Islamic ritual, however, this approach is more problematic. In the Central Asian context the ambivalent relationship between Islam and music has been discussed by several ethnomusicologists, in greatest detail in Afghanistan, where the debate on the permissibility of music has historically been particularly sharp.[24] Among the Uyghurs the situation has historically been more relaxed, yet in reports from early twentieth-century Xinjiang both sides of the debate were represented in popular thought. One strand of the argument held that the hair of the ass of the Antichrist is made from the strings of musical instruments, which will entice people to follow him on the Day of Judgment; however, Uyghur musicians defended themselves with the belief that the prophet David (Dawut) was the inventor of music.[25]

The difficulties with treating the recitation of sacred texts as musical performance have been amply discussed in the literature, notably in Kristina Nelson's 2001 study of Qur'anic recitation. As the directly transmitted word of God, the Qur'an should not be associated with the ambivalent category of music, yet Qur'anic recitation draws directly on the musical rules of *maqām*. As Nelson argues, the close relationship between musical and ritual performance is acknowledged, if uncomfortable, within Islamic discourse.[26] Racy notes that many *tarab* musicians were employed as *muezzin* (one who gives the call to prayer) or as Qur'anic reciters.[27] The most famous of all Egyptian singers, Umm Kulthum, learned as a child to recite the Qur'an and perform *qasida* sung poems about the Prophet.[28] Likewise, Maryam's skills as a *büwi* are based in part on the musicality of her performance.

The field of Sufi ritual practices, notably the *sama* ritual, is more comfortably drawn into the sphere of ethnomusicology, especially in South Asia where categories have perhaps been more relaxed, where *sama* rituals are accompanied by musical instruments and many *qawwal* ritual singers perform regularly on world music stages. In her ethnography of speaking and performance in the male ritual sphere of Qawwali, Shemeem Abbas explores aspects of the communication between *qawwal*, whom she has no problem in terming musician, and audience. Like Racy, Abbas focuses on the production of ecstasy (*kefiat*) in the audience by vocal repetition (*takrar*), body language, humor, and eye contact.[29] Regula Burckhardt Qureshi shifts the focus to the ways in which hierarchical order and spirituality are negotiated audibly in Qawwali.[30] Discussing the traditionally low status of the Qawwali musician, she argues that the *qawwal* is the sole mouthpiece, who speaks musically for all and articulates all the relationships around him. Clearly this responsibility invests the *qawwal* with much power over his audience. The way to control this musical power, she argues, is to give the audience religiously legitimized social and economic power over him. Qureshi's discussion of power, ritual, and musical practice in this exclusively male sphere resonates with Doumato's gendered analysis of marginalized women's ritual practices in Saudi Arabia. I will further explore aspects of these links between music, power, and gender below. Having explored the possibilities for reading the *khätmä* ritual as musical performance, I now turn to the problems concerning women's association with what is locally understood as musical performance.

Showing Myself

In the course of my early fieldwork in this area, I confronted several issues arising from the dichotomy of ritual and music in Islamic belief and practice, issues that highlight the gendered nature of this dichotomy. The first issue arose from my own unfortunate desire to play music. I have played the *dutar* long-necked lute for several years. This was a very useful entry into my earlier research topic on the highly prized *muqam* repertoire,[31] and a source of much pleasure over the years. On previous visits to the village, this habit had been regarded benignly, and I was often invited to play and especially to sing (rather badly) for the amusement of our hosts. I was aware, however, that this was unusual behavior. There was only one woman in the nearby villages who might be remotely termed a singer, having taught herself to play the *dutar* and sing classic Uyghur folk songs by listening to the radio. People spoke of her jokingly, and after she married her husband forbade her to sing in public.

During our 2009 visit, we came across a new teahouse in the local town, which employed a very passable group of musicians to sing *muqam* and folk songs for the customers. My husband volunteered my services as a musician to the owner, an offer that was enthusiastically accepted. There was a large, all-male crowd at the teahouse, and it crossed my mind that this might be seen as inappropriate, but the lure of playing with these fine musicians was too strong; I climbed up onto the stage and played and sang several excerpts from the *muqam* with them. The assembled men applauded loudly, the musicians winked and said I could join their band any time, and I was enjoyably back at my old gender boundary-crossing game.

The second issue arose from my continued association with professional musicians from Ürümchi. We invited Sanubar Tursun, a prominent and much-loved singer and *dutar* player, to stay in the village to get some respite from the ongoing crackdown in Ürümchi. Sanubar is a member of a prominent musical family from the northern town of Ghulja. She released a series of VCDs[32] in the 1990s featuring her own compositions, which were very much in the traditional style of her home region, performed solo with *dutar* or supported by her brothers on other traditional instruments. These albums were very popular and widely imitated, and she became something of a national icon. The whole extended family was insistent that we ask her to sing at a *mäshräp*: a common type of celebratory community gathering. Again, this was an activity that might be problematic with the authorities. We consulted them and were allowed to go ahead as long as we kept the numbers small. Inevitably the word spread, and hundreds of villagers arrived on carts and motorbikes and squeezed into the family orchard hoping to catch a glimpse of the star, but the event passed decorously and all seemed content.

It transpired, however, that all were not content. My husband told me some days later that he had met with a childhood friend who was now a *damolla*, a prominent male cleric in the official local religious hierarchy. Apparently some people had said to him, "Why did the English visitors hold a *khätmä* ritual and then just a few days later 'do Satan's business' inviting a singing star from Ürümchi?" Here the musical performance was drawn as diametrically opposed to the sacred business of the ritual, and their juxtaposition was inappropriate. The *damolla* also opined that it was not suitable for me to "show myself" in front of an all-male audience at the tea shop. I was not overly worried by this: it seemed to represent a more conservative view than was general among the local people, and my husband, happily, treated it merely as a juicy ethnographic tidbit. One of the leading younger *büwi* had come to the *mäshräp* to hear Sanubar and had comfortably taken the seat of honor next to Sanubar and myself. Nonetheless, I was concerned that our activities were seen in some quarters as a problem and afraid that some of the *büwi* might be upset by our musical activities.

I consulted with two young women who were close relatives and was surprised that they broadly agreed with the *damolla*. "If we were proper Muslims we should cover ourselves completely, long sleeves, our faces," they said, "but we don't do things properly here." This linked the problem of "showing myself" in the sense of public performance to the wider issue of women's veiling in a most direct and personal way. It was also revealing for me in terms of my research. The *damolla* had in fact neatly summarized the whole nexus of gender, ritual, and performance for me.

The situation regarding veiling in Xinjiang is complex, and a woman's social status and occupation are clearly marked by her choice of headwear. For rural Uyghur women, the normal headgear is a light, usually brightly patterned, headscarf tied behind the neck under the hair. Women with higher religious and social status (for example *büwi* or *haji* who have visited Mecca) pin their scarf under the chin in public, and a few older religious women cover their faces. Urban professional women go unveiled; indeed the veil is banned for government workers and students. In contrast to this, many other urban Uyghur women in recent years, following the spread of reformist or orthodox trends in religious practice,[33] have adopted a more severe "Arab" style of veiling, as it is locally termed, covering the head and neck, and sometimes the *niqab* covering for the face.

In previous visits I had gone about the village unveiled, but in 2009 the family women encouraged me to wear a headscarf and insisted I do so when religious people (the *damolla* or *büwi*) came to the house. Veronica Doubleday writes tellingly of her experience of adopting the veil in 1970s Afghanistan: "Adopting the veil was a far bigger step than I ever imagined: it took me right inside Herati psychology and affected me deeply. Ironically this symbol of oppression had liberating aspects for me": it minimized difference and drew less attention from men. But Doubleday also remarks how the veil modified her own public behavior: she lowered her head and cast her eyes down. "I experienced the way in which the veil breeds a submissive attitude in women. . . . I also understood that the veil is very addictive."[34] I had less trouble putting it on, perceiving rather than an absolute choice (to veil or not to veil) a range of veiling practices that acted as markers of social status or a political choice. I also found the village women's headscarf light and practical to wear. However, the limits of this perceived flexibility soon became apparent, and the problems came when I wanted to take it off. Once I had adopted the headscarf, the family women were quick to point out that I should be consistent: the *büwi* would be surprised if I turned up one day in a headscarf and was spotted the next day going about the village or the local town without it.

Such dilemmas and choices are a commonplace in fieldwork and are part of the process of learning and familiarization.[35] Benedicte Grima writes of her fieldwork experiences in northern Pakistan and Afghanistan, noting her personal transition from outsider to woman: "Linguistic competence and adherence to rules of cultural etiquette gave me more of the status and treatment of a woman insider." Such status had clear benefits for her fieldwork; her understanding of the (female) Pashtun code of shame and honor helped her gain confidence and access to activities and discussions meant only for women.[36] These dilemmas also helped me to understand the complex negotiations that Uyghur women make in their own assertions of status and identity within the context of religious tradition and the socialist, modernizing state. The problem of women and musical performance is equally revealing of these negotiations and closely linked to the issue of veiling.

The prohibitions on women's public singing and dancing are well documented across the Islamic world. They may be more or less restrictive across time and place. Grima notes that in Pashtun culture in 1980s northern Pakistan, dancing and singing

> are shameful for women outside of specific contexts, such as weddings, due to their implicit nature as entertainment. Such behavior is the job of *dəms*, low-status entertainers hired at weddings and other festivities. . . . If word were spread that a woman had engaged in *dəm* behavior outside of its licit context, her family's honor would be marred and her men would have to take severe measures against her, such as killing her or ostracizing her.[37]

Writing on 1970s Herat, Doubleday describes the scandalous reputation of professional female musicians, who were not in fact prostitutes but widely regarded as such: "dangerously free," they went unveiled in the home and could argue and barter with strange men.[38] Again, drawing on her personal experiences of learning and eventually performing with these women, Doubleday describes the scandalized reaction of her Herati friends when she joins the band: her actions impacted on not only her own reputation but also her husband's and his teachers'.[39] Moreover, she herself absorbs these attitudes: "I felt uncomfortable singing for men, highly conscious of their admiration and aware that I was granting a rare, almost erotic, delight. . . . I had become infected with a Herati sense of shame."[40] Sadly, perhaps, I felt more as if I was providing comic delight for the teahouse audience in the local town, yet the *damolla*'s disapproval points to an equivalent set of values that equate women's public musical performance with shame.

In her chapter on Egyptian belly dancers and the recent trend of renouncing the profession to take the veil, Karin Van Nieuwkerk reviews a range of the contemporary writings of Islamist clerics. She cites the contemporary Islamist writer Al-Qaradawi, who explains that Muslim women avoid flirtatious movements, cast down their eyes, and do not mingle with men. Female performers are thus antithetical to proper Muslim women and belong to the category of "infidels." Van Nieuwkerk also cites Marilyn Tadros, who argues that women are the main focus of religious discourses on art. According to these texts, women exist to provoke the sexual instinct and should therefore be hidden away from sight. Art exists to provoke sexuality, and thus art is an evil that requires repentance.[41]

Maintaining Respectability

How much are the experiences of women under the Pashtun social code or the writings of Islamists in Cairo relevant to contemporary Xinjiang? Geographically distant from the Islamist heartland and controlled by secular government, in Xinjiang the state supports a huge network of arts institutes and performing troupes within which women may study and work professionally in dance, instrumental, and vocal performance and where female singers and dancers fill the television schedules and populate the shelves of music shops in bazaars across the region. Accounts by older-generation singers attest to the efforts of the state in the early stages of Communist rule in Xinjiang to establish this status quo. Pashsha Ishan is probably the most renowned Uyghur female singer of the twentieth century. Like so many of China's minority divas, she sang for Chairman Mao in the Great Hall of the People in Beijing, her songs filled Xinjiang's airwaves in the late 1970s and 1980s, and she was rewarded by the state for her contribution with a seat on the Chinese People's Political Consultative Conference. She recounts how government cultural workers came to her home when she was a young girl and proposed to the family that she go to Ürümchi to become a professional singer. "My parents were not willing at first," she recalls, "but the cadres did thought work on them [*zuole sixiang gongzuo*], and then they agreed."[42] Even with established role models available, similar tales of family resistance to girls pursuing careers in music or dance are still very common today.

Equally, the historical process in this region is far from one of straightforward secularization. Changing attitudes in other parts of the Islamic world impact readily on attitudes within Xinjiang. As Edmund Waite's research attests, reformist or orthodox currents have flowed into the region over the last two decades,[43] and Muslims in Xinjiang are themselves engaging in the debates of the kind delineated by Al-Qaradawi above. It is perhaps noteworthy that the *damolla* who regarded our family *mäshräp* as "Satan's business" studied Qur'anic recitation in Egypt. The remarks of my female relatives on veiling also display an active, if idealized, awareness of standards of religious behavior beyond the Uyghur region.

Although such attitudes have gained ground in recent years, the *damolla*'s comment struck me as lying outside the norms of Uyghur society, as our friend Sanubar is the most highly respected female singer of her generation, with a broad fan base that crosses the urban-rural divide. Through the time spent with her in 2009 in and around our family village, I was able to observe how she presented herself to the wider public, and I was struck by the care with which she preserved her reputation. Her concern and her strategies to maintain respectability are instructive in the context of this discussion.

As Jay Dautcher has vividly described, Uyghur hospitality is a fiercely competitive game of demonstrating status, and one of the many strategies for establishing prestige is the ability to invite a respected musician to play for a gathering.[44] Although this was primarily a male game, Sanubar was also a frequent target of such invitations, and she negotiated them with care. She told me, "If I am asked to play somewhere and the men are drinking, I say to them, very nicely, 'I will play a couple of songs since you have invited me, but I am busy. I will go and get on with my business and you can stay and drink.' Then I play two songs, no more, and I get up and go."[45] On the final day of her visit, we found ourselves unwittingly inveigled into the same teahouse where my enthusiasm for singing had got the better of me. Sanubar was conducted to the finest private room and served with an impressive array of choice fruits and dishes. Then she was asked if she would be kind enough to sing a couple of songs for the crowd outside. Sanubar was polite but firm. She had not expected to be brought here and had no intention of singing. "I don't like places like this," she said, "you can't guarantee that the men will show respect." The owner begged her to reconsider; a large crowd had gathered to hear her and would be terribly disappointed if she did not appear. Sanubar was unmoved, and we stayed in our private room for another hour until a senior representative of the assembled group of men, a teacher and *haji*, came to beg for her favor on behalf of the crowd. Only then did she acquiesce and performed precisely two songs for the crowd amidst a reverential hush, with such calm and readiness that it occurred to me that she had been simply waiting for this move from the audience.

Channeling Charisma

Sanubar exercises tight control over her musical performance and identity, but she is empowered to do so by her star status, her urban background, and her position within a respected musical family. For village women such strategies are distant, yet it seems to me that within the framework of religious tradition, women who desire the forms of expression and creativity otherwise offered by music-making can find these outlets in the ritual activities of the *büwi*. I discussed these ideas with my longtime research associate Rahila Dawut, an Ürümchi-based Uyghur anthropologist who has worked with women's ritual groups across the Uyghur region. We talked about the kinds of women who might become *büwi*. "A *büwi* has charisma and a good voice," she said. "She can control other women, and control the ritual. Many are relatives of religious men. Sometimes they may be women who were a bit wild in their youth."[46]

This last point chimed with my impressions of some of the *büwi* I had met. The diminutive Maryam was indeed a person of great charisma, still beautiful under a black and gold embroidered veil, whose recitation had almost instant power to provoke weeping. She herself was reticent about her past, but the family women were quick to fill in the details. "Maryam became a *büwi* after seeing ghosts," they said. "She is a real *bakhshi* [shamanic healer]. When she was young she was wild, she had a lover. Even now she likes to talk and laugh." Clearly not the character traits of a good Muslim woman as defined by Al-Qaradawi, and traits that might have brought her to serious harm at the hands of her family, but channeled into ritual expression these same attributes have enabled her to become the most powerful and respected *büwi* in the locality.

Also striking is the story of conversion after seeing ghosts, with its shamanic overtones that are explicitly recognized by my informants. This kind of dream conversion seems to be common among *büwi*. Aygul, the younger *büwi* gave me this account:

> After I had my second child I was not well, and I had no time for my prayers for a few years. Then one morning around 3:00 a.m. I had a dream. A fine old man with a handsome beard sitting on a carpet came towards me from the sky. I was in a graveyard, and he lectured me about the Qur'an. I was very afraid. I had developed a liver illness, and I thought I would die. At that time my youngest child was only six months old; I was so scared. After that dream I woke up, and I understood myself. This was twelve years ago. Since then I have been praying and reading the Qur'an.[47]

Such accounts, intriguingly, are echoed in van Nieuwkerk's discussion of Egyptian belly dancers, several of whom during recent decades have publically repented of their "sinful" profession, adopted the *hijab*, and given accounts of their dream conversions.[48] Doubleday provides another interesting parallel in her account of Mother of Nebi in Herat. She was a well-known performer as a child, who loved to sing and dance for other women at weddings, and she thrived on audience attention. She married a highly religious man and after a few years suffered a nervous breakdown that was diagnosed as spirit possession. She was cured by a hereditary healer, became his disciple, and began to divine through voluntary spirit possession. Doubleday comments that through this she built up a circle of women around her, the work brought her prestige and money, and enabled her to slip through her husband's net.[49]

Writing Gender; Gendered Writing

In writing this chapter I have used a more reflexive style than I am accustomed to, in order to integrate my fieldwork experiences and the insights they gave me into the gendered nature of the nexus of musical and ritual performance in Islam. Curiously, this new focus on women's expressive culture, and no doubt the extended exposure to the body of literature relating to this sphere (almost exclusively penned by women), have perceptibly impacted on my own ethnographic style. The literature and my field experiences have also impelled a focus on gender and power in ritual practice and religious discourse and the ways in which it is negotiated by individual female musicians and ritualizes. Subtle prohibitions prevent rural women from participating as musicians in the celebratory *mäshräp* gatherings that are the most common public context for music making in village life, although they do commonly participate in dancing. Women's opportunities for musical expression are instead provided within the private ritual sphere associated with mourning and grief. I suggest that the role of *büwi* ritualist offers rural Uyghur women a socially sanctioned outlet for religious, emotional, and artistic expression; a community beyond the family and village structures; and the opportunity to develop and exert authority and charisma.

Notes

1. Rachel Harris, "Reggae on the Silk Road: The Globalisation of Uyghur Pop," *China Quarterly* 183 (2005): 627–43; Rachel Harris, *The Making of a Musical Canon in Chinese Central Asia: The Uyghur Twelve Muqam* (Aldershot, UK: Ashgate Press, 2008).

2. "an ability to transform oneself . . . not afforded to men," Sabine Trebinjac, "Femme, seule et venue d'ailleurs: Trois atouts d'un ethnomusicologue au Turkestan Chinois," *Cahiers de Musiques Traditionnelles* 8 (1995): 59–68.

3. Catherine Lutz, "Emotion, Thought, and Estrangement: Emotion as a Cultural Category," *Cultural Anthropology* 1, no. 3 (1986): 287–309.

4. For a detailed account of the events, see James A. Millward, "Introduction: Does the 2009 Urumchi Violence Mark a Turning Point?" *Central Asian Survey* 28, no. 4 (2009): 347–60.

5. For details on mourning practices in preliberation Uyghur society, see Ildikó Bellér-Hann, *Community Matters in Xinjiang 1880–1949: Towards a Historical Anthropology of the Uyghur* (Leiden: Brill, 2008), 284–300. For details on ritual practices associated with Barat, see pp. 355–62.

6. I have changed the names of the ritualists at their request.

7. More widely known as Sha'ban.

8. Zhou Ji, *Zhongguo Xinjiang Weiwu'erzu Yisilanjiao Liyi Yinyue* (Taipei: Xinwenfeng chuban gongsi, 1999); Rachel Harris, "National Traditions and Illegal Religious Activities in Chinese Central Asia," in *Sounds of Power: Music, Politics and Ideology in the Middle East, North Africa and Central Asia*, ed. Laudan Nooshin (Aldershot, UK: Ashgate Press, 2009), 165–85.

9. Bellér-Hann, *Community Matters*, 355–60.

10. Zhou, *Zhongguo Xinjiang*; Harris, "National Traditions."

11. Some of the Sufi lodges do set aside separate *khaniqa* for women, but home-based rituals are far more prevalent; see Bellér-Hann, *Community Matters*, 324.

12. Elizabeth Fernea, *Guests of the Sheik: An Ethnography of an Iraqi Village* (New York: Knopf Doubleday Publishing Group, 1995); Catharina Raudvere, *The Book and the Roses: Sufi Women, Visibility, and Zikir in Contemporary Istanbul* (London: I. B. Tauris, 2002).

13. Judith Hoch-Smith and Anita Spring, *Women in Ritual and Symbolic Roles* (New York: Plenum Press, 1978).

14. Eleanor Abdella Doumato, *Getting God's Ear: Women, Islam and Healing in Saudi Arabia and the Gulf* (New York: Columbia University Press, 2000), 37–38.

15. Ildikó Bellér-Hann, "Making the Oil Fragrant: Dealings with the Supernatural among the Uyghurs in Xinjiang," *Asian Ethnicity* 2, no. 1 (2001): 15.

16. Doumato, *Getting God's Ear*, 8.

17. Rubie Watson, "Chinese Bridal Laments: the Claims of a Dutiful Daughter," in *Harmony and Counterpoint: Ritual Music in Chinese Context*, ed. Bell Yung, Evelyn S. Rawski, and Rubie S. Watson (Palo Alto, CA: Stanford University Press, 1996), 129.

18. Ali Jihad Racy, *Making Music in the Arab World: The Culture and Artistry of Tarab* (New York: Cambridge University Press, 2003): 54–65.

19. Raudvere, *Book and the Roses*.

20. Christine R. Yano, *Tears of Longing: Nostalgia and the Nation in Japanese Popular Song* (Cambridge, MA: Harvard University Press, 2002).

21. Steven Feld, *Sound and Sentiment: Birds, Weeping, Poetics and Song in Kaluli Expression* (Philadelphia: University of Pennsylvania Press, 1990).

22. Yano, *Tears of Longing*, 120, 121.

23. See, e.g., Judith Becker, *Deep Listeners: Music, Emotion and Trancing* (Bloomington: Indiana University Press, 2004); Steven Friedson, *Dancing Prophets: Musical Experience in Tumbuka Healing* (Chicago: University of Chicago Press, 1996); Richard C. Jankowsky, "Music, Spirit Possession and the In-Between: Ethnomusicological Inquiry and the Challenge of Trance," *Ethnomusicology Forum* 16, no. 2 (2007): 185–208; Gilbert Rouget, *Music and Trance: A Theory of the Relations between Music and Possession* (Chicago: University of Chicago Press, 1985).

24. John Baily, *Music of Afghanistan: Professional Musicians in the City of Herat* (Cambridge: Cambridge University Press, 1988); John Baily, *Can You Stop the Birds Singing? The Censorship of Music in Afghanistan* (Copenhagen: Freemuse, 2001); Veronica Doubleday, "The Frame Drum in the Middle East: Women, Musical Instruments and Power," *Ethnomusicology* 43, no. 1 (1999): 101–34; Hiromi Lorraine Sakata, "The Complementary Opposition of Music and Religion in Afghanistan," *World of Music* 20, no. 3 (1986): 33–41.

25. Ildikó Bellér-Hann, *The Written and the Spoken: Literacy and Oral Transmission among the Uyghur* (Berlin: Anor, 2000): 40.

26. Kristina Nelson, *The Art of Reciting the Qur'an* (Cairo: American University in Cairo Press, 2001).

27. Racy, *Making Music in the Arab World*, 25.

28. Virginia Danielson, *The Voice of Egypt: Umm Kulthum, Arabic Song, and Egyptian Society in the Twentieth Century* (Chicago: University of Chicago Press, 1997), 21, 144.

29. Shemeem Burney Abbas, *The Female Voice in Sufi Ritual: Devotional Practices of Pakistan and India* (Austin: University of Texas Press, 2002).

30. Regula B. Qureshi, *Sufi Music of India and Pakistan* (Cambridge: Cambridge University Press, 1986).

31. See Harris, *Making of a Musical Canon*.

32. A simple form of digital video technology.

33. See Edmund Waite, "The Emergence of Muslim Reformism in Contemporary Xinjiang," in *Situating the Uyghurs: Between China and Central Asia*, ed. Bellér-Hann, Césaro, Harris, and Smith (Aldershot, UK: Ashgate Press, 2007), 165–81.

34. Veronica Doubleday, *Three Women of Herat* (London: Cape, 1988), 65.

35. See, e.g., Fernea, *Guests of the Sheik*.

36. Benedicte Grima, *The Performance of Emotion among Paxtun Women: "The Misfortunes Which Have Befallen Me"* (Austin: University of Texas Press, 1992), 16–26.

37. Ibid., 30.

38. Doubleday, *Three Women of Herat*, 157–213.

39. Ibid., 195.

40. Ibid., 211.

41. Karin Van Nieuwkerk, "On Religion, Gender, and Performing: Female Performers and Repentence in Egypt," in *Music and Gender: Perspectives from the Mediterranean*, ed. Tullia Magrini (Chicago: University of Chicago Press, 2003): 273–74.

42. Pashsha Ishan, interview, April 1998, Ürümchi.
43. Waite, *Emergence of Muslim Reformism.*
44. Jay Dautcher, *Down a Narrow Road: Identity and Masculinity in a Uyghur Community in Xinjiang China* (Cambridge, MA: Harvard University Press, 2009); see also Harris, *Making of a Musical Canon.*
45. Sanubar Tursun, personal communication, July 2009, Shahyar.
46. Rahila Dawut, personal communication, August 2009, Ürümchi.
47. Aygul, interview, July 2009, Shahyar.
48. Van Nieuwkerk, *Religion, Gender, and Performing,* 277–78.
49. Doubleday, *Three Women of Herat,* 109.

Chapter Eighteen

Bodies, Gender, and Worldviews

Me-mot Spirit Mediums in the Jingxi Region of Guangxi

Xiao Mei

The core behavior of religious or faith systems generally revolves around how people establish contact with the supernatural. Anthony Wallace summarizes twelve kinds of religious behavior globally: prayer, music, physical experience, exhortation, reciting codes, simulation, mana or taboo, feasts, sacrifice, congregation, inspiration, and symbolism.[1] But the basis for distinguishing different types of religious practitioners within a religious or faith system generally lies in its choice of the diverse forms of liaising with the supernatural.

For instance, in China, practitioners who serve as intermediaries between supernatural gods (*shen* 神) and ghosts (*gui* 鬼)[2] and human beings through possession and trance are generally known as *wu* 巫, or "spirit mediums." Daoist priests, in contrast, adopt liturgy and ritual, using talismans and mantras. Of course, Daoist ritual skills, used to avert calamity and pray for well-being, have their origins in skills that mediums have practiced in different historical periods, like folk medicine, rain prayers, interpretation of dreams, divination, and summoning the soul—indeed, the Daoists' use of talismans and mantras derives directly from mediumism. But the main difference between them is that the Daoists do not make the gods descend by using their own bodies to "journey to the other world" (*zouyin* 走阴); whereas the subjects of this chapter, the *me-mot* mediums of the Zhuang people in Debao and Jingxi Counties in the southwest of the Guangxi Zhuang Autonomous Region, near the border with Vietnam, make the gods descend, visualize ghosts, and enter the formless world.

An integral part of any ritual enactment is its rich spectrum of sound: a wide range of vocal utterances as well as other sounds made by musical instruments and ritual objects. This ritual soundscape completes the meaning and efficacy of the ritual, including symbolic meaning of different sounds, perhaps particularly as a channel or facilitator of communication with the spirit world. Since the different types of ritual specialists produce different ritual soundscapes, I start the discussion by explaining them.

There is a variety of types of spirit mediums in China. There are both male and female mediums, going right back to the terms *wu* (female) and *xi/ji* 觋 (male) in the section on the Chu kingdom in the ancient *Conversations of the states* (*Guoyu* 国语).[3] My own fieldwork in Guangxi shows two situations regarding gender classification, one consistent with the biological sex of the practitioner, one not: that is, whether mediums are biologically male or female, when performing as mediums they adopt the role of female. But whether male or female, they all have the experience of having encountered intractable calamity, either personal (e.g., incurable illness or mental disorder) or domestic (e.g., frequent illness or death in the family), and it is only through becoming a medium that they can be released from such calamities.

In ancient records, such as the *Zhouli* 周礼 (Rites of Zhou) from the second century BCE, we find a division of labor between the male *xi* and the female *wu*. Some scholars have claimed that they were possessed by different gods or even that male mediums were possessed by gods, female mediums by "souls" (*hun* 魂) or "spirits" (*ling* 灵). But research shows that the role of *tongji* 童乩 (in Hokkien dialect, *dang-ki*, a medium connecting with the gods), once thought to be only filled by men, is in fact also filled by women.[4] And female mediums can act as intermediaries both between people and gods and between people and ghosts (dead souls).

So I consider that, apart from gender, a more significant typological distinction for mediums is still the *methods* by which they communicate with the supernatural. That is, although male and female mediums both have the ability to be possessed by gods and ghosts, the means by which they are possessed are different. For instance, we might differentiate the type who perform rituals to lead dead souls or investigate the cause of sickness by means of possession or visitation by a god or ghost from the type who through a vision or dream obtain techniques of spiritual transmission in the underworld (e.g., an ancestral lineage of the formless world) and master a set of skills of the medium's journey through formal rituals like "opening the eyes" (*kaiguang* 开光), "donning the headgear" (*jiamian* 加冕), or "crossing the passes" (*guoguan* 过关), on which journey they are able actively to seek out gods and ghosts.[5]

In the contents and methods of mediums' ritual practice, it is important to distinguish whether they make the medium's journey or can actively manipulate spirits. This also influences the nature and venue of their performance: rituals performed within the private domestic sphere, for curing illness, enhancing fertility, or bringing out dead souls, may be officiated by either type of medium. Conversely, mediums who perform rituals in the public domain, like those discussed in this chapter, are generally those who can undertake the medium journey, actively visiting and manipulating gods and ghosts in order to achieve various ritual goals, transmitting news from the formless world on behalf of the souls of the ancestors and deceased kin of their followers and patrons.

In China, spirit mediums may practice independently but also often officiate over rituals in collaboration with other folk ritual specialists such as Daoist or Buddhist priests. In this collaboration, they mainly utilize their ability to journey to the underworld and "make the gods descend," investigating problems in the supernatural formless world.[6]

In Jingxi County the *me-mot* have a close relationship with lay Zhengyi Daoist priests known as *daogong*. The *daogong* not only play a major role during the process of someone becoming a medium but also need to practice rituals for averting calamity and seeking blessing along with the medium. So how do their ritual practices differ? What kinds of competition, collaboration, and influences are there between them? This chapter seeks to explain the relation of *me-mot* mediums and Daoist priests in the Jingxi region from the perspective of gender and their use of the body and singing styles during rituals, and to explore the local social structure and worldview revealed by these relations. Therefore, this chapter is divided into three sections. Section one explains the relation of *me-mot* mediums and Daoist priests in the Jingxi region from the perspective of gender. Section two discusses the different ritual practices of *me-mot* and Daoists. Finally, I comment on the differences between their music-making and ritual soundscapes.

Daoism and *Mot* from a Gender Perspective

The most popular forms of folk religion in the Jingxi region are the indigenous polytheistic faiths of the two systems of the *me-mot* mediums and folk Daoist priests (the latter also permeated by Buddhist and Confucian values). These two systems subsume four categories of ritualists (see table 18.1).

Table 18.1. Types of ritual specialists

	Local term	Chinese term	Local Chinese gloss	Gender
Daoist system	*pouta:u*	*daogong* 道公	*yang* 洋 (foreign) *daogong*	male
	poumo	*mogong* 魔公	*tu* 土 (local) *daogong*	male
Mot system	*me mot*		*mopo* 魔婆, *wupo* 巫婆	female
	mot da		*monan* 魔男	male

In fact, though here I focus on the common local dichotomy between *mot* and *dao*, local ritual specialists go beyond these two systems and four types.[7] In the "Daoist system" here, *pou*[45] is an appellation given to the husband's father, *ta:u* is the local pronunciation of the *dao* of Daoism, and *mo* refers to a ritualist. The main distinctions between *daogong* and *mogong* are the different scripts and language they use. The *daogong* uses ritual scriptures written in Chinese characters, pronounced in the Guiliu 桂柳 dialect of the southwestern official language system; whereas the *mogong*'s texts are written in the "square letters" of the local Zhuang script[8] and pronounced in local dialect.

In the *mot* system, *me* designates a woman who has given birth to children, *mot* (like the *mo* of *mogong*, often glossed in Chinese as *mo* 魔, similar to *wu*) means a "spirit medium." Becoming a *mot* is not restricted to women; men can take on this role and are then called *mot da*, the qualifying morpheme *da* being added to designate biological maleness. Once these men have become *mot*, they act exactly the same as their female counterparts for ritual performance, taking on feminine traits through cross-dressing. The common characteristic of these mediums is the behavioral mode that centers on trance and their common capability of "clairvoyance" or "communicating with ghosts."

Both systems of ritualists have their respective genealogies of grand masters and successors, but in the Daoist system, there is no record of female ritualists so far. That is, in a lineage containing *daogong*, if the fate of succession falls upon a female, then she can never become a *daogong*, only a *mot*. Therefore, in the popular belief system, the sexual distinction between *dao* and mot is that Daoist ritualists are male, *mot* ritualists female (see fig. 18.1).

Different Ritual Functions of *Dao* and *Mot*

In their ritual practice, are there divisions of labor and distinctions between the female *mot* and the male *dao*? Some Western scholars have posited a taxonomy of dualistic relations of male-female and public-private,[9] for example, the private domain is gendered female and the public domain male. In addition, the twin notions of central cult and peripheral cult have also been used to distinguish between central practices, which uphold mainstream morality, usually gendered male and public, and women's possession cults, regarded as peripheral and potentially read as subversive or as providing compensation for women's marginalized position in society.[10] However, the local belief system in the Jingxi region is more complex. *Me-mot* can perform rituals independently and openly in public contexts, just like the *daogong*. For instance, I attended a ritual performed by a *me-mot* for "guaranteeing well-being" (*bao ping'an* 保平安) in the Guanyinmiao temple of Hurunshan on behalf of thirteen households of a neighborhood of the local township[11] and the "inviting Chang'e" ritual performed by the *me-mot* every year on the fifteenth day of the eighth moon on behalf of the entire community of Longguang village.[12] Major "grand offering" (*dajiao* 大醮) rituals to the earth god (*tudigong* 土地公) for the entire community are also held every three years during the intercalary twelfth moon,

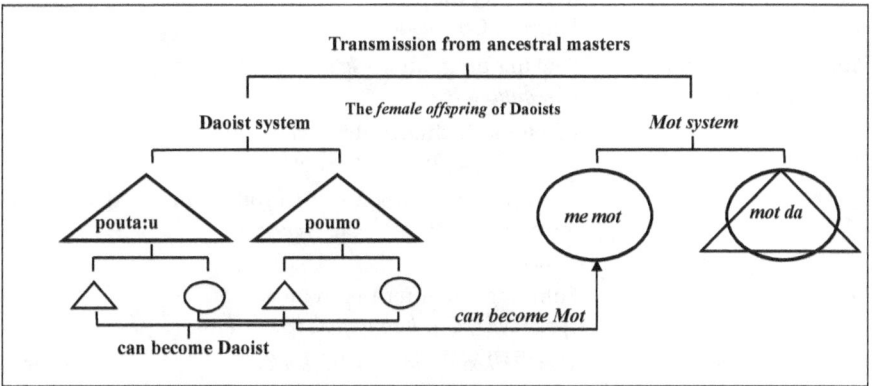

Figure 18.1. Gendered lines of transmission among *daogong* and *me-mot*.

for which at least three *daogong* and three *me-mot* must officiate. Meanwhile, *daogong* can also help *me-mot* enact some private domestic rituals, such as those relating to childbirth. The key distinction between their division of labor is not public or private but their different limitations in capability.

These distinctions are listed in table 18.2. As you can see, some rituals may be performed independently by either the *me-mot* or the *daogong*; some are performed by both in collaboration; some may only be performed by one or the other. For instance, most rituals to seek pregnancy for an infertile couple belong exclusively to the *me-mot*. She leads the souls of the couple to enter the "garden" that is responsible for children and to select a flower from it. Since the garden belongs to the formless world, the *me-mot* relies on her capacity to journey to the other world to lead them there. "Retrieving the soul" of people with a long-term incurable illness, too, can only be performed by the *me-mot*; the *daogong* is not capable of this, since the ritual depends on the *me-mot*'s gift of clairvoyance. Her method of diagnosis is mainly "inspecting the clothes" (θa:i^{45}θi^{2323}, Ch. *kan yifu* 看衣服) of the client in order to determine what kind of ritual is necessary to heal them.

Conversely, let us consider a ritual that the *me-mot* cannot perform, like "smashing the hells"—the ritual performed by both Daoists and Buddhists to liberate the dead soul from purgatory. One might suppose that since the *me-mot* is able to journey to the other world, she would be able to visualize the hells that are part of what is generally considered the underworld. So why can't the *me-mot* visit the hells? As they told me, "The Daoists journey to the hells, they have secret techniques; we can't go to the hells, we journey in the heavens." This distinction yields an important clue: the other world of the hells and the formless other world in which the *me-mot* journey are two distinct areas, one beneath the earth, and the other in the heavens. So what are the "secret techniques" of the *daogong*? According to the *me-mot*, "The Daoists have texts (*shu*),

Table 18.2. Roles of *me-mot* and *daogong* in some rituals in Jingxi County

Healing rituals	Retrieving the soul (*ʔa:u⁵³ kʰwan⁵⁴*, Ch. *shouhun* 收魂)	m	
Rituals for childbirth and children	Seeking pregnancy (*kʲau³¹ wa⁵⁴*, Ch. *qiuhua* 求花)	m*	d
	For smooth childbirth[a] (*hat⁴⁴kiu³¹ wa⁵⁴*, Ch. *jia huaqiao* 架花桥)	m*	d
	Protecting baby upon its first full moon (*an²³²³¹ wa⁵⁴*, Ch. *anhua* 安花)	m*	d
	Fulfilling vow after pregnancy (*poi³¹wa⁵⁴*, Ch. *huanhua* 还花)		m/d
Ancestor worship	*khən²³²³koŋ⁴⁵ tso²³²³*, Ch. *jizu* 祭祖	d	d/m
Blessing rituals	Celebrating longevity (*pou²³²³li:ŋ³¹*, Ch. *zhushou* 祝寿)	m	d
	Seeking promotion (*da:ŋ⁵⁴ dau³¹*, Ch. *qiansheng* 迁升)	m	d
	Escorting the gods (*so:ŋ⁴⁵: θi:n⁵⁴*, Ch. *songshen* 送神)	m	d
	Grand offering for the community (*da⁵⁴ zhao⁵⁴*, Ch. *dajiao* 大醮)		d/m
	"Raising the star"[b] (*ta:i³¹ θəŋ⁵⁴*, Ch. *taixing* 抬星)	m	
	Settling the gods (*an²³²³ θi:n⁵⁴*, Ch. *anshen* 安神)	m	d
Exorcism	Minor	m	d
	Major		m+d
Mortuary rituals	Funeral		d/m
	Smashing the hells (*po⁴⁵ nio²³²³*, Ch. *poyu* 破狱)	d	
	Burial of people who died away from home (*tai⁵⁴ wai²¹⁴ wa:ŋ³¹*, Ch. *hunqianzang* 魂迁葬)	d	

Note: This is a selective, not complete, list of representative rituals performed by *mot* and *dao* in the Jingxi region. m* means a higher ratio of *mot* than *dao*; m/d means that *mo* and *dao* both perform, with *mot* in charge and *dao* subsidiary; d/m means the other way round; m+d means that both must officiate.

a. The ritual for smooth childbirth (lit. building the child bridge) is performed when the woman is five to seven months pregnant, but a woman only does this once in her lifetime, ensuring that her future pregnancies will also run smoothly by means of this bridge.

b. "Raising the star": in local belief, everyone's fate belongs to their own heavenly star. If someone is suffering from bad fortune, it means that their personal star has fallen down, thus requiring it to be raised again to its position on high. This ritual segment is usually subsumed within other rituals.

they have talismans (*fu*), they are the 'great man' (*dazhangfu* 大丈夫)." Clearly, their secret techniques are their ritual manuals, talismans, and mantras. Daoist cosmology holds that the soul of the deceased either ascends to the realm of the immortals or descends to the hells; thus in order to rescue the soul of one who has descended to the "bitter sea" of the hells, they must smash the hells of the underworld and release the soul. But smashing the hells is a product of the Buddhist theory of karmic rebirth, which was adapted by the Daoists as early as the Northern and Southern dynasties (420–589 CE). Thus we can see that the reason the *me-mot* are unable to journey to the hells is not because their powers of clairvoyance are deficient, but because the hells do not belong to their own "other world." For the indigenous culture of the Zhuang, the hells are actually part of the concepts of an external "civilization" or faith.

Physical and Singing Styles

Thus the different sources of power of the *me-mot* and *daogong* explain why they have formed different means of solving problems. We can explore these differences further through the distinct physical and singing styles they adopt in their rituals.

In August 2005, I attended a "settling the gods for sacrificing to the ancestors" (*jizu anshen* 祭祖安神) ritual at the house of the Huang family in Kangshangtun hamlet of Anning village, with both *me-mot* and *daogong* presiding. The practitioners were a Daoist also surnamed Huang and his assistant, the *me-mot* Jintang, and village women offering incense. The ritual specialists face the host's altar (Ch. *shentai* 神台 holy platform), the *daogong*'s altar to the right, the *me-mot*'s to the left. The *daogong* sits on a chair; the *me-mot* sits cross-legged on a mat on the ground. Though both are performing for the same ritual, their responsibilities are distinct.

The *daogong* first "sweeps away filth" (*saohui* 扫秽) by reciting the scriptures, accompanying himself with small cymbals, "burning the memorial" (*shaobiao* 烧表), "ascending to the constellations" (*shanggang* 上罡), and "depicting talismans" (*huafu* 画符). After registering all the names in the "setting up the altar" (*shetan* 设坛) ritual, he goes on to perform a sequence of rituals: "settling the gods" (*anshen* 安神), "untying the passes" (*jieguan* 解关), "settling the fences" (*anlan* 安栏), and "escorting away calamity" (*songzai* 送灾 to escort away the Yama kings of the underworld and the White Tiger). Finally he "escorts the gods away" (*songshen* 送神).

At the start of the ritual, the *me-mot* "invites the ghosts" (çə:n^{2323}pa^{214}, Ch. *qinggui* 请鬼) of her own ancestral masters to occupy her body. She then dons her clothing and headgear, like a military general donning his tabard and armor, and lowers the veil to cover her face. In trance, she begins the medium's journey, singing as she does so, all along inspecting and seeking images of

Figure 18.2. A male *mot*. Photograph by author.

Figure 18.3. Making the medium's journey. Photograph by author.

the souls of the family members, on the way meeting all kinds of gods (of the stove, doorway, water, field, tree, mountain, etc.),[13] going from the house to the village, outside the village, through mountains and forests, right up to the "street of heaven" (*tianjie* 天街 like a market where items pertaining to people's fate, such as stars, may be bought), constantly beseeching the gods to give her directions.

Since she sits on a mat called a "saddle-pad" throughout the ritual, the *me-mot*'s ritual performance is mainly through song. No matter how many gods, ghosts, and human beings are presented, and regardless of their attitudes and emotions, they are mainly realized through the trance of the *me-mot* and occasionally with other practitioners in ritual; basically, it is a monodrama. What is distinctive is that this kind of interpretation through monologue is different from *Daiyan* style (a genre of character representation) drama; here an individual provides access to various events, settings, and characters, storytelling in a combination of narrative and successive characters within a story.

Besides singing songs, the *me-mot* utilizes various sound styles: spoken parts; solo recitation using the traditional pronunciation of certain words, which is slightly different from that of current local dialect; reciting verse; incantation; chanting, which appears to be less closely tied to speech tones than recitation; onomatopoeia, as well as instruments; all of which constitute the soundscape spectrum.

For example, an almost silent weak voice of incantation guarantees the procedures of pleasing gods, admitting souls, and eradicating woes; as to the spoken parts of the ritual, the *me-mot* behaves like a medium to speak for the family. Solo recitation tells us that the *me-mot* is with the gods on behalf of a possessed ancestor or speaks for gods directly. Recitation comes from Daoist scriptures, which serve as a means of eradicating woes; whereas onomatopoeia, such as "pu . . . ," which is like a horse's sneeze, means they feel tired, it's time to change.

One crucial segment is seeking out the souls lost in the fields and mountains; the host household is only guaranteed well-being once all of its lost souls have been summoned back. On the journey the *me-mot* also has to pass the "grave land" of the host household, where with her assistance the host can meet the deceased ancestors; at this moment, they can use the *me-mot*'s mouth to speak out their own demands and answer the questions of the living descendants. With the *me-mot* as intermediary, the ancestors may speak out the source of the afflictions besetting the household. This is another crucial stage in assessing the power of the *me-mot*.

Now the *daogong* suddenly instructs the host to catch and kill a rooster. He performs the rituals of "escorting away the Thunder King" (*song leiwang* 送雷王) and "untying the passes [obstacles] of the three realms" (*jie sanjie guan* 解三界关). The phrase *untying the passes* means breaking evil spirits to avoid disaster under the guidance of Daoist theology. The term *sanjie* means three realms: the human realm (*renjie* 人界), the realm of the gods (*xianjie* 仙界), and that of ghosts (*guijie* 鬼界). This ritual was added at the spur of the moment, and, when I asked why, Huang *daogong* replied that while the *me-mot* was passing through the grave land, she "saw" that the family was involved in bitter verbal wrangling, so they needed the "untying the passes of the three realms" ritual. But although the *me-mot* is the one who "saw" it, it is the *daogong* who has to use his ritual skills to resolve the obstacles. This is an example of the interaction of the *me-mot* and *daogong*.

Throughout the ritual sequence, I note, in the sacrificial rituals performed by the *daogong*, the household members offering incense at the main household altar and that of the *daogong* are all male, while it is the women of the household who are mostly assembled around the altar of the *me-mot*. But, in the ritual sequences of the *daogong*, apart from the complex ritual procedures of untying the passes, which attract people to crowd round, the *daogong*'s other activities in reciting the scriptures have virtually no audience—it is as if he is talking to himself. The situation of the *me-mot*, on the other hand, is completely different: the household women are assembled all around her from start to finish, following her journey by burning paper artifacts (money, clothes, *maolang* 茅郎 doll effigies), and, as she gleans information from the other world, responding to and awaiting a dialogue with the spirits of the ancestors occupying her body. I also note that, apart from her demanding that the *daogong* should add the untying the passes ritual after she had "seen" the grave-land dispute, there are other segments where the two have to interact, such as the *me-mot*'s use of the red paper cuts, made by the *daogong* to symbolize a bridge, for her own rituals of making a bridge at her altar in order to "open up a road" for the children of the host household and solve their problems.

This domestic ritual illustrates the differences arising between the *me-mot* and *daogong* while performing together with a similar ritual purpose. Apart from their different ritual spaces, ritual itineraries, methods, and contents, the means of using their bodies and singing are also distinctive, as I will now show.

Me-mot No Face, *Daogong* No Closed Eyes

No face means that the face of the *me-mot* is almost entirely covered by the veil of her headgear throughout the whole ritual, and, what is more, behind her veil she "sees" through closed eyes; what she sees is the formless world, which the *daogong* cannot see. This distinction reveals the different sources of power of the *me-mot* and *daogong*. As to the shared ritual of exorcism, the *daogong* recites the liturgical text, with incantations and talismans, while the *me-mot* "closes her eyes in trance and responds to whatever she sees." As to ritual music, in her exposition the *me-mot* relies on being possessed by the spirits and thus "sees" ($\theta a{:}i^{45}\theta i^{2323}$, as opposed to $ko{:}i^{53}$, the verb for seeing the material world) the formless world through her closed eyes. Thus her singing seems improvisatory and random: she interacts closely with her followers, and her subjects adhere closely to secular life.[14] When she can see different scenes and figures on her journey or is possessed by different gods and ghosts, her vocal utterances may also change in singing tone, timbre, and style of recitation as well as the content expressed. The capability of the *me-mot* is in her power of entering into the formless world, whereas the "magic power" of the *daogong* derives from his reliance on the ritual manuals and on the power of the talismans and mantras of his Daoist order.

The Oral-Literate Dichotomy of Me-mot and Daogong

The *me-mot* performs the ritual content through oral narration (singing), while the *daogong* recites and sings according to the text of his ritual manuals. This distinction between oral and textual leads to different ritual languages. As mentioned above, the *daogong* uses the Guiliu dialect of southwestern Chinese official language, while the *me-mot* uses local Zhuang dialect. In melodic style, the *daogong* sings in a standard Daoist liturgical style transmitted from the Maoshan lineage, while the *me-mot* mostly adopts the local "mountain song" (*shan'ge*) style. The *me-mot* draws on generally available musical forms for her ritual and does not have exclusive specific musical knowledge. However her

Figure 18.4. A *daogong* reciting from his ritual manual. Photograph by author

adaptation of these forms is skilled. The *me-mot* should obey strict norms of poetic construction, following the rules and forms of lyrics in five- or seven-word verse, sentence by sentence, to form a song in the specific rhyming style of her journey.

The *me-mot*'s use of rhyme works according to a unique principle. It is a kind of mixture of different rhymes: the antecedent line uses a final rhyme, while the rhyme of the consequent line lies in the middle of the line. Called a "waist-foot rhyme" (*yaojiaoyun*), it is the most prevalent principle in Zhuang folk song. The following diagrams show examples of five- and seven-word rhyming. Boxes mark the rhymes, where the square means an end rhyme and the triangle means a middle rhyme.

Five-word verse:

"When I took my first step out of the door, heavy tears fell down my cheek."

Nap^{21} mi^{31} tou^{54} ta:i^{214} at^{44},   nam^{13} that^{44} lei^{214} pan^{31} naŋ^{45}
            ▲   ■

Seven-word verse:

"Like a guest, this flower [the *me-mot*] learned about rituals from the gods who have money and books"

No:k^{55} tsou^{2323} ma^{31} ha:k^{55} lok^{21} leu^{13} j$\boxed{\text{ei}}$^{31} pa^{214} lou^{13} m$\boxed{\text{ei}}$^{31} ŋən^{31} θei^{54} koŋ^{45}koŋ^{45}

▲ ■

As has been mentioned, the singing of the *me-mot* has an improvisatory character, for she sings whatever she sees in the course of the ritual journey. The syntax is also varied, combined into a new kind of verse with five-word antecedent lines and seven-word consequent lines, or the other way around. The structure can be made more complicated by adding an opener at the beginning of a three- or five-word verse, followed by a tail at the end. Whatever the structure turns out to be, the rule of rhyme must be consistent.

Apostrophe + three-sentence verse + interjection:

ja^{214} lei^{31}

wan^{31} nai^{54} tsu^{2323} than^{54} luŋ^{31} o:k^{55} t$\boxed{\text{oŋ}}$^{214},
▲

thin^{54} khai^{54} tsu^{2323} tan^{54} f$\boxed{\text{oŋ}}$^{214} o:k^{55} l$\boxed{\text{ən}}$^{31}
■ ▲

Me^{214} na:ŋ^{31} te^{2323} jo^{54} t$\boxed{\text{ən}}$^{54} o:k^{55} l$\boxed{\text{o}}$^{214}
■ ▲

n$\boxed{\text{o}}$^{214} lən^{31}
■

According to the changes in her walking and the ability of her singing and constructing poetic rhymes, the local people identify whether a *me-mot* is efficacious. As to reception, the local people understand the songs of the *me-mot*, but not the liturgy of the *daogong* (see table 18.3).

Therefore, the apparent distinction between oral and literate traditions is only an external phenomenon. Because of the *me-mot*'s bodily character, her possessions are always hard to fix in text. Moreover, as she is a spiritual intermediary, her role is always changing in various ritual settings in order to speak for different spirits and ghosts; her singing always derives from multiple sources. The *me-mot* sings songs corresponding to what she has seen using different content and tone during her possession.

Table 18.3. Performative distinctions between *daogong* and *me-mot*

	Daogong system	*Me-mot* system
Source of power	Daoist liturgy and talismans	Trance and possession
Style of expression	Text-based literate tradition	Oral tradition
Language	Southwestern official language	Local dialect
Melodic style	Daoist liturgical style	Folk song
Physical expression	"No closed eyes"	"No face"
Textual content	Composed	Improvised
Role within ritual	Stable	Fluid
Cultural identity	Imperial power	Local popular culture

On the ritual journey, the *me-mot* carries a chain and a plate, both made of brass. She strikes the plate ($pəŋ^{31} ma^{13}$) with the chain ($θ_i^{55}θa{:}k^{55}$) held in her left hand, producing a regular beat, and moves an unfolded fan in her right hand back and forth to the rhythmic beat of the chain. The chain symbolizes a horse, the plate symbolizes a manger, and the fan denotes a sword and whip. All these signify that the *me-mot* makes her ritual journey on horseback. The sound of the chain striking the plate can be heard as the clip-clop of horses' hooves; it not only provides a percussive rhythm for the singing of the *me-mot* but also serves as a linking and transitional force between phrases and periods. This constitutes the principal soundscape. These, together with the gestures made by the *me-mot's* right hand with the fan, create a performance mimicking horse-back riding.

The *me-mot* takes whatever she sees (or hears) on her ritual journey into the invisible world as the subject of her singing. The technical consequences of this are the relatively great length of the narrative section and the unfolding and cyclic character of the structure of the tunes. The tunes primarily consist of four or five notes. Although a number of different sections are produced throughout the ritual journey, all are built on one basic tune.

In example 18.1, the first four bars constitute the basic tune, made up of an antecedent and a consequent. The fifth and sixth bars serve as a middle section, and the last four bars are a nearly exact repetition of the first four bars. This basic principle underlies the expanded narrative, producing a kind of verse-chorus form: a + b + a + c + a + d + a ... as shown in example 18.2. The individual "verses" vary in meter, rhythm, or melody.

As to the *daogong*, once he has mastered the powers of ritual manuals, incantations, and talismans, then whatever the rituals (exorcism, healing illness, selecting auspicious days for house building, interpreting horoscopes, untying the obstacles, mortuary rituals, communal offerings, etc.), he will enact his ritual skills according to a fixed procedure; his role is unchanging from beginning to end of the ritual.

Example 18.1. Basic tune of the *me-mot*.

The Relationship of Me-mot and Daogong

A popular story in the Jingxi region about *daogong* and *me-mot* relates how in ancient times they were older brother and younger sister. The older brother made his living as a *daogong*, so in order to enable his sister to make a living too, he cut off half his sleeve and gave it to her; the sleeve became the veil of the *me-mot*'s headgear, enabling her to become a medium. And this is why nowadays we can see the sleeve of the *daogong* is cut shorter than normal.

In fact, the *me-mot* relies on the *daogong* in two aspects when she becomes sure of her destiny as a medium. First, every *me-mot* has a genealogy of ancestral

Example 18.2. Verse-chorus form in the *me-mot's* song.

ritual masters (which may include the titles of both gods and deceased *mot*, both male and female), and so, before she embarks on the medium's journey, she must request these spirits occupy her body to provide her source of power. But since most *me-mot* are more or less illiterate, she depends on the *daogong* to write down her mediumistic genealogy in Chinese characters and to offer it up to her own "grand master shrine" (Ch. *zushilou* 祖师楼) to confirm her genealogy in the formless world. Second, in her ritual of donning the headgear to become a medium, the *me-mot* needs to invite the *daogong* to bestow mantras and talismans, some of which she learns to perform herself. The possession of her genealogy of ancestral masters implies that the *me-mot* owns, and is capable of directing, the military forces of the ancestral masters in the formless world; the talismans and mantras of the *daogong* supplement her own magical powers.

Once in the *me-mot's* inner room I saw her carefully writing characters—what she was actually doing was practicing depicting talismans and copying out mantras and secret formulas! She was basically illiterate, but, over the course of knowing her for several years, I found that she was becoming keen to learn the written characters of ritual manuals. Thus—unlike our initial impression of a ritual division of labor whereby the *me-mot* can only discover problems through "seeing" the formless, whereas the task of resolving these problems is then consigned to the *daogong*—over the *me-mot's* career of practicing ritual, there is a constant potential for learning from the *daogong* and thereby enhancing her own ability to solve problems herself.

Therefore, in her ritual practice, the *me-mot* in the Jingxi region is not only clairvoyant but can also practice ritual skills; she can not only perceive problems but solve them. At the same time as expanding the use of her bodies, she expands the types of rituals she can perform and their scope. It is precisely through the *me-mot's* further adoption of Daoist elements that she is not merely a spiritual intermediary with the formless world but at the same time has the power to solve problems. Thus, historically, while Daoism's liturgy and magical techniques (like talismans and mantras) originally derived from ancient *wu* mediums, in a specific society, the two distinct faith systems of Daoists and mediums have never ceased to amalgamate.

Although the Daoism of the Jingxi region derives directly from Han Chinese culture, the local Zhuang people, including the mediumistic faith system represented by the *me-mot*, have also gradually absorbed the concept of imperial orthodoxy from Han Chinese culture. Still, however much official imperial power (as represented by maleness and the *daogong*) may be regarded as a legitimate supporter of the *me-mot*'s ritual practice, it still cannot entirely supplant the formless world that coexists with the material world in the Zhuang belief system. According to the Zhuang, afflictions arising in the material world must have roots in the formless world, and the Zhuang still need the eyes of the medium in order to "see" the formless world.

Thus we can now understand why both the *me-mot* and *daogong* often officiate in the same ritual. Major rituals for well-being in the public domain also require the *me-mot* to act on behalf of the villagers to ensure that their family line will prosper by visiting the spirits of the formless world and "raising the star" on behalf of her patrons. All this at the same time, the *daogong* is performing parallel rituals, reciting ritual manuals, mantras, using talismans, and so on, offering to heaven and earth and exorcizing demons. This implies that the coexistence of so-called public and private domains in Zhuang social structure similarly embodies an affirmation of parallelism. Lineage transmission, symbolized by female fertility, is not merely a private family affair; it also forms a communal emblem for people's aspirations. Both "private" and "public" domains require a structural equilibrium between the material and formless worlds. And, while the Daoist chanting embodies the written scripture, the *me-mot* sing and embody the invisible world by means of a varied, improvised sound spectrum.

Notes

This chapter derives from fieldwork on spirit mediums in Guangxi, southwest China, documented more extensively in Chinese in Xiao Mei, "Chang zai wulu shang," in *Zhongguo minjian yishi yinyue yanjiu, Huanan juan*, ed. Tsao Pen-Yeh [Cao Benye] (Shanghai: Shanghai yinyue xueyuan chubanshe, 2007), 328–494. Note also the ritual excerpts on the accompanying DVD. I am grateful to Dr. Stephen Jones for his insightful comments and help with editing this article.

1. Antony Wallace, *Religion: An Anthropological View* (New York: Random House, 1966), chap. 1.

2. I give most terms in standard Chinese, which is a lingua franca in the region, sometimes adding local pronunciations, such as in table 18.2. Where local pronunciations are given, superscript numbers indicate pitch levels. In the Sino-Tibetan language family, to which the Zhuang speech group belongs, tones differentiate meaning. Thus pou^{45} indicates that the word begins at the 4th pitch level and rises to the 5th pitch level.

3. For the relation of ancient mediums to rain prayers in modern Shaanbei, see Xiao Mei, "Huwu yujue qi ganlin: Xibei (Shaanbei) diqu qiyu yishi yu yinyue diaocha zongshu," in *Zhongguo minjian yishi yinyue yanjiu, Xibei juan*, ed. Tsao Pen-Yeh (Kunming: Yunnan renmin chubanshe, 2003).

4. Cai Peiru, "Quansuo tianrenzhiji de nüren: Nü tongji de xingbie tezhi yu shenti yihan," *Qinghua daxue renleixue congkan* 4 (Taipei: Tangshan chubanshe, 2001): 5–20.

5. Such mediums may resemble "shamans," and some Chinese scholars have described them thus; e.g., for Guangxi, see Gao Yaning, "Guangxi Jingxi xian Zhuangren nongcun shehuizhong me^{214}. mot^{31}. (mopo) de yangcheng guocheng yu yishi biaoyan" (master's thesis, Taiwan guoli qinghua daxue renleixue yanjiusuo, 2000); for the *xiangtong* of southwest Shandong, Chen Yanjiao, "Zhongyuan 'samanjiao': Luxinan Shawoxiang yishi biaoyan" (master's thesis, Shanghai daxue shehuixue xi, 2005). However, I avoid the term, with its association with particular geographical areas and the proliferation of definitions; cf. Fiona Bowie, *The Anthropology of Religion: An Introduction* (Oxford: Blackwell, 2000), 194–96.

6. In Chinese folk practice, we also sometimes find the untainted eyes of children being used in conjunction with the Daoist priest or *yinyang* master to diagnose problems. Such children evoke the original meaning of the term *tongji*—in south Gansu, for instance, the ritual in which children are used to diagnose problems is called "fulfilling the light" (*yuanguang*).

7. David Holm's taxonomy for nearby areas includes "female spirit mediums, vernacular priests (*mogong*), ritual masters (*shigong*) of the Meishan tradition, and Daoist priests (*daogong*) of a self-styled Maoshan lineage." See David Holm, *Killing a Buffalo for the Ancestors: A Zhuang Cosmological Text from Southwest China* (DeKalb, IL: Southeast Asia Publications, Center for Southeast Asian Studies, 2003). Apart from the *shigong* (not discussed in this chapter), in Jingxi some *daogong* also combine elements from folk Buddhism and Daoism.

8. The earliest evidence for the script used by the *mogong* is a carved stone inscription from 682 CE in Shanglin County in Guangxi. The script still has widespread folk currency. Related publications include Su Yongqin, ed., *Gu Zhuang zi zidian* (Nanning: Guangxi minzu chubanshe, 1989); Liang Tingwang, ed., *Gu Zhuang zi wenxian xuanzhu* (Tianjin: Tianjin guji chubanshe, 1992).

9. Michelle Rosaldo, "Women, Culture and Society: A Theoretical Overview," in *Women, Culture and Society*, ed. Michelle Rosaldo and Louise Lamphere (Palo Alto, CA: Stanford University Press, 1974), 67–88.

10. I. M. Lewis, "Spirit Possession and Deprivation Cults," *Man*, n.s., 1, no. 3 (1966): 307–29; I. M. Lewis, *Ecstatic Religion: A Study of Shamanism and Spirit Possession* (London: Routledge, 2003).

11. Xiao, "Chang zai wulu shang," 344–60.

12. Liu Shulin, "Guangxi Baode xian Longguang xiang Longguang cun bayue shiwu 'qing Chang'e' (wa:i^{214}. na:g^{31}. hai:i^{54}) yishi diaocha baogao," in *Zhongguo minjian yishi yinyue yanjiu, Huanan juan*, ed. Tsao Pen-Yeh (Shanghai: Shanghai yinyue xueyuan chubanshe, 2007), 495–528.

13. For a full list, see Xiao, "Chang zai wulu shang," 383–85.

14. Marina Roseman also discusses the singing of spirit mediums during ceremonial healing performances in her study of the Temiars. By following the path that is shown by a spirit guide, the medium sings of the route traversed by the spirit guide during its travels. The path links spirit guide, medium, and other ceremonial participants; see Marina Roseman, *Healing Sounds from the Malaysian Rainforest: Temiar Music and Medicine* (Berkeley: University of California Press, 1993), 6. *Me-mot* in Jingxi have similar characteristics.

Chapter Nineteen

Vegetarian Sisters

New Configurations of Gender in Buddhism in Southern Fujian

Hwee-San Tan

The theorizing of gender in Chinese society has been a subject of much scrutiny in the past several decades and continues to generate much interest. The topic of women and gender roles in Buddhism, however, is only recently burgeoning.[1] Traditionally in China a woman's role in religion was expected to be that of a worshipper of deities, household ritualist (taking charge of the worshipping of the husband's ancestors), and pilgrim; if women were ritualists, they were shamans or spirit mediums.[2] Women's role in Buddhist liturgical music is, as yet, not on the research radar.

This chapter will examine the rise of *caigu* (菜姑 lit. vegetarian sister), a type of female lay Buddhist found in the Minnan region of Fujian Province on the southeastern coast of China. The *caigu* not only live in and run small temples but they also fulfill the role of ritual performers in rites for the dead. In Minnan, liturgical music in the Buddhist rites for the dead has a variety of singing styles and repertoires, and today, because of sociopolitical changes in twentieth century China that have had an impact on religions and their social structures, the *caigu* have become the main purveyors of these rites and their music. At the same time, the male counterparts of *caigu*—the *caiyou* (菜友 vegetarian friends), a group who previously predominated the ritual scene—are now dwindling in number. Institutionally ordained monks join them to comprise the three types of ritualist who perform private rites for the dead, each occupying a somewhat separate ritual sphere yet also complementing the others.

The *caigu* phenomenon in Minnan is exceptional as far as women's roles in Chinese religion are concerned but has hitherto been little studied outside China.[3] It also raises some questions: How did the *caigu* and *caiyou* traditions arise? What are the *caigu*'s roles as performers of the *gongde* ritual (功德 lit.

merit) for the dead, vis-à-vis the *caiyou* or institutional monks? Certainly the *caigu*'s rise as *gongde* ritualists highlights a change in women's place in society and new perceptions of gendered power relations in the People's Republic of China, but where do the *caigu* stand in the still male-dominated domain of Buddhism? Has their acceptance influenced or changed the traditional conception of gender within the religion? Based largely on ethnographic research while also drawing much from textual material and musical analysis, this chapter investigates the *caigu* phenomenon to examine how the representation of gender and changing gender roles in Buddhism are manifested through their ritual and musical performance.

Caigu and *Caiyou* in Minnan

Caigu do not shave their heads like ordained nuns, but they live as a community in small temples. They are easily distinguishable by the loose grey top and trousers commonly worn by Buddhist laymen or women. They observe the daily morning and evening lessons and all calendric dates and related rituals as performed in any Buddhist monastery.[4] The *caigu* live and practice like the monastics, and, in today's Minnan society, they also serve the local community in familial rites for the dead, the performance of which is known in Minnan as *zuo gongde* (做功德).[5]

Where do *caigu* belong within the Buddhist milieu? In general, the Buddhist community is divided into two main groups, monastic and lay. The former, those who renounce lay life, is further divided into five categories: *biqiu* (比丘, Skt. *bhikṣu* fully ordained monk), *biqiuni* (比丘尼, Skt. *bhikṣuni*, fully-ordained nun), *shami* (沙弥, Skt. *sramanera*, male novice), *shamini* (沙弥尼, Skt. *sramaneri*, female novice) and *xuejienu* (学戒女, Skt. *siksamana*, a novice-in-waiting).[6] The second category consists of the *youposai* (优婆塞, Skt. *upāsaka*, male lay Buddhist) and *youpoyi* (优婆夷, Skt. *upāsika*, female lay Buddhist), both known in Chinese as *zaijia jushi* (在家居士 stay home lay Buddhists). Lay Buddhists need not live in the monastic community, as they do not renounce lay life. They undertake to become confirmed Buddhists by pledging the *san guiyi* (三皈依 Taking refuge in the triple gem) and may vow to observe five or ten precepts.[7]

Unlike ordained nuns who take the tonsure and pledge to observe 348 Buddhist precepts (rules of abstention), *caigu* keep their full head of hair. Like lay Buddhists, *caigu* undertake the ten precepts. Yet, as *caigu* give up lay life to live in temples and practice like monastics, they are seen as different from lay Buddhists, who usually practice the religion from home and lead an ordinary family life; at the same time, *caigu* cannot be considered *siksamana*, since many have never been married and they do not become ordained after the two-year period. *Caigu* is thus a category that falls in somewhere between an ordained nun, a *siksamana* novice nun, and an *upāsika* female lay Buddhist. They could be seen as "noncommittal" *siksamana*, since some do take the full vows to become an ordained nun at some point in their lives. Many, however, remain unordained. Just like ordained clerics, *caigu* adopt the term *chujia* (出家 leave home) for what they do. Another term commonly used to describe the *caigu* way of practice is *daifa xiuxing* (带发修行 practicing with a full head of hair). They also usually have an ordained monk as their *shifu* (师父 lit. teacher-father). As they are half-lay, half-institutionalized, are active *gongde* ritualists, and have a close relationship with institutional monasteries through their teacher, I refer to them as semi-institutional ritualists.

It is not clear when and how the *caigu* tradition arose. But certainly by the beginning of the twentieth century, with the decline in number of ordained nuns and a growth in *caigu* numbers, this tradition has become more conspicuous. As with many traditions, some *caigu* practitioners are keen to embellish its beginnings. One young *caigu* told me that their tradition came about when a young daughter of an imperial official in Minnan wanted to give up lay life to become a Buddhist nun.[8] The family objected; but failing to dissuade the young girl, they built a temple for her to devote her life to Buddhist practice, on the condition that she did not shave her head. From then on, my informant suggested, practicing with a full head of hair became popular in Minnan. A written source suggests a similar beginning:[9] a small temple named Shijiasi (释伽寺) in Quanzhou was said to have been built in the early Ming period (late fourteenth century) by a local government minister whose daughter lost her betrothed before the marriage could take place. As it was the custom in those days that she should remain chaste and not marry, the minister built a small nunnery for her to practice Buddhism.

In the early 1900s, the term *caigu* was used to refer to women who were members of *zhaijiao* (斋教 vegetarian sects) living in *zhaitang* (斋堂 vegetarian halls).[10] *Zhaijiao* were viewed as popular or even heretical sects and not officially recognized by orthodox Buddhists.[11] In the early 1960s, there were 19,986 temples throughout China with laywomen in residence; these temples were most likely vegetarian halls to which women retired in old age.[12] In Fuzhou, northern Fujian, I was informed that *caigu* exist there, but, just as observed by Welch, they are usually women who observe vegetarianism and choose to live in a temple in their old age, mainly either because of lack of family support or personal religious sentiments. Clerics told me that, unlike in Minnan, it is rare to find *caigu* in Fuzhou running temples or serving as ritualists.[13]

In earlier times, *caigu* in vegetarian sects, unlike Buddhist *caigu* today, did not have a Buddhist monk as a teacher-mentor, nor did they strictly follow the teachings of Buddhism. The Buddhist reform movement of the early twentieth century was most vibrant in Minnan; monks including the renowned Taixu and Hongyi actively spread the teachings of orthodox Buddhism and discouraged practices that were incompatible with its original tenets. Monasteries were restructured, modern *sangha*[14] education was established, and lay Buddhists were galvanized. These had a great impact in revitalizing Buddhism. Influenced by the new political and social conditions and by the teachings of the Buddhist reformists, some *caigu* of *zhaijiao* sects began to reform their practice and thinking, with many turning to orthodox Buddhism.[15]

Of course, not all *caigu* were originally members of "heretical" sects. Revolutionary change brought about by the May Fourth movement and the establishment of the PRC also greatly affected urban women's roles and lives, allowing them to break from social mores of Confucianism that tied them to their family, and in particular to men, and gain economic independence.[16] The rise of *caigu* as a distinct group was an example; some women left home to live in temples, choosing to dedicate their lives to the practice of religion. Some were widows,[17] while others chose this path after receiving spiritual calling.[18]

In those early days, *caigu* lived either by tending their own small plot of land or by receiving donations from incense visitors to the temple.[19] Subsequently, some *caigu* began to run the temples they lived in; some even built their own small temples. According to a census carried out in Xiamen in 1990, out of a total of ten *zhaitang* temples that were left in the city, six were *caigu*-run.[20] In Quanzhou up to 1949, there were at least twenty small *caigu*-run temples.[21] In the late nineteenth century, missionaries in Fujian noted that infanticide was particularly rife there:[22] baby girls were often drowned or abandoned to die. As *caigu* temples grew in the first half of the twentieth century, baby girls were often abandoned at these temples. *Caigu* thus became the custodians of these girls, raising them and sending them to school. But these girls are also taught to recite sutras and incantations and to perform rituals. Many girls who grew up in *caigu* temples also ended up as *caigu*. Up until the late 1990s, almost all the *caigu* temples I visited had girls of different ages living within their walls; the one-child policy introduced in the reform era under the PRC meant that families who wanted sons were abandoning newborn daughters so that they could have another child.

Sister Miaolian, a *caigu* now in her eighties who runs Tongfosi (铜佛寺) in Quanzhou city, agreed that women came into prominence as *caigu* during the Republican period. According to her, one of the reasons women in Minnan prefer *caigu* status (once this model became acceptable in society) rather than becoming nuns is because of the copious precepts ordained nuns must adhere to. Women who want to practice Buddhism fear that they would not be able to comply with all the stipulated vows and follow the restricted life of a nun. Many therefore prefer to practice without becoming ordained, gradually adding to the number of precepts that they could keep.

Here, a brief word must be said about gender concepts and the status of nuns in Mahayana Buddhism; as recent studies have unraveled, Buddhist scriptural portrayals of gender and gender roles are not without contradictions and ambivalence. Gender understanding in Buddhism has been subject to varying interpretations during different periods and in different locations and contexts.[23] Although, in China and other countries where Mahayana Buddhism is practiced, nuns have been able to receive full ordination since the *bhikṣuni* (order of nuns) lineage was established in the fifth century, paradoxes remain in the attitudes to women's role and ability to attain enlightenment.[24] Nuns are subject to more than 300 vows, while ordained monks must observe only 250. The Buddhist law also prohibits nuns from retaking their vows again if they return to laity, while monks are allowed to retake vows up to seven times. Thus if what Sister Miaolian said is true, this restriction is very likely another deterrent to women becoming nuns.

Traditionally, the concept of impurity in women has been linked to the process of procreation; the ideology of female pollution was another obstacle to women attaining full Buddhahood. Thus, among the purgatory acts that developed in rites for the dead was the "blood bowl" ceremony (*xuepen yi* 血盆仪), although this rite is no longer performed.[25] While Mahayana Buddhism expounds the egalitarian view that all sentient beings, men or women, ordained or lay, are capable of attaining the potentials of a Buddha (that is, Enlightened Being), women are said to possess Five Obstacles (*nivaranas*) that prevent them from attaining enlightenment.[26] At the same time that Mahayana scriptures contain narratives of the attainment of Buddhahood by women, it corroborates that this is possible only through the male body. Thus in Mahayana Buddhism, it is believed, if you are born a female, pious practice in this life could lead to rebirth in a male body and hence to the attainment of Buddhahood.[27] In a predominantly patriarchal Confucian China, this no doubt explains the low status of nuns in traditional Chinese society as observed by Western scholars.[28] Given all the above factors involving the stigmatization and negative portrayal of nuns, it is not surprising that the number of nuns has been much lower than that of monks and that the *caigu* do not readily proceed to the major step of taking tonsure.[29]

Sister Miaolian also said that in earlier times nuns were rarely seen in public; this meant nuns had less freedom of movement. Keeping their hair made *caigu* less conspicuous and thus gave them more mobility. This was indeed a common view shared by other elderly *caigu* in Xiamen; some said keeping their head unshaven is more "convenient" (*fangbian* 方便).[30] Thus few women and girls become ordained, because they are not prepared to commit fully despite wanting to practice like the monastics. The compromise was therefore to become *caigu*.

Changing religious conditions and ideology during the Republican era also helped to provide the impetus for the *caigu* to become a distinct group. The success of the Buddhist Reform movement in the early twentieth century did not rest solely upon the forward thinking of eminent monks like Xuyun, Taixu, and Hongyi: the combined efforts and huge support of Buddhist laymen (the most famous being Yang Wenhui, a Confucian scholar who became a devout Buddhist and who founded a Buddhist printing house) also strengthened the role of the lay Buddhists, men and women alike.[31] The act of *nianfo* (念佛 reciting the names of Buddha) became only one of many ways to practice modern Buddhism; education and public sutra lectures for the ordinary laypeople became more widespread.

In the early twentieth century, *caigu* were mostly illiterate because education for women was still rare; some learned passages from the scriptures and the daily rituals from their teacher-monk by rote. By the 1930s, at the height of the Buddhist reform movement, there were more opportunities for Buddhist women to receive education; Sister Miaolian was among the few who benefited from this development. Today, the new generation of *caigu* is even more fortunate. Many attend the Buddhist colleges for women in Xiamen, Quanzhou, and Fuzhou, graduating with better job prospects and opportunities.

Caiyou Male Ritualists

In urban Minnan, there is also a category of male lay *gongde* ritualists known as *caiyou*. Like the *caigu*, *caiyou* take the Triple Refuge with a teacher-monk, swear to the five or ten precepts and observe vegetarianism. Unlike the *caigu*, however, they do not renounce lay life but marry and live at home.[32] Since the Tang dynasty, there are records of lay religious societies formed by laymen under the leadership of one or more monks.[33] Members of such societies gather for vegetarian feasts, sutra recitation, or other activities to gain merit. After the tenth century, popular religious sects influenced by Buddhism, Daoism, and Confucianism began to spread. Over time, these came to be referred to as vegetarian sects (*zhaijiao* 斋教), as their members observed strict vegetarianism. Some stayed predominantly religious, while others took on political aspirations and became secret societies; one such, which began as a Buddhist sect but gradually developed syncretic and political leanings, was the White Lotus Society (白莲教 Bailian jiao).[34]

During the Ming and Qing dynasties, new religious societies continued to evolve. Lay ritual activities, in particular, flourished under Zhu Yuanzhang, the first Ming emperor, who was for a brief time a Buddhist novice (*sramanera*). He decreed that anyone (priest or lay) who had taken the Three Refuges and the five or ten Buddhist precepts could "set up altars in the open, or in cities or villages."[35] This sanctioned the existence of lay religious specialists. By the late nineteenth century, sectarian religions such as the Longhua jiao (龙华教) and Xiantian jiao (先天教) were rife, the former spreading to Fujian from the Zhejiang region and the latter from Jiangxi province. These sects built temples, but priests associated with them did not obtain proper ordination certificates; some kept their heads unshaven and led normal family lives, but they were known to perform rites for the dead "all in the manner of the sangha."[36] A careful study by Dutch sinologist J. J. M. de Groot of Ming and Qing legal codes, in which many anti-Buddhist measures could be found to restrict the number of ordained monks and nuns, led him also to conclude: "The number of consecrated clergy sinks into insignificance compared with those who remain unconsecrated, and who therefore more in name and dress than in reality belong to the clerical class. They form a caste of priests who for the laity perform religious functions, principally for the redemption and salvation for the dead."[37] By the late nineteenth century, however, sectarian religions in Minnan had almost disappeared because of severe persecution by the Qing government.[38] Vegetarian sects, in particular the Longhua sect, are still active in Taiwan today.[39] Though not officially recognized by orthodox Buddhists, *zhaijiao* members observe vegetarianism and undertake the Triple Refuge and the five lay precepts, and the underlying teachings of *zhaijiao* are based on Buddhism. Although Longhua, Xiantian, and other such sectarian religious societies no longer exist in Xiamen, it is possible that the *caiyou* phenomenon there may be a legacy of the vegetarian sects. Local historians I spoke to told me that *caiyou* were more active as *gongde* ritualists before the Communist period. Written records of vegetarian sects still extant in Zhejiang after the Boxer Rebellion stated that their members performed rituals for those in need.[40] In Fuzhou during the Republican era, a type of male religious society known as Chanhe doutang (禅和斗堂 lit. Dipper's Hall) provided mutual support for its members; in the event of death, members performed rites for the dead in return for a meal. Today in Minnan, however, the number of *caiyou* is gradually declining. Although I did come across some young *caiyou* in Quanzhou, Sister Miaolian told me they are not "proper" *caiyou* as they do not observe vegetarianism.[41]

Caigu as *Gongde* Ritualists: Context and Role

As mentioned above, *caigu* have strong links with institutional monasteries through their teacher. They observe the daily lessons and all other regular "practicing" activities found in institutional monasteries. In *caigu*-run temples, morning service takes place at 5:00 a.m. and evening lessons at 4:00 p.m., just as in institutional monasteries. On new-moon or full-moon days (*chuyi shiwu* 初一十五) or special commemoration days of the Buddha or a Bodhisattva, *caigu* may lead a small congregation in a sutra recitation service; a midday vegetarian meal is provided for those who attend. On occasion, *caigu* perform simple rituals such as reciting sutras in the temple in return for a small fee. Today, *caigu* are most prominent as performers of *gongde* (lit. merit): a structured set of postfunerary rites thus called because the merits accrued from performing the rites help to deliver the soul to the western paradise of Amitabha Buddha or to a better rebirth. *Gongde* are private services paid for by individual families and performed on some or all of the seventh and forty-ninth days and the first and third anniversary after death. The service is generally held in a temple but may take place in a private home.

As testified by Sister Miaolian of Tongfosi in Quanzhou and other elderly *caigu* in Xiamen, *caigu* rarely took on the role of *gongde* ritualists before 1949, and they most certainly did not perform in private homes. The change of role has to be understood in the context of social and economic changes in postsocialist China. With improved economic means and, in particular, support from overseas Chinese who are now able to renew kinship links, demand for *gongde* has risen in both urban and rural areas. Despite considerable relaxation of antireligious policies after 1979, in the cities, lavish funerals are still frowned upon by local authorities.[42] In Xiamen, for instance, the dead are cremated within twenty-four hours of death. The body may be placed at a funeral parlor during that time, but no religious ceremonies are allowed there. In Quanzhou, the body is allowed to lie in state at home for up to three days. Thus, for most, one of the ways to compensate for the simplicity of rites in funerals is to hold *gongde* memorial rites, which are seen as legitimate because they are considered a part of Buddhist ritual. Families who can afford the expense will thus arrange for a *gongde* performance on at least one of those aforementioned days. Recently, performances in private homes, which tend to be undertaken by younger *caigu*, are becoming more common.[43] The increasing demand for *gongde* means more ritualists are needed. The demand for *caigu* as *gongde* ritualists can be further attributed to the following reasons. First, following the post–Cultural Revolution religious revival, many large monasteries of learning now ban *gongde*.[44] This, and the reluctance of more erudite monastic Buddhists to be involved in *gongde*, thus created a niche for *caigu*. Second, *caigu* temples that used to have lands to farm are losing them to urbanization due to rapid economic development since the 1980s; performing *gongde* has thus become a means of survival for some *caigu* temples. Third, a *gongde* performed in a *caigu* temple costs less because these temples are less religiously prestigious than monasteries; for lower-income families, the *caigu* are a good second choice. Last but not least is the *caigu*'s willingness to accommodate certain religious customs that institutional Buddhists now eschew: for example, the burning of paper objects is still a common part of *caigu gongde*, as is the turning of the paper wheel to symbolize rescuing the dead from the depths of hell (see outline of ritual in table 19.1).

In Quanzhou, several *caigu* temples frequently hold *gongde*. Tongfosi, in the heart of the city, holds them almost daily, in addition to those at private homes. In imperial times, *gongde* tended to be opulent and lengthy affairs, but today families with modest income may have a half- or one-day ritual; those who can afford it may command a three-day ritual. When the number of *caigu* in one temple is insufficient for a *gongde*, those from other temples are enlisted. Thus *caigu* form a close and very mobile network. However, not all *caigu* temples perform *gongde*. Suyansi (宿燕寺) in Jinjiang is an example; its location halfway up a mountain may be one reason for the lower demand for *gongde* there. Instead, since they do attract local tourists and incense visitors during weekends and holidays, they raise income by selling vegetarian meals.

Patrons can pay more to have the prestigious rite of releasing Flaming Mouth (放焰口 *fang yankou*), or officially titled Yogacara rite of feeding Flaming Mouth (瑜伽焰口施食集要 *yuqie yankou shishi jiyao*), included in a *gongde*. Translated into Chinese in the eighth century by the Indian tantric master Amoghavajra from the *Saving the Flaming Mouth hungry ghost dharani sutra* (*Jiuba Yankou tuoluoni jing* 救拔焰口陀罗尼经), it tells of Buddha's disciple Ananda's encounter with a hungry ghost named Flaming Mouth (Yankou) who had a throat like a needle and flame spewing from his mouth. Whenever he tried to eat, his food would turn to ashes, so he was constantly hungry. In the wheels of transmigration, this is the lowest of the six paths. This salvation rite became an intrinsic part of rites for the dead during the Tang dynasty. It fell into disuse after the ninth century, but, when the Mongols came into power, it was revived and has remained popular ever since.

While *caigu* may perform the similar but smaller-scale Mengshan rite of feeding (蒙山施食仪, see table 19.1), the larger Yankou rite requires the help of monks. The key figure in this rite is the *Jin'gang shangshi* (金刚上师 Vajra high master), who should be a monk of high standing and experience, as the ritual process involves his symbolic transformation into the representation of *Dizang pusa* (地藏菩萨 Bodhisattva Ksitigarbha). He then gains the power to open the throats of the hungry ghosts so they can feed. These beings will then be exhorted to repent their sins to gain a better rebirth. Even in institutional contexts, ordained nuns never perform the role of the Vajra high master. In a *caigu* temple, a monk will need to be invited to perform the task, and *caiyou* are also often enlisted to assist in the ritual ceremony. Although in Taiwan today it is not uncommon to have nuns perform in the supporting roles of acolytes (a minimum of six are needed to recite the Yankou text),[45] I have never seen *caigu* take part in the actual rite; instead, they help with the steward duties of replenishing tea, passing the tray of food for the high master to feed the hungry ghosts, and so on. Only on one occasion, elderly sister Miaolian performed on the bell and drum at a *caigu* temple.

From the above description, we see the rise and acceptance of *caigu* by society as religious practitioners and ritualists. Within the Buddhist circle by the 1990s, *caigu* who run temples are allowed to become members of the committee of the Buddhist Association (佛教协会). Thus the *caigu* now occupy a growing, if still marginal, place in religious society in Fujian. Although specific rites such as *Fang Yankou* are still taboo, women's crossover into the traditionally male domain constitutes a significant socioreligious change in modern society.

The Ritual Role of the *Caiyou*

It is more difficult to locate *caiyou* as they live at home and are not based at temples. *Caiyou* are in theory male lay Buddhists (*zaijia jushi*) who are serious about their religious and spiritual pursuits. Some may shave their heads and wear the grey *jushi* garb, but they do not necessarily perform the role of ritualists.[46] By the end of the nineteenth century, *caiyou* in Minnan were acting as *gongde* ritualists. During my fieldwork at the end of the 1990s, their number was dwindling. From my observations of *caiyou* in Quanzhou, only one, Tianpei, who was in his fifties, wore *jushi* clothing. Younger ones, although they do shave their heads, sport everyday clothes when not performing rituals. Once during a *gongde* in a *caigu*-run temple, both *caiyou* and ordained monks were invited to preside over the *gongde*. During the ritual, they donned the *jiasha* (伽沙, Skt. *Kasaya*), ritual robes worn by monks; since *caiyou* also shave their heads, it is difficult to tell the difference between lay and ordained in a ritual context. Thus, *caigu* may rely on the services of *caiyou* when necessary (in this context it was a gongde service of considerable scale), and since the number of *caiyou* is diminishing today, they in turn collaborate with monks from large monasteries.

Although many monasteries ban *gongde*, this does not prevent monks living in those monasteries from performing them in private outside. As this is stigmatized as being mercenary and seen as a distraction from serious religious learning, the more erudite and higher-ranking monks eschew such practices; but rank-and-file monks may be lured by the profit motive. Thus, at times, ordained monks enlist the help of lay *caiyou* (or the reverse may happen) to make up the numbers for outside *gongde*.

Gongde Rite of Merit: Ritual Process and Music

The *gongde* is an aggregation of several, sometimes autonomous, rites. Depending on the financial abilities of the family, a *gongde* today usually lasts from half a day to three, or occasionally up to five, days. The length of the *gongde* largely determines the type of scriptures and rites that can be included. For a half- or one-day rite, it is common to perform the *shuichan* (water penitence, see table 19.1). This is based on the three-volume Penitence text, *Cibei sanmei shuichan* (慈悲三昧水忏 The compassionate samadhi water penitence), said to have been compiled by the Tang-dynasty monk Zhixuan.[47] For a *gongde* of three days or more, the ten-volume *Lianghuang baochan* (梁皇宝忏 Precious penitence of Emperor Liang) is often used.[48] If the family can afford the expenses, longer *gongde* may also include the rite of releasing Flaming Mouth, in which the services of monks of higher learning are required. Apart from the main penitence texts, a *gongde* also invariably includes the smaller rites of *jingtan* (净坛 purification of the altar), *shanggong* (上供 the offering), and, in the absence of the more specialized rite of releasing Flaming Mouth (performed separately in the evening), the smaller scale *Mengshan shishiyi* (Mengshan feeding rite), the *gongde* closing with *huixiang* (回向 the transference of merit, see table 19.1).[49]

Gongde rites are performed in turn at two altars: the *fotan* (佛坛 Buddha altar) and the *lingtan* (灵坛 spirit altar). The first is the main altar where the Buddhist pantheon is revered. The second, a temporary altar set up especially for *gongde*, is reserved for worshipping the dead. Each of the smaller rites begins at the Buddha altar; on completion of a rite, the ritualists then proceed to perform the same rites at the spirit altar. The main penitence texts are performed only before the Buddha altar; following the recitation of each section or volume, the ritualists proceed to the spirit altar to transfer the merits to the soul. Table 19.1 shows a basic outline of a one-day *gongde* that would be performed by both *caigu* and *caiyou*.

Table 19.1. Basic outline of a one-day *gongde* performed by *caigu* and *caiyou*

Morning
1. Purification at the Buddha altar (演净 *yanjing*)
2. Invocation of the soul at the Spirit altar (引魂 *yinhun*)
3. "Turning the wheel" (牵藏 *qianzang*)—performed outdoors
4. "Bathing the soul'" (沐浴 *muyu*)—performed outdoors
5. Penitence (拜忏 *Baichan*) (vol. 1) at the Buddha altar
6. Offering (上供 *shanggong*)
Afternoon
7. Penitence (vol. 2)—same as above
8. Penitence (vol. 3)—same as above
Early Evening
9. The "small" feeding rite of Mengshan (*Xiao Mengshan*)[1]
10. Transference of merit (回向 *huixiang*)
11. Burning the spirit house (烧灵厝 *shao lingcuo*)

1. Mengshan recitation and exhortation rite of bestowing food (*Mengshan shishi niansong shuofayi*). It is a rite to feed beings in all realms, compiled in the twelfth century by the Indian monk Aksobhya Vajra and named after Mount Mengshan, on which he lived. To accrue further merit for the dead, salvation rituals such as the smaller-scale Mengshan rite or the large-scale Yogacara rite of feeding the hungry ghost (瑜伽焰口施食集要 *Yuqie yankou shishi jiyao*) must be included in a *gongde*.

Buddhist vocalization comprises two main types of delivery referred to collectively as *changnian* (唱念) or *changsong* (唱诵), translatable respectively as "sing" and "recite."[50] These terms seem to imply that Buddhist vocalization falls neatly into two categories, one very melodious, one less so. On a broad surface level, this is indeed true, but on a deeper level, there are many complex melodic implications in both forms. Very often, the textual form designates the type of vocalization. For example, both the *zan* (赞 lit. praise), a textual structure ranging from six to ten lines, with various numbers of syllables, and the *ji* (偈, Skt. *Gatha*), texts in verses of four or eight lines, each having five or seven syllables, are metered and songlike; these therefore come under the sung category. *Jing* (经 Sutra texts), *zhou* (咒 incantations), and *wenshu* (文疏 announcement texts) are recited. These are less melodious but are by no means intoned on a single pitch or on a limited number of pitches.[51] For our present purposes I will focus on the sung forms, *zan* and *ji*, which I will refer to as hymns for convenience.

In Minnan several bodies of hymn tunes are found in the *gongde* ritual. Minnan ritualists use the term *diao* (调 here meaning style)[52] when describing each of these different corpora. Three hymn styles are identified: *waijiang diao* (外江调 lit. beyond the river style), *Fuzhou diao* (福州调 Fuzhou being the capital of Fujian province) and *caiyou diao* (vegetarian friend style). One single hymn text may be sung in any of these three styles. As the transmission of Buddhist hymn singing is an oral tradition, the tune of a hymn text, in whichever style, may be slightly varied depending on singer and in particular, geographical areas. However, the broad outline of its melody is still mostly discernible.

Waijiang diao, so called because it originated in the large monasteries in the central provinces of Jiangsu and Zhejiang and hence from beyond the Min River with which Fujian province is generally associated, is the hymn-singing style adopted in monasteries and temples all over China today and commonly used in daily, ceremonial, and calendric rituals.[53] As this style is more or less homogenous, I will expediently use the term *national style* when referring to what the Minnanese call *waijiang* style. Hymns in national style are commonly used in rituals of *xiuxing* (修行 personal cultivation). This is a repertoire of tunes characterized by slow, drawn-out tempo and very melismatic melodies. This, in theory, is to allow practitioners to contemplate the meanings of the lyrics and enhance religiosity.[54] As national style melodies are long and slow, in the context of a *gongde*, in which subrites are copious, the *caigu* only use this style occasionally, and usually only when performing before the Buddha altar.[55]

The second hymn style found in Minnan is *Fuzhou diao* (Fuzhou style); I was informed by the *caigu* in Minnan[56] that it is thus called because it originated in Fuzhou, the capital of Fujian province. Miaolian also told me that they used this style in *gongde* because it does not take up as much time as hymns in the national style, and, when they are pressed for time, they might use the *caiyou* style. I will come back to this below. Given the copious rites in a *gongde*, it is not surprising that the ritualists need to perform in a hymn style that will allow them to get through the rites in a reasonable amount of time, particularly when a patron pays for only a half-day or one-day ritual. Commercial reasons therefore play a part in the type of hymn style used in *gongde*.

Expanding my fieldwork later to the Fuzhou area, I confirmed that what the *caigu* called Fuzhou-style hymns are indeed close variants of hymn melodies found in Fuzhou; but there this style is referred to by local monks as *chanhe diao* (Chan [Zen] harmony style).[57] This style developed in the monasteries in and around Fuzhou, in particular two large ordination monasteries, Yongquansi (涌泉寺) in Fuzhou's Gushan and its more urban counterpart Xichansi (西禅寺). Up to the early Republican period, Yongquansi was a famous ordination center for monks not only from Fujian but also from Taiwan and even Malaysia, Singapore, and the Philippines. It is therefore not surprising that the hymn style from these monasteries has spread to other parts of Fujian and even abroad. Benfa, the abbot of Tianwangsi (天王寺) in Changle, one of the few monks left in the Fuzhou area knowledgeable about *Chanhe* hymns, told me that before the 1950s they were commonly used in Yongquansi and other Fuzhou monasteries not only in *gongde* rituals but also in the daily lessons. But the post–Cultural Revolution generations of monks residing in large monasteries such as Yongquansi and Xichansi are mostly from other parts of China. Thus, the *waijiang* national style of the large teaching monasteries of Zhejiang and Jiangsu, these being the main places where younger monks are ordained and trained, became the one used in monasteries in Fuzhou today, consigning the *Chanhe* style to *gongde* rituals.

Comparing the *zan* text *Jieding zhenxiang* (戒定真香 The true incense of abstention and meditation), a four-phrase hymn each of nine syllables, in the national and Fuzhou style, I found that it was not simply a matter of speed that differentiates the two styles; the same hymn texts in these two styles not only have different melodies but different rhythmic patterns for the accompanying ritual percussion instruments (see ex. 19.1).[58]

Today, then, Fuzhou style is most prevalently used by the *caigu* and *caiyou* when performing *gongde* rituals. According to Sister Miaolian, this style is preferable to the national style because the hymns are "faster."[59] To understand what Sister Miaolian means by fast, I compared the *zan* text *True incense of abstention and meditation* (*Jieding zhenxiang*) sung in the Fuzhou style by some *caigu* in Minnan with that sung in the Chanhe style by Fuzhou monk Venerable Benfa, and again in the national style by monks from the Nanputuosi (南普陀寺) monastery in Xiamen. When sung by the *caigu* in Minnan dialect, the hymn took 1 minute 22 seconds (twenty-six syllables per minute), whilst Benfa's version sung in Fuzhou dialect took 1 minute 33 seconds (twenty-three syllables per minute). In comparison, the same hymn text sung in the national style lasted 4 minutes 30 seconds (ca. eight syllables per minute). The time

Example 19.1. "True Incense Hymn" in national and Fuzhou styles. Sources (a) Hu Yao, "Tianningsi changsong," in *Zhongguo fojiao yinyue xuancui*, ed. Tian Qing (Shanghai: Shanghai Yinyue Chubanshe, 1993), 207–39; (b) sung by Venerable Benfa. Transcription by author.

difference between the *caigu* version and the Fuzhou monk Benfa's rendition is not huge, as they are basically variations of the same tune; but, as we have seen in example 19.1, the national style not only is more melismatic but it is also sung at a slow, leisurely pace when performed in the context of the daily morning and evening lessons, symbolic of the sangha's religious devoutness.[60]

As hymns sung in the national style take much longer to get through, in practice, particularly in the context of modern-day *gongde* when there are copious ritual elements to get through in a short time, it is not surprising the *caigu* prefer to use the Fuzhou style. However, my research shows that the singers may sing hymns in the national style in a *gongde*, but they adapt the melody by using fewer ornaments and singing at a faster pace.[61] I have found this practice to be more prevalent among institutional ordained monks, many of whom are from other parts of China and are thus unfamiliar with Fuzhou-style hymns. Since the *caigu* have a larger repertoire of Fuzhou-style hymns at hand, they do not need to risk tainting a hymn style that is symbolic of their personal spiritual cultivation.

Caiyou style is thought to have developed in Minnan and is sometimes called *bendi diao* (本地调 local style).[62] *Caigu*, young and old alike, know of this style; however, older *caigu* dismiss its short, simple melodies as *zhizhi hengheng* (支支哼哼 lit. humming or twittering) and therefore *bu zhuangyan* (不庄严 not solemn enough). As mentioned earlier, *caigu* only use this style when really pressed for time. This attitude of the elderly *caigu* has also influenced the younger generation. One young *caigu* told me that they tend not to learn the *caiyou* style at all because it is not reverent enough and its use would be disrespectful to the Buddha.[63] In Quanzhou, Xiamen, and Huian, this style is declining among younger *caigu*, and the indigenous Minnanese monks of the older generation who knew this style well are dying out.

It is possible that some of the tunes in *caiyou* style are derived from local folk tunes, but this requires further research. The influence of *nanyin*, a vocal-instrumental ensemble and a classical genre typical of the Minnan region, on *caiyou* style is negligible, as the melodies in this genre are very melismatic in contrast to the short, simple melodies in *caiyou* style. The only tune shared both in *nanyin* and Buddhist hymn is that of the hymn tune titled "Nanhai guanyin zan" (南海观音赞). It is possible that the former adopted the tune from the Buddhist tradition.

As mentioned earlier, in *gongde* there is also an altar set up separately for the soul (*lingtan*). Here, the soul has to be exhorted to repent past sins so as to be reborn. Apart from repeated recitation of the Amitabha and Heart Sutras, incantations such as the dharani of Grand Compassion and Rebirth in Pure Land, a large corpus of *tanwang zan* (叹亡赞 laments for the dead) exists for use at this altar. These songs are didactic in function and content. Over a hundred texts exist in this repertoire, varying greatly in length and prosody. The texts can be grouped into three broad categories according to their didactic functions; table 19.2 below shows the categories and the number of texts in each group.[64]

Table 19.2. Grouping of *tanwang zan* as found in *Chanlin zanji* (Collection of hymns from Chan monasteries)

1. *Jishou guiyi zan* (稽首皈依赞 prostrate and take refuge hymns)	24
2. *Tanwang mianci* (叹亡勉词 lament and encourage the dead)	48
3. *Tanshu gujin* (叹述古今 lamenting the past and present)	71

In comparison to the number of texts, the melodic repertoire is small, since texts having the same prosody often use one and the same melody; this is not dissimilar to other Chinese musical system of *qupai*, in the sense that a label or title may be ascribed to a body of hymn texts sharing the same prosody.[65] It is interesting to note that while hymns sung before the Buddha altar may be in any of the three singing styles—national *waijiang*, regional Fuzhou, or local *caiyou*—the melodies for laments for the dead are only in the Fuzhou and *caiyou* styles.[66]

Since this repertoire is a regional one, ordained monks from those large monasteries that still perform *gongde* are often not familiar with this repertoire, as many of the younger generation are from other parts of China and do not speak the dialect. Those who perform *gongde* regularly become gradually more familiar with this repertoire and even learn a few hymn tunes through listening to others or learning from *caigu*. One monk from Nanputuosi told me that he asks a young *caigu* to record Fuzhou-style hymns and laments (sung in Mandarin) on cassette so that he can learn them.[67] The ordained *gongde* ritualists too feel the need to sing in Fuzhou style, partly because it takes less time and also because they think that patrons like the hymn style.[68]

Changing Roles for Female *Caigu*

We see from this study how gender relations are played out between the female *caigu* and male ritualists, both ordained monks and *caiyou* ritualists, via hymn-singing styles in Buddhist *gongde*. A crucial musical element in *gongde* is the *tanwang zan* laments sung to edify the spirit. As *caigu* gain a dominant position in the *gongde* niche, these women also become the main purveyors of the Fuzhou musical style, considered more appropriate than the local *caiyou* style, which is gradually dying out. In a way, Fuzhou style raises the respectability of *caigu* and endorses their identity as *gongde* ritualists.

Despite a gradual change in gender attitudes within the modern Buddhist *sangha* and society as a whole, fundamental Buddhist notions concerning the female body continue to demonstrate religious ambivalence toward women, as demonstrated by the restriction on women in the role of Vajra high master in the Yankou rite. The underlying value and ideal that one has to reach for the goal of gender transformation in order to attain higher spiritual aptitude inherently limit women's potential for spiritual leadership.

Yet today *caigu* have become an important part of the Buddhist socioreligious structure in Minnan society. Emerging as new religious actors, they represent the empowerment of women in religion and in society. As *gongde* ritualists, they enter into and foster a symbiotic relationship with the ordained institutional Buddhists and the lay *caiyou*. In the end, the groups mutually benefit as each fills the gap left open by the other; yet as can be seen, to a degree, they are also interdependent. The *caigu* tradition not only configures new gender relationships but also serves to mediate between socioreligious structures.

Notes

1. Since the founding of Sakyadhita International Association of Buddhist Women at a meeting in Bodhgaya, India, in 1987, many studies on women in Buddhism have emerged. See, e.g., Karma Lekshe Tsomo, *Buddhist Women across Cultures* (Albany: State University of New York Press, 1999); Karma Lekshe Tsomo, ed., *Buddhist Women and Social Justice: Ideals, Challenges, and Achievements* (Albany: State University of New York Press, 2004); Ellison Banks, *Women's Buddhism, Buddhism's Women: Tradition, Revision, Renewal* (Boston, MA: Wisdom, 2000); Martine Batchelor, *Women on the Buddhist Path* (London: Thorsons, 2002).

2. Daniel Overmyer, "Women in Chinese Religions: Submission, Struggle, Transcendence," in *From Benares to Beijing: Essays on Buddhism and Chinese Religion in Honour of Prof. Jan Yun-Hua*, ed. Koichi Shinohara and Gregor Schopen (Oakville, ON: Mosaic Press, 1991), 91–120.

3. For Chinese articles on *caigu*, see Lin Sha, *Huashuo Xiamen* (Xiamen: Xiamen Daxue Chubanshe, 1999), 258–62; Yu Cheng, "Quanzhou Minjian de Guanyin Xinyang," in *Quanzou Licheng Wenshi Ziliao*, ed. Fu Jinxing, Lin Nansheng, and Hong Henian. (Quanzhou: Zhongguo Renmin Zhengzhi Xieshang Huiyi, 1995), 13:114–21; Gao Lingyin, Zheng Mengxing, Su Mingtong, Li Qixian, and Chang Jiayou, *Xiamen Zongjiao* (Xiamen: Lujiang Chubanshe, 2002), 15–25, 38–61.

4. Here *monastery* denotes a large institution of learning that operates in accordance with established rules; smaller establishments of other types are called *temples*. The Chinese 寺 (*si*) does not differentiate between the two. See Holmes Welch, *The Practice of Chinese Buddhism 1900–1950* (Cambridge, MA: Harvard University Press, 1967), chap. 5.

5. Performing such rites is known in other regions by different terms: in many places, it is simply referred to as *zuo foshi* (做佛事) or *zuo daochang* (做道场).

6. I give these terms in their Sanskrit rather than Pali, as the former is used in Mahayana Buddhism. I also provide the pinyin only in Mandarin and not in Minnanese.

7. Taking the Triple Refuge is to affirm commitments to the Triple Gems: the Buddha, Dharma (teachings of the Buddha), and Sangha (monastic community). The five precepts are to refrain from killing, taking what is not given, telling lies, sexual misconduct, and taking intoxicants; the ten lay precepts include commitment to vegetarianism plus avoidance of taking untimely food; viewing dancing, singing, and grotesque forms of entertainment; using cosmetics and ornaments; using high, luxurious seats or beds; and accepting gold and silver.

8. Sister Yulian, personal communication, August 1997.

9. Fu Jinxing, *Quanshan caipu* (Hong Kong: Huaxing Chubanshe, 1992), 155.

10. Charles Brewer Jones, *Buddhism in Taiwan: Religion and the State 1660–1990* (London: Routledge-Curzon, 1999), 14–30.

11. In Xiamen, *zhaijiao* groups such as Longhua and Xiantian were active until they were persecuted by the Qing government. See J. J. M. de Groot, *Sectarianism and Religious Persecution in China* (Taipei: Literature House, 1963). *Zhaijiao* sects are no longer found in Minnan. For *zhaijiao* in Taiwan, see Gao Xianzhi, *Taiwan zongjiao* (Taipei: Zhongwen Tushu, 1995); and Lin Meirong, *Taiwan de zhaitang yu yanzi: Minjian fojiao de shijiao* (Taipei: Taiwan Shufang Chuban Youxian Gongsi, 2008).

12. Welch, *Practice of Chinese Buddhism*, 419.

13. Overmyer, "Women in Chinese Religions," 109, notes the existence of lay women ritualists in Zhejiang, but it is unclear whether these are like the *caigu*. *Caigu* exist also in neighboring Chaozhou and in parts of Southeast Asia; see Mercedes Dujunco, "Taiguo, Malaixiya, Xinjiapo Chaozhou gongdeban sangzang yishi zhong 'xuepen' de zhanxian jiqi shehui he lishi yinsu de kaolu," *Dayin* 3 (2010): 28–59.

14. A word in Pali or Sanskrit meaning the Buddhist community.

15. See Gao, Lin, and Hong, *Xiamen Zongjiao*, 52.

16. Western observers in the nineteenth century noted that women were not infrequently driven to suicide by autocratic mothers-in-law and cruel husbands. See James Johnston, *China and Formosa: The Story of the Mission of the Presbyterian Church of England* (London: Hazell, Watson & Viney, 1897), 42.

17. The Confucian tradition of chaste widows was strong in Minnan. Research shows that Tongan county had the greatest number of steles erected to commemorate chaste widows; see Yan Lishui, *Qiu shi ji* (Xiamen: Lujiang Chubanshe, 1992), 79–81.

18. An account of Yang Jiagu, the founder of Suyansi Temple in Quanzhou, relates an encounter with a mysterious woman who led her to a cave where she began meditating and practicing Buddhism. She attracted worshippers and later built a temple which became Suyansi. It was believed that she had been guided by a bodhisattva. See Feilubin Suyansi Bianji Weiyuanhui, *Feilubin suyansi wenlian zhensuo jiniankan* (Manila: HI-Q, 1983), 91–93.

19. Feilubin, *Feilubin Suyansi*, 1983; Gao, Lin, and Hong, *Xiamen Zongjiao*, 55–61; Yu, "Quanzhou Minjian," 119.

20. Lin, *Huashuo*, 261.

21. Yu, "Quanzhou Minjian," 114–21.

22. Johnston, *China and Formosa*, 30.

23. Diana Paul, *Women in Buddhism* (Berkeley, CA: Asian Humanities Press, 1980).

24. When the bhikṣuni order in India disappeared in the tenth century, no full ordination of nuns was allowed. Following an international full ordination of bhikṣuni organized by Taiwan's Foguangshan (佛光山) Monastery in Bodhgaya in 1998, the tradition of ordination for nuns has been revived.

25. It can still be found in parts of Southeast Asia; see Dujunco, "Taiguo, Malaixiya," 2010.

26. The Five Obstacles or Hindrances are sensual desire, anger or ill will, boredom or lack of concentration, restlessness or worry, and doubt.

27. The Lotus Sutra narrates the story of the eight-year-old daughter of the dragon king Sagara, who attains enlightenment. Doubted by some of Buddha's disciples to be capable of achieving Buddhahood, she transforms herself into a man. See Lucinda Joy Peach, "Social Responsibility, Sex Change and Salvation: Gender Justice in the 'Lotus

Sutra,'" *Philosophy East and West* 52, no. 1 (2002): 55–56; see also Kathryn A. Tsai, "The Chinese Buddhist Monastic Order for Women: the First Two Centuries," *Historical Reflections*, 8, no. 3 (Fall 1981): 1–20.

28. See Overmyer, "Women in Chinese Religions,"1991.

29. In 1925, there were approximately a million monks and nuns in China (excluding wandering monks). Nuns consisted of one-tenth of this number. See Karl Ludwig Reichelt, *Truth and Tradition in Chinese Buddhism: A Study of Chinese Mahayana Buddhism* (Copenhagen, 1927), chap. 10. See also Welch, *Practice of Chinese Buddhism*, 1967.

30. Sister Jugu, manager of Mituosi (弥陀寺) and Feigu of Yanshou Tang (延寿堂), personal communication, both in Xiamen (November 13, 2000).

31. Venerable Master Xingyun's Foguangshan order in Taiwan, with its worldwide branches and lay associations, has a much larger percentage of nuns than monks. For a study of the Foguangshan order, see Stuart Chandler, *Establishing a Pure Land on Earth: The Foguang Buddhist Perspective on Modernization and Globalization* (Honolulu: University of Hawaii Press, 2004); for a historical survey of Buddhism in Taiwan, see Charles Brewer Jones, *Buddhism in Taiwan*; and for a study of Buddhist nuns in Taiwan and Sri Lanka, see Cheng Wei-Yi, *Buddhist Nuns in Taiwan and Sri Lanka: A Critique of the Feminist Perspective* (London: Routledge, 2007).

32. I have come across a further type of lay Buddhist ritualist in the Minnan region who are known as *xianghua heshang* (香花和尚 incense-flower monks); for a more detailed study of this type of ritualists, see Hwee-San Tan, "Journey through the Underworld: Music and Meaning in a Folk Buddhist Ritual for the Dead," in *Power, Beauty and Meaning: Eight Studies on Chinese Music*, ed. Luciana Galliano (Florence: Leo S. Olschki Editore, 2005), 223–51.

33. Kenneth K. S. Ch'en, *Buddhism in China: A Historical Survey* (Princeton: Princeton University Press, 1964), 294.

34. See Barend J. Ter Haar, *The White Lotus Teachings in Chinese Religious History* (Leiden: Brill, 1992).

35. Shi Huanlun, *Shishi jigu lue xuji* (Yangzhou: Jiangsu Guangling Guji Keyin She, 1992).

36. Lian Lichang, *Fujian mimi shehui* (Fuzhou: Fujian Renmin Chubanshe, 1988), 32.

37. de Groot, *Sectarianism*, 98.

38. For studies of sectarian religions in China, see de Groot, *Sectarianism*; and Overmyer, "Women in Chinese Religions."

39. Based on my own observations in Taiwan in the early 2000s, although vegetarian sects are on the decline because of the growing popularity of Buddhism, there are several Longhua sect vegetarian halls that are still active. For a history of the origin of *zhaijiao* and their development in Taiwan, see Jiang Canteng and Wang Jianchuan, *Taiwan zhaijiao de lishi guancha yu zhanwan* (Taipei: Xinwenfeng, 1994).

40. See ibid., 11.

41. Sister Miaolian, personal communication, July 1997.

42. Post-1949 lavish funerals were frowned upon, and the Chinese Communist Party set about reforming funeral practices; see Martin K. Whyte, "Death in the People's Republic of China," in *Death Ritual in Late Imperial and Modern China*, ed. James L. Watson and Evelyn S. Rawski (Berkeley: University of California Press, 1988), 289–316; and Donald E. MacInnis, *Religion in China Today: Policy and Practice* (Maryknoll, NY: Orbis, 1989).

43. Up to 1989, it was against government policy to hold religious rites at home; see MacInnis, *Religion*, 146.

44. Criticism of performing rites for the dead, particularly for private families for commercial gain, grew after Taixu's early twentieth-century reforms. Thus, even before 1949, some monasteries in Zhejiang and Jiangsu regions had already stopped. See Welch, *Practice of Chinese Buddhism*, 197–98. Today some monasteries ban them, while others perform a "cleaned-up" form; see also Hwee-San Tan, "Saving the Soul in Red China: Music and Ideology in the *Gongde* Ritual of Merit in Fujian," *British Journal of Ethnomusicology* 11, no. 1 (2002): 119–40.

45. In the temples of Foguangshan in Taiwan, nuns commonly perform in *Yankou* rites, though not in the role of Vajra high master.

46. My paternal grandfather was a Buddhist *jushi* in Singapore; he shaved his head and was always dressed in *jushi* grey clothing. As a child, I thought he was a Buddhist monk but realized when I was much older that he was a *jushi* who practiced piously at home.

47. In lieu of the water penitence, other texts such as the *Jingang baochan* (金刚宝忏 Precious penitence of the diamond sutra) or *Dizang pusa benyuanjing* (地藏菩萨本愿经 Sutra of the original vows of Bodhisattva Ksitigarbha) may also be used.

48. Emperor Wudi (502–49 CE) of the Liang dynasty decreed that a penitential ritual be compiled to save the soul of his empress following a dream that she had turned into a serpent after her death. The ten-volume penitence was compiled by the Chan master Baozhi.

49. The concept of the transference of merit is an important one in Mahayana Buddhism and particularly in *gongde*, whereby merits accrued from the recitation of sutra or penitence texts and the bestowing of food on sentient beings are aggregated and passed on to the deceased to help secure their passage to the western paradise of Amitabha Buddha.

50. Some scholars use the term *chant* to describe Buddhist vocal performance; since *chant* is a very generic term and tends to imply intonation on the same note or a limited range of notes, I prefer to avoid the term in this writing.

51. For a detailed study, see Tan, "Saving the Soul."

52. In Chinese musical theory, the term *diao* may be used to convey the concept of both key and mode; with the development of Chinese opera, the term *qiangdiao* or *diaoqiang* may also refer to singing style in different operatic forms. See *Zhongguo yinyue cidian*, ed. Zhongguo yishu yanjiu yuan, yinyue yanjiusuo (1985): 81. In this case, the term *diao* refers to a repertoire of tunes in a recognizable singing style.

53. Note that this nationally adopted hymn-singing style is called different names in different regions; in Taiwan, it is referred to as *haichaoyin* (sound of the waves); in other places, it is known as *shifang yun* (melodies of the ten directions, referring to monasteries of high learning, *shifang conglin*) or *conglin diao* (conglin style).

54. See Pi-yen Chen, "The Contemporary Practice of the Chinese Buddhist Daily Service: Two Case Studies of the Traditional in the Post-traditional World," *Ethnomusicology*, 46, no. 2 (2002): 226–49, for a further study of this form of vocalization in the monastic daily lessons.

55. For a more detailed comparison of one and the same *zan* text sung in the *waijiang* and Fuzhou styles by monks and *caigu*, see Tan, "Saving the Soul."

56. For example, Sister Miaolian, personal communication, July 1997.

57. Venerable Benfa, personal communication, November 1998.

58. In the daily and ceremonial rituals in large monasteries, hymns are accompanied only by percussion instruments that are more or less unique to Chinese Mahayana Buddhism; these include *daqing* (大磬 large bronze bowl), *yinqing* (引磬 hand-held

bowl), *dangzi* (铛子 small hand-held gong), *muyu* (木鱼 wooden fish), and *bo* (钹 small cymbals).

59. Sister Miaolian, personal communication, July 1997.

60. For further discussion on this and a comparative score of the hymn, see Tan, "Saving the Soul."

61. For the musical example, see Tan, "Saving the Soul," 131.

62. Cai Junchao, personal communication, July, 1997.

63. Sister Huigen, personal communication, November 1998.

64. For more detailed analyses of the texts, see Hwee-San Tan, "Sounds for the Dead: Ritualists and Their Vocal Liturgical Music in the Buddhist Rite of Merit in Fujian, China" (PhD diss., University of London, 2003), chap. 3.

65. Chinese musicologist Yuan Jingfang has found that in temples in and around Beijing, *qupai* labels are still commonly used to identify hymn tunes. See Yuan Jingfang, "Zhongguo beifang foqu 'shi dayun,'" *1998 nian foxue yanjiu lunwenji: Fojiao yinyue*, ed. Caituan Faren Foguanshan Wenjiao Jijinhui (Taipeixian, Sanchongshi: Foguang Wenhua Shiye Youxian Gongsi, 1998), 237–88. In Fujian today, the younger generation of monks and *caigu* are hardly aware of this *qupai* system, as it is no longer used to designate hymn tunes.

66. Regional styles of hymn singing, particularly the repertoire found in rites for the dead, exist in other parts of China. See Liu Jianchang "Wutai foyue," *Zhongguo fojiao yinyue xuancui*, ed. Tian Qing (Shanghai: Shanghai Yinyue Chubanshe, 1993), 253–98; Shi Huiyuan, "Chaozhou foyue," *Zhongguo fojiao yinyue xuancui*, ed. Tian Qing (Shanghai: Shanghai Yinyue Chubanshe, 1993), 207–39.

67. Shi Guoman, personal communication, August 1997.

68. Shi Huayu, personal communication, August 1997.

Selected Bibliography

Bai Xianyong, ed. *Shidan baotian yuzanji* [A lust so extensive that it can wrap up the sky]. Taipei: Tianxia yuanjian, 2009.
Banks, Ellison, ed. *Women's Buddhism, Buddhism's Women: Tradition, Revision, Renewal.* Boston: Wisdom, 2000.
Baptandier, Brigitte. *The Lady of Linshui: A Chinese Female Cult.* Palo Alto, CA: Stanford University Press, 2008.
Baranovitch, Nimrod. *China's New Voices: Popular Music, Ethnicity, Gender, and Politics, 1978–1997.* Berkeley: University of California Press, 2003.
Barkin, Elaine, and Lydia Hamessley, eds. *Audible Traces: Gender, Identity and Music.* Zurich: Carciofoli, 1999.
Barlow, Tani E., and Angela Zito, eds. *Body, Subject, and Power in China.* Chicago: University of Chicago Press, 1994.
Batchelor, Martine. *Women on the Buddhist Path.* London: Thorsons, 2000.
Bellér-Hann, Ildikó. *Community Matters in Xinjiang 1880–1949: Towards a Historical Anthropology of the Uyghur.* Leiden: Brill, 2008.
Bender, Mark. "A Description of *Jiangjing* (Telling Scriptures) Services in Jingjiang, China." *Asian Folklore Studies* 60, no. 1 (2001): 101–33.
Birch, Cyril. *Scenes for Mandarins: The Elite Theater of the Ming.* New York: Columbia University Press, 1995.
Blake, Fred C. "Death and Abuse in Chinese Marriage *Laments*: the Curse of Chinese Brides." *Asian Folklore Studies* 37 (1978): 13–33.
Brownell, Susan. "The Body and the Beautiful in Chinese Nationalism: Sportswomen and Fashion Models in the Reform Era." *China Information* 13, no. 2–3 (1998): 36–58.
———. "Gender and Nationalism in China at the Turn of the Millennium." In *China Briefing 2000*, edited by Tyrene White. Armonk, NY: M. E. Sharpe, 2000.
Brownell, Susan, and Jeffrey N. Wasserstrom, eds. *Chinese Femininities, Chinese Masculinities: A Reader.* Berkeley: University of California Press, 2002.
Butler, Judith. *Gender Trouble: Feminism and the Subversion of Identity.* London: Routledge, 1990.
Cai Fulian, and Chen Bo. "Liangshan Yizu Bimo wenxian 'Niri Erguo' yu kujiage 'Mama de nü'er' bijiao yanjiu" [A comparative study of Yi nationality Bimo scripture "Niri Erguo" and the marriage-crying song "Mother's Daughter"]. *Liangshan Minzu Yanjiu* 19 (October 2009): 130–38.
Cai Peiru. "Quansuo tianrenzhiji de nüren: Nü tongji de xingbie tezhi yu shenti yihan" [Women shuttling between heaven and mortals: Gender features and physical implications of female spirit mediums]. In *Qinghua daxue renleixue congkan* 4, 5–20. Taipei: Tangshan chubanshe, 2001.

Cass, Victoria. *Dangerous Women: Warriors, Grannies, and Geishas of the Ming.* Lanham, MD: Rowman and Littlefield, 1999.
Chau, Adam Yuet. *Miraculous Response: Doing Popular Religion in Contemporary China.* Palo Alto, CA: Stanford University Press, 2006.
Cheng Qin. "Hua'er zhong de nüxing he nüxing de Hua'er" [Women in *Hua'er* and *Hua'er* sung by women]. Master's thesis, Xibei minzu daxue, 2005.
Cheng Wei-Yi. *Buddhist Nuns in Taiwan and Sri Lanka: A Critique of the Feminist Perspective.* London: Routledge, 2007.
Chŏn Hwaja [Quan Huazi]. "Jiantan Chaoxianzu minzu shengyue de tedian" [A brief discussion of Korean vocal music characteristics]. *Renmin Yinyue* 10 (1984): 36–39.
Chow, Rey, "On Chineseness as a Theoretical Problem." *Boundary* 2, no. 25 (1998): 1–24.
Dai Ning. "Ming Qing shiqi Qinhuai qinglou yinyue wenhua chutan" [A preliminary study of the Qinhuai pleasure quarter's musical culture in Ming and Qing]. *Zhongguo Yinyuexue* 3 (1997): 40–54.
Dautcher, Jay. *Down a Narrow Road: Identity and Masculinity in a Uyghur Community in Xinjiang China.* Cambridge, MA: Harvard University Press, 2009.
de Kloet, Jeroen. *China with a Cut: Globalisation, Urban Youth and Popular Culture.* Amsterdam: Amsterdam University Press, 2010.
DeNora, Tia. *Music in Everyday Life.* Cambridge: Cambridge University Press, 2000.
Doubleday, Veronica. "The Frame Drum in the Middle East: Women, Musical Instruments and Power." *Ethnomusicology* 43, no. 1 (1999): 101–34.
———. *Three Women of Herat.* London: Cape, 1988.
Doyle, James. *The Male Experience.* Dubuque, IA: Wm. C. Brown, 1989.
Du Yaxiong. "Taomin Hua'er" [Taomin *Hua'er*, phallicism and fertility cults]. *Longyuan Wenhua* 2 (1997): 14–20.
DuBois, Thomas D. *The Sacred Village: Social Change and Religious Life in Rural North China.* Honololu: University of Hawaii Press, 2005.
Egan, Ronald. "The Controversy over Music and 'Sadness' and Changing Conceptions of the *Qin* in Middle Period China." *Harvard Journal of Asiatic Studies* 57, no. 1 (1997): 5–66.
———. *The Problem of Beauty: Aesthetic Thought and Pursuits in Northern Song Dynasty China.* Cambridge, MA: Harvard University Asia Center, 2006.
Fan Lizhu. "The Cult of the Silkworm Mother as a Core of Local Community Religion in a North China Village: Field Study in Zhiwuying, Baoding, Hebei." In *Religion in China Today*, edited by Daniel Overmyer. Cambridge: Cambridge University Press, 2003.
Farquhar, Judith. *Appetites: Food and Sex in Post-Socialist China.* Durham, NC: Duke University Press, 2002.
Frith, Simon, and Angela McRobbie. "Rock and Sexuality." *Screen Education* 29 (1978): 5–9, 12–15.
Fung, Anthony, and Michael Curtin. "The Anomalies of Being Faye (Wong): Gender Politics in Chinese Popular Music." *International Journal of Cultural Studies* 5, no. 3 (2002): 263–90.
Garber, Marjorie. *Vested Interests: Cross-Dressing and Cultural Anxiety.* New York: Routledge, 1992.

Gilmartin, Christina K., Gail Hershhatter, Lisa Rofel, and Tyrene White, eds. *Engendering China: Women, Culture and the State*. Cambridge, MA: Harvard University Press, 1994.
Gladney, Dru. "Representing Nationality in China: Refiguring Majority/Minority Identities." *Journal of Asian Studies* 53, no. 1 (1994): 92–123.
Goodman, Bryna, and Wendy Larson, eds. *Gender in Motion: Divisions of Labour and Cultural Change in Late Imperial and Modern China*. Lanham, MD: Rowman and Littlefield, 2005.
Graddol, David, and Joan Swann. *Gender Voices*. Oxford: Blackwell, 1989.
Halberstam, Judith. *Female Masculinity*. Durham, NC: Duke University Press, 1998.
Harrell, Stevan. *Ways of Being Ethnic in Southwest China*. Seattle: University of Washington Press, 2001.
Harrell, Stevan, Bamo Qubumo, and Ma Erzi. *Mountain Patterns: The Survival of Nuosu Culture*. Seattle: University of Washington Press, 2000.
Harris, Rachel. *The Making of a Musical Canon in Chinese Central Asia: The Uyghur Twelve Muqam*. Aldershot, UK: Ashgate Press, 2008.
———. "Reggae on the Silk Road: the Globalization of Uyghur Pop." *China Quarterly* 183 (2005): 627–43.
Hawkins, Stan. *The British Pop Dandy: Male Identity, Music and Culture*. Farnham, UK: Ashgate, 2009.
Henriot, Christian. *Prostitution and Sexuality in Shanghai: A Social History, 1849–1949*. Cambridge: Cambridge University Press, 2001.
Hershatter, Gail. *Dangerous Pleasures: Prostitution and Modernity in Twentieth-Century Shanghai*. Berkeley: University of California Press, 1997.
———. *Women in China's Long Twentieth Century*. Berkeley: University of California Press, 2007.
Honig, Emily. "Maoist Mappings of Gender: Reassessing the Red Guards." In *Chinese Femininities, Chinese Masculinities*, edited by Susan Brownell and Jeffrey Wasserstrom, 255–68. Berkeley: University of California Press, 2002.
Hua Wei. "Ma Xianglan yu Mingdai houqi de qutan" [Ma Xianglan in the music drama world of the late Ming]. *Xiqu Xuebao* 12 (2007): 55–82.
Huang, Martin, ed. *Male Friendship in Ming China*. Leiden: Brill, 2007.
———. *Negotiating Masculinities in Late Imperial China*. Honolulu: University of Hawaii Press, 2006.
Hung, Eric. "Performing 'Chineseness' on the Western Concert Stage: The Case of Lang Lang." *Asian Music* Winter/Spring 2009, 131–48.
Jacka, Tamara. *Women's Work in Rural China: Change and Continuity in an Era of Reform*. Cambridge: Cambridge University Press, 1997.
Jarman-Ivens, Freya, ed. *Oh Boy! Masculinities and Popular Music*. London: Routledge, 2007.
Jin Jiang. *Women Playing Men: Yue Opera and Social Change in Twentieth-Century Shanghai*. Seattle: University of Washington Press, 2009.
Jing Jun. *The Temple of Memories: History, Power, and Morality in a Chinese Village*. Palo Alto, CA: Stanford University Press, 1996.
Johnson, Bruce, and Martin Cloonan. *Dark Side of the Tune: Popular Music and Violence*. Aldershot, UK: Ashgate, 2009.

Johnson, Elizabeth L. "Grieving for the Dead, Grieving for the Living: Funeral Laments of Hakka Women." In *Death Ritual in Late Imperial China*, edited by James L. Watson and Evelyn Rawski, 135–63. Berkeley: University of California Press, 1988.

———. "Singing of Separation, Lamenting Loss: Hakka Women's Expressions of Separation and Reunion." In *Living with Separation in China: Anthropological Accounts*, edited by Charles Stafford, 27–52. London: Routledge Curzon, 2003.

Jones, Andrew. *Like a Knife: Ideology and Genre in Contemporary Chinese Music*, New York: Cornell University Press, 1992.

Jones, Stephen. "Living Early Composition: An Appreciation of Chinese Shawm Melody." In *Analysing East Asian Music: Patterns of Rhythm and Melody*, edited by Simon Mills, 25–112. Musiké 4 (The Hague: Semar, 2010).

———. *Ritual and Music of North China*. Vol. 1, *Shawm Bands in Shanxi*. Aldershot, UK: Ashgate, 2007, with DVD.

———. *Ritual and Music of North China*. Vol. 2, *Shaanbei*. Aldershot, UK: Ashgate, 2009, with DVD.

Kang Xiaofei. "In the Name of Buddha: The Cult of the Fox in Contemporary Northern Shaanxi." *Minsu Qu Yi* 138 (2002): 67–109.

Karpf, Anne. *The Human Voice: The Story of a Remarkable Talent*. London: Bloomsbury, 2006.

Killick, Andrew. *In Search of Korean Traditional Opera: Discourses of Ch'anggŭk*. Honolulu: University of Hawaii Press, 2010.

Kipnis, Andrew. "Zouping Christianity as Gendered Critique? The Place of the Political in Ethnography." *Anthropology and Humanism* 27, no. 1 (2002): 80–96.

Ko, Dorothy. "The Written Word and the Bound Foot: A History of the Courtesan's Aura." In *Writing Women in Late Imperial China*, edited by Ellen Widmer and Kang-i Sun Chang, 74–100. Stanford, CA: Stanford University Press, 1997.

Koskoff, Ellen, ed. *Women and Music in Cross-Cultural Perspective*. Urbana: University of Illinois Press, 1989.

Kraef, Olivia. "Strumming the 'Lost Mouth Chord'—Discourses of Preserving the Nuosu-Yi Mouth Harp." In *Music as Intangible Cultural Heritage: Policy, Ideology and Practice in the Preservation of East Asian Traditions*, edited by Keith Howard. Farnham, UK: Ashgate Press, 2012.

———. *Yi frauen in Peking—zu problemen ethnischer und weiblicher identität im kontext der Chinesischen reformpolitik* [Yi women in Beijing—issues of ethnic and gender identity in the context of Chinese reform policies]. Master's thesis, Freie Universität Berlin, 2003.

Kraus, Richard. *Pianos and Politics in China: Middle-Class Ambitions and the Struggle over Western Music*. Oxford: Oxford University Press, 1989.

Lam, Joseph S. C. "The Presence and Absence of Female Musicians and Music in China." In *Women and Confucian Cultures in Premodern China, Korea, and Japan*, edited by Dorothy Ko, JaHyun Kim Haboush, and Joan R. Piggott, 27–52. Berkeley: University of California Press, 2003.

Lee, Tong Soon. "Grace Liu and Cantonese Opera in England: Becoming Chinese Overseas." In *Lives in Chinese Music*, edited by Helen Rees, 119–44. Urbana: University of Illinois Press, 2009.

Li Juan. "Minzu yinyuexue zhong de shehui xingbie yanjiu: Yige xinke dute que yijiu bianyuan de yanjiu shijiao" [Gender research in ethnomusicology: A new but still marginal angle]. *Zhongguo Yinyuexue* 1 (2006): 134–37.
Lin Meirong. *Taiwan de zhaitang yu yanzi: Minjian fojiao de shijiao* [The vegetarian halls and mountainside temples of Taiwan: A perspective of folk Buddhism]. Taipei: Taiwan Shufang Chuban Youxian Gongsi, 2008.
Link, Perry, Richard P. Madsen, and Paul G. Pickowicz, eds. *Popular China: Unofficial Culture in a Globalizing Society*. Lanham, MD: Rowman and Littlefield, 2002.
Lipman, Jonathan M., and Stevan Harrell, eds. *Violence in China: Essays in Culture and Counterculture*. Albany: State University of New York Press, 1990.
Litzinger, Ralph. "Tradition and the Gender of Civility." In *Chinese Femininities, Chinese Masculinities: A Reader*, edited by Susan Brownell and Jeffrey N. Wasserstrom, 412–34. Berkeley: University of California Press, 2002.
Liu Dalin. *Zhongguo gudai xing wenhua* [Sexual culture in ancient China]. Yinchuan: Ningxia Renmin Chubanshe, 1993.
Liu Fei-wen. "Women Who De-silence Themselves: Male-Illegible Literature (*Nüshu*) and Female-Specific Songs (*Nüge*) in Jiangyong County, Hunan Province, China." PhD diss., Syracuse University, 1997.
Liu Xin. *In One's Own Shadow: An Ethnographic Account of the Condition of Post-Reform Rural China*. Berkeley: University of California Press, 2000.
Louie, Kam. *Theorizing Chinese Masculinity: Society and Gender in China*. London: Cambridge University Press, 2002.
Louie, Kam, and Louise Edwards. "Chinese Masculinity: Theorizing Wen and Wu." *East Asian History* 8 (1994): 135–48.
Louie, Kam, and Morris Low, eds. *Asian Masculinities: The Meaning and Practice of Manhood in China and Japan*. London: Routledge Curzon, 2003.
Lowry, Kathryn A. *The Tapestry of Popular Songs in 16th- and 17th-Century China: Reading, Limitation, and Desire*. Leiden: Brill, 2005.
Lum, Casey Man Kong. *In Search of a Voice: Karaoke and the Construction of Identity in Chinese America*. Mahwah, NJ: Lawrence Erlbaum, 1996.
Lutz, Catherine. "Emotion, Thought, and Estrangement: Emotion as a Cultural Category." *Cultural Anthropology* 1, no. 3 (1986): 287–309.
Ma Linying. *Yizu funü wenhua* [The culture of Yi women]. Chengdu: Sichuan Minzu Chubanshe, 1995.
Magrini, Tullia, ed. *Music and Gender: Perspectives from the Mediterranean*. Chicago: University of Chicago Press, 2003.
Martin, Fran. "The Perfect Lie: Sandee Chan and Lesbian Representability in Mandarin Pop Music." *Inter-Asia Cultural Studies* 4, no. 2 (2003): 264–79.
Martin, Fran, and Larissa Heinrich. *Embodied Modernities: Corporeality, Representation, and Chinese Cultures*. Honolulu: University of Hawaii Press, 2006.
McClary, Susan. *Feminine Endings: Music, Gender and Sexuality*. Minnesota: University of Minnesota Press, 2002.
McLaren, Anne E. "Competing for Women: The Marriage Market as Reflected in Folk Performance in the Lower Yangzi Delta." *Intersections: Gender and Sexuality in Asia and the Pacific* 16 (2008). http://intersections.anu.edu.au/issue16/mclaren.htm.

———. *Performing Grief: Bridal Laments in Rural China.* Honolulu: University of Hawaii Press, 2008.
———. "Women's Work and Ritual Space in China." In *Chinese Women, Living and Working,* edited by Anne McLaren, 169–87. London: Routledge Curzon, 2004.
Meintjes, Louise. "Shoot the Sergeant, Shatter the Mountain: The Production of Masculinity in Zulu *Ngoma* Song and Dance in Post Apartheid South Africa." *Ethnomusicology Forum* 13, no. 2 (2004): 173–201.
Melvin, Sheila, and Jindong Cai. *Rhapsody in Red: How Western Classical Music Became Chinese.* New York: Algora, 2004.
Min Tian. "Male *Dan*: the Paradox of Sex, Acting, and Perception of Female Impersonation in Traditional Chinese Theater." *Asian Theater Journal* 17, no. 1 (2000): 78–97.
Mitsui, Toru, and Shūhei Hosokawa, eds. *Karaoke around the World: Global Technology, Local Singing.* London: Routledge, 1998.
Moskowitz, Marc L. *Cries of Joy, Songs of Sorrow: Chinese Pop Music and Its Cultural Connotations.* Honolulu: University of Hawaii Press, 2010.
Mueggler, Erik. *The Age of Wild Ghosts: Memory, Violence, and Place in Southwest China.* Berkeley: University of California Press, 2001.
Myers, John E. *The Way of the Pipa: Structure and Imagery in Chinese Lute Music.* Kent, Ohio: Kent State University Press, 1992.
Ning Ying. "Yanbian Chaoxianzu namdo minyo, pansuoli chuanji moshi diaocha" [Elementary study on the transmission of Namdo folk songs and Pansori in Yanbian Chaoxian ethnic group]. *Hundred Schools in Art* 5 (2008): 38–43.
Ōki Yasushi. *Chūgoku yūri kūkan: Min shin shinwai gijo no sekai* [The Chinese pleasure quarter: The world of Nanjing courtesans]. Tokyo: Seidosha, 2002.
———. *Fū Bōryū "Sanka" no kenkyū: Chūgoku Mindai no tsūzoku kayō* [Research on Feng Menglong's "Mountain Songs": Ming dynasty folk songs]. Tokyo: Keisō Shobō, 2003.
Overmyer, Daniel. *Local Religion in North China in the Twentieth Century: the Structure and Organization of Community Rituals and Beliefs.* Leiden: Brill, 2009.
———. "Women in Chinese Religions: Submission, Struggle, Transcendence." In *From Benares to Beijing: Essays on Buddhism and Chinese Religion in Honour of Professor Jan Yun-Hua,* edited by Koichi Shinohara and Gregor Schopen, 91–120. Oakville, ON: Mosaic Press, 1991.
Pacini Hernandez, Deborah. "'Cantando la Cama Vacia': Love, Sexuality and Gender Relationships in Dominican Bachata." *Popular Music* 9, no. 3 (1990): 351–67.
Park, Chan E. *Voices from the Straw Mat: Toward an Ethnography of Korean Story Singing,* Honolulu: University of Hawaii Press, 2003.
Paul, Diana. *Women in Buddhism.* Berkeley, CA: Asian Humanities Press, 1980.
Peach, Lucinda Joy. "Social Responsibility, Sex Change and Salvation: Gender Justice in the 'Lotus Sutra.'" *Philosophy East and West* 52, no. 1 (2002): 50–74.
Pease, Rowan. "Yanbian Songs: Musical Expressions of Identity among Chinese Koreans." PhD diss., University of London, 2001.
Perry, Elizabeth. "Rural Violence in Socialist China." *China Quarterly* 103 (1985): 414–40.

Pu Yongguang. *Sichuan Liangshan Yizu chuantong wudao yanjiu* [Research on the traditional dances of the Liangshan Yi]. Beijing: Minzu Chubanshe, 2005.
Qi Kun. *Lishide shanshi: Shanghai Nanhui sizhuyue qingyinde chuancheng yu bianqian yanjiu* [Historical exegesis: Study of transmission and change of *qingyin* groups in the *sizhu* music of Nanhui in Shanghai]. Shanghai: Shanghai yinyuexueyuan chubanshe, 2007.
Qiao Jian, Liu Guanwen, and Li Tiansheng. *Yuehu: tianye diaocha yu lishi zhuizong* [Music households: Fieldwork and historical traces]. Nanchang: Jiangxi renmin chubanshe, 2002.
Ren Jiahe, ed. *Kusang ge* [Funeral laments]. Shanghai: Shanghai wenyi chubanshe, 1988.
Roberts, Rosemary A. *Maoist Model Theater: The Semiotics of Gender and Sexuality in the Chinese Cultural Revolution (1966–1976)*. Leiden: Brill, 2010.
Rosaldo, Michelle Z., and Louise Lamphere, eds. *Women, Culture and Society*. Palo Alto, CA: Stanford University Press, 1974.
Roseman, Marina. *Healing Sounds from the Malaysian Rainforest: Temiar Music and Medicine*. Berkeley: University of California Press, 1993.
Sang Ye. *China Candid: The People on the People's Republic*, edited by Geremie R. Barmé with Miriam Lang. Berkeley: University of California Press, 2006.
Schein, Louisa. "Gender and Internal Orientalism in China." *Modern China* 23, no. 1 (1997): 69–98.
———. *Minority Rules: The Miao and the Feminine in China's Cultural Politics*. Durham, NC: Duke University Press, 2000.
Schimmelpenninck, Antoinet. *Chinese Folk Songs and Folk Singers: Shan'ge Traditions in Southern Jiangsu*. Leiden: CHIME foundation, 1997.
Shang Wei. "*Jin Ping Mei* and Late Ming Culture." In *Writing and Materiality in China*, edited by Judith T. Zeitlin and Lydia H. Liu. Cambridge, MA: Harvard University Asia Center, 2003.
Shepherd, John. "Music and Male Hegemony." In *Music and Society: The Politics of Composition, Performance and Reception*, edited by Richard Leppert and Susan McClary, 151–72. Cambridge: Cambridge University Press, 1987.
Sieber, Patricia Angela. *Theaters of Desire: Authors, Readers, and the Reproduction of Early Chinese Song-Drama, 1300–2000*. New York: Palgrave Macmillan, 2003.
Song Bang-song, "*Kwangdae Ka*: A Source Material for the Pánsori Tradition," *Korea Journal* 16, no. 8 (1976): 26.
Song Geng. *The Fragile Scholar: Power and Masculinity in Chinese Culture*. Hong Kong: Hong Kong University Press, 2004.
Stock, Jonathan. *Huju: Traditional Opera in Modern Shanghai*. Oxford: Oxford University Press, 2003.
———. "Reconsidering the Past: Zhou Xuan and the Rehabilitation of Early Twentieth-Century Popular Music." *Asian Music* 26, no. 2 (1995): 119–35.
Stokes, Martin, ed. *Ethnicity, Identity and Music: The Musical Construction of Place*. Oxford: Berg, 1994.
Sugarman, Jane. *Engendering Song: Singing and Subjectivity at Prespa Albanian Weddings*. Chicago: University of Chicago Press, 1997.
Sutton, Donald S. *Steps of Perfection: Exorcistic Performers and Chinese Religion in Twentieth-Century Taiwan*. Cambridge, MA: Harvard University Press, 2003.

Tan Daxian. *Zhongguo hunjia yishi geyao yanjiu* [A study of Chinese bridal ritual songs]. Taipei: Shangwu yinshuguan, 1990.

Tan, Hwee-San. "Journey through the Underworld: Music and Meaning in a Folk Buddhist Ritual for the Dead." In *Power, Beauty and Meaning: Eight Studies on Chinese Music*, edited by Luciana Galliano, 223–51. Florence: Leo S. Olschki Editore, 2005.

Tang Baoxiang. *Yu Zhenfei chuan* [A biography of Yu Zhenfei]. Shanghai: Wenyi chubanshe, 1997.

Thorpe, Ashley. "Only Joking? The Role of the Clown and Percussion in *Jingju*." *Asian Theater Journal* 22, no. 2 (2005): 269–92.

Thrasher, Alan. *Sizhu Instrumental Music of South China: Ethos, Theory and Practice*. Leiden: Brill, 2009.

Tian Liantao, ed. *Zhongguo shaoshu minzu chuantong yinyue* [Traditional music of China's minorities]. Vols. 1 and 2. Beijing: Zhongyang Minzu Daxue Chubanshe, 2001.

Trebinjac, Sabine. "Femme, seule et venue d'ailleurs: Trois atouts d'un ethnomusicologue au Turkestan Chinois." *Cahiers de Musiques Traditionnelles* 8 (1995): 59–68.

Trippner, Joseph. "Die *Shaonien* in Ch'inghai" *Folklore Studies* 1 (1952): 264–305.

Tsomo, Karma Lekshe, ed. *Buddhist Women and Social Justice: Ideals, Challenges, and Achievements*. Albany: State University of New York Press, 2004.

Tuohy, Sue. "The Sonic Dimensions of Nationalism in Modern China: Musical Representation and Transformation." *Ethnomusicology* 45, no. 1 (2001): 107–31.

Turino, Thomas. *Music as Social Life: The Politics of Participation*. Chicago: University of Chicago Press, 2008.

Van Gulik, R. H. *Sexual Life in Ancient China*. Shanghai: Shanghai People's, 1990 [orig. ed. 1961].

Walser, Robert. *Running with the Devil: Power, Gender, and Madness in Heavy Metal Music*. Middletown, CT: Wesleyan University Press, 1993.

Wang Baohua. "Shiqi nian zhong hongse geju nüxing xingxiang suzao de tezheng fenxi" [An analysis of female roles in revolutionary opera]. *Zhongguo Yinyuexue* 4 (2006): 96–100.

Wang, Jing. *Brand New China: Advertising, Media, and Commercial Culture*. Cambridge, MA: Harvard University Press, 2008.

Wang Yuejin. "Mixing Memory and Desire: *Red Sorghum*, a Chinese Version of Masculinity and Femininity." *Public Culture* 2, no. 1 (1989): 31–53.

Watson, Rubie S. "Chinese Bridal Laments: The Claims of a Dutiful Daughter." In *Harmony and Counterpoint: Ritual Music in the Chinese Context*, edited by Bell Yung, Evelyn S. Rawski, and Rubie S. Watson, 107–29. Palo Alto, CA: Stanford University Press, 1996.

Willoughby, Heather. "The Sound of Han: *P'ansori*, Timbre and a Korean Ethos of Pain and Suffering," *Yearbook for Traditional Music* 32 (2000): 17–30.

Witzleben, J. Lawrence. *'Silk-and-Bamboo' Music in Shanghai: The Jiangnan Sizhu Instrumental Ensemble Tradition*. Kent, OH: Kent State University Press, 1995.

Wong, Cynthia P. "Women and Music I." In *Garland Encyclopedia of World Music*. Vol. 7, *East Asia: China, Japan, and Korea*, edited by Robert C. Provine, 401–4. London: Routledge, 2001.

Wong, Deborah, and Elliot, Mai. "I Want the Microphone: Mass Mediation and Agency in Asian-American Popular Music." *Drama Review* 38, no. 3 (1994): 152–67.

Wu Cuncun. *Homoerotic Sensibilities in Late Imperial China.* London: Routledge Curzon, 2004.

Wu Fan. *Yinyang gujiang: zaizhixu kongjianzhong* [Daoists and shawm bands in the ordering of space]. Beijing: Wenhua yishu chubanshe, 2007.

Xiang Yang. *Shanxi yuehu yanjiu* [Study of *yuehu* of feudal China in Shanxi]. Beijing: Wenwu chubanshe, 2001.

Xiao Mei. "Chang zai wulu shang" [Singing on the journey of the medium]. In *Zhongguo minjian yishi yinyue yanjiu, Huanan juan* [Studies of Chinese folk ritual music, South China vols.], edited by Tsao Pen-Yeh [Cao Benye], 328–494. Shanghai: Shanghai yinyue xueyuan chubanshe, 2007, with DVD.

——. "Huwu hujie qi ganlin: Xibei (Shaanbei) diqu qiyu yishi yu yinyue diaocha zongshu" [The buzz of praying for sweet rainfall: Field survey of ritual and music of rain prayer in the northwest (Shaanbei) region]. In *Zhongguo minjian yishi yinyue yanjiu, Xibei juan* [Studies of Chinese folk ritual music, Northwest vol.], edited by Tsao Pen-yeh [Cao Benye], 419–88. Kunming: Yunnan renmin chubanshe, 2003, with DVD.

Xiu Jun, and Jian Jin. *Zhongguo yueji shi* [History of Chinese female musical entertainers]. Beijing: Zhongguo wenlian chuban gongsi, 1993.

Yang, Mayfair Mei-hui. *Spaces of Their Own: Women's Public Sphere in Transnational China.* Minneapolis: University of Minnesota Press, 1999.

Yang Mu. "Erotic Musical Activity in Multiethnic China." *Ethnomusicology* 42, no. 2 (1998): 199–264.

——. "On the *Hua'er* Songs of North-Western China." *Yearbook for Traditional Music* 26 (1994): 100–116.

Yang Xifan. *Zang Yi zoulang de yuewu wenhua yanjiu* [Research on the music and dance culture of the Tibetan Yi corridor]. Beijing: Minzu Chubanshe, 2009.

Yano, Christine, R. *Tears of Longing: Nostalgia and the Nation in Japanese Popular Song.* Cambridge, MA: Harvard University Press, 2002.

Yeh, Catherine Vance. "Reinventing Ritual: Late Qing Handbooks for Proper Customer Behavior in Shanghai Courtesan Houses." *Late Imperial China* 19, no. 2 (1998): 1–63.

Yeh, Nora. "Wisdom of Ignorance: Women Performers in the Classical Chinese Music Traditions." In *Women, Gender, and Culture*, edited by Marcia Herndon and Susanne Ziegler, 157–72. Wilhelmshaven: Florian Noetzel, 1990.

Yoshihara, Mari. *Musicians from a Different Shore: Asians and Asian Americans in Classical Music.* Philadelphia: Temple University Press, 2007.

Yu Xia. "Yuexi tujiazu kujia ge de zhuti xinli fenxi" [A psychological analysis of wailing songs in wedding of Tujia nationality in western Hubei]. *Zhongnan Minzu Daxue Xuebao*, 1 (2004): 152–55.

Yue Meiti. *Jinsheng jinshi: Yue Meiti kunqu wushi nian* [This life as a young male: Yue Meiti's fifty years' career of performing *kunqu*]. Beijing: Wenhua yishu chubanshe, 2008.

Yue Meiti, and Yang Hanru. *Linfeng duqu: Yue Meiti jinsheng biaoyan yishu* [Handsome and musical: Yue Meiti's performance artistry of the commoner young man role]. Taipei: Shitou chuban gufen youxian gongsi, 2006.

Yung, Bell. *The Last of China's Literati: The Music, Poetry and Life of Tsar Teh-yun*. Hong Kong: Hong Kong University Press, 2008.
Zeitlin, Judith T. "The Gift of Song: Courtesans and Patrons in Late Ming and Early Qing Cultural Production." *Hsiang Lectures on Chinese Poetry*, edited by Grace S. Fong, 1–46. Vol. 4. Montreal: McGill University Centre for East Asian Research, 2008.
———. "'Notes of Flesh' and the Courtesan's Song in Seventeenth-Century China." In *The Courtesans' Arts: Cross-Cultural Perspectives*, edited by Martha Feldman and Bonnie Gordon, 75–99. New York: Oxford University Press, 2006.
Zeng Lingshi. "Yizu huobajie de 'duhuo' ge"[The "duhuo" songs of the Yi torch festival]. In *Zhongguo Yinyue* (1998, no. 2): 72–74+69.
Zeng Ming, Luo Qu, Aniu Shiri and Jilang Wuye. *Da Liangshan Meigu Yizu minjian yishu yanjiu* [Research on the folklore of the Meigu Yi in Liangshan]. Chengdu: Sichuan Minzu Chubanshe, 2004.
Zeng Suijin. "Liangshan Yizu kouxian yinyue de fenlei jiqi tedian" [On the classification and characteristics of the music of the mouth harp of the Liangshan Yi]. *Zhongyang Yinyue Xueyuan Xuebao*, no. 3 (1987): 20–25.
Zhang Jun. *Wo shi xiaosheng* [I am a young male actor]. Shanghai: Cishu chubanshe, 2008.
Zhang Yanqin. "Zhangzi shuoshu jiqi xijuhua qingxiang" [Story-telling in Zhangzi and its tendency of dramatization]. *Minsu Quyi* 151 (2006): 31–96.
Zhang Yingjin. "Ideology of the Body in *Red Sorghum*: National Allegory, National Roots, and Third Cinema." *East-West Film Journal* 4, no. 2 (1990): 38–53.
Zhang Zhentao. "Nü yueshou yu nü changjia" [Female instrumentalists and singers]. *Xinghai yinyuexueyuan xuebao*, no. 3 (2009): 43–49.
Zhao Zongfu. *Hua'er tonglun* [A survey of *hua'er*]. Xining: Qinghai renmin chubanshe. 1989.
Zheng, Su. "Redefining Yin and Yang: Transformation of Gender/Sexual Politics in Chinese Music." In *Audible Traces: Gender, Identity and Music*, edited by Elaine Barkin and Lydia Hamessley, 153–76. Zurich: Carciofoli Verlagshaus, 1999.
———. "Women and Music II." In *Garland Encyclopedia of World Music*. Vol. 7, *East Asia: China, Japan, and Korea*, edited by Robert C. Provine, 405–10. London: Routledge, 2001.
Zheng Tiantian. *Red Lights: The Lives of Sex Workers in Postsocialist China*. Minneapolis: University of Minnesota Press, 2009.
Zhong Xueping. *Masculinity Beseiged? Issues of Modernity and Male Subjectivity in Chinese Literature of the Late Twentieth Century*. Durham, NC: Duke University Press, 2000.
Zhongguo yishu yanjiuyuan yinyue yanjiusuo, ed. *Zhongguo jinxiandai yinyuejia zhuan* [Biographies of recent and contemporary musicians]. Shenyang: Chunfeng wenyi chubanshe, 1994.
Zhou Ji. *Zhongguo Xinjiang Weiwu'erzu Yisilanjiao liyi yinyue* [China's Xinjiang Uyghur Islamic ritual music]. Taipei: Xinwenfeng chuban gongsi, 1999.
Zhou Kaimo. "Minjian yishi zhong de nüxing juese: Yinyue xingwei jiqi xiangzheng yiyi" [Female roles, musical behaviors and their symbolism in folk rites: A case study of Chinese Bai people's ritual music]. *Yinyue Yishu* 1 (2005): 64–72.

Contributors

RUARD ABSAROKA is a PhD candidate at SOAS, University of London, where he has lectured on music in East Asia and on ethnomusicology courses. His research interests include the impact of digital technologies on informal, independent musicking. Following fieldwork in China his doctoral dissertation focuses on urban musical geographies and networks in Shanghai. He is also an active musician in London.

RACHEL HARRIS is senior lecturer at SOAS, University of London, where she teaches ethnomusicology and the musics of Central Asia and China. She is the author of *Singing the Village* (Oxford University Press, 2004) and *The Making of a Musical Canon in Chinese Central Asia* (Ashgate, 2008). Her current research interests focus on Islamic soundscapes, working with rural women in Xinjiang. She is engaged with outreach projects relating to Central Asian and Chinese music, including recording projects, musical performance, and consultancy for the Aga Khan Music Initiative.

STEPHEN JONES has been documenting living traditions of folk music in rural China since 1986. A cofounder of CHIME, from 1993 to 2005 he held research fellowships at SOAS, University of London. He is also a violinist in leading early music ensembles in London. He is author of *Folk Music of China: Living Instrumental Traditions* (Oxford University Press, 1995), *Plucking the Winds* (CHIME, 2004), *Ritual and Music of North China*, two volumes with DVDs (Ashgate, 2007, 2009), and *In Search of the Folk Daoists of North China* (Ashgate, 2010).

FRANK KOUWENHOVEN is a music researcher from Leiden, Holland, and cofounder of the European Foundation for Chinese Music Research (CHIME). He studied English language and literature at the University of Utrecht. Since 1986, he has carried out extensive fieldwork on Chinese music in close cooperation with his partner Antoinet Schimmelpenninck. He is the main editor of the *CHIME* journal, a concert organizer and a producer of books, films, and exhibitions on Chinese music.

OLIVIA KRAEF is a lecturer and PhD candidate with the Seminar of East Asian Studies (Institute of Chinese Studies) at Freie Universitaet Berlin, Germany. Kraef began conducting research on the Nuosu-Yi of Liangshan, Sichuan Province, in early 2002 as part of her master thesis on gender and intellectual migration. Her doctoral dissertation focuses on Nuosu-Yi music, cultural policy, and change in Liangshan.

JOSEPH LAM is director of the Confucius Institute at the University of Michigan and professor of musicology in the School of Music, Theatre and Dance, the University of Michigan. A musicologist and sinologist, Lam specializes in the musics and cultures of southern Song (1127–1275), Ming (1368–1644), and modern China (1900 to present). Lam regularly lectures in the United States, mainland China, and Asia. His most recent publications include "Music and Masculinities in Ming China" (*Asian Music*, 2011), and *Songdai yinyueshi lunwenji: lilun yu miaoshu* (Historical studies on Song dynasty music: Theories and narratives; Shanghai Conservatory of Music Press, 2012). Currently, he is working on a monograph entitled *Kunqu, the Classical Opera of Globalized China.*

ROWAN PEASE is a senior teaching fellow at SOAS, University of London, and editorial manager of *The China Quarterly*. She completed her PhD on songs of the ethnic Koreans living in northeast China in 2001, and she has since published several book chapters on the Korean pop wave Hanliu in China. She is currently researching China's Korean music during the Cultural Revolution.

ANTOINET SCHIMMELPENNINCK was a cofounder of CHIME. A Sinologist and amateur musician, she did extensive research on Chinese music from 1986 until her death in 2012. She was a main editor of the *CHIME* journal, a producer of books and films on Chinese music, and author of *Chinese Folk Songs and Folk Singers:* Shan'ge *Traditions in Southern Jiangsu* (CHIME, 1997).

HWEE-SAN TAN is a visiting lecturer at Middlesex University in London. Since completing her PhD at SOAS in 2003, she has held lecturing posts at Durham University, University College Dublin, and University of Surrey. She has published in *Asian Music, British Journal of Ethnomusicology*, and *The World of Music*. She has several book chapters and has also published articles in Chinese.

SHZR EE TAN is a lecturer in music at Royal Holloway, University of London, an active musician in the United Kingdom and Singapore, and author of *Beyond 'Innocence': Amis Aboriginal Song in Taiwan as an Ecosystem* (Ashgate, 2012). She has published articles in *Ethnomusicology Forum, Journal of American Folklore*, and *Music, Sound and Moving Image*, among other academic publications. Her research interests include new media, diaspora and music, and music and politics.

XIAO MEI is a professor of ethnomusicology at Shanghai Conservatory of Music. She has been collecting, coordinating, and studying traditional, folk, and ritual music of Han and ethnic groups in China such as Mongolian, Zhuang, Oroqen, Naxi, and Hmong peoples over several decades. She has written, edited, and published many articles and books (in Chinese) such as *Tianye de huisheng: Yinyue renleixue biji* (Echo on the field: Notes on the anthropology of music; Xiamen 2001, Shanghai, 2010), and *Zhongguo dalu minzu yinyuexue shidi kaocha, 1900–1966: Biannian yu ge'an* (Ethnomusicological fieldwork in mainland China, 1900–1966: Chronicle and cases; Shanghai, 2007).

JUDITH T. ZEITLIN is Professor of Chinese Literature in the Department of East Asian Languages and Civilizations at the University of Chicago. In addition to many articles and several edited volumes, she is the author of two books, *The Phantom Heroine: Ghosts and Gender in Seventeenth-Century Chinese Literature* (University of Hawai'i Press, 2007) and *Historian of the Strange: Pu Songling and the Chinese Classical Tale* (Stanford University Press, 1993). The recipient of numerous grants and fellowships, including a Guggenheim, she is currently writing a book on the culture of musical entertainment in early modern China and cocurating an exhibition on the visual culture of Chinese opera.

TIANTIAN ZHENG holds a PhD in anthropology from Yale University and teaches as professor of anthropology at State University of New York, Cortland. She is the author of the following books on sex, gender, and the state: *Red Lights* (winner of the 2010 Sara A. Whaley Book Prize from the National Women's Studies), *Ethnographies of Prostitution in Contemporary China* (winner of the 2011 Research Publication Book Award from the Association of Chinese Professors of Social Sciences in the United States), *Sex-Trafficking, Human Rights, and Social Justice* (editor), *HIV/AIDS through an Anthropological Lens* (lead author; Dubuque: Kendall Hunt Publishing, 2011), and *Ethical Research with Sex Workers: Anthropological Approaches* (coauthor; New York: Springer, 2013).

Index

agency, 4, 5, 20, 67, 137, 184
All Men are Brothers (*Shuihu zhuan/ji*), 88, 102
alterity, 9, 15–6, 75, 155, 164, 180, 230, 239
androgyny, 1–2, 128, 131, 142, 202. *See also* female impersonators
Anita Mui, 152
Anthology of Folk Music of the Chinese Peoples, 3, 30, 31, 32, 188–91, 193
artist, 12, 17, 42–3, 67–69, 72, 74, 88, 95, 118, 132, 138, 141–43, 146–47, 177, 180, 188, 201–4, 206, 236; folk (*minjian yiren*), 182, 192
asaniu, 213, 216, 222n83
audiences, 3, 11, 15–16, 18–19, 50, 52–53, 87–93, 95, 97, 100, 102–4, 105n12, 110–11, 119, 122–23, 128, 133–36, 140, 143–48, 158, 190, 192, 196, 202, 212, 216, 218, 235–37, 238, 240, 242, 256
authenticity, 1, 7, 9, 10, 16, 19, 137, 181–82, 185, 195, 235. See also *yuanshengtai*

backward (*luohou*), 9, 28
bangzi, 119, 177. *See also* opera
Baranovitch, Nimrod, 5, 7, 9, 186
bars, 10, 17, 66, 70–74, 76–77, 79, 82–85, 129, 131, 172, 183. *See also* karaoke
beauty, 1, 15, 72, 168, 189; competitions, 212, 217
Beijing opera (*jingju*), 11, 15–16, 135–36, 191, 200n64
biography, 31, 91, 104n4, 133, 196

body, 6, 15, 48, 67, 69, 97, 102, 171–72, 184–85, 233, 235, 249, 253, 256, 262, 269, 272, 280; language, 119, 237. *See also* embodiment
boy, 7, 14–15, 49, 54, 119, 123, 132, 172, 184, 202, 213; band, 202, 216; Happy Boys, 2, 9; Super Boys, 2. *See also* masculinity
Buddhism, 264n7, 265, 268–71, 281n1, 282n18, 283n31, 283n39; Mahayana, 268–69, 281n6, 284n49, 284n58
Buddhist, hymns, 20, 276–80, 284n53, 284n58, 285n65; precepts, 266, 268, 270, 281n7; reform movement, 267, 269, 270
Butler, Judith, 6, 13
büwi, 231–33, 236, 238–39, 242–44

caigu. *See* vegetarian sisters
caizi. *See* Confucianism, scholars
CCP. *See* Chinese Communist Party
Cantonese opera, 9, 15, 107–11. *See also* opera
Cantopop, 152, 155, 201
ch'anggŭk, 187–90
Cheng, Sammi, 152, 154–55
Chinese Communist Party, 29, 75, 117, 188, 205, 241, 271, 283n42; cultural policy, 298; ideology, 205, 214
Ch'oe Ryŏryŏng, 196
Chŏn Hwaja, 190
chou (clown), 18, 90, 135, 139, 142
Chow, Rey, 147
civilized (*wenming*), 82, 115–17
class, 11–12, 14–15, 18, 21, 27–28, 35, 49, 68, 72, 74, 78, 114–16, 135, 143, 157, 184, 200n59, 271

302   INDEX

classical music (Western), 8, 128, 132–40, 143–44, 146–47
clothing, 1, 13, 68, 70, 75, 107, 123, 128, 139, 141, 203–4, 208, 226, 251, 253, 256, 274. *See also* cross-dressing
cock rock, 7, 185
colonialism, 9, 10, 187, 199n37. *See also* postcolonial
community, 19, 32, 107, 152, 155, 175n24, 231, 233–34, 238, 244
concubine, 11, 26, 67; male, 131
Confucianism, 18, 30, 32, 123, 187, 269, 282n17; ideas on music, 2, 17, 34–35, 56, 117–18; ideology, 10, 14, 26, 117–19, 249; scholars (*caizi*), 11, 12, 17, 27, 44, 58, 68, 88, 90–97, 106n19, 109, 135, 140, 142–43, 146, 270
conservatories, 8, 129, 133, 139, 146, 181, 183, 186, 192, 195, 215, 224
cosmopolitanism, 10, 15, 18, 21, 31, 91, 142–44, 147
courtesans, 6, 12, 17, 41–63, 66–70, 78, 105n12, 194
cross-dressing, 11, 16, 21, 22n2, 250. *See also* female: impersonators
crying, 1, 2, 20, 35, 61, 102, 105n8, 128, 158–59, 162, 194, 212, 228, 230–36, 242
Cui Jian, 186
cultural difference. *See* alterity
Cultural Revolution, 7, 117, 127, 131, 168, 190, 194, 207, 214, 219n14, 227
culture, 17, 28, 177, 184–85; courtesan, 17, 41–42, 70, 87; expressive, 4, 6, 36, 122, 243; intangible, 195; minority, 206; 217–18, 253; national, 20, 218, 230; popular, 5, 11, 16, 18, 138, 142, 163; ritual, 30
cultured (*wenming*). *See* civilized
Cusick, Suzanne, 185–86
cute, 131, 202–3

dan, 14–16, 90, 191. *See also* female: impersonators
dance, 6, 9, 28, 32, 67, 71–72, 77, 85, 88, 138, 154, 166, 172, 181, 183, 201, 204, 208, 212, 216, 233, 239–43

Daoism, 4, 12, 19, 28, 30–33, 113–14, 117, 121, 124, 247, 249–51, 253, 256–57, 260, 262–63, 264n7, 270
daughters, 31, 86, 96, 112, 162–63, 168–69, 175n24, 196, 205, 208–9, 211, 213, 215, 227–28, 230, 267–68
demographics, 21, 144–45, 148
Deng Lijun (Teresa Teng), 2, 7, 204
diaspora, 2, 9, 21, 144, 272
difference. *See* alterity
Doubleday, Veronica, 239–40, 243
Dragon Ball Z, 137–39
dreams, 41, 77, 109, 132, 140, 169, 243, 247–48, 284n48
dualisms, 10, 35, 230; *wen-wu*, 11, 27, 35, 135, 138, 147–48
duets, 48, 75, 77, 110, 213, 216–17
duhuo, 211–13, 217

East Asia, 9, 145; cultural industry, 18, 142; musicianship, 139
embodiment, 20, 89, 112, 135–36, 145–47, 235, 263
emotion, 43, 46, 52–59, 67, 88, 90–93, 95, 102–3, 111, 133, 135, 137–38, 140, 142–43, 159, 181, 185–87, 192, 196, 210–11, 214, 229–36. *See also* crying
emasculation, 9–10, 24n53, 27, 73, 123
empowerment, 18, 242, 281
entrepreneurs, 10, 17, 28, 67, 70–74, 78–79
erotic, 42, 47, 49, 72, 79, 96, 162, 240; erotica, 12; eroticization, 19, 206, 213, 217–18
ethnic minorities. *See* minority nationalities
ethnography, 4, 6, 8, 13, 27, 37n17, 67, 236, 243, 266
ethnomusicology, 3–5, 34, 224–28, 229, 235–36
exoticization, 9, 19, 145, 182, 195, 206, 235

family, 4, 13–15, 27, 68, 112–16, 123, 135, 157, 162, 166–67, 169, 173, 182, 207, 210–12, 225, 227, 230, 234,

238–42, 248, 255–56, 263, 266–68, 270, 274
fans, 1–2, 15–16, 111, 132–34, 136, 140, 144–46, 148, 152–54, 183, 195, 197, 204, 241
fantasy, 7, 75, 79, 142, 147, 163, 179, 216
Faye Wong, 136, 152–55
female: audiences, 18, 134, 141–42, 144–46; deities, 32, 164; exogamy, 13, 211; identity, 178–79, 217, 224–28; impersonators, 15–6, 89; performance, 1–2, 4–5, 8, 10, 67, 105n12, 145, 156–58, 166–73, 240; ritualists, 19–20, 33, 231–34, 249–51, 264–69, 280–81; sexuality, 6, 18 (*see also* sexuality); subordination, 26–27, 36, 74–79, 118, 131; voices, 185–87, 192
feminism, 73; feminist scholarship, 3, 17–18, 160, 181
femininity, 1–2, 8–9, 14–16, 27, 30, 74–75, 79, 83, 128, 186, 197, 201, 215, 227, 250; feminization, 8, 31–32, 123
fieldwork, 39n39, 67, 112, 158, 162, 181, 216, 219n14, 225, 263, 266
Flaming Mouth ritual (*fang yankou*), 273, 275
folk songs, 31–32, 156–59, 163, 186, 211, 237, 258; collection, 3, 32 189; erotic, 4, 13, 156, 170–72; festivals, 161–62, 166; professional, 182–84, 188, 190–92, 195; revolutionary, 179, 184, 186. See also *hua'er*; *shan'ge*; song
Frith, Simon, 5, 7, 183–85, 197

Gao Lian, 90
gardens, 49–50, 66, 77, 96–97, 251
gay, 21, 128–31, 140, 152, 154, 155, 202. See also homosexuality; lesbian; queer
gender: asymmetry, 26–27, 36, 74–79, 118; discrimination, 207; identities, 5–6, 18, 68, 72–75, 79, 133, 142, 239, 242; performance of, 1–2, 5–7, 10, 13, 15, 19, 79, 133–34, 136, 140–44, 170, 184–86, 195, 215; relations, 6, 10, 207, 214, 217, 234, 249, 280–81; roles, 1, 34–36, 206–7, 265–66; studies, 4–5, 10. See also dualisms; feminism: feminist scholarship; taboos
girls, 1, 10, 27, 36, 71, 82–85, 162, 171–72 188, 194, 202, 207, 211, 231, 241, 267–69; iron, 2; Super Girls, 1–2, 6–7, 203; Twelve Girls Band, 8. See also daughters
globalization, 3, 132, 135, 138, 143, 147, 183
gods (*shen*), 11, 13, 27–28, 32–33, 46, 124, 157, 162–68, 247–57, 259
goddesses, 163–66. See also female deities
Guan Yu (Guan Gong), 11, 89, 98–100, 135–36. See also dualisms: *wen-wu*
Guangxi, 205, 247–48
guchui. See shawm bands
guqin. See qin

Han: culture, 234, 263; musical traditions, 4, 31, 35, 191; relations with minorities, 130, 175n24; scholars, 205, 211, 214
healing, 33, 234, 242–43, 264n14. See also spirit medium
hegemony, 32, 75
heroes, 11–12, 17, 59, 73, 87–90, 99–100, 102–3, 116, 135–37, 163, 212; Byronic, 18, 134, 142, 147
heroines, 59, 73, 146, 152, 154, 157, 168, 189, 191
High School Musical, 204
homosexuality, 5, 14, 21, 128–31. See also gay, lesbian, queer
hostesses, 17, 27, 66–67, 70–79
Hou Fangyu, 91
Hou Shaokui, 87, 98–103
hua'er, 157–73. See also folk songs: festivals
huju, 15–16, 35. See also opera
husband, 21, 67, 77, 90, 107, 109–10, 158, 162, 167–68, 173, 175n23, 182, 188, 211, 227, 237–38, 240, 265

hxohxo. See mouth harp

identity, 68, 74–75, 142, 145, 147–48, 184, 197, 215, 239, 242, 260, 280
idols, pop, 11, 16, 18, 21, 142, 144, 183, 185, 201
improvisation, 13, 19, 43, 159, 162, 178–79, 235, 260, 263
inequality, 4, 158, 234
instruments, 8–9, 11, 67, 74, 112, 119–20, 179, 190, 207–8, 217, 236, 238, 244n58, 255, 277; instrumental ensembles, 30–32, 35, 117, 120, 190, 215, 235, 279; instrumentalists, 198nn9–10, 209, 220n32; instrumental music, 3, 8, 11, 30–31, 34, 35, 92, 112, 120, 122–23, 135, 207, 215. *See also* piano; *qin*
Internet, 1–2, 137, 139, 142, 146, 195. *See also* YouTube
Islam: and gender, 20, 34, 175n24, 229, 231, 234, 236–37, 239–41, 243; Muslim, 164, 175, 179, 235, 239–40, 242

Jade Hairpin (*Yuzanji*), 89, 93, 95–97, 105n18
jazz, 21, 29, 115, 118, 127–30, 179
Jike Qubu, 216–17, 219n17, 221n50, 221n52, 223nn104–5
Jingju. See Beijing opera
Jones, Andrew, 186, 199n31
junzi, 135, 142. *See also* dualisms

Kang Shinja, 189, 192, 196
karaoke, 10, 17, 27, 66–67, 70–77, 79, 82, 84, 86, 109, 172, 183, 216, 217
khätmä, 231–32, 234, 236–38
Korean, 3, 18–19, 139, 142, 145, 177, 181, 182, 185, 187–88, 190–92, 194–97, 199n37, 199n43, 202
Koskoff, Ellen, 5, 6
kunqu, 11, 16–17, 30, 35, 42, 43, 52, 87–93, 95, 99–100, 102–4, 104n1, 104n4, 105n8, 105n12, 120. *See also* opera

labeled melodies (*qupai*), 42, 53, 117, 280, 285n65
Lady Gaga, 154, 203
laments: marriage, 4, 13–14, 18, 20, 23n18, 32, 156–60, 172, 193–94, 211–12, 234, 279, 280
Lang Lang, 132–48
lesbian, 1, 6. *See also* homosexuality; gay; queer
Li Sisong, 21, 201, 203
Li Yuchun, 1–3, 20, 203
Li Yundi, 8, 18, 132–48
Liang Chenyu, 41, 64n34, 65n42, 89, 105n10
Liangshan, 102, 205, 207–10, 212–18, 219n16, 220n35
Lin Chong, 89, 100, 100–103
lire'er, 211–12, 221n59
listener, 3, 7–8, 16, 44, 46–50, 59, 65n41, 141, 179, 198n18, 204, 209, 236; listening, 46, 49, 102, 109, 120, 166, 212, 214–15, 226, 237
Liszt, 141
literacy, 26, 28, 207
literati, 11–12, 42–43, 49–50, 54, 69–70, 93, 95
Liu Sola, 177–80
Louie, Kam, 11, 17–18, 87–88, 135–36, 139, 140, 143

Madonna, 152, 154
male-centrism, 226
Mandopop, 5, 7, 152, 155, 201–4
Mao Zedong, 9, 20, 188, 241; Maoist, 5, 70, 73, 75, 123, 144, 161, 206
marginalization, 3–4, 12, 105n12, 115, 154–55, 234, 237, 250
marriage, 4, 13, 20, 26–27, 36n2, 160, 162, 167, 173, 175, 207, 211, 213–14, 221n61, 234, 267. *See also* laments
masculinity, 5, 7–8, 11–12, 14, 18, 27–28, 67–79, 88–89, 92–93, 96–97, 100, 102–4, 113, 122, 135, 138–40, 142–46, 148, 182, 185–87, 196, 202, 230; crisis of, 17
McClary, Susan, 7, 16, 34, 118–19, 122
me-mot, 19, 247–63

media: new media. *See* Internet; YouTube
Mei Lanfang, 15
men. *See* masculinity
metaphor, 12, 29, 46, 58, 65n40, 120–21, 138–39, 160, 170, 208, 214
Miaolian, 268–73, 276–77
migrants, 71–72, 82–86. *See also* diaspora
Ming dynasty, 41–79, 138, 270
minority nationalities, 4, 9, 19, 20, 39n38, 84, 164, 177, 182, 195, 198, 205–7, 214–15, 225, 227, 241. *See also* Korean; Nuosu; Uyghur; Zhuang nationality
minyue, 8–9
misogyny, 9, 26, 34
modernity, 3, 8–9, 30, 124, 221n53
monk, 110, 170, 226, 265–67, 269–71, 273–76, 279–80, 283n29, 284n46, 285n65
Monkey King, 139
Moore, Allan, 185, 186, 197
morality, 7, 13–15, 89–90, 93, 96, 112, 119, 135, 157, 159, 161, 167, 213, 227–28, 233, 250
mouth harp (*hxohxo*), 19, 205–11, 214, 216–17, 219n16, 220n32, 220n45, 221n54, 223n105
mother, cult of, 32, 39n40, 207–9, 216, 218, 220n32, 221n62
MTV, 136
musicology, 3–5, 224
music industry, 3, 5, 21, 66, 83, 85, 116, 123, 140, 142, 145–46, 201–2, 204, 206
musical style, 3–4, 6–7, 16–20, 30, 35, 42, 53, 64n21, 117–18, 123, 133–34, 138, 141, 177, 179, 181, 183–85, 197, 204, 238–39, 243, 257, 280, 284n52, 285n66
musicians: professional, 9, 12, 114, 182, 187–88, 197, 229, 238; amateur, 9, 12, 114, 197
musiking, 92–103

nostalgia, 41, 47, 59–60, 95, 145, 235
notation: *dianban*, 52–53

Nuosu, 19, 205–18; songs, 210–23

opera, 2, 5, 7, 10–12, 14, 16, 21, 28–37, 42, 63n3, 68, 89, 91, 107, 110, 115–16, 119, 124, 127, 135–36, 138, 164, 166, 177, 179, 188, 189, 191, 194, 199n43, 200n64, 284n52. *See also* Beijing opera; Cantonese opera; *huju*; *kunqu*; *yueju*
original ecology (*yuanshengtai*), 177, 194–95, 197
other/othering. *See* alterity

Pak Chŏngnyŏl, 188–90, 192–94
Pan Bizheng, 89, 93, 95–97, 99
p'ansori, 19, 182, 185–89, 190, 192, 194, 196–97, 199n39, 199n43
Park Chan, 187
parody, 16
patriarchy, 6, 10, 14, 17–18, 26, 34, 73, 117, 123–24
penitence, 274–75, 284n47, 284n48, 284n49
Peony Pavilion (*Mudanting*), 11, 89, 95
performance: contexts, 10, 13, 87 91, 133, 140, 156, 160, 166, 214, 229, 235, 240, 250; gender relations, 1, 6, 9–10, 14–17, 173, 206, 213–14, 234–35, 250, 266; gender reversals in, 1–23, 36, 67, 88–93, 95, 104, 133, 135, 141–49, 156, 181–84, 186, 188, 191, 194–97, 206, 209, 213–14, 229, 234–38, 243, 248; practice, 11, 91–92, 97, 104, 105n12, 138, 160, 234, 237
performativity, 6, 13
phallocentrism, 100, 119, 123, 126n33, 288
piano, 8, 11, 132–48, 192, 203, 227
pleasure quarters, 59, 79n4, 105
Plum Blossom Award (*meihua jiang*), 91
politics, of performance, 9–10, 144; of gender, 229
pollution. *See* taboos
popular culture, 5, 11, 16, 18, 71, 134, 138, 140, 142, 144, 163, 186, 195, 215, 235, 260

popular music, 1–7, 10, 17–18, 20–21, 59, 63n3, 66, 75, 123–24, 129, 142, 144, 179, 181–86, 192–97, 201–4, 211, 215–26, 229, 230, 238
postcolonial, 10, 186
power, 4–7, 10, 11, 14–20, 26–36, 79, 73–78, 80n18, 85, 90–91, 115–17, 135, 137–38 144–48, 154, 159, 173, 179, 181, 197, 205, 231, 234–37, 242–43, 253, 256–57, 260–63, 273, 281
prostitution, 13–14, 27, 67–72
Pyŏn Yŏnghwa, 194, 197–98

qin, 8–12, 29–30, 86, 106n24, 114, 119–20
qing (love, desire, sentiment), 44, 47, 53–60, 64n31
Qing dynasty, 14, 41, 42, 68, 89, 186, 195, 213, 270–71, 282n11
queer, 4–5. See also homosexuality, gay, lesbian
Qubi Awu, 214–16, 218
qupai. See labeled melodies
Qur'an, 231–32, 236, 241, 243

race, 7, 70, 180, 184
rap, 29
reality shows, 1, 16
reception, 97, 122, 133, 143–44, 259
recording, 71, 138, 140, 145, 178, 190, 194
repertoire, 11, 12, 18, 30, 34, 84, 114, 117–24, 136–38, 140, 145, 156–60, 182, 188, 190, 211, 212, 214, 216, 237, 265, 276, 279–80, 284n52, 285n66
repetition, 6, 17, 34, 47–48, 59–60, 82, 84, 120–21, 232, 237, 260, 279
revolutionary, 2, 17, 22n12, 75, 179, 182, 184, 190, 191, 206, 268
rhythm, 7, 16, 50, 92, 100, 103, 122, 132, 137, 159, 186, 191–92, 196, 232, 260, 277
Ri Kŭmdŏk, 188, 193, 197
ritual, 2, 5, 6, 9, 12, 18, 19, 20, 27–35, 37n9, 39n38, 60, 70, 76, 199, 112, 114, 117, 118, 119, 120–21, 24, 156–58, 160, 166, 171, 212, 214, 224, 226, 229, 231, 232–38, 242–44, 247–63, 264n6 264n7, 265–81, 282n13, 282n32; reversal, 6. See also Flaming Mouth ritual; khätmä
ritualist, 19–20, 229, 244, 249, 250, 265–67, 270–81, 282n13, 282n32, 285. See also büwi
rock music, 2, 5, 7–10, 49, 123, 130, 177, 181, 183, 185–87
romanticism, 35

sadness in music, 46, 59, 60, 63, 209, 288. See also emotion; crying
sanqu, 17 42–44, 50–54, 59–60, 63n3, 64n21, 65n48
scholarship, 3, 4, 11, 41, 130, 226
scream, 2, 66, 179
sectarian religions, 33, 270, 271
separation, 60, 65n42
sex, activity, 4, 5, 10, 12–18, 67–68, 72–79, 85–97, 116, 118, 119, 121, 124, 128–31, 139, 156–57, 159–62, 172–73, 182, 184, 211, 213, 216, 226, 228, 248, 250, 281n7
sexual politics, 10, 21, 71, 73, 90, 139, 148
sexuality, style and image, 1, 2, 7, 14–15, 93, 97, 128, 142, 154, 178, 203, 240
shan'ge, 18, 32, 156–73, 213
Shanghai, 4, 15, 21, 30, 31, 32, 37, 71, 91, 127–31, 204, 224
shawm bands, 4, 7–8, 12, 18, 28, 29–31, 34, 36n2, 112–24, 126n27
Shin Okhwa, 118, 189, 192
shuquanqi, 93, 95–96
Singapore, 21, 82–86, 152, 155, 201, 204, 277, 284
singers, 3, 7, 10, 12, 18, 19, 21, 30, 32, 38n32, 43–44, 46–53, 65n50, 68, 74–75, 78, 82–85, 107, 110–11, 124, 127, 129, 131, 142, 152, 154, 157–73, 177–78, 181–97, 201–3, 206, 211–18, 223n97, 229, 235–38, 241, 276, 279
singing, 6, 7, 13, 15–17, 20–21, 28–33, 42–52, 60, 63n3, 66–79, 84, 88–89,

92, 96–97, 100, 102–3, 107, 109–11, 156–97, 198n11, 201, 205–16, 221–23, 235–42, 249, 253, 255, 257, 259–60, 264–65, 276, 279–80, 281n7, 284n52, 285n66. *See also* vocal style
Single Sword Meeting (*Dandaohui*), 89, 104, 106
son, 10, 27, 116, 121, 123, 134, 157, 211, 233
song-and-dance troupes, 9, 195
songs: suite, 42, 44, 46–49, 53, 56, 60, 62; and birds, 46, 59, 60, 196, 235; as gift, 13, 43, 59, 62, 140, 163–64, 210; lyrics, 10, 42–44, 48–49, 52–63, 75–77, 130, 152, 157–62, 172–73, 176, 183, 212, 258; [woodblock] illustrations, 43–44, 65n42; modern ethnic, 214. *See also* Nuosu: songs; original ecology
soundscape, 29–30, 97, 247, 249, 255, 260
spirit medium, 4, 31, 33, 247–63, 265. *See also* ritualist; *wu*
spirit possession, 243, 247–50, 259, 262
Stock, Jonathan, 4, 15, 16, 35
subjectivity, 16, 92
subversion, 2, 6, 11, 33, 118
Sugarman, Jane, 6
Sun, Stefanie, 201–2
superstar, 1, 132, 136, 144, 145, 147
symbolism, 6, 11, 155, 209–10, 247, 273, 279

taboos, 6, 13, 124, 157–58, 162, 206, 209–10, 213–18, 220n34, 222n72, 247, 273
taitai, 21, 107, 110
Taiwan, 2, 5, 55–58, 75, 83, 181, 202, 204, 271–73, 277, 288
theatre, 10, 14–15, 89. *See also* opera
timbre, 7, 12, 92, 120, 181–92, 196–98, 257. *See also* musical style; vocal style
tourism, 9, 19, 206, 208, 217, 226, 273
tradition, 12–3, 18–21, 26–35, 47, 54, 68–78, 87–97, 100–7, 110, 112, 117–18, 122–24, 133, 142–47, 156–73, 183–85, 187–99, 205–18, 221n53, 223, 224, 228–29, 245, 237–39, 242, 255, 259, 260, 265, 274, 276, 282n17
trance, 19, 33, 247, 250, 253, 255, 257, 260. *See also* spirit possession
transgender, 5. *See also* cross-dressing
transnational, 3, 139, 143–48
transvestism, 16. *See also* cross-dressing
Tursun, Sanubar, 238, 241, 242

Uyghur, 9, 20, 200n64, 229–46; *muqam*, 9, 229, 237

vegetarian sisters (*caigu*), 20, 265–81
veiling practices, 238–41
violence, 8, 11–12, 18, 28–29, 37n11, 38n38, 113, 115–18, 123–24, 126n38, 143, 230–31
vocal style, 4, 6, 7, 16–19, 135, 179, 183–86, 191, 196

Washing Silk (*Huanshaji*), 89, 105n10
Watson, Rubie, 13–14, 234–35
weeping. *See* crying
wen-wu. See dualisms
wife, 73, 77, 100, 102, 183, 219n11, 227, 230. *See also* marriage
women: education, 26, 27, 158, 162, 172, 216, 268, 270; oppression, 4, 29, 39n45, 160, 167, 239. *See also* female; femininity
worldviews, 249
wu (spirit medium), 247–50, 263. *See also* spirit medium
wusheng, 88

Xiao Mei, 224–28, 247
xiqu. See opera

Yan Song, 91
Yanbian, 181–93, 197
Yang Mu, 4, 13, 221n58
yankou. See Flaming Mouth ritual
Yano, Christine, 235–56
Yi nationality, 205. *See* Nuosu
youth culture, 16, 133 139, 147, 185, 194–96, 210, 242
YouTube, 2, 136

yuanshengtai. See original ecology
Yue Meiti, 87, 93–97, 104
Yue opera, 15, 25, 289

Zhang Jun, 91–92
Zheng, Su, 3, 26, 35, 186
Zhuang nationality, 19, 20, 247, 263, 298

www.ingramcontent.com/pod-product-compliance
Lightning Source LLC
Chambersburg PA
CBHW021650230426
43668CB00008B/572